The Cambridge Companion to the
Nazi-Soviet War

The Nazi-Soviet War was the largest and most brutal theatre of the Second World War, fought between two of the most ruthless states ever to exist. Bringing together twenty-four of the most accomplished authors in both German and Soviet history, this Cambridge Companion provides the most authoritative and yet highly accessible guide to the conflict. Each chapter examines a key aspect of the war, from war planning, the opposing forces, and the campaigns, to criminality and occupation, alliances, the home fronts, and post-war legacies and myth-making. The authors demonstrate that the Nazi-Soviet War was not only a conventional clash of arms in which millions of soldiers fought in titanic battles, but also an unconventional war in which soldiers and security forces murdered countless non-combatants. It was a war of resources, industry, mobilisation, administration, and popular support, with implications that still drive European security debates today.

DAVID STAHEL is Associate Professor of History at the University of New South Wales. He has authored or edited ten previous works about aspects of the Nazi-Soviet War, including *Operation Barbarossa and Germany's Defeat in the East* (2009), *Joining Hitler's Crusade* (2016), *Retreat from Moscow* (2019), and *Hitler's Panzer Generals* (2023).

Cambridge Companions to History

Cambridge Companions to History provide accessible and thought-provoking introductions to key topics, eras, places, and figures, invaluable to both the student and scholar. Edited by leading academics, each volume contains specially commissioned essays by a team of expert contributors from around the world, presenting cutting-edge research and suggesting new paths of inquiry for the reader. Companions are designed not only to offer a comprehensive overview of their chosen topic, but also to provoke debate and discussion. Like the highly successful Cambridge Companions to Literature and Cambridge Companions to Philosophy series, these volumes are ideal for use by students and will be of interest also to the curious general reader.

A full list of recent titles in the series can be found at the following address: www.cambridge.org/history-companions

The Cambridge Companion to the
Nazi-Soviet War

Edited by

DAVID STAHEL

University of New South Wales

Shaftesbury Road, Cambridge CB2 8EA, United Kingdom

One Liberty Plaza, 20th Floor, New York, NY 10006, USA

477 Williamstown Road, Port Melbourne, VIC 3207, Australia

314–321, 3rd Floor, Plot 3, Splendor Forum, Jasola District Centre,
New Delhi – 110025, India

103 Penang Road, #05-06/07, Visioncrest Commercial, Singapore 238467

Cambridge University Press is part of Cambridge University Press & Assessment,
a department of the University of Cambridge.

We share the University's mission to contribute to society through the pursuit of
education, learning and research at the highest international levels of excellence.

www.cambridge.org
Information on this title: www.cambridge.org/9781009656696

DOI: 10.1017/9781009656733

First published 2026

Cover image: A Soviet propaganda poster from 1944 by K. Avvakumov, which was
originally printed above the slogan 'Death to German Fascist Invaders!'

A catalogue record for this publication is available from the British Library

Library of Congress Cataloging-in-Publication Data
Names: Stahel, David, 1975– editor
Title: The Cambridge companion to the Nazi-Soviet War / edited by David Stahel,
University of New South Wales, Canberra.
Description: Cambridge, United Kingdom ; New York, NY : Cambridge University
Press, 2026. | Series: Cambridge companions to history | Collection of essays by Jeff
Rutherford and 23 others. | Includes bibliographical references and index.
Identifiers: LCCN 2025015687 | ISBN 9781009656696 hardback | ISBN
9781009656726 paperback | ISBN 9781009656733 ebook
Subjects: LCSH: World War, 1939–1945 – Soviet Union | World War, 1939–1945 –
Campaigns – Eastern Front | World War, 1939–1945 – Campaigns – Soviet Union |
Germany – History – 1933–1945 | Soviet Union – History – 1925–1953
Classification: LCC D764 .C34 2026
LC record available at https://lccn.loc.gov/2025015687

ISBN 978-1-009-65669-6 Hardback
ISBN 978-1-009-65672-6 Paperback

Contents

Figures

Maps

All maps are courtesty of *When Titans Clashed: How the Red Army Stopped Hitler, Revised and Expanded Edition* by David Glantz and Jonathan M. House, published by the University Press of Kansas © 2015. www.kansaspress.ku.edu. Used by permission of the publisher.

Contributors

OLEG BEYDA is the Hansen Lecturer in Russian History at the University of Melbourne. He is a multilingual historian focussing on diaspora studies (the first and second waves of migration from Russia after 1917) and the Second World War in Europe. His book *For Russia with Hitler* was published in 2024.

JONATHAN BRUNSTEDT is Associate Professor of History and Arts & Humanities Fellow at Texas A&M University. Among other works, he is the author of *The Soviet Myth of World War II: Patriotic Memory and the Russian Question in the USSR* (Cambridge University Press, 2021).

RICHARD CARRIER is Associate Professor of Military History at the Royal Military College of Canada. He is a contributor to and the co-editor of *Italy and the Second World War: Alternative Perspectives* (Brill, 2018) and the author of *Mussolini's Army against Greece, October 1940–April 1941* (Routledge, 2021).

JÖRG ECHTERNKAMP is Senior Research Director at the Center for Military History and Social Sciences of the Bundeswehr, Potsdam. He is also head of the 'Military History after 1945' research department and Adjunct Professor of Modern History at Martin Luther University, Halle-Wittenberg.

MARK EDELE is the inaugural Hansen Professor in History at the University of Melbourne. He is the author of eight books, including *Soviet Veterans of the Second World War* (Oxford University Press,

2008), *Stalin's Defectors* (2017), and *Stalinism at War: The Soviet Union in World War II* (Bloomsbury Academic, 2021).

WENDY Z. GOLDMAN, Paul Mellon Distinguished Professor, Carnegie Mellon University, is a political and social historian of the Soviet Union. Her work covers women, industrialization, Stalinist repression, and the Second World War. Her most recent book (with Donald Filtzer) is *Fortress Dark and Stern: The Soviet Home Front during World War II.*

DAVID HARRISVILLE is a Learning Designer on the staff of Brown University and has taught history at the University of Wisconsin–Madison and Furman University. He is the author of *The Virtuous Wehrmacht: Crafting the Myth of the German Soldier on the Eastern Front, 1941–1944* (Cornell University Press, 2021).

GRANT T. HARWARD completed his PhD in history at Texas A&M University in 2018. He was an Auschwitz Jewish Center Fellow, Fulbright Scholar to Romania, and US Holocaust Memorial Museum Fellow. Cornell University Press published his book *Romania's Holy War: Soldiers, Motivation, and the Holocaust* in 2021.

ALEXANDER HILL is Professor in Military History at the University of Calgary. He is the author of *The Red Army and the Second World War* (Cambridge University Press, 2017) and other books and articles on the Soviet armed forces. His most recent publication is *The Routledge Handbook of Soviet and Russian Military Studies* (Routledge, 2025).

IAN ONA JOHNSON is the P. J. Moran Family Associate Professor of Military History at the University of Notre Dame. He is the author or editor of three books, including *Faustian Bargain: The Soviet-German Partnership and the Origins of the Second World War*, published by Oxford University Press in 2021.

ALEX J. KAY is Senior Lecturer in the Department of History at the University of Potsdam and lifetime Fellow of the Royal Historical

Society. He has published five acclaimed books on Nazi Germany, including *Empire of Destruction* (2021), the first comparative, comprehensive history of Nazi mass killing.

HIROAKI KUROMIYA is Professor of History Emeritus, Indiana University, and author of several books on Stalin and his era, which include *Stalin, Japan, and the Struggle for Supremacy over China, 1894–1945* (2023), and *Stalin: Profiles in Power* (2005).

EVAN MAWDSLEY is a Professorial Research Fellow and former Professor of International History at the University of Glasgow. He is the author of several books on Russian history and the Second World War, notably *Thunder in the East: The Nazi-Soviet War, 1941–1945* (Bloomsbury Academic, 2016).

HENRIK MEINANDER, Professor of History at the University of Helsinki, has focused his research on Finnish and Nordic twentieth-century history, with an emphasis on sport, wartime, and social history of ideas. Among many others, his most recent work is *Mannerheim, Marshal of Finland: A Life in Geopolitics* (Hurst, 2023).

ROGER R. REESE is Professor of History at Texas A&M University. His research specialty is the social history of the Imperial Russian and Soviet armies. He has authored numerous articles, book chapters, and books, most recently *Russia's Army* (University of Oklahoma, 2023).

GEOFFREY ROBERTS is Emeritus Professor of History at University College Cork. His books include *Stalin's Wars: From World War to Cold War, 1939–1953* (Yale University Press, 2006), *Stalin's General: The Life of General Zhukov* (Icon Books, 2012), and *Stalin's Library: A Dictator and His Books* (Yale University Press, 2022).

JEFF RUTHERFORD is Professor of History at Xavier University. He is the author of *Combat and Genocide on the Eastern Front: The German Infantry's War* (Cambridge University Press, 2014) and co-author with Adrian Wettstein of *The German Army on the Eastern Front: An Inner View of the Ostheer's Experiences of War* (Pen and Sword, 2018).

BEN H. SHEPHERD is Reader in History at Glasgow Caledonian University. He specializes in German military history from 1914 to 1945. He is currently writing a new history of the Waffen-SS, a companion volume to his work *Hitler's Soldiers: The German Army in the Third Reich*, published by Yale University Press in 2016.

DAVID STAHEL is Associate Professor at the University of New South Wales in Australia. He has published seven books with Cambridge University Press covering different aspects of the Nazi-Soviet War, including *Operation Barbarossa and Germany's Defeat in the East* (2009), *Operation Typhoon* (2013), and *Hitler's Panzer Generals* (2023).

ALEXANDER STATIEV teaches Russian and Soviet history at the University of Waterloo, Canada. He has published books and articles on pro- and anti-Soviet resistance during the Second World War, Soviet counter-insurgency, Russian and Romanian military history, Soviet deportations, Russian war memory, Ukrainian fascism, and mountain warfare.

DAVID R. STONE is the William E. Odom Professor of Russian Studies at the US Naval War College. He received his PhD in history from Yale University and is the author of several books and numerous articles on Russian/Soviet military history.

ROMAN TÖPPEL is co-editor of the award-winning edition of Hitler's *Mein Kampf* and author of an internationally acclaimed study of the Battle of Kursk. He is currently working on an edition of the private war diaries and letters of Field Marshal Erich von Manstein.

ADRIAN E. WETTSTEIN is Senior Academic Adviser at the Military Academy at ETH Zurich (MILAK). He has published a number of books and articles on European armies in the age of the world wars, focussing on military thinking, tactics, and organization. He is the author of *Die Wehrmacht im Stadtkampf 1939–1942* (Ferdinand Schöningh, 2014).

BASTIAAN WILLEMS is Lecturer in the History of War in Twentieth-Century Europe at Lancaster University. He recently published *Violence in Defeat: The Wehrmacht on German Soil 1944–1945* (Cambridge University Press, 2021) and co-edited *Reflections on Perpetration and Complicity under Nazism and Beyond: Compromised Identities?* (Bloomsbury Academic, 2023).

DAVID STAHEL

Introduction

History is a product of the time in which it is written. This should not surprise us since each generation has its own interpretation of the past, which is easily impacted by the events of the present. Writing the history of the Nazi-Soviet War in the 2020s against the backdrop of resurgent warfare in Eastern Europe – war that draws so directly from interpretations (many of which are disputed) of the period 1941–1945 – makes our task unusually complex but all the more important. The temptation to use and abuse history is nothing new, but amid an active information war the value of first-rate scholarship and established expertise cannot be overestimated. To that end, I am deeply appreciative for the time and support of so many leading scholars.

If the Cambridge Companion series imagines a non-professional audience, predominately those unfamiliar with a period, it is perhaps important to frame what this volume is and is not. The *Cambridge Companion to the Nazi-Soviet War* is at its core a military history because the conflict is the common denominator that cannot be separated from the events. This need not be controversial, since the best military histories today, as reflected in this volume, defy narrow categorisation and embrace the diversity of the humanities. Scholarly military histories are not the patriotic pulp that dominates a percentage of the literature in the field, but every academic discourse confronts popular challenges, which only underwrite the importance of corrective, evidence-based studies. The Nazi-Soviet War is a case in point. The ideological nature of the conflict and enduring divisions that resulted from its conclusion shaped decades of literature, with many partisan authors and institutions fighting a paper war over its representation. In the early post-war decades, the quality of many publications was dubious – and sometimes fanciful – but the end of the Cold War proved an intellectual renaissance. Longstanding tensions disappeared, while the opening of former Soviet and Eastern European archives provided an abundance of new evidence to correct and confirm past narratives.

Beyond the challenge of agenda-driven narratives, the early histories of the Nazi-Soviet War also suffered from being one-dimensionally focused on the military campaign. This is hardly surprising since the centrality of the 'battle narrative' predominated throughout the military history genre. With only a few exceptions, this narrowly 'operational' focus shaped western accounts of the Nazi-Soviet War until the 1990s and continues to dominate the field in Russian-language literature today. When researched and well-written, the battle narrative certainly has its place in military history, but it is inadequate for identifying context and causality in warfare. Indeed, because of what it historically ignored, it inadvertently (and incorrectly) attributed an undue importance to generals and armies when explaining events. Not surprisingly, therefore, the intellectual tradition of framing history through 'great men' has also pervaded military history, and the Nazi-Soviet War is no exception. The centrality of Hitler and Stalin, as well as their leading generals, dominates the 'top-down' perspective of the war, but this is slowly changing as increasingly more institutional, cultural, and social research into the war is conducted. This reflects the changes in military history from the late twentieth century towards a more philosophically diverse and methodologically rich discourse that is sometimes called 'new military history' or 'war and society'. This has redefined the field from narrowly dogmatic operational histories to a truly interdisciplinary study of the phenomenon of war. It is this intellectual evolution that informs our history of the Nazi-Soviet War. As Stephen Morillo has asserted, 'many contemporary military historians have begun to examine these universalist assumptions, and an alternative view has emerged that places military decisions and systems in their social and cultural context, and then tries to assess them in their own historicized terms'.[1] In layman terms, military histories have increasingly drawn upon a far wider disciplinary lens. The possibilities granted by exploring war through political, sociological, economic, environmental, intellectual, and psychological contexts have transformed the field and enriched our understandings. Many of these new perspectives have shaped the work of this volume's author base, and while no claim is made to fundamentally rewrite the Nazi-Soviet War, it is the most authoritative and wide-ranging synthesis available.

There are seven conceptual themes to this book, subdivided into twenty chapters. Capturing the vast dimensions of the Nazi-Soviet War is a challenge for any study, and the size constraints imposed by a volume for the Cambridge Companion series require some hard choices to be made. This book cannot claim to have covered every subject of relevance, but it does capture many of the most important. The big picture of the war emerges, and it is one that equally considers both the German and Soviet perspectives, as well as their main allies.

Given the space constraints, as well as an anticipated undergraduate readership, contributors were recommended to limit their citation to more essential texts (as opposed to highly specific studies or archival references) and, where possible, to preference English-language sources. This is not to suggest the contents of these chapters are not overwhelmingly informed by a deep familiarity with the German and/or Russian literature, as well as past archival research – every contributor's publication history speaks to this. The concept here is to provide useful further readings for newcomers to the field, which are readily accessible to them both physically and linguistically.

Part I deals with pre-war German and Soviet relations, especially as conceived by Hitler and Stalin in the years immediately preceding Operation Barbarossa. While the ideological divide shaped the conflict, it belies the complexities of the relationship, which from the 1920s to the early 1930s included an important period of intensive military exchange and cooperation. Part II considers the standing of the German Wehrmacht and Soviet Red Army, both as organisational institutions built and managed from above but also as organic societies of men (and in the Soviet case also women), whose motivation and upkeep are equally important to their survival and endurance. Part III is the longest section of the book, taking a chronological look at the major German and Soviet campaigns of the war from 1941 to 1945. Barbarossa, Stalingrad, Kursk, Leningrad, Bagration, and Berlin are by no means the only campaigns of the war, but they are the best known and each meaningfully represents the conflict in its period. Part IV explores the parallel wars each side waged against civilian populations, domestically or foreign. While the scale of the violence and number of victims varied between them, it was their willingness to target non-combatants that epitomised German and Soviet methods. Part V is devoted to the colossal social, cultural, and economic effort of both the German and Soviet societies to maintain their respective war efforts. In a conflict that was existential for both sides, the mobilisation was total and militarisation of the home fronts soon blurred the distinction between civilian and soldier. Part VI situates the Nazi-Soviet War in a transnational context by illuminating the significance of political, economic, and direct military aid through both Allied and Axis countries. The Nazi-Soviet conflict was by no means limited to Central and Eastern Europe; global resources sustained it, each alliance configuration was contingent upon it, and more than thirty nationalities directly participated in the fighting,[2] which in the context of a world war meant the repercussions were truly universal. Part VII traces the conflict's fraught memory politics and politicised history of commemoration through the past eighty years. Recognising the rupture in national narratives that 1941–1945 represents, the power that this period exerts is as cautionary in its terrible cost as it is unifying in its defiance of imagined tyranny and violence.

Clearly, this short volume attempts a good deal, but its brevity is also its strength. The Nazi-Soviet War is the largest-scale conflict ever fought. More than thirty million people died in the period 1941–1945 (soldiers and civilians), and many times that number experienced its horror. If the devil is in the details, this volume is merely an introduction. It is a primer, not only for the events themselves but for the scholarship that shapes the field. While the sources that constitute each chapter will point to their own specialised literature, the volume distinguishes itself in a number of ways from comparable literature.

First, this study is a delicate balancing act, representing each side of the conflict in both subject matter and expertise. Histories of the Nazi-Soviet War are overwhelmingly written from one side or the other, and even those that purport to represent both sides seldom have truly equal representation or equal expertise in that representation. This is not a criticism of past works; it is simply a comment on the mountain of primary and secondary material pertaining to each side, as well as the obvious language barriers. Yet for these reasons an anthology of the Nazi-Soviet War probably makes the most sense for grappling evenly with the vast scale of the conflict.

Second, it cannot be lost on any of the contributors in preparing their chapters, or presumedly the readers of this book, that it has been produced in the era of what Chancellor Olaf Scholz determined to be a *Zeitenwende* – an historic turning point – in German and European history. It was only in 2016, in the preface to Evan Mawdsley's majestic *Thunder in the East: The Nazi-Soviet War 1941–1945*, that Professor Hew Strachan suggested what the book 'tells us about modern war and its lessons has also lost immediacy'. Indeed, Strachan concluded that the historic departure from high-intensity, industrialised warfare 'may be increasingly remote from current perspectives on war, at least within Europe', but that this fact 'is no reason to forget it'.[3] Strachan was not wrong at the time, but such analysis illustrates how we view and what we draw from the past. It goes without saying that the Nazi-Soviet War looks alarmingly different today. The intractable east-west divide has dashed the hopes of a united post–Cold War world, while in many respects, the reality of modern warfare in the 2020s looks decidedly less modern. For all that has changed, the Russo-Ukrainian War suggests remarkable continuity with its 1941–1945 predecessor: the aggressor seeks the political and cultural elimination of the rival state, the war quickly transitioned from a blitz campaign to costly attritional fighting, it is sustained by divergent political alliances, its justification reinforces competing worldviews, it is framed by irreconcilable territorial claims, it is underwritten by an increasingly global arms race, the battlespace is marked by constant technical evolutions, and civilians have been purposefully and consistently targeted. The similarities were metaphorically illustrated when a Ukrainian volunteer group searching for recent war dead reported, 'When you dig into a trench you find a trench from World War II.' Not surprisingly, they have also recovered soldiers from the Nazi-Soviet War in the same places they are searching.[4] Of course, analogies with the past only extend so far, but given the frightening realities of the Nazi-Soviet War, any parallels with the war in Europe today are a sobering proposition and a reminder of what historical study offers us.

Notes

1 Stephen Morillo and Michael F. Pavkovic, *What Is Military History?* (Medford, MA: Polity Press, 2018), p. 55.
2 These nationalities were not all independent counties at that time, but this need not diminish the significance of their participation.
3 Evan Mawdsley, *Thunder in the East: The Nazi-Soviet War 1941–1945* (London: Bloomsbury, 2016), p. xvi.
4 Andrew E. Kramer, 'A Current War Collides with the Past: Remnants of World War II in Ukraine', *New York Times* (18 July 2023).

Part I

Conceptions of War

1

German-Soviet Relations and Military Collaboration in the Inter-war Period

On 23 August 1939, Nazi Foreign Minister Joachim Ribbentrop arrived in Moscow to finalise a non-aggression pact with Stalin's Soviet Union. 'To most of us it will seem almost incredible that Russia should do something which, of purpose or in effect, will help Germany in her plans for aggression', the *Manchester Guardian* recorded in shock.[1] When news of the final pact became public the following day, editors at the *New York Times* predicted war across Europe within a week.[2] They were nearly right: Germany invaded Poland on 1 September 1939. Great Britain and France reluctantly followed their pledges to Poland and declared war, marking the formal beginning of the Second World War in Europe.

Though the Nazi-Soviet Pact stunned contemporary observers, the decision for partnership – and the military, economic, and intelligence cooperation it portended – had a long prehistory. The first tentative steps towards the Molotov-Ribbentrop Pact had been taken even before the First World War had ended. Following the successful October Revolution in Petrograd in 1917, Vladimir Lenin and his Bolshevik Party opened peace negotiations with Imperial Germany. When Soviet negotiators, anticipating an imminent revolution in war-torn Germany, tried to delay a final settlement, the frustrated German High Command responded by launching a fresh offensive, advancing 150 miles eastward in just seven days. Facing military catastrophe, the Bolsheviks hastily agreed to the Treaty of Brest-Litovsk on 3 March 1918.[3] The terms Germany imposed were draconian: the Bolsheviks gave up claim to vast swathes of territory, which collectively contained nearly a third of the Russian Empire's population and more than half of its industrial capacity.[4] Nevertheless, in this moment of defeat, the seeds of later cooperation were planted. The Bolsheviks, internationally isolated and facing growing prospects of civil war, almost immediately dispatched a trade delegation to Berlin to purchase much-needed industrial goods, particularly locomotives and railway equipment.[5]

Meanwhile, in the west, Germany's spring offensives had failed to win the war. In October 1918, as Allied forces advanced eastward, the German Supreme Army Command ceded its near-dictatorial control of German politics to civilian leaders, hoping to pass the blame for Germany's rapidly approaching defeat.[6] Germany's new government opened armistice talks on 7 November. Four days later, they concluded a ceasefire that brought an end to hostilities on the Western Front. The exact terms to be imposed on defeated Germany would be determined the following year at a conference to be hosted in Paris.

Even as the victorious allies negotiated the terms of that treaty, however, the German General Staff sought to begin working to reverse Germany's military defeat. In December 1918 Karl Radek, a prominent Bolshevik revolutionary, had secretly travelled to Berlin to assist Germany's communists in seizing power. That attempt failed, and Radek was arrested. While detained in Moabit prison in Berlin, he began to develop a relationship with a number of senior German military officers of the reorganised German army, the *Reichswehr* (Defence Force), who were interested in the possibility of a partnership with Soviet Russia against Britain and France.[7] In April 1919 the Reichswehr's leading post-war figure, General Hans von Seeckt, approved a proposal from Radek to dispatch a representative to Moscow to help open channels between Moscow and the German military.[8]

On 7 May 1919, the Allies delivered the 440-page Treaty of Versailles to the German Foreign Minister. Under its terms, Germany was to be stripped of its colonies and 10 per cent of its land area, as well as assigned reparations to be paid to the victors. The German General Staff – the 'brain' of the army – was to be disbanded, and the army itself was to be reduced in strength to just 100,000 men, of whom no more than 4,000 could be officers. Germany was further barred from the production or possession of military aircraft, tanks, heavy artillery, submarines, chemical weapons, and most other modern instruments of war. To enforce these terms, the Allies established an Inter-Allied

Military Control Commission (IAMCC) of more than 1,300 officers and men whose task was to oversee the dismantling of German military industry and the destruction of its surplus arms.[9] Versailles was viewed as so catastrophic by Germany's military leaders that they held a secret conference to discuss the possibility of resuming the war. But concluding such a course was impossible; they instead set about surreptitiously undermining the terms of the treaty.[10]

Further events would soon draw Germany and Soviet Russia towards partnership. Beginning in August 1918, the Allies had intervened in the Russian Civil War, seeking to undermine the communists; from November, the Soviets had also found themselves embroiled in war with newly independent Poland, a state that had been partially carved out from German territory. Hoping for Russian victory, General Seeckt wrote, 'Poland must and will be wiped off the map, with our help, through internal weakness and Russian action. Poland's fall will be that of one of the key columns supporting the Treaty of Versailles.'[11] As the Polish-Soviet War reached its crescendo in 1920, the German military did what it could to aid the Red Army.[12]

Seeckt would soon have a chance to do much more. Following a failed military coup in Berlin in March 1920, he became Chief of the Troop Office, a thinly veiled successor to the German General Staff. Despite ideological concerns about the Soviet regime in Moscow, Seeckt strongly favoured collaboration with the Soviet military as a means of evading the restrictions of Versailles and developing a future ally equally committed to overturning the European order established after the First World War.

He found willing partners in the Soviet Union. Leon Trotsky played a key role in leading the Red Army to victory in the Russian Civil War. At the end of the war, the Soviet military was in disastrous shape, lacking uniforms, weapons, and – in Trotsky's estimation – politically reliable professional officers. Trotsky wanted foreign assistance in professionalising and modernising the Red Army. At the same time, in the face of disastrous economic conditions, Vladimir Lenin promulgated the 'New Economic Policy', which permitted limited free enterprise and created opportunities for foreign investment.

Seeckt was eager to take advantage of both prospects. In particular, he hoped to relocate military-industrial work that was banned under the terms of Versailles to Soviet Russia. Trotsky was also enthusiastic, as German investment might assist in modernising Soviet military industry. Both men were particularly interested in aviation, viewing it as critical to the future of warfare. In 1921, Seeckt began to seek out corporate partners willing to take the risk of setting up factories in the USSR. After receiving surreptitious guarantees from the Reichswehr against financial losses, German aviation pioneer Hugo Junkers agreed to send representatives to meet with Leon Trotsky in Moscow in December 1921.[13] At that meeting, Trotsky offered Junkers the lease of an automobile plant near Moscow named Fili, agreeing to purchase a large number of the aircraft to be produced there in order to guarantee its solvency. This agreement with Junkers would prove the beginning of an expansive network of German-funded or managed military industrial facilities in the USSR. Over the next eleven years, the Red Army would negotiate agreements with 255 different German firms, many of them mediated by the Reichswehr.[14]

Amid these growing economic ties, Weimar Germany and Soviet Russia also pursued closer diplomatic relations. On 16 April 1922, during a pan-European economic summit in Italy, German and Soviet diplomats left the deliberations to conclude their own bilateral agreement. The Treaty of Rapallo, as it was known, marked the first normalisation of relations between any capitalist state and Soviet Russia. It was intended by its authors to help both states escape their own international isolation.[15]

In early 1923, the Weimar German government claimed – on dubious grounds – it was no longer capable of making reparations payments to the Allies. The French government responded by occupying Germany's industrial heartland, the Ruhr, to forcibly extract payment. The Ruhr Crisis greatly damaged the young Weimar Republic and led to decisions in Berlin which would trigger hyperinflation. In addition, this public demonstration of the country's military weakness led Seeckt to expand commitments to the (recently renamed) Soviet Union.[16] Two meetings held in Moscow that spring led to further commitments to cooperate, including agreements for direct investment by the Reichswehr in Soviet military industry, with the understanding that Soviet factories would produce munitions for the Reichswehr should a general war break out.

By the summer of 1923, the Reichswehr had active investments in two large-scale industrial concerns. The first was the Junkers aviation plant at Fili, still in the process of organisation. The second was a chemical weapons complex near Samara called Bersol, managed by the German firm Stolzenberg AG, whose task was to manufacture chemical weapons and gas shells for both armies. Despite considerable investment from both Germany and the USSR, however, both facilities failed to meet expectations, in part because of the tremendous difficulties of operating in post-civil-war Russia. By 1924, the Bersol plant employed nearly 1,400 people and had two large plants undergoing modernisation, but had failed to produce any of the half million gas shells expected annually, nor any of the chemical weapons agents specified in its contract.[17] The Junkers concession at Fili had also grown to become a major industrial complex – employing more than 1,500 people – but it had only assembled 73 aircraft of mixed quality.[18]

Facing concerns about these corporate ventures in the USSR, the German ambassador in Moscow, Count Ulrich von Brockdorff-Rantzau, met with Trotsky on 9 June 1924. Agreeing about the mixed success of the corporate ventures, they agreed to instead concentrate on expanding military-to-military cooperation. To assist the Soviet Air Force, the Reichswehr would begin dispatching 'consultants' to train Soviet pilots, mechanics, and engineers in August. The Soviets reciprocated by sending a representative to participate in Reichswehr manoeuvres and training courses that year, a programme that would soon expand greatly and eventually include stays by 156 senior Soviet officers of up to a year at a time.[19]

As part of this change in strategy, on 15 April 1925, the Reichswehr accepted a Soviet offer to lease Lipetsk Air Base in south-central Russia. At this facility, Seeckt intended to train a new generation of pilots, develop German aviation doctrine, and test new aircraft prototypes. In exchange, the Soviet military required access to all German technology at the facility, as well as assistance with training pilots and mechanics alongside their German counterparts. To maintain the fiction that the German military was not involved, twelve 'retired' officers were duly dispatched to serve as the core training staff. After shipping a number of prefabricated buildings from Germany, the base began to receive its first pilots in June 1925.[20]

In March 1926, the German government welcomed a Soviet negotiating team to Berlin. Their visit eventually resulted in the Treaty of Berlin, renewing the Treaty of Rapallo and pledging the neutrality of each side in the event that either state went to war with a third party. Even as those terms were being concluded, Soviet military representatives met privately with Seeckt and senior Reichswehr officers to pitch what they called the 'Big Programme' of expanded collaboration. The Reichswehr did not accept all of the Soviet proposals but did agree to open a new joint armoured-warfare training and testing facility in the USSR, to expand joint officer training, exchange technical information (including submarine blueprints), and continue the production of military equipment in the USSR. Critically, the Reichswehr did not inform Germany's government of its decisions.[21]

Following these meetings, the Soviets and Germans expanded their ambitions for their joint facilities, agreeing to increase the technical work performed at Lipetsk and finalising arrangements for two new facilities. The first was a chemical weapons testing facility at Podosinki, just twelve miles from central Moscow. Its task was to work on new deployment techniques for chemical weapons, particularly in conjunction with air power. The Reichswehr dispatched a team of twelve German scientists and military officers to the site in September 1926, where they almost immediately began research under the close supervision of Soviet officers.[22] Even as they arrived, Soviet and German negotiators also finalised the terms of the joint armoured warfare training and testing ground, now codenamed 'Kama', to be established in Kazan – some 400 miles east of Moscow.[23]

In December 1926, as this network of bases grew, the first of a series of public scandals revealed to the world the scope and scale of Soviet-German cooperation. Despite their private enthusiasm for partnership with the Reichswehr, Soviet leaders were embarrassed by the revelations that they were working with arch-reactionary German military officers who had butchered communist revolutionaries in 1919 and 1923. As such, they demanded a 'political pause' – a halt to the further expansion of joint facilities. They also required that future cooperation be resumed on a 'legal basis' – that is, with the approval of the government in Berlin, whose limited knowledge and oversight had led to the scandals in the first place.[24] The Reichswehr, now headed by General Wilhelm Heye, agreed.[25] Perhaps to his surprise, Heye discovered that the German government largely supported secret rearmament measures in the USSR – provided they had some degree of oversight.[26]

Meanwhile, in the face of mounting evidence that the German army and navy were both evading Versailles on a large scale, British and French leaders disagreed over how to respond. The British government of Stanley Baldwin preferred the policy of 'appeasement'. The term was first used in reference to Germany in 1919 by a member of Lloyd George's cabinet, who had suggested a policy of reintegrating Germany into the European political and economic order by lifting the restrictions of Versailles over time.[27] The French, by contrast, sought to stringently enforce German disarmament. In part because of French strategic dependence on Britain, London eventually triumphed. There was no reaction to public revelations of the secret German rearmament programme, except for the withdrawal of the IAMCC inspectors whose task had been to supervise German disarmament in the first place. In its final report, the IAMCC warned, 'Germany has never disarmed, has never had the intention of disarming, and for seven years had done everything in her power to deceive and "counter-control" the Commission appointed to control her disarmament.'[28]

Having faced no consequences for its violations of Versailles, the German government greenlit the further expansion of the cooperative programme in the USSR in early 1928.[29] Not long after, in a sign of the improved atmosphere and increasing lack of concern about secrecy, the new head of the Reichswehr's *Truppenamt* (Troop Office), General Werner von Blomberg, made a lengthy in-person visit to the various facilities in the USSR.[30] Traveling for much of the trip in the company of Kliment Voroshilov, the Soviet Commissar of Defence, he was impressed by the extent of the joint facilities. At that juncture, a much larger chemical weapons base had just opened at Tomka near Samara in Central Russia, replacing the one at Podosinki. In addition, the engineering team in place at the armoured warfare training ground at Kama had begun experimenting with rudimentary armoured vehicles while awaiting the arrival of prototypes from Germany. And at Lipetsk, the German staff had further expanded their training programme, which had already grown to more than 180 pilots and engineers by the end of the previous year.[31] The only unsatisfactory point from Voroshilov's perspective was that Blomberg refused to commit to fighting Poland should a new Polish-Soviet War break out – something the tiny Reichswehr was ill-prepared to do in any case.[32]

With the end of the political pause, several other new initiatives began. In the spring of 1929, the armoured warfare facility at Kama started its first full armoured warfare training course, with twenty students drawn from both militaries. Classes were divided between theory and practice. Students were expected to master the basic functions of the tank – driving, communication, loading, and shooting. Rather tellingly, Soviet students dressed up the dummies on the target range in Polish and Czech uniforms.[33] This programme was greatly aided by the arrival of the first armoured vehicles in May 1929. These included a mix of Soviet-owned tanks purchased abroad and German armoured vehicle prototypes, which had been shipped to the USSR disguised as agricultural tractors to fool any Allied inspectors or spies who might be monitoring them.[34] These were used both to teach students driving and to provide opportunities for testing and development.

With the arrival of armoured vehicles, that last task – technical development – became one of Kama's primary missions. Three companies had won contracts to work at Kama: Krupp, Rheinmetall, and Daimler. All three dispatched engineering teams alongside their prototypes to the facility, where they lived alongside the officers in training, seeking to put their prototypes to the test and draw lessons for future designs. The technical work they performed at Kama between 1929 and 1933 had a huge impact on German tank design and production. Most of the engineers involved in designing German tanks during the Second World War gained their initial experience working at Kama. And most of the tanks used by Germany through 1943 – the Panzers I, II, III, and IV – were products of the lessons learned from the prototype testing performed at Kama.[35] It should be noted that much of this process was collaborative between the Soviet and German engineering teams, with each borrowing technology from the other.[36] The Soviets also made extensive technical changes to their tank designs based on the joint work carried out at Kama.

Much the same process of training and technical development was playing out some 500 miles away at Lipetsk. By 1929, the school had grown to host more than 400 German and Soviet officers and men. As at Kama, as the training programme expanded, technical testing did too.

There would soon be 115 engineers, designers, and test pilots in Lipetsk's research division alone.[37] Their main task was to test new aircraft and equipment, ranging from radios to parachutes. Between 1930 and 1933, six different German aviation firms – of the seven extant in Germany at that time – would send nearly two dozen different aircraft prototypes to Lipetsk to be flown by test pilots and evaluated by the Reichswehr's experienced aeronautical team in residence there. Like Kama, the technical work at Lipetsk provided the basis for the manufacture of combat aircraft for the next decade. The observation, borrowing, and outright theft of German prototypes at Lipetsk were tremendously useful to the Soviet Union's own ongoing aviation programme; one civilian designer sued the Soviet Union in international court for patent infringement.[38]

At the chemical weapons facility Tomka, the research programme was somewhat different. It centred on attempts by joint Soviet and German research teams to develop new technologies and tactics for chemical warfare. The great ambition was to determine whether the sorts of chemical agents used in the First World War – phosgene, chlorine, and mustard gas – could be used in conjunction with evolving technologies of war to either carpet bomb enemy cities from the air or spray chemical agents from advancing tanks. To that end, Tomka had a small fleet of aircraft and 'chemical tanks', which were used to drop chemical bombs or spray chemical agents on a testing ground, often full of caged test subjects – dogs and rabbits. By mid-1931, both sides increasingly drew the conclusion that chemical warfare – barring major technical advances – did not work well with their developing doctrines of mobile, high-speed warfare.[39] This would be one factor in its non-use in Europe during the Second World War.

The height of Soviet-German military cooperation was reached in 1931. The following spring, to Soviet dismay, the Reichswehr began to scale back its commitments in Russia. The ostensible reason was cost-cutting in the face of the Great Depression. But, in fact, convinced that the British and French would not intervene, the German military had become increasingly audacious about resuming testing and weapons production in Germany in violation of Versailles. Well before Hitler came to power, the German Ministry of Defence had already approved plans to expand the size of the army from ten to twenty-one divisions and begin tooling up German industry for long-term rearmament.[40] As one officer recorded in 1932, the only reason for maintaining the facilities in the USSR was the political relationship with the Red Army.[41]

Stalin had also decided to embark on a military build-up, though on a much larger scale than the Germans.[42] After exiling Trotsky, Stalin had risked civil war with a grand scheme to collectivise Soviet agriculture in 1929. Under this programme, the Soviet state nationalised farmland and seized grain from Soviet peasants; the grain was then sold abroad in order to buy industrial and military equipment, primarily from Germany and America.[43] Amid the horrific famine collectivisation produced, Soviet military spending and production skyrocketed. Thanks in part to more than a decade of German assistance, the USSR had developed the foundations to become a world leader in aircraft and tank production. Soviet tank production grew from 26 in 1929 to 3,121 in 1932.[44] By the following year, Soviet planners estimated in the event of war they could produce up to 40,400 armoured vehicles and more than 13,000 aircraft a year, figures dwarfing any other country in the world.[45]

Even as the Soviet and German armies grew, the political landscape shifted. In July 1932, Adolf Hitler's Nazi Party became the largest party in the Reichstag, winning 37.3 per cent of the vote. It was not quite enough to seize power but greatly undermined efforts then underway to block Hitler from power. Attempts by senior Reichswehr officers to bar Hitler from office floundered amid concerns that much of the army was sympathetic to the Nazis.[46] In this context, on 30 January 1933, Hitler accepted President Paul von Hindenburg's offer to form a new government. Within two months, the Nazis established dictatorial control over much of the country and began to reorient Germany's foreign policy.

There was, naturally, some alarm in Moscow, especially as Hitler's book *Mein Kampf* had explicitly called for the destruction of the USSR. But Stalin, interpreting the Nazi revolution in class terms, still considered the Nazi takeover as better for Soviet interests than victory by the Social Democrats, communism's main rival with Germany's working class.[47] Hitler's early decision to renew the 1926 Treaty of Berlin and his public statements in 1933 that he was 'determined to cultivate friendly relations' with the USSR also assuaged some Soviet concerns.[48] Nevertheless, given Hitler's willingness to ignore Versailles, the various facilities in the USSR soon became redundant – such testing and training could now be conducted in Germany. By September 1933 the last of the joint bases closed, followed by most of the major German-funded military-industrial concerns. With the end of cooperation came a rapid deterioration in Soviet-German relations.

Meanwhile, Hitler's priority was accelerating German rearmament. He soon ordered the mass production of tanks (January 1934), tripled the size of the army (June 1934), re-established the German Air Force (February 1935), and reintroduced conscription (March 1935). By that juncture, the French Minister of War concluded privately that Germany already possessed the strongest army in Europe.[49] The British and French were nevertheless slow to react. France reduced the size of its army by 10 per cent in 1933 and only began real rearmament efforts in 1936.[50] Great Britain waited even longer: Chancellor of the Exchequer Neville Chamberlain ordered further drastic cuts to the country's already anaemic defence spending as late as 1937.[51] As a result, Hitler grew increasingly bold as he violated the last remaining terms of Versailles.

Only one state seemed to possess the capacity and will to stop Germany in the early stages of this new arms race: the USSR. Stalin's Red Army was, on paper, the strongest in Europe. And following the end of military cooperation, the USSR began taking a series of steps seemingly designed to contain Hitler. In December 1933, the Politburo officially endorsed the strategy of 'collective security' – building a network of partnerships with capitalist states to improve Soviet security.[52] This led to the Franco-Soviet and Czechoslovak-Soviet Treaties of Mutual Assistance, both signed in 1935.[53] Six months later, the Comintern in Moscow announced the 'Popular Front', whereby Communist parties were ordered to cease attacks against other left-wing parties and, instead, seek to build coalitions against Fascism. Nevertheless, behind the scenes, Soviet diplomacy made it clear that Stalin had never entirely abandoned the prospect of a partnership with Berlin, as the USSR signed a new trade agreement with Nazi Germany in April 1935 and repeatedly proposed the resumption of earlier military cooperation to German officials.[54]

Though the door remained open to rapprochement, Soviet-German relations plunged to a new nadir, driven by public rhetoric, ideological hostility, and strategic competition. It was the Munich Conference in September 1938 which provided a spur for both leaders to revisit the prospect. Despite his bloodless victory in acquiring the Sudetenland from Czechoslovakia, Hitler was disappointed, having not gotten the short, victorious war he sought.[55] Stalin was also irate in Munich's aftermath. The USSR had not been invited to the conference despite its alliances with Czechoslovakia and France.[56] This was in part due to the fact that the USSR was in the midst of a vast, bloody purge of its military, intelligence, and diplomatic services, which left it seemingly useless as a potential ally from the perspectives of London and Paris.

As a result, German and Soviet diplomats began a new round of trade talks that included the possibility of renewed military collaboration in December 1938.[57] Those talks stalled until March 1939, largely because Hitler still hoped for a pact with neighbouring Poland against the USSR. But, following Hitler's seizure of the remainder of Czechoslovakia, Neville Chamberlain issued a security guarantee to Poland – again without consulting the USSR. Now certain that Poland was his adversary, Hitler ordered preparations to invade. Concluding that Soviet neutrality would be hugely beneficial, just weeks later, Hitler relayed word to the Soviet Commissariat of Foreign Affairs that 'a new Rapallo stage should be achieved in Soviet-German relations'.[58] Beginning in May, talks resumed about forging a new economic and political partnership.

For Stalin, cooperation with Germany meant territorial gains, the resumption of military-industrial cooperation, and the possibility of remaining neutral while Britain, France, and Germany exhausted each other in a war in Western Europe.[59] But, hoping to raise the price Hitler would pay for Soviet partnership, Stalin invited an Anglo-French negotiating team to Moscow. The night they arrived, Stalin informed the Politburo he intended to open final negotiations with Hitler.[60] Two weeks later, on 23 August German Foreign Minister Joachim von Ribbentrop arrived in Moscow. Following a few final concessions, Ribbentrop affixed his name alongside Vyacheslav Molotov's on the pact that would bear their names. Their agreement partitioned Eastern Europe into spheres of influence and pointed towards the resumption of economic exchange on a mass scale.

Secure in the east, Hitler invaded Poland on 1 September 1939. As German forces rapidly overran the western portions of the country, Stalin – surprised at the pace of German success – ordered the Red Army to invade from the east on 17 September. The two armies began meeting the following day.[61] For the next twenty-two months, despite

Figure 1.1 A Soviet political commissar and senior German officers in discussion at Brest-Litowsk, September 1939. Source: ullstein bild via Getty Images.

mutual suspicion, Berlin and Moscow would be partners in the conquest of much of Europe. Between them, they would invade fourteen sovereign states during that time, often assisting each other in the process. The Soviets helped provide navigational aids to German aircraft during their invasion of Poland, assisted in the arming and deception operations of German commerce raiders in the Pacific and Atlantic, and even invited the Germans to open a naval base near the Soviet port of Murmansk, which began operations in November 1939.[62] In exchange, the Germans agreed to assist the Soviets in their invasion of Finland by supplying Soviet naval vessels; they also agreed to dispatch officers and engineers to the USSR to assist Soviet military industry.[63] Most significantly, negotiators also signed a series of economic agreements, which made the two economies heavily interdependent and helped make Hitler's war in the west possible. By 1940, the USSR had pledged to deliver a million tons of grain, 900,000 tons of oil, 800,000 tons of iron, 500,000 tons of phosphates, 100,000 tons of chrome, as well as copper, cobalt, molybdenum, nickel, tin, and wolfram in exchange for renewed technical assistance and vast quantities of German military and industrial equipment.[64]

Figure 1.2 German generals Mauritz von Wiktorin (left) and Heinz Guderian (center) with Soviet general Semyon Krivoshein (right) during the German-Soviet military parade in Brest-Litovsk on 22 September 1939. Source: AFP via Getty Images.

The seeming success of their partnership brought tensions, however. Hitler resented Germany's growing economic dependence on the USSR and its continuing neutrality in the war against Great Britain. The Soviets were concerned with Nazi intentions and activities in the Balkans and Finland following the sudden defeat of France in June 1940; troops moved rapidly to annex Estonia, Latvia, Lithuania, and Romanian Bessarada in the summer of 1940. They also invaded the Romanian territory of North Bukovina, which had not been included in the Molotov-Ribbentrop Pact, alarming Berlin in turn.[65] To address these growing difficulties, in November 1940 Ribbentrop invited Molotov to Berlin. In exchange for full Soviet entry into the war, Hitler and Ribbentrop offered a new agreement on spheres of influence, covering much of the rest of the world. But Molotov, following Stalin's orders, took a 'tough line' and refused to consider such terms until past agreements were honoured to the full. Nevertheless, a Soviet counter-offer on a military alliance followed not long after the conference. It came too late: Hitler had already decided upon war. On

18 December 1940 he issued Directive Number 21, ordering preparations for Operation Barbarossa – the invasion of the Soviet Union.[66]

Beginning on 22 June without a formal declaration of war, more than three million Axis soldiers invaded the USSR. Despite months of warnings, Operation Barbarossa achieved nearly complete surprise against a Red Army still recovering from Stalin's purges. The result was chaos and carnage: over the course of the next six weeks, the unprepared Red Army would suffer staggering losses of roughly a quarter-million casualties per week.[67] More than thirty million people would die in Eastern Europe over the next four years. Two decades of Soviet-German cooperation had succeeded in overturning the European order, only to lead to a war of annihilation between Berlin and Moscow.

Notes

1 'The Russo-German Pact', *Manchester Guardian*, 23 August 1939, p. 8.

2 P. J. Philip, 'France Prepares to Stop Germany', *New York Times*, 23 August 1939, p. 1; 'Reich and Soviet Sign 10-Year Pact', *New York Times*, 24 August 1939, p. 1.

3 A. Beevor, *Russia: Revolution and Civil War, 1917–1921* (London: Viking, 2022), pp. 145–150, 155.

4 V. Sebestyen, *Lenin: The Man, the Dictator, and the Master of Terror* (New York: Pantheon Books, 2017), pp. 341–343.

5 R. Haigh, D. Morris, and A. Peters, *German-Soviet Relations in the Weimar Era: Friendship from Necessity* (Totowa, NJ: Barnes and Noble, 1985), p. 28.

6 F. L. Carsten, *The Reichswehr and Politics, 1918–1933* (Berkeley: University of California Press, 1966), p. 6.

7 G. Hilger and A. G. Meyer, *The Incompatible Allies: A Memoir-History of German-Soviet Relations, 1918–1941* (New York: Hafner, 1971), p. 73.

8 V. Vourkoutiotis, *Making Common Cause: German-Soviet Secret Relations, 1919–1922* (New York: Palgrave MacMillan, 2007), p. 44.

9 R. Shuster, *German Disarmament after World War I: The Diplomacy of International Arms Inspection, 1920–1931* (London: Routledge, 2006), p. 27.

10 W. Groener, *Lebenserinnerungen: Jugend, Generalstab, Weltkrieg*, ed. F. von Gaertringen (Göttingen: Vandenhoeck und Ruprecht, 1957), p. 503.

11 G. Schramm, 'Basic Features of German Ostpolitik, 1918–1939', in *From Peace to War: Germany, Soviet Russia, and the World, 1939–1941*, ed. Bernd Wegner (Providence, RI: Berghahn Books, 1997), p. 23.

12 Y. Dyakov and T. Bushuyeva, eds., *The Red Army and the Wehrmacht: How the Soviets Militarized Germany and Paved the Way for Fascism, from the*

Secret Archives of the Former Soviet Union (Amherst, NY: Prometheus Books, 1995), p. 32.

13. Vourkoutiotis, *Making Common Cause*, pp. 122–123.

14. I. O. Johnson, *Faustian Bargain: The Soviet-German Partnership and the Origins of the Second World War* (New York: Oxford University Press, 2021), p. 46.

15. C. Fink, *The Genoa Conference: European Diplomacy, 1921–1922* (Chapel Hill: University of North Carolina Press, 1993), p. 152.

16. Haigh, Morris, and Peters, *German-Soviet Relations*, pp. 92–93.

17. S. Gorlov, *Sovershenno Sekretno: Alianz Moskva-Berlin, 1920–1933* (Moscow: Olma Press, 2001), pp. 104–105.

18. W. Wagner, *Hugo Junkers Pionier der Luftfahrt – seine Flugzeuge* (Bonn: Bernard und Graefe Verlag, 1996), pp. 217–229.

19. Johnson, *Faustian Bargain*, pp. 70, 75.

20. Ibid., pp. 84–85.

21. Gorlov, *Sovershenno Sekretno*, p. 172.

22. Ibid., pp. 134–135.

23. Dyakov and Bushuyeva, eds., *The Red Army and the Wehrmacht*, pp. 164–170.

24. Gorlov, *Sovershenno Sekretno*, p. 93.

25. M. Zeidler, *Reichswehr und Rote Armee, 1920–1933: Wege Und Stationen einer ungewöhnlichen Zusammenarbeit* (Munich: Oldenbourg Verlag, 1994), pp. 149–153.

26. W. Deist, 'The Rearmament of the Wehrmacht', in *Germany and the Second World War, Volume I: The Build-Up of German Aggression*, ed. Wilhelm Deist, Manfred Messerschmidt, Hans-Erich Volkmann, and Wolfram Wette (Oxford: Clarendon Press, 1990), p. 382.

27. Martin Gilbert, *The Roots of Appeasement* (London: Weidenfeld and Nicolson, 1966), p. 52.

28. B. Whaley, *Covert German Rearmament, 1919–1939: Deception and Misperception* (Frederick, MD: University Publications of America, 1984), p. 33.

29. Zeidler, *Reichswehr und Rote Armee*, p. 153.

30. J. Erickson, *The Soviet High Command: A Military-Political History, 1918–1941* (London: Frank Cass, 2001), pp. 263–265.

31. Dyakov and Bushuyeva, eds., *The Red Army and the Wehrmacht*, p. 157.

32. Erickson, *The Soviet High Command*, p. 265.

33. K. Müller, So lebten und arbeiteten wir 1929 bis 1933 in Kama (unpublished memoir, 1972), pp. 29, 34.

34. A. Nekrich, *Pariahs, Partners, Predators: German Soviet Relations, 1922–1941*, ed. and trans. Gregory Freeze (New York: Columbia University Press, 1997), p. 78.

35. M. Habeck, *Storm of Steel: The Development of Armor Doctrine in Germany and the Soviet Union, 1919–1939* (Ithaca, NY: Cornell University Press, 2003), p. 226.

36. W. Spielberger, *Die Motorisierung der Deutschen Reichswehr 1920–1935* (Stuttgart: Motorbuch, 1995), p. 282.

37. Johnson, *Faustian Bargain*, p. 150.

38. Famed aviation pioneer Hugo Junkers tried to sue the Soviet government through the Permanent Court of Arbitration at The Hague on the grounds that the first Soviet monoplane bomber, the TB-1, was largely derivative of his own work, borrowing its design and corrugated aluminium wings from Junkers's own designs; it did not help that the aircraft was produced exclusively at Fili, the aircraft factory that Junkers's corporation had modernised and managed for a number of years. Johnson, *Faustian Bargain*, p. 150.

39. Johnson, *Faustian Bargain*, pp. 139–141, 159.

40. A. Tooze, *The Wages of Destruction: The Making and Breaking of the Nazi Economy* (New York: Viking Penguin, 2007), p. 26.

41. Zeidler, *Reichswehr und Rote Armee*, p. 304.

42. See D. R. Stone, *Hammer and Rifle: The Militarization of the Soviet Union, 1926–1933* (Lawrence: University Press of Kansas, 2000).

43. R. Suny, *The Soviet Experiment: Russia, the USSR, and the Successor States* (Oxford: Oxford University Press, 1998), p. 224.

44. S. Zaloga and J. Grandsen, *Soviet Tanks and Combat Vehicles of World War Two* (London: Arms and Armour Press, 1988), p. 108.

45. L. Samuelson, *Soviet Defence Industry Planning: Tukhachevskii and Military-Industrial Mobilization, 1926–1937* (Stockholm: Stockholm Institute of East European Economies, 1996), pp. 208–209.

46. E. W. Bennett, *German Rearmament and the West, 1932–1933* (Princeton, NJ: Princeton University Press, 1979), p. 277.

47. S. Kotkin, *Stalin, Volume II: Waiting for Hitler, 1929–1941* (New York: Penguin Press, 2017), p. 119.

48. Nekrich, *Pariahs, Partners, Predators*, p. 60.

49. S. Schuker, 'France and the Remilitarization of the Rhineland, 1936', *French Historical Studies*, 14 (1986), p. 322.

50. M. Thomas, 'French Economic Affairs and Rearmament: The First Crucial Months, June–September 1936', *Journal of Contemporary History*, 27:4 (October 1992), p. 660.

51. B. Bond and W. Murray, 'The British Armed Forces, 1918–1939', in A. R. Millett and W. Murray, eds., *Military Effectiveness, Volume II: The Interwar Period* (Boston: Unwin Hyman, 1988), pp. 98–130; 103.

52. J. Haslam, *The Soviet Union and the Struggle for Collective Security in Europe, 1933–1939* (New York: St. Martin's Press, 1984), p. 145.

53. Z. Steiner, *The Triumph of the Dark: European International History* (Oxford: Oxford University Press, 2011), pp. 94–95.

54. M. Zeidler, 'German-Soviet Economic Relations During the Hitler-Stalin Pact', in B. Wegner, ed., *From Peace to War: Germany, Soviet Russia, and the World, 1939–1941* (Providence, RI: Berghahn Books, 1997), p. 97.

55. M. Messerschmidt, 'Foreign Policy and Preparation for War', in *Germany and the Second World War, Volume I*, pp. 672–673.

56. Z. Steiner, 'The Soviet Commissariat of Foreign Affairs and the Czechoslovakian Crisis in 1938: New Material from the Soviet Archives', *The Historical Journal*, 42:3 (September 1999), pp. 751–779.

57. E. Ericson III, *Feeding the German Eagle: Soviet Economic Aid to Nazi Germany, 1933–1941* (Westport, CT: Praeger, 1999), pp. 28–30; Johnson, *Faustian Bargain*, p. 202.

58. I. Maisky, *The Maisky Diaries: Red Ambassador to the Court of St. James, 1932–1943*, ed. G. Gorodetsky (New Haven: Yale University Press, 2015), p. 203.

59. R. Moorhouse, *The Devil's Alliance: Hitler's Pact with Stalin, 1939–1941* (New York: Basic Books, 2014), p. 15.

60. Kotkin, *Stalin: Waiting for Hitler*, p. 657.

61. Roger Moorhouse, *Poland 1939: The Outbreak of World War II* (New York: Basic Books, 2020), pp. xxix, 195.

62. T. Philbin, *The Lure of Neptune: German-Soviet Naval Collaboration and Ambitions, 1919–1941* (Columbia: University of South Carolina Press, 1994), p. 99.

63. Johnson, *Faustian Bargain*, pp. 213, 218–219.

64. R. J. Sontag and J. S. Beddie, eds., *Nazi-Soviet Relations 1939–1941: Nazi-Soviet Relations, 1939–1941: Documents from the Archives of the German Foreign Office* (Washington, DC: Department of State, 1948), pp. 260–264.

65. Johnson, *Faustian Bargain*, p. 223.

66. Ibid, p. 131.

67. D. Glantz and J. House, *When Titans Clashed: How the Red Army Stopped Hitler* (Lawrence: University Press of Kansas, 2015), pp. 33–34, 391.

2

Political Thinking and Strategic Planning for Hitler's *Lebensraum* in the East

This chapter examines the background strategy to the invasion and pacification of the Soviet Union on the part of Hitler as commander in chief of the German armed forces and of German military leadership in general. The Nazi dictator saw human existence as a struggle between superior and inferior races. For the Germans to continue to remain first among the races, he believed they needed to conquer the agriculturally fertile living space (*Lebensraum*) to their east at the expense of a racially inferior Slavic population. This population, in turn, would be decimated and enslaved to serve the needs of its new masters. Hitler called for the annihilation of what he perceived as the Judeo-Bolshevik leadership class of the Soviet Union, headed by the dictator Josef Stalin but ultimately controlled by the forces of international Jewry. Overrunning the European Soviet Union, finally, would secure the Reich a colossal economic bounty, a base of economic resources Hitler considered sufficient for it to make a play for global supremacy.[1]

This invasion strategy had ideologically driven brutality baked into it. It did not, however, determine the decision for when to invade. And it gives us pause to consider the willingness of German military leadership to sign up for such an ambitious, ruthless undertaking. This chapter thus examines the pressures and opportunities Hitler experienced in the evolving wartime situation that persuaded him to attack when he did, along with the attitudes of the senior officer corps of the German army and Luftwaffe. The timing and planning of the attack were shaped by military, political, logistical, economic, and diplomatic considerations. Also crucial in shaping German leadership decisions were the roles of military intelligence, or rather the lack of it, and unexpected events. The chapter also considers the military, ideological, logistical, and economic factors involved in shaping the intensely severe, racially suffused pacification policies envisioned for the freshly overrun regions.

2.1 Timing the Invasion

Germany's long-term motives for invading the Soviet Union did not themselves determine the timing of the invasion. Opportunistic in international as in domestic affairs, Hitler chose to attack in 1941, considerably earlier than the mid-1940s time frame he had originally outlined to his military and diplomatic chiefs in 1937.[2] He did so in response to emerging pressures and opportunities.

Hitler's turn against the Soviet Union evolved across the second half of 1940. Following the fall of France, the dictator hoped Britain would make peace with Germany. He was aware, moreover, of the long-term dangers posed by Britain's continuation of the war. Despite the setback Britain had suffered with the fall of France, she commanded ongoing access to global supplies, an unmatched naval strength, and the manpower and resources of her empire and commonwealth. Britain could blockade Germany, as she had to eventually ruinous effect during the Great War. This time around, Germany possessed more occupied territory and hence supply lines for its domestic population, but there were limits to these chains of supply and Germany was shut off from global markets. Longer-term, Britain's ongoing participation in the war made it increasingly likely that the United States eventually would be drawn in on her side.

When Britain, under its new prime minister Winston Churchill, refused to come to terms, Hitler was compelled to recognise that he lacked any immediate means of bending Britain to his will. The Luftwaffe could not defeat the Royal Air Force. The German navy, the *Kriegsmarine*, was too small, particularly following losses during the Norway campaign, to guard any invasion fleet in the English Channel against the numerically superior Royal Navy.[3] Any 'peripheral' strategy to force Britain to terms by knocking away her props in and around the Mediterranean, such as the Suez Canal and the Gibraltar naval base, would have depended on mutual cooperation by the mutually distrustful nationalist Spain, Vichy France, and Germany's Axis ally fascist Italy. Moreover, the only service branch advocating such a strategy, the Kriegsmarine, was very much the junior branch of Germany's armed forces. Strategy, then, dovetailed with ideology, as Hitler came to believe that the best, indeed only, means of forcing the British to negotiate was to demoralise them into doing so by conquering the Soviet Union and thereby removing their only remaining hope of a powerful continental European ally.[4]

Yet while Hitler first expressed an interest in invading the Soviet Union sooner rather than later on 31 July 1940, he would not settle irrevocably on that course until the autumn. His growing resolve was reinforced by the worsening state of Soviet-German relations during the second half of 1940.

Privately, neither dictatorship harboured any illusions that the Nazi-Soviet non-aggression pact of August 1939 constituted anything more than a mutually beneficial breathing space in which to prepare for an eventual clash. Hitler's alarm button was activated when, in the summer of 1940, the Soviet Union used the breathing space to overrun the Baltic states, then pressure Romania to relinquish its eastern territories of Bessarabia and Bukovina. The latter move particularly rattled the dictator due to the threat it apparently posed to the Romanian oil fields at Ploesti, upon which Germany was especially dependent.[5] These were defensive moves by Stalin, designed to create a buffer zone against the Reich rather than offensive preliminaries, but Hitler chose not to see them that way.

Stalin, fearful himself of the apparent strength of Germany's diplomatic position, urged Foreign Minister Vyacheslav Molotov to play hardball in the face of German suggestions that the Soviet Union turn its attention from its interests in the eastern Baltic, the Balkans, and the Dardanelles to the Persian Gulf, Iran, and India. The increasingly prickly tone of Soviet-German diplomatic relations became all too clear during Molotov's visit to Berlin in November 1940.[6] The prospect of invading the Soviet Union also presented Hitler with numerous economic temptations. Its grain, oil, and other resources promised an economic bonanza far in excess not just of that provided

Figure 2.1 Russian Foreign Minister Vyacheslav Molotov and his German counterpart Joachim von Ribbentrop walk past a line of troops outside a train station in Berlin, November 1940. Source: Laski Diffusion/Getty Images.

by the conquered territories of western Europe but also of the limited economic benefits of the Nazi-Soviet pact itself.[7]

Hitler also perceived enticing opportunities in attacking the Soviet Union early. To an outside eye, the Red Army appeared in poor shape in 1940. Stalin had purged it of some of its best commanders during the late 1930s, and soldiers had performed poorly during the Winter War against Finland of 1939–1940. The flipside of this state of affairs, as Hitler saw it, was that the Red Army was also undergoing a radical reorganisation and might therefore grow more formidable over the coming years.[8] On this count, too, attacking the Soviet Union sooner rather than later seemed to make military sense.

2.2   Intelligence Failures

Yet the Führer, the Army High Command (*Oberkommando des Heeres*, or OKH), and the military intelligence on whom they extensively based their judgements seriously overestimated the extent of the Red Army's weaknesses. The damage Stalin's purges had inflicted on the Red Army was less severe than they supposed. They also underestimated the number of troops the Red Army would be able to mobilise in the event of invasion, and overlooked the possibility that the Soviets would uproot much of their Europe-based industry and ship it eastward for reassembly beyond both the Ural Mountains and German bombing range.[9]

That the German leaders were so wide of the mark came down to three things. The first was the innate tendency of German military planners and intelligence specialists to underestimate Soviet fighting power. This was based on recent history: the poor showing of the Red Army during the Winter War and of the Tsar's army during the Great War. Second was the disdainful anti-Slavism that German military leadership shared extensively with Nazi leadership,[10] and third was the inadequacies of the German military intelligence department responsible for monitoring the Soviet Union's military capabilities.

Foreign Armies East (*Fremde Heere Ost*, hereafter FHO), the army office charged with overall responsibility for gathering intelligence on the Soviet Union, defined 'East' as encompassing not just the Soviet Union but also southeast Europe, Turkey, Iran, Scandinavia, and the Far East. Overseeing intelligence gathering across such a vast area were just fifteen officers. They also had to reckon with a lack of German agents in high places, no means of deciphering Soviet radio traffic, intensive Soviet border security, and insufficient aerial reconnaissance.[11] Many of their prognostications were hopelessly vague; they read too much into Soviet failings against the Finns, and they passed up a golden opportunity to examine Soviet military capabilities first-hand across the boundary of the German- and Soviet-controlled zones of occupied Poland.

2.3   Military Complacency and Force Comparisons

The dangerously inaccurate picture of Red Army capabilities that the FHO painted encouraged German army leadership to perceive an invasion of the Soviet Union as an unparalleled opportunity to show off. On the whole, German army leadership was loath to pass on the prospect of waging a continental campaign across copious flat, open terrain, suited to the kind of manoeuvre warfare that the panzer divisions excelled at. It was a prospect that presented the army with far greater opportunity to shine than the long-range intercontinental war, heavily reliant on air and sea power, that Hitler contemplated eventually waging against Britain and the United States. Added to all this was an inflated confidence in the German army's own tactical and operational abilities following its triumph over the French.[12]

Reinforcing such attitudes was a set of comparisons between German and Soviet forces on land and in the air. The Red Army outnumbered the German army, but not extensively, and the German army could count itself superior on several other counts. Overall, however, German military planners overestimated their own strengths just as they underestimated their enemy's. German soldiers were better-trained and, generally, better-educated than their Red Army opponents, and many rural Red Army recruits, particularly from the Ukraine, felt embittered towards Stalin's regime in the traumatic wake of collectivisation. On the other hand, Red Army soldiers from urban backgrounds had reason to be grateful for Soviet economic policies; education levels had risen dramatically in both rural and urban areas, and there was a network of military training camps and organisations. The Germans' own edge was softened by reduced training times dictated by the wartime need to get growing numbers of officers and men into the field, and by the dwindling number of new recruits from the youngest, fittest age groups.[13]

When it came to hardware, even though the Germans' use of the versatile 88mm anti-aircraft gun would narrow the gap, the Soviets commanded vastly more artillery than the Germans. Soviet mechanised corps were in a complex process of re-organisation, while the panzer divisions had already completed theirs before the invasion, and the vast majority of Red Army tanks were technically inferior to the Germans' medium Mark III and Mark IV Panzers. On the other hand, much of the Reich's panzer force comprised obsolescent Mark Is and Mark IIs, and Czech light tanks were easy prey for Soviet artillery and medium and heavy tanks. The formidable Soviet T-34, meanwhile, would prove a nasty surprise for the Germans after the invasion had started.[14]

The Germans had clearer advantages in air power. On the Soviet side, excellent models such as the Yak-1 fighter and the Sturmovik ground attack plane were coming into service, but were still few in number. Pilot training remained of a poor standard, and the Red Army air force overall was in a state of painful transition. The Germans, with the Messerschmitt 109, Stuka, and Heinkel, possessed superior fighters and bombers. Their crews were largely handpicked, highly trained, and extensively battle-hardened following a succession of campaigns stretching back to the Spanish Civil War. In the wake of Stalin's purges, they were also more daring and offensive-minded than their Soviet opponents. On the other hand, with large numbers of German aircraft committed against the British, the Luftwaffe could deploy no more than two-thirds of its full strength against the Soviet Union. It also lacked the kind of strategic bomber force that might have devastated Soviet industry further east; rather, its task – one it would initially fulfil to devastating effect where it could concentrate sufficient strength – was to provide support for the army's ground operations.[15]

2.4   The Invasion Plan

Hitler's Führer Directive 21, issued on 18 December 1940, contained the blueprint of the plan for invading the Soviet Union. It was codenamed Operation Barbarossa, after the twelfth-century German king and Holy Roman emperor. The invasion force would comprise three million men organised into more than 150 divisions across three army groups.[16] Yet the campaign plan they would follow placed too much faith in German advantages and paid too little heed to how limited those advantages would be in the context of a campaign that would be taking on so much.

'The bulk of the Russian army stationed in western Russia,' Hitler proclaimed, 'is to be destroyed in a series of daring operations spearheaded by armoured thrusts. The organized withdrawal of intact units into the vastness of interior Russia must be prevented.'[17] The Germans would then drive into the heart of the Soviet Union to take Leningrad and the Baltic states (the task of Army Group North); the economically essential regions of the Ukraine, the Donbass, and later the Caucasus (the task of Army Group South); and Moscow (the task of Army Group Centre). In order to achieve all these objectives, the Germans would need to advance rapidly along a wide front and reach their targets at the very latest before winter came. They were tasked with eventually establishing a line east of Moscow, from Archangel to the River Volga, from which the Luftwaffe would bomb Soviet factories beyond the Urals. Two-thirds of German land forces would then be withdrawn, while the remaining third would man the Reich's new eastern frontier.[18]

But meeting all these targets would be rendered even more onerous by the fact that the army's panzer divisions were unevenly distributed across the army groups. They were arranged into four *Panzergruppen* (tank armies), but a mass encirclement of Soviet troops of the kind the OKH envisaged would require allocating two such *Panzergruppen* to whichever of the three army groups was conducting that particular manoeuvre. It was a matter of simple mathematics to grasp the fact that only one army group at a time would be able to achieve such a feat, while the others would need to make do with one *Panzergruppe* apiece. Furthermore, at the time of the invasion only about a sixth of the German army's divisions were mechanised or motorised; the rest would need to largely rely on slower horse-drawn supply.[19] One in fact almost perceives two armies – a modernised, mechanised and motorised force at the technological and tactical cutting edge, and a much larger, more technologically backward one resembling its 1914–1918 predecessor.

All this would inevitably slow the German advance by requiring the panzers to wait for the infantry to catch up. Even an army group with two *Panzergruppen* at its disposal, then, would find it harder to seal off and destroy cauldrons of encircled Soviet troops without enabling sizeable numbers of such troops to slip the net, return to their own lines, or form partisan groups in the German rear.

Hitler and the OKH agreed that two *Panzergruppen* should be allocated to Army Group Centre for the initial breakthrough and encirclement along the frontiers, but they disagreed over what should happen next. General Franz Halder, the OKH chief of staff, wanted to recommit the bulk of the armour on Army Group Centre's front in a drive on Moscow. Halder believed that Stalin would feel compelled to commit the Red Army's remaining forces to defending the Soviet Union's political and administrative centre, and the Germans would then be able to annihilate them. Hitler, however, placed more importance on objectives to the north and south. He believed that seizing the economic targets of the Ukrainian breadbasket, the Donbass industrial region, and the oil of the Caucasus was a surer way of defeating the Soviet Union, and that capturing Leningrad, named as it was after the Soviet Union's founder, would damage Soviet morale fatally.[20] Rather than disagree in vain to Hitler's face, Halder opted to appear to go along with the Führer's wishes, while surreptitiously steering the staff chiefs of the three army groups to prioritise their own major targets and ignore 'objections from the stratosphere'.[21] Having the high command working at such cross-purposes was hardly a recipe for smooth military operations.

The Luftwaffe was also committed to Barbarossa on a scale that it risked being unable to meet. Such was the numerical weakness of the Luftwaffe forces deployed in the east that they were unable to provide equal air cover for all three army groups. Strongest of all, with the great majority of Stuka dive bombers at its disposal, was *Luftflotte* (Air Fleet) 2 (II and VIII *Fliegerkorps* (Air Corps), assigned to the Army Group Centre area of operations. Army Group South could call upon *Luftflotte* 4 (IV and V *Fliegerkorps*) and the limited benefit of allied Romanian air power. The weakest allocation of air power was *Luftflotte* I, assigned to Army Group North, which contained one solitary *Fliegerkorps*. Overall, like the *Panzergruppen*, the *Luftflotten* could only provide force in sufficient strength to only one army group at a time.[22] The Kriegsmarine, meanwhile, was assigned only a subsidiary role in the invasion. Its main focus was on the eastern Baltic, where it would provide cover from maritime attack to the forces of Army Group North advancing on Leningrad.[23]

Speed was essential to the success of Barbarossa, for the longer it lasted, the less likely the prospect of German victory. Failure to beat the Soviets before winter would confront the Germans with the same fate as had befallen Napoleon in 1812. Even if the Germans were not driven out of the Soviet Union, their opponent's vastly greater population and material resources would make it increasingly difficult for them to prevail in a lengthy campaign – for Germany's economic means would fall considerably short in such a scenario. For one thing, it suffered severe shortages in industrial labour and crucial economic resources such as fuel and rubber. Furthermore, for too long during the first half of the war, the German economy was beset by bureaucratic chaos and a plethora of competing economic agencies. As a result, resource allocation was haphazard, and Hitler's general lack of interest in economic matters left Fritz Todt (his Minister of Munitions until his untimely death in an air crash in January 1942) without the Führer's effective backing to drive through the necessary rationalisation measures.[24]

Meanwhile, Germany's resources were perilously overstretched by the need to anticipate the intercontinental war that Hitler envisaged waging against Britain and the United States once the Soviet Union had been defeated. Thus many of the resources that might have been ploughed into mechanising and motorising the German army to the necessary level were earmarked for the Luftwaffe and Kriegsmarine – even though both branches had generally yet to benefit from them by the time of Barbarossa – in the cause of taking on the Reich's western enemies.[25]

It was under these inauspicious circumstances that General Eduard Wagner, chief army quartermaster, was charged with ensuring the supply of Barbarossa. Wagner recognised the poor conditions of the Soviet road network on which the Germans would have to rely during the campaign's opening phase. In the autumn of 1940, in order to try and overcome this logistical challenge, strict controls were imposed on the army's fuel consumption. Yet by the spring of 1941 the army still only held three months' worth of consumption in reserve. Wagner also pooled most of the infantry divisions' motorised transport in a central reserve, for distribution by each army group across their formations, but infantry divisions that did not benefit would have to rely on Polish *Panje* horse-drawn wagons. After the opening phase of the invasion, the distances involved in the further advance eastward would compel the army to rely on the Soviet railway network. But the German military's general, long-standing underestimation of the importance of logistics; insufficient coordination between German military and civilian transport bodies; and the Soviets' ability to wreck or remove track, locomotives, rolling stock, and maintenance equipment in the face of the German advance would combine to cripple German efforts in that area.[26]

Such was the contrast between Barbarossa's ambitions and the means at its disposal that it appears to reflect a collective sense of delusion. While the military chiefs had not fallen under Hitler's spell unquestioningly, their critical faculties had been increasingly blunted over the previous eight years. The Luftwaffe had always leaned markedly towards the Führer; it owed its very existence to the National Socialist regime, and its commander in chief was Hermann Göring. More generally, its breakneck expansion from nothing during the 1930s meant that, overall, its senior officer corps had not developed a sounder strategic and logistical grasp.[27]

The erosion of objective professionalism within the army's senior ranks had been a longer, more complex process. Even older, more conservative officers had long shared some of the Nazi movement's ideological conviction, particularly anti-Bolshevism. The army leadership had gained from the political murder of the leadership of the SA (*Sturmabteilung*, a paramilitary organization backed by the Nazi Party) in 1934 and had shown its gratitude – and surrendered its independence – by swearing an oath of loyalty to the Führer himself. Senior officers who remained critical of the regime were sacked or sidelined – or, like Halder, reconciled themselves to the regime for the sake of their careers.[28]

The first years of the war brought successive swift and (in the case of the fall of France) stunning victories that cemented Hitler's undeserved but much-trumpeted reputation as the 'greatest warlord of all time'.[29] The hubris that now increasingly infected the senior corps, not to mention Hitler's material bribery of several of its number, combined with ideology and rosy intelligence prognostications to secure a largely uncritical reception for the Barbarossa plans. Not only Halder but also many field commanders felt enormous professional self-confidence and superiority over the Red Army.[30] Officers who were more sceptical of the invasion plan generally avoided voicing their concerns openly. Moreover, they lacked any better ideas themselves for winning either the campaign or the war. This in itself reflects the strategic predicament in which Germany found itself; unable to bring Britain to terms by any other means, and correctly perceiving the long-term dangers of that ongoing situation, it opted for a solution that, if not entirely beyond its capabilities, left too little margin for error.

2.5 Allies and Complications

Even less margin remained after events set back the invasion start date from May to June. In the winter of 1940–1941, Italy had invaded Greece from Italian-occupied Albania. But the substandard Italian forces were badly mauled by a doughty Greek defence, benefiting from British military aid. This threatened Barbarossa's southern flank and compelled Hitler to divert forces to conquer Greece. Then in March 1941, following the pro-German Yugoslav government's joining of the Tripartite Pact

Figure 2.2 Benito Mussolini and Adolf Hitler visit the German army's headquarters in Mauerwald, East Prussia, 26 August 1941. Source: Library of Congress/Corbis/VCG via Getty Images.

with Germany, Italy, and Japan, a coup in Belgrade persuaded Hitler that military intervention was needed there also.[31] The Axis campaign in south-east Europe during the spring of 1941 lasted the better part of two months. Yet it was not the decisive factor in delaying Barbarossa; that distinction went to the myriad logistical problems caused by the spring thaw in the Soviet Union and by the disruption it inflicted to the airfields, supply routes, and other infrastructure the Germans would need to utilise during the invasion's opening weeks.[32] This was another factor that Operation Barbarossa's military planners overlooked.

The roles allotted to Germany's allies in Barbarossa were of marginal strategic significance at most. Finland, Romania, Italy, Hungary, and Slovakia would all come to be involved with varying degrees of commitment. These were determined by factors including these countries' domestic political power balances, the ideological and – sometimes at each other's expense – territorial ambitions of their governments, how far their fear of the Soviets trumped their concerns about making common cause with Hitler, and how worried they were that sitting out the campaign might leave them in a weaker state militarily, diplomatically, and economically.[33] Hitler envisaged an important role for Finland in helping the Germans seize the port of Murmansk and saw Romanian involvement as important in preventing any Soviet move on the Ploesti oil fields. The Slovaks and Hungarians were only engaged by the Germans at the onset of the invasion, largely serving as useful sources of security manpower in the occupied rear areas of Army Group South. Likewise, the Italians, whom Hitler sought to confine to the 'parallel war' in the Mediterranean, did not feature in German strategic planning for Barbarossa. This did not stop Mussolini from gatecrashing the operation, with a comparatively small but initially well-resourced military commitment, largely in the hope of sharing in both the glory of smashing Bolshevism and the resulting economic and territorial pickings.[34]

2.6 Securing *Lebensraum*

The ruthlessness the German invaders would exercise, whether against Soviet POWs, front-line Red Army units, or rear area civilians, was driven partly by Hitler's ideological detestation of 'Judeo-Bolshevism', shared extensively by the military leadership, along with a contempt for 'backward' Slavic peoples. There was also economic motivation; the army leadership had concluded that the Soviet transport system would struggle to support the supply of fuel and ammunition to the troops, let alone food, and so ordered them to live off the land – a euphemism for plundering the occupied population to a fatal extent. Similarly, the vast numbers of Red Army POWs Barbarossa's planners envisaged taking would be left exposed and starving so that, in a speedy campaign with acutely tight supply margins, the Germans need not expend time, shelter, or provisions on them.[35]

Moreover, according to General Halder, Hitler asserted that German occupation troops would need to exercise terror in order to keep occupied civilians under control.[36] Thus would they compensate for their own low numbers due to the vast majority of troops being earmarked for front-line fighting. This approach also chimed with an influential tradition within the German military of severe occupation security policies pursued in the name of 'harsh military necessity'.[37]

Occupied territory would eventually be divided into civilian-administered Reich *Commissariats* (administrative entities directly controlled by powerful governors, often acting directly on Hitler's instructions), but while the military campaign was ongoing the army would administer much of the occupied Soviet Union itself. Its jurisdiction would stretch from the front and the immediate operational zone, westwards through a belt of rear areas administered by the individual field armies, culminating in the army group rear areas North, Centre, and South. Apart from Estonians, none of the ethnic groups under German occupation were to be granted 'favourable' racial status, though there was a pecking order from Jews at the bottom up to Latvians and Lithuanians.[38]

The inadequate numbers of troops allocated to rear area security would need support in policing tasks. Most ominously, this included extensive reliance on the SS and Police. The Wagner-Heydrich agreement of 26 March, drawn up between the army's chief quartermaster and the head of the Reich Security Service (*Sicherheitsdienst*, hereafter SD), set out arrangements for eliminating 'emigrants, saboteurs, and terrorists' and gave the SS full powers to combat such threats within the army's jurisdiction. SS and Police units, meanwhile, would rely on the army for practical matters, such as supply and accommodation.[39] In practice, the agreement would provide cover for annihilating an ever more widely defined set of enemies, eventually including all Jews on German-occupied Soviet soil – an undertaking in which the army would soon be involved, its senior officer corps having largely buried its qualms about the conduct of the SS in its jurisdiction during the Polish campaign.[40] The SS and Police units assigned to the east initially comprised four 'task forces' or *Einsatzgruppen*, with personnel drawn from the SD, Gestapo, and Criminal Police. These would be augmented by a cavalry brigade and two infantry brigades of the Waffen-SS and by numerous battalions from the heavily militarised Order Police.[41]

German soldiers, depending on their age, had been subjected to a barrage of Nazi propaganda in civilian life, particularly if they were young enough to have gone through the Nazi youth movement and the Reich Labour Service. Now, the army took responsibility for indoctrinating them further in order to accept the supposedly cruel necessity of what war against the Soviet Union would require of them. Among other things, they were informed that the invasion of the Soviet Union was a pre-emptive strike. They were also issued with a set of broad, ruthless guidelines. The Barbarossa Decree and the Guidelines for the Conduct of the Troops instructed them to distrust the population and Red Army prisoners; to see them as treacherous, cruel, and devious; and to exercise the utmost ruthlessness against them. Both the army and the SS were to single out and execute captured Soviet commissars, the political officers of the Red Army.[42]

Ultimately, however, the ruthlessness that the German invaders would display during Barbarossa would backfire. The calculation was that it would terrorise the Soviets into submission, but it would in fact provoke intensifying Soviet resistance, both at the front and in the occupied areas.[43]

2.7 Conclusion

The aim of invading the Soviet Union, the decision for when to attack, and the conduct of the invasion and pacification were founded on the alternative realities that Hitler and the German military leadership created for themselves. Hitler's alternative ideological reality was of an arrangement of human affairs based on the notion of superior and inferior races. Defeating, destroying, and exploiting the Soviet Union, he believed, was essential to maintaining the status of the Germans as *the* superior race. The alternative military reality that drove the decision to invade derived from Hitler's belief that defeating the Soviet Union was the best means of persuading Britain to make peace. The fact that Hitler arrived at this conclusion, and that the military leadership backed him, also reflected the lack of viable strategic options open to Germany.

The planning of Operation Barbarossa itself, meanwhile, was rooted in an alternative reality in which the supposed tactical and operational brilliance of the German army and Luftwaffe would overcome the daunting array of challenges that invading the Soviet Union would present. This perspective was based not just on ideological contempt for 'inferior' eastern peoples but also on the Germans' stratospheric self-belief following the fall of France, on an inadequate intelligence operation whose findings reinforced it, and on the long-standing logistical blind spot in the German military mindset. Finally, ideologically suffused measures to cow the Red Army and pacify the newly occupied areas were founded on the self-defeating notion that indiscriminate harshness brought success. Such was the groundwork for Germany's eventual failure across every dimension of its war against the Soviet Union.

Notes

1 On the literature concerning how long-term Hitler's foreign policy goals were, see Ian Kershaw, *The Nazi Dictatorship: Problems and Perspectives of Interpretation*, 4th ed. (London: Bloomsbury, 2015), chapter 6.

2 Ian Kershaw, *Hitler 1936–1945: Nemesis* (London: Penguin, 2000), pp. 46–51.

3 Gerhard L. Weinberg, *A World at Arms: A Global History of World War II*, 2nd ed. (Cambridge: Cambridge University Press, 2005), pp. 116–118.

4 Kershaw, *Hitler 1936–1945*, pp. 330–331.

5 Jürgen Förster, 'Germany's Acquisition of Allies in South-East Europe', in Horst Boog, Jürgen Förster, Ernst Klink, Rolf-Dieter Müller, and Gerd R. Ueberschär, eds., *Germany and the Second World War. Volume IV: The Attack on the Soviet Union* (Oxford: Oxford University Press, 1996), p. 392.

6 William son Murray, *Luftwaffe* (London: Allen and Unwin, 1985), pp. 67–68.

7 Adam Tooze, *The Wages of Destruction: The Making and Breaking of the Nazi Economy* (London: Penguin, 2007), pp. 411–413, 418.

8 Craig Luther, *Barbarossa Unleashed: The German Blitzkrieg through Russia to the Gates of Moscow, June–December 1941* (Atglen, PA: Schiffer, 2014), pp. 144–148.

9 See Chapters 5 and 6 of this volume.

10 Jürgen Förster, 'Hitler's Decision in Favour of War against the Soviet Union', in Horst Boog, Jürgen Förster, Ernst Klink, Rolf-Dieter Müller, and Gerd R. Ueberschär, eds., *Germany and the Second World War. Volume IV: The Attack on the Soviet Union* (Oxford: Oxford University Press, 1996), pp. 30–38.

11 Magnus Pahl, *Fremde Heere Ost: Hitlers militärische Feindaufklärung* (Berlin: Ch. Links Verlag, 2011), pp. 60, 71–75.

12 Ben H. Shepherd, *Hitler's Soldiers: The German Army in the Third Reich* (London: Yale University Press, 2016), pp. 121–122.

13 See Chapters 4–6 of this volume.

14 Ibid.

15 Christoph Bergström and Andrey Mikhailov, *Black Cross, Red Star: Air War over the Eastern Front. Volume I: Operation Barbarossa 1941* (Pacifica, CA: Pacifica Military History, 2000), pp. 5–18.

16 Albert Seaton, *The German Army 1933–45* (London: Weidenfeld and Nicolson, 1982), p. 175.

17 Robert M. Citino, *The German Way of War: From the Thirty Years' War to the Third Reich* (Lawrence: University Press of Kansas, 2005), quotation from p. 292.

18 Geoffrey P. Megargee, *Inside Hitler's High Command* (Lawrence, KS: University Press of Kansas, 2000), p. 131.

19 Ernst Klink, 'The Military Concept of the War against the Soviet Union: Land Warfare', in Horst Boog, Jürgen Förster, Ernst Klink, Rolf-Dieter Müller, and Gerd R. Ueberschär, eds., *Germany and the Second World War. Volume IV: The Attack on the Soviet Union* (Oxford: Oxford University Press, 1996), pp. 317–318.

20 David Stahel, *Operation Barbarossa and Germany's Defeat in the East* (Cambridge: Cambridge University Press, 2009), pp. 61–63.

21 Christian Hartmann, *Halder: Generalstabschef Hitler 1938–1942*, 2nd ed. (Paderborn: Schöningh, 2010), quotation from p. 281.

22 Horst Boog, 'The Military Concept of the War against the Soviet Union: The German Air Force', in Horst Boog, Jürgen Förster, Ernst Klink, Rolf-Dieter Müller, and Gerd R. Ueberschär, eds., *Germany and the Second World War. Volume IV: The Attack on the Soviet Union* (Oxford, Oxford University Press, 1996), pp. 362–370.

23 Ernst Klink, 'The Military Concept of the War against the Soviet Union: The German Navy', in Horst Boog, Jürgen Förster, Ernst Klink, Rolf-Dieter Müller, and Gerd R. Ueberschär, eds., *Germany and the Second World War. Volume IV: The Attack on the Soviet Union* (Oxford, Oxford University Press,1996), pp. 376–385.

24 Richard Overy, *War and Economy in the Third Reich* (Oxford: Oxford University Press, 2002), pp. 199–202, 251–253, 293; Tooze, *The Wages of Destruction*, pp. 433–436, 455.

25 Tooze, *The Wages of Destruction*, pp. 429–440.

26 Luther, *Barbarossa Unleashed*, pp. 62–64; Hugh Davie, 'The Influence of Railways on Military Operations in the Russo-German War 1941–1945', *Journal of Slavic Military Studies*, 30, 2 (2017), pp. 321–346.

27 Murray, *Luftwaffe*, pp. 7–8.

28 Förster, 'Hitler's Decision', pp. 30–38.

29 Jürgen Förster, 'Ideological Warfare in Germany 1919 to 1945', in Ralf Blank, Jörg Echternkamp, Karola Fings, Jürgen Förster, Winfried Heinemann, Tobian's Jersak, Armin Nolzen, and Christoph Rass, eds., *Germany and the Second World War, Volume IX. Part One: German Wartime Society 1939–1945. Politicization, Disintegration and the Struggle for Survival* (Oxford: Oxford University Press, 2008), quotation from p. 530.

30 See, for example, Hans-Heinrich Wilhelm, 'Guderian', in Ronald Smelser and Enrico Syring, eds., *Die Militärelite des Dritten Reiches: 27 Biographische Skizzen* (Frankfurt am Main: Ullstein, 1997), p. 195.

31 Detlef Vogel, 'German Intervention in the Balkans', in Gerhard Schreiber, Bernd Stegemann, and Detlef Vogel, eds. *Germany and the Second World War, Volume Three. The Mediterranean, South-East Europe, and North Africa 1939–1941* (Oxford: Oxford University Press, 1995), pp. 479–485;

Craig Stockings and Eleanor Hancock, *Swastika over the Acropolis. Re-interpreting the Nazi Invasion of Greece in World War II* (Brill: Leiden, Boston, 2013).

32 Boog, 'The German Air Force', p. 376.

33 See Chapter 17 of this volume.

34 David Stahel, ed., *Joining Hitler's Crusade: European Nations and the Invasion of the Soviet Union, 1941* (Cambridge: Cambridge University Press, 2018), pp. 1–157; Boog, 'The German Air Force', p. 365; Förster, 'Germany's Acquisition of Allies', pp. 422, 427.

35 See Chapter 13.

36 Kershaw, *Hitler, 1936–1945*, p. 356.

37 For a brief overview and further literature, see Shepherd, *Hitler's Soldiers*, p. 53.

38 See Chapter 13.

39 Jürgen Förster, *Die Wehrmacht im NS-Staat: Eine strukturgeschichtliche Analyse* (Munich: Oldenbourg, 2007), p. 87.

40 See Chapter 13.

41 Peter Longerich, *Holocaust: The Nazi Persecution and Murder of the Jews* (Oxford: Oxford University Press, 2010), p. 184; Adrian Weale, *The SS: A New History* (London: Abacus, 2010), pp. 140–141.

42 Shepherd, *Hitler's Soldiers*, pp. 126–130.

43 See Chapter 13.

3

Stalin's Political Delusions and Military Preparations for War with Nazi Germany

Soviet dictator Iosif V. Stalin took seriously the inevitability of war with foreign powers. He developed strategies and plans for using the Red Army to export socialist revolution abroad. To this end, over the course of the 1930s, Stalin built the Soviet Union into a militarised fortress at great cost to general national welfare. Indeed, in 1939–1940, by means of war and threat of force, Stalin successfully expanded Soviet territory by absorbing smaller states to the west of the country. All the same, Adolf Hitler's attack on the Soviet Union on 22 June 1941 took Stalin by surprise, raising the spectre of a humiliating defeat as German forces swiftly advanced on the Soviet capital Moscow by October 1941. Although Stalin recovered quickly and eventually led the country to victory, Hitler's attack marked the biggest crisis for both Stalin and the Soviet Union up to that point. How was it possible for Stalin to be caught backfooted? Even though the Soviet people did not say so publicly, there is no doubt that they privately asked one another this question. His hubris, delusions, and the very system he had built were responsible for this abject failure.

3.1 War, Revolution, and Strategy

War meant revolution to Stalin. He did not fear war. Rather, he welcomed war as a catalyst for revolution.[1] The Russo-Japanese War of 1904–1905 led to the 1905 Revolution in Russia, creating the preconditions for overthrowing the centuries-old autocracy. This in fact took place in two stages in 1917, amid bleak military confrontations with the

Central Powers during World War I. The February Revolution over-threw Tsarism, while the October Revolution brought the Bolsheviks to power. The Bolshevik Revolution was quickly followed by foreign military intervention and civil war. After three years of fighting, the Bolsheviks beat back the enemy and consolidated their power over much of the former Tsarist Empire. Then Stalin, adroitly concealing his political and military ambitions, expanded Soviet influence into Asia (Mongolia and China, in particular). In 1939 and 1940, Stalin waged war against Poland and Finland, expanding Soviet territory and annex-ing much of the remaining territory of the former Russian Empire. World War II ended up creating a Soviet socialist camp in central-eastern Europe and Asia. Content with his victory over Hitler in 1945, Stalin fully expected that a World War III was inevitable and that such a war would eliminate the capitalist camp and create a socialist world.[2]

As a convinced Marxist, Stalin inherently believed that contradictory economic goals among the imperialist capitalist countries would lead them to war.[3] His role as a revolutionary was to accelerate or at least facilitate 'struggle, conflicts and wars between our enemies' as a catalyst for socialist revolution.[4] To this end, Stalin used any means available, including provo-cation, subversion, camouflage, and disinformation. Thus, throughout the 1920s and 1930s and culminating in World War II, the Soviet Union consistently (and often secretly) intervened in foreign countries, its attempts to stir revolution in Germany in 1923 being one of the earliest and best known. More notably, Moscow interfered secretly in Mongolia ('Outer Mongolia') and created the first Soviet satellite state there ('Mongolian People's Republic') in 1924. Simultaneously, Stalin fostered and encouraged Chinese nationalism against all powers that claimed an imperialist stake there, extending military, financial, and political aid to the Chinese Communists. In 1927, he encouraged and supported the Chinese Communists in their failed attempt to take power. Their failure turned the nationalists decisively against Moscow.[5] In 1929, the Soviet Union suc-cessfully waged a brief war against China to retain its colonial possessions in Manchuria. Stalin's attempts to communise Manchuria in the process proved unrealisable at the time. In 1929–1930, Stalin secretly intervened militarily in Afghanistan, although he failed to retain pro-Soviet power there. From 1933 and 1934 onward, Stalin covertly meddled in Xinjiang

(Chinese Turkestan), deploying military and secret police forces there and turning it into a virtual Soviet satellite.

Then, in 1939, in collusion with his arch-enemy, Hitler, Stalin waged war against Poland and Finland. After destroying Poland, he annexed and quickly sovietised eastern Poland ('Western Ukraine' and 'Western Belarus'). Lev D. Trotskii, Stalin's bitter rival in exile in Mexico, welcomed this expansion of Soviet power: 'Since Stalin's Bonapartist dictatorship rests not on private but on state property, the Red Army's invasion of Poland must virtually bring with it the liquidation of private capitalist property in order thereby to bring the régime of the occupied territories into line with the régime in the USSR.'[6] Declaring war against Finland, Stalin designed a plan to make it into a Soviet satellite[7] but was faced with unexpectedly strong Finish resistance. He was forced to abandon his plan and concluded a peace with modest territorial gains. In 1940, however, using the threat of military force, Stalin managed to annex and sovietise Bessarabia (roughly today's Moldova), Northern Bukovina, Estonia, Latvia, and Lithuania. In light of this, Stalin's famous slogan 'Socialism in One Country,' not to mention the constant peace campaign he promoted before World War II, would appear to have been mere political cover.

Indeed, Stalin systematically and meticulously militarised Soviet society in preparation for a final showdown with its capitalist enemies. Before Stalin began to take Hitler's threat seriously, there is little evidence that Moscow believed that it faced a realistic danger of war from capitalist enemies. The infamous 1927 'war scare' occasioned by the rupture of diplomatic relations with Great Britain was deliberately inflated by Moscow. Nor did Japan's invasion of Manchuria in 1931 and the foundation of Manzhouguo the following year present any serious threat of war to the Soviet Union: in fact, Stalin appears to have engineered Japan's invasion as part of his strategy to entrap Japan and destroy Japanese imperialism in China.[8] Stalin harnessed perceived capitalist hostility towards the Soviet Union, the first openly anti-capitalist Communist regime, to convince the Soviet people of the need to divert national resources from consumption to military build-up. He proved very successful in this endeavour, never shrinking from the use of terror as he saw fit.

Stalin lived by politics and believed in the 'all-conquering power of Bolshevism' (*vsesokrushaiushchaia sila bolshevizma*). On any number of occasions, he emphasised that strength was what mattered in politics. After World War II, for instance, Stalin told the British labour delegation that 'the weak are neither pitied nor respected. Only the strong are taken into account.'[9] The 'revolution from above', launched by Stalin in the late 1920s, was geared explicitly in Stalin's mind towards enhancing the country's military capacity by siphoning off national resources from agriculture and concentrating them in the building of heavy industry at the cost of light industry. One cannot fight war with cotton, Stalin and his allies often argued against their opponents (such as Nikolai I. Bukharin), who feared Stalin's radical policy would politically antagonize the peasantry and threaten the Soviet government.[10] To this end, Stalin essentially rid the Soviet economy of market relations and instituted a centrally planned economy.

Of course, Stalin was not a blind believer in power but a realist. In 1930, when widely regarded military strategist Mikhail N. Tukhachevskii proposed an all-powerful, modernised Red Army, an instrument with which to conquer the world and export socialist revolution, Stalin questioned his plan as an overambitious, wholesale militarisation of Soviet society. Given the country's economic backwardness, Stalin called the plan an unrealistic, Utopian, 'bureaucratic maximalist' play with numbers, 'worse than any kind of counterrevolution'. Two years later, however, Stalin apologised to Tukhachevskii for his earlier criticism, accepted some of his ambitious goals, and accordingly updated the Soviet strategy to build a formidable Red Army capable of confronting any coalition of capitalist countries, ultimately dealing them a decisive military defeat.[11] Over the course of the 1930s, Stalin did indeed transform the country into a 'warfare state', marked by 'a total and absolute integration of the military, the economy, and the society for war and conflict'.[12]

Stalin's change of mind regarding Tukhachevskii's maximalist plan portended a change in Soviet war plans that took place in the mid-1930s: the 'PR' series, with a 'defensive/counteroffensive' strategy against Poland and Romania as the primary adversaries, gave way to the 'GP' series, with a strategy of combining covert mobilisation, surprise, and pre-emption against Germany and Poland, now regarded as the Soviet Union's primary foes. The Red Army adopted the guiding principle of 'deep operations', which was more comprehensive 'than the contemporaneous German notion of Blitzkrieg' and envisaged the

Figure 3.1 Marshal Kliment Voroshilov (right) talking to Joseph Stalin (left) after the vote on the new constitution of the USSR, also known as the 'Stalin constitution', 5 December 1936. Source: SNEP/AFP via Getty Images.

'prospect of either limiting or banishing protracted combat from the battlefields of future war'. Simultaneously, Stalin is said to have forbidden 'instruction in strategy at the newly created Academy of the General Staff, asserting that he alone was the source of Soviet strategy'. From then until June 1941, pre-emption lurked 'in the background of Soviet war planning'.[13] The assertion of nineteenth-century German strategist Carl von Clausewitz that war is a continuation of politics by other means suited well the hubris of the twentieth-century Soviet dictator. In October 1938, while publicly proclaiming his peace campaigns, Stalin grumbled privately that Soviet propagandists were wrong to think that the Bolsheviks were pacifists. No, he emphasised, they were not at all against offensives or any kind of war. Stalin made clear that there could be instances when the Soviet Union would attack capitalist countries to liberate the proletariat. Of course the Bolsheviks 'cry for defence', he continued, but 'it is a *veil*. Everyone masquerades, and *we too masquerade*. You live with wolves, and you howl with wolves.'[14]

His rapprochement with Tukhachevskii notwithstanding, Stalin came to suspect the Soviet strategist of harbouring 'Red Bonapartism' and had him executed in 1937. Nor did Tukhachevskii's main rival in strategic thinking, Aleksandr A. Svechin, survive Stalin's terror: he, too, was executed in 1938, accused of being a 'counterrevolutionary'. Stalin thus killed his two outstanding Soviet strategists to safeguard his own autocratic hubris, to the detriment of the security of the country. Yet Svechin's doctrine on wars of 'attrition' (*izmor*) rather than Tukhachevskii's wars of 'annihilation' (*sokrushenie*) proved prophetic of Stalin's fight for survival in the war against Hitler's Nazi Germany.[15]

The executions of Tukhachevskii and Svechin were part of Stalin's decapitation of the Soviet military high command. Stalin's actions made no sense to outside observers and Germany's political and military leaders, Hitler included. As Stalin sounded the tocsin of the danger of military attack from outside forces, he actively worked to destroy the Red Army from within. Germans looked on in disbelief. Gloating over Stalin's destruction of the Red Army, Hitler called him 'crazy' (*gehirnkrank*, literally 'sick in the brain'): 'His bloody regime can otherwise not be explained.'[16] Had Stalin been beaten by Hitler in the war that came within a few years, Hitler's and others' assessment of Stalin's actions would have been hailed as prescient. Yet it was Hitler, not Stalin, who was beaten in the duel.

Contrary to widely accepted views, Hitler was not a mere military 'dilettante', constantly quarrelling with his commanders over military decisions.[17] Yet Hitler still could not fully trust his commanders and other important men in his government. Near the end of the war, when Hitler realised that his defeat was certain, he told his interlocutor:

> My disciples have not yet had time to attain their full manhood. I should really have had another twenty years in which to bring this new *élite* to maturity, an *élite* of youth, immersed from infancy in the philosophy of National Socialism. The tragedy for us Germans is that we never have enough time . . . . A Germany, cemented by a single faith and National Socialist in body and soul . . . would have been invincible . . . . We lacked men moulded in the shape of our ideal . . . . Our generals and diplomats, with a few, rare exceptions, are men of another age, and their methods of waging war and conducting our foreign policy also belong to an age that is passed.[18]

With hindsight, in 1969 Seweryn Bialer echoed Hitler's reckoning:

> The success of Hitler's political designs depended to a large extent on his ability to subordinate the military establishment to his will. Stalin started

the war with an army which was his creation from the lowest command levels to the highest during the years of the Great Purge and after; never was his effective control over Red Army commanders in doubt.

Having little respect for his generals, Bialer claimed that Hitler relied on 'his own initiative and judgment concerning military operations', while Stalin 'never considered the conception and planning of military operations his paramount strength, his major interest, or the measure of his absolute authority. He was more willing to listen to his generals, more willing to correct his errors (while, of course, refusing to acknowledge them).'[19] Moreover, it should be acknowledged that the economy and the military forces Stalin built proved capable of sustaining a total war against Nazi Germany.

One should not unduly credit Stalin with political foresight, however. Stalin's cruelty, which matched Hitler's, meant that he had no compunction in using Soviet soldiers as cannon fodder. It is instructive to note that the war casualties for the victorious Soviet Union (approximately 7.5 million combatants, excepting 3 to 4 million deaths of POWs)[20] far exceeded those for the defeated Nazi Germany (4 to 5 million). Stalin criminalised surrender to the enemy under any circumstances as treachery and had far more soldiers executed for alleged cowardice, insubordination, and desertion than Hitler (some 158,000 versus 15,000). Stalin offered the Soviet soldiers no choice but to fight to their deaths.

The hubris of Stalin as a dictator certainly compared well with that of Hitler. Stalin aspired to 'total leadership', an idea supported by Stalin's favourite military commander and strategist, Boris M. Shaposhnikov.[21] When 'total leadership' went astray, the entire country was threatened with collapse. His ultimate victory notwithstanding, Stalin's miscalculation in June 1941 proved an unqualified historic blunder.

3.2 Preparations for War

Like many other world political leaders, Stalin was not overly concerned with Hitler's ascent to power in Germany in 1933. He considered social democracy ('social fascism') a more serious threat than Nazism. With numerous agents and informants in high places in Germany and other countries, Stalin soon came to realise that Hitler's talk of Bolshevism as his life enemy was more than mere political bloviating. By 1935, abandoning his views on 'social fascism', Stalin threw his support behind the coalition of all anti-Nazi and anti-fascist forces (the 'popular front'). Stalin knew that war with Germany was not imminent: Germany was not yet ready. However, he was also aware of Hitler's plans, revealed to his inner circle in December 1936, that the 'German army must be ready for commitment within four years' and that the 'German economy must be ready for war within four years'.[22]

A past master himself of disinformation, Stalin was tormented by suspicions of disinformation by his enemies. In 1937, he said to his intelligence operative, 'It's turned out that, in our intelligence organ, there is a whole group of masters of this business, working for Germany, Japan, and Poland. Intelligence is where for the first time in twenty years we have been trounced.'[23] Accordingly, Stalin's Great Terror eliminated (killed, arrested, or fired) 275 (or 68 per cent) of 450 Soviet foreign intelligence officials in Moscow and abroad. For 127 consecutive days in 1938, fearful Soviet intelligence officials failed to submit any formal intelligence briefs to Stalin.[24]

Stalin did not seem overly worried, however, deeming it unlikely that Germany would risk war with the Soviet Union before solving its imperialist conflicts with Britain. Stalin's thinking was guided by the lessons of history: Napoleon's adventure in Russia was conclusively defeated; in World War I, Germany under Kaiser Wilhelm II collapsed by waging a two-front war (against which many sage strategists had warned); by contrast, the phenomenal success of Prussia under Otto von Bismarck was achieved at least partially by maintaining peace with Russia. Stalin had good reason to believe that Hitler would not be reckless towards the Soviet Union,[25] notwithstanding Hitler's adventures in Europe (such as the *Anschluß* and the annexation of Sudetenland in 1938 and the destruction of Czechoslovakia in 1939).

Several additional reasons inclined Stalin to assume as late as 1939 that Hitler's attack was not imminent. The German military lacked a sufficient amount of key raw materials such as oil, manganese, grain, and rubber to conduct full-scale war. The negotiations that led to the Nazi-Soviet rapprochement (Molotov-Ribbentrop Pact of August 1939) started as economic negotiations. Moreover, Stalin and Hitler were united against the liberal world order dominated by Britain, France, and the United States. In Stalin's view, nationalisms, including National Socialism and Fascism, were a potent political force to be used against the imperialists. The Communist Soviet Union and Fascist Italy had gotten along just fine until the mid-1930s. Karl Radek, a Bolshevik loose cannon who often revealed too much of Stalin's privileged thoughts, spoke on several occasions in the 1920s and 1930s for Nazi-Soviet cooperation (by which the cleverer Soviets would be able to use the foolish Nazis as unwitting 'pacemakers' (*Schrittmacher*) of Communism).[26] Stalin considered it possible to pit Germany against Britain and France, allowing them to destroy (or at least weaken) one another and only then intervene to deliver the coup de grace to Nazi Germany (and possibly other imperialist powers as well). Furthermore, his theoretical strategy of annihilation notwithstanding, Stalin deemed frontal military attack dangerous and ineffectual. In 1924, he apparently told China's nationalist leader Chiang Kaishek, who was asking for Soviet help in building a strong army, 'You don't need excessive forces. The armed forces are the last resort. You must exhaust all other means to lead the enemy to collapse before using arms.' Such means included disinformation, deception, subversion, 'reflexive control', and vicarious war. It was exactly what Stalin did to Japan in China from 1937 to 1945.[27] Stalin's advice to Chiang was in line with the wise counsel of Sun Tzu, the famous strategist of ancient China: 'To break the enemy without fighting is the best of the best.'[28]

All the same, at Stalin's orders, Soviet military build-up and war preparations accelerated apace. The size of the Soviet armed forces climbed from 1 million in 1934 to 1.3 million in 1935–1936 and to more than 5 million by June 1941. Although the Soviet forces were still somewhat smaller than the 7 million or so of the Wehrmacht already in the war in Europe, Moscow still had a vast capacity to mobilise several millions more to surpass the German forces.[29] The gross output of the Soviet defence industry skyrocketed more than 1,600 per cent from 1933 to 1940.[30]

At least until 1940 Stalin was confident that he would prevail. At the eighteenth congress of the Communist Party in March 1939 ('Congress of Victorious Socialism'), for instance, Stalin openly rebuffed foreign observations that his Great Terror had weakened the Soviet system. On the contrary, he asserted, the Soviet Union was now internally united, and in the event of war, the front and the rear were stronger in the Soviet Union than in any other country. Stalin warned his adversaries, 'We don't fear threats from aggressors and are ready to respond with double punches to a blow from warmongers who attempt to violate the sanctity of the Soviet borders.'[31] In the summer of 1939, Stalin had, for all intents and purposes, neutralised the threat from the east (Japan) by soundly beating it at the Battle of Khalkhin Gol (Nomonhan). Concluding a non-aggression pact with Germany on 23 August 1939 (the 'Molotov-Ribbentrop Pact'), Stalin hoped to pit Germany against Britain and France. Having neutralised the Soviet threat for now, Hitler proceeded to attack Poland on 1 September, in violation of the German-Polish declaration of non-aggression of 1934, whereupon Britain and France declared war on Germany. Stalin gloated over the effect on Britain and France, which he correctly suspected had wanted Nazi Germany and the Communist Soviet Union to attack and destroy each other. Now Stalin had every reason to hope that the war Hitler unleashed would weaken Britain and France, as well as Germany itself. On 17 September 1939 Stalin unilaterally broke the Soviet-Polish non-aggression pact of 1932 and invaded Poland. Germany and the Soviet Union together conquered Poland easily and quickly, partitioning it in accordance with the Molotov-Ribbentrop Pact.

The 'Winter War' Stalin launched against Finland in November 1939 in violation of the Soviet-Finnish non-aggression pact of 1932 proved a rude awakening. The seemingly decisive victory at Khalkhin Gol was deceptive, for the commander of Japan's main fighting units appears to have been a Soviet mole.[32] Even though Stalin ultimately beat the Finns and grabbed chunks of territory, Stalin was shocked by the poor performance of his soldiers. He won the victory only at extraordinary human cost, presaging his fight against Nazi Germany. The Soviet forces lost more than 130,000 soldiers (dead or missing), almost five times as many as the Finnish losses. If the injured were included, the Red Army recorded almost 4,000 casualties a day.[33] Khrushchev later noted of the Soviet losses, 'A victory at such a cost was actually a moral defeat.' He recorded Stalin's anger at Kliment E. Voroshilov, the Red

Army Commander and People's Commissar of Defence, in a gathering at Stalin's dacha:

> Stalin jumped up in a white-hot rage and started to berate Voroshilov. Voroshilov was also boiling mad. He leaped up, turned red, and hurled Stalin's accusations back into his face. 'You have your self to blame for all this!' shouted Voroshilov. 'You're the one who annihilated the Old Guard of the army; you had our best generals killed!' Stalin rebuffed him, and at that, Voroshilov picked up a platter with a roast suckling pig on it and smashed it on the table.[34]

Of course, Voroshilov had supported Stalin's orders to execute army commanders in 1937–1938. If this episode is not apocryphal, it must have been a sobering reminder for everyone present that the Red Army's poor fighting ability had been exposed and its reputation severely damaged for the entire world to see.

The Pyrrhic victory in Finland in March 1940 was followed soon after by another disappointment for Stalin: the fall of Paris to Germany in June 1940. Instead of being weakened by a war of attrition, Hitler appeared to have conquered with ease much of Europe, with the exception of Britain. On the one hand, Germany now could battle Britain with the vast resources of its newly acquired lands. On the other hand, Hitler envied and privately admired the might of the British Empire – and might still strike a deal with Britain. In that case, Hitler would turn his attention on his lifelong enemy to the east, the Soviet Union.

Stalin took up the challenge and addressed the issue head on, displaying remarkable dictatorial leadership in the process. At a meeting he convened to discuss the problems posed by war against Finland, he humiliated the military command. Singling out some of them individually, Stalin scolded all of them for not adjusting to the demands of modern warfare. Addressing A. P. Kovalev, Army Commander Second Rank, he said, 'You are an able man, but you have some hidden pride that won't let you adjust your self. Accept your drawbacks and readjust yourself, then will things get going.' Humbled, Kovalev merely said, 'Yes, Comrade Stalin.'[35] Voroshilov, whom Stalin removed from command of the Soviet forces in the middle of the Winter War, was praised for his deferential prostration to the dictator: 'It does not often happen around here that a People's Commissar speaks so openly about his own shortcomings.'[36] Stalin convened a four-day meeting in April 1940 to address the problems the Red Army had faced in the war. Stalin brushed aside every argument the military commanders made to explain the Red Army's weaknesses, including the terror of 1937–1938. The harsh winter conditions in Finland were also brushed off as irrelevant. He said, 'All the Russian army's major victories were won in wintertime. Alexander Nevsky against the Swedes, Peter I against the Swedes in Finland, Alexander I's victory over Napoleon. We are *a northern country*.' He excoriated the Red Army commanders for being hopelessly spoilt from the easy victories against Japan and Poland in 1939. Those battles were 'merely a military stroll', 'trifles, not a war'. Stalin berated the military leaders for not taking care of the mundane issues of soldiers' needs, such as warm clothes and boots, food on the battlefield, and the like. He attended every session, listened to and responded to every speaker, and made numerous suggestions. In the end, he reassured the fazed and despondent commanders that it was fortunate that the Red Army had had the chance to get the experience of modern war 'not from German aviation but in Finland, with God's help'.[37] It was as much self-consolation as reassurance for his commanders.

All the same, Stalin remained concerned about the war readiness of the Red Army. He understood correctly that the Germans thought little of the Red Army's capacity to fight. He had to ask himself whether Hitler would seize the golden opportunity to realise his dream of crushing his enemy before subduing Britain. Stalin began a feverish overhaul of the Red Army. According to Viacheslav M. Molotov, Stalin's right-hand man, Stalin reckoned that the Red Army would be ready to take on the Wehrmacht only in 1943.[38]

3.3   The Blunder

If Stalin's assessment was correct that the Red Army would not be ready to fight Nazi Germany until 1943, its failure in the initial phases of the war in 1941 should have been expected – and yet it was not. How does one account for the scale of the Soviet disaster and the degree of Stalin's shock in 1941?

A great deal has been written within and outside Russia about Stalin's blunder in June 1941. What is clear is that Stalin had become increasingly aware of the burden and loneliness of his position as dictator. He often referred to himself in the third person singular and claimed that 'Stalin' meant the Soviet Union. Stalin was a political mastermind. Unlike Hitler, Stalin was cautious and always kept the end-game in view. In his early political gambles, Stalin had proved triumphant: his inner-party struggles against rivals such as Trotskii and Nikolai I. Bukharin, his audacious 'revolution from above', and the Great Terror. The only humiliation he had endured was the Winter War, but he was able to console himself that it had been a trial by fire and that it had ended well. The Faustian bargain Stalin struck with Hitler in August 1939 was a gamble of a different order. It was mutually beneficial in the short run, but would it prove Stalin right in the end? This was the question that tormented him.

Stalin was both confident and anxious. His hubris and power as a dictator was on full display. On 7 November 1940, after the celebration of the anniversary of the October 1917 Revolution, Stalin excoriated and abased the entire coterie of powerful men with abandon. Addressing the shortcomings of the Red Army, he said:

> I am busy at this every day now, meeting with designers and other specialists .... But I am the *only* one dealing with all these problems. None of you could be bothered with them. I am out there *by myself* .... Look at me: I am capable of learning, reading, keeping up with things every day – why can you not do this? You do not like to learn; you are happy just going along the way you are, complacent. You are squandering Lenin's legacy .... People are thoughtless, do not want to learn and relearn. *They will hear me out and then go on just as before.* But I will show you, if I ever lose my patience. (You know very well how I can do that.) I shall hit the fatsos so hard that you will hear the crack for miles around.

'Everyone stood straight', according to an eyewitness, 'and listened quietly; clearly no one ever expected J.V. [Stalin] to come out with such scolding. There were tears in Voroshilov's eyes.'[39]

If Stalin was nervous, Hitler was not, and in the summer of 1940 he was determined to attack the Soviet Union (although the exact timing was to be decided in due course). He provoked Stalin with an invitation to join the tripartite with Italy and Japan (signed in September 1940). In November, Hitler happily rejected the conditions Stalin demanded for joining it and proceeded the following month to order Operation Barbarossa. It was a product of Nazi hubris that vastly underestimated the potentiality of the Red Army. Soon after, Stalin began to receive a stream of warnings concerning Hitler's intention from agents placed high in the political and military establishments of Germany, Japan, China, and elsewhere. In April 1941, to Hitler's dismay,[40] Stalin concluded a neutrality pact with Japan, formally securing the east, and began moving Soviet troops from the east to the west before 22 June 1941.[41]

Sensing Germany's preparations for war against the Soviet Union, Stalin started covert mobilisation, drafting offensive war plans, the last being completed just before Hitler attacked the Soviet Union. In fact, it appears that Moscow had a plan (if not a decision) for an offensive to be started on 12 June 1941.[42]

Nevertheless, Stalin was cagey and played it safe. In the months leading up to June 1941, the two dictators performed a remarkable game of deception. Amid feverish preparation for war, Stalin felt confident he had outfoxed Hitler by faithfully observing the pact and economic deals they had struck in 1939. Stalin forbade his forces from responding to obvious and numerous minor military provocations by the German side. Hitler was convinced that by amassing his troops on the Soviet borders, he could mislead Stalin: he would not attack the Soviet Union before taming Britain; the military build-up on the Soviet borders was not to attack the Soviet Union but to extract necessary concessions from Stalin so as to be able to concentrate on crushing Britain. In this gamble, Stalin was the loser. On 17 June 1941, five days before Hitler's attack, Stalin received an intelligence brief on the imminence of German attack based on information from a Soviet mole in Germany. Stalin angrily rejected it, returning it with a note to V. N. Merkulov, the chief of state security: 'You can tell your "source" in the Ger[man] air force staff to go f[uck] his mother. He's not an "informer" but a *disinformer*.'[43] When the Soviet forces subsequently were attacked on 22 June, he could not bring himself to address the nation. He commanded his henchman Molotov to speak.

Clearly Stalin had fallen into the kind of trap with which he was intimately familiar. According to a former Soviet secret police official,

> Stalin, who was his own intelligence boss and who liked to take a personal part in the cloak and dagger business, warned his intelligence chiefs time and again to keep away from hypotheses and 'equations with many unknowns' . . . . He used to say: 'An intelligence hypothesis may become your hobby horse on which you will ride straight into a self-made trap.' Stalin wanted raw intelligence material: he often interjected during his conferences with intelligence chiefs, 'Don't tell me what you think, give me the facts and the sources!'[44]

As is always the case, the hubris and delusions of a dictator did Stalin in.

3.4   Conclusions

If Stalin's hubris did him in, it was also his hubris that saved him and his country. Quickly recovering from the shock of his life, Stalin rallied his country. He was confident that the vast size and almost limitless reserves of the Soviet Union could outlast Hitler's assault. After all, he had plans for military offensives and had made preparations for war as well. The country, however, was ready for neither offensive nor defensive war in June 1941. In response, he tempered his natural hubris with a willingness to listen to his subordinates. For his part, Hitler understood Stalin and what he meant to the Soviet Union. After Germany's defeat at the battle of Stalingrad in 1943, according to German Foreign Minister Joachim von Ribbentrop, Hitler said, 'One could perceive what one man could mean to a nation. Any other nation would have broken down under the blows of 1941 and 1942. Russia owed her victory to this man, whose iron will and heroism had rallied the people to renewed resistance.'[45]

Ironically, as it turns out, Stalin's blunder in June 1941 may have helped the nation, albeit at enormous human and material cost. In December 1941, after Japan's Pearl Harbour Attack, Winston Churchill dispatched Anthony Eden to Moscow to urge Stalin to join the war against Japan. Stalin responded by saying that it would be better to let Japan attack the Soviet Union:

> War would be unpopular with our people if the Soviet Government were to take the first step. If, on the other hand, we were attacked, the feelings

of the Soviet people would be very strong. We have seen this in the present war in the West. Hitler attacked us, and because we were attacked, the Soviet people have shown a wonderful unity and great heroism and readiness to sacrifice themselves.[46]

Stalin thus turned his blunder and defeat into a message heralding the triumph of the Soviet people.

Notes

1 See Stephen Kotkin, *Stalin, Vol. 1, Paradoxes of Power, 1878–1928* (New York: Penguin Press, 2014), pp. 556–558. For the opposite view stressing Stalin's 'defensive' stance, see Geoffrey Roberts, *Stalin's Wars: From World War to Cold War, 1939–1953* (New Haven, CT: Yale University Press, 2008).

2 See Feliks I. Chuev, *Molotov Remembers. Inside Kremlin Politics: Conversations with Felix Chuev*, ed. and with an introduction and notes by Albert Resis (Chicago: I.R. Dee, 1993), p. 63.

3 For Stalin as a Marxist, see Erik Van Ree, *The Political Thought of Joseph Stalin* (London: Routledge, 2002). For thoughts that underpinned Stalin's foreign policy, see Jonathan Haslam's works, particularly *The Spectre of War: International Communism and the Origins of World War II* (Princeton, NJ: Princeton University Press, 2021).

4 See his 1925 speech in I. V. Stalin, *Sochineniia*, vol. 7 (Moscow: Politizdat, 1953), p. 27.

5 Ten years later, Moscow would furtively resume military intervention in support of China against Japan's full-scale military aggression in China.

6 Quoted in Jonathan Haslam, *The Spectre of War: International Communism and the Origins of World War II* (Princeton, NJ: Princeton University Press, 2021), p. 335.

7 See Aleksandr Gogun, *Oshibka 1941* (Kherson: Oldi-Plius, 2021), pp. 58–59.

8 See Hiroaki Kuromiya, *Stalin, Japan, and the Struggle for Supremacy over China, 1894–1945* (London: Routledge, 2023), chapter 3.

9 Sergei Radchenko, 'Joseph Stalin', in Steven Casey and Jonathan Write, eds., *Mental Maps in the Early Cold War Era, 1945–68* (London: Palgrave-Macmillan, 2011), p. 28.

10 Kuromiya, *Stalin*, p. 89.

11 See 'Moia otsenka byla slishkom rezkoi', *Istoricheskii arkhiv*, 1998, nos. 5–6, pp. 147–152.

12 James J. Schneider, *The Structure of Strategic Revolution: Total War and the Roots of the Soviet Warfare State* (Novato, CA: Presidio, 1994), p. 2.

13 Bruce W. Menning and Jonathan House, 'Soviet Strategy', in John Ferris and Evan Mawdsley, eds., *Cambridge History of the Second World War*, vol. 1 (Cambridge: Cambridge University Press, 2015), pp. 215–218.

14 N. N. Maslov, 'I.V. Stalin o "Kratkom kurse istorii VKP(b)"', *Istoricheskii arkhiv* 5 (1994), p. 13 (emphasis added).

15 These two concepts were not necessarily mutually exclusive in Svechin's thinking, however. See David R. Stone, 'Misreading Svechin: Attrition, Annihilation, and Historicism', *Journal of Military History*, 76 (July 2012).

16 See Ian Kershaw, *Hitler 1936–45: Nemesis* (New York: W.W. Norton & Company, 2000), p. 44.

17 See Roman Töppel, 'Unbelehrbar? Hitler als militärischer Entscheider', in Martin Clauss and Christoph Nübel, eds., *Militärisches Entscheiden. Voraussetzungen, Prozesse und Repräsentationen einer sozialen Praxis von der Antike bis zum 20. Jahrhunder* (Frankfurt am Main: Campus Verlag, 2020), pp. 341–364, and Töppel, 'Hitler était-il un dilettante militaire?', *Guerres & Histoires*, hors série no. 16 (November 2023), pp. 98–101.

18 See *The Testament of Adolf Hitler; The Hitler-Bormann Documents, February–April 1945*, ed. François Genoud, trans. from the German by R. H. Stevens, and with an intro. by H. R. Trevor-Roper (London: Cassell, 1961), p. 59.

19 Seweryn Bialer, ed., *Stalin and His Generals* (New York: Pegasus, 1969), p. 42.

20 See V. N. Zemskov, 'O masshtabakh liudskikh poter' SSSR v Velikoi Otechestvennoi voine (v poiskakh istiny)', *Voenno-istoricheskii arkhiv*, 9 (2012), pp. 67–68 (the three to four million deaths of Soviet POWs are not included), and Rüdiger Overmans, *Deutsche militärische Verluste im Zweiten Weltkrieg* (Munich: R. Oldenbourg, 2000), pp. 285–286 and 294. Little consensus exists on the scale of Soviet combatant losses. The estimate of 7.5 million is at the low end of various Russian and Western estimates, some of which are twice as high. See, for example, Michael Ellman and S. Maksudov, 'Soviet Deaths in the Great Patriotic War: A Note', *Europe-Asia Studies*, 46, no. 4 (1994), pp. 617–680.

21 Schneider, *The Structure of Strategic Revolution*, p. 248.

22 See Joachim C. Fest, *Hitler*, trans. Richard and Clara Winston (London: Weidenfeld and Nicolson, 1974), p. 538.

23 Quoted in Ervin Stavinskii, *Zarubiny. Semeinaia rezidentura* (Moscow: Olma Press, 2003), p. 374.

24 *Ocherki istorii rossiiskoi vneshnei razvedki*, vol. 3 (Moscow: Mezhdunarodnye otnosheniia, 1997), p. 17.

25 See Stalin's remarks in 1940 quoted in M. Ia. Gefter, *Iz tekh i etikh let* (Moscow: Progress, 1991), pp. 261–262.

26 See *Deutschland und Sowjetunion 1933–1941. Dokumente aus russischen und deutschen Archiven. Bd. 1: 30 Januar 1933–31 Dezember 1934* (Oldenbourg: Verlag München, 2014), p. 1319.

27 Quoted in Kuromiya, *Stalin*, pp. 3, 23.

28 Sun Tzu, *On the Art of War: The Oldest Military Treatise in the World*, trans. Liones Giles (London: Luzac & Co., 1910), p. 17.

29 This became clear not long after Hitler's attack on the Soviet Union. See David Stahel, *Operation Barbarossa and Germany's Defeat in the East* (Cambridge: Cambridge University Press, 2009).

30 Robert W. Davies, Mark Harrison, and Stephen G. Wheatcroft, eds., *The Economic Transformation of the Soviet Union, 1913–1945* (Cambridge: Cambridge University Press, 1994), p. 299.

31 I. V. Stalin, *Sochineniia*, vol. 1 (14), ed. Robert H. McNeal (Stanford, CA: Hoover Institution, 1967), pp. 344, 268.

32 See Hiroaki Kuromiya, 'The Mystery of Nomonhan, 1939', *Journal of Slavic Military Studies*, 24 (2011), pp. 4, 659–677.

33 Stephen Kotkin, *Stalin: Waiting for Hitler, 1929–1941* (New York: Penguin, 2017), p. 748.

34 *Khrushchev Remembers* (Boston: Little, Brown and Co., 1970), pp. 154, 156.

35 Alexander Chubaryan and Harold Shukman, eds., *Stalin and the Soviet-Finnish War, 1939–1940* (London: Routledge, 2014), p. 192.

36 Ivo Banac, ed., *The Diary of Georgi Dimitrov, 1933–1949* (New Haven: Yale University Press, 2003), p. 128.

37 Chubaryan and Shukman, eds., *Stalin and the Soviet-Finnish War, 1939–1940* (quotes are from pp. 179–180, 267, and 272).

38 Chuev, *Molotov Remembers*, p. 22.

39 Banac, ed., *The Diary of Georgi Dimitrov, 1933–1949*, pp. 133–134.

40 Kershaw, *Hitler 1936–45*, p. 364.

41 See Pavel Sudoplatov, *Raznye dni tainoi voiny i diplomatii. 1941 god* (Moscow: Olma Press, 2001), p. 368, as well as a testimony by an American military attaché in Moscow: *Memoirs of Ivan D. Yeaton, USA (Ret.) 1919–1953* (Stanford, CA: Hoover Institution, 1976), p. 30. The Japanese also noticed the troop moves at the time: Miyasugi Hiroyasu, 'Nihon no taiSo jōsei handan to jōhō katsudō, 1939–1941', *Seiji keizai shigaku* 55, no. 2 (2019), pp. 10–14.

42 Menning and House, 'Soviet Strategy', p. 227. On Stalin's offensive plans of that time in general, see Gogun, *Oshibka 1941*. On the controversial issue of whether Stalin actually planned a pre-emptive strike against Germany, see careful assessments by Jürgen Förster and Evan Mawdsley, 'Hitler and Stalin in Perspective: Secret Speeches on the Eve of Barbarossa', *War in History*, 11, no. 1 (2004), pp. 61–103, and Evan Mawdsley, 'Crossing the Rubicon: Soviet Plans for Offensive War in 1940–1941', *International History Review*, 25, no. 4 (2003), pp. 818–865.

43 Kuromiya, *Stalin*, p. 150 (emphasis Stalin's).

44 Alexander Orlov, *Handbook of Intelligence and Guerrilla Warfare* (Ann Arbor: University of Michigan Press, 1963), p. 10.

45 Joachim von Ribbentrop, *The Ribbentrop Memoirs* (London: Weidenfeld and Nicolson, 1954), pp. 169–170.

46 Quoted in Anthony Eden, *The Memoirs of Anthony Eden: The Reckoning* (Boston: Houghton Mifflin, 1965), p. 349.

Part II

Opposing Forces

DAVID HARRISVILLE AND
JEFF RUTHERFORD

4
____

The *Ostheer*: Leadership, Command, Motivation, and Experience

On the eve of Operation Barbarossa, Nazi Germany dominated the European continent due in large part to its army's efficiency. Unlocking the firepower-dominated battlefield of the First World War, the German army restored movement and achieved a series of unprecedented quick and decisive victories between 1939 and 1941 that seemingly ensured the Third Reich's hegemony. The attack on the Soviet Union, however, failed to follow the scripts of previous campaigns. The *Ostheer* – Germany's eastern army – attacked on 22 June 1941 with roughly 3 million men, 3,648 tanks, and 7,146 artillery pieces.[1] Over the course of the year, they were joined by more than 700,000 troops from allied nations.[2] Of the approximately 18 million men who served in Germany's armed forces during the war, about 10 million deployed to the Eastern Front.[3] The *Ostheer* would suffer devastating casualties, losing over 3 million dead, missing, or captured by the end of 1944, and its destruction sealed the fate of the Third Reich.[4] Operation Barbarossa thus served as the opening round of a savage war that both fundamentally altered the German army and played the predominant role in the defeat of Hitler's Germany.

Several interlocking factors allowed the Germans to achieve continental hegemony and gave them the confidence to achieve another quick and decisive victory against the Red Army. In June 1941, the Germans possessed a relatively experienced and cohesive officer and non-commissioned officer (NCO) corps. This leadership effectively applied the Prusso-German army's traditional 'way of war' to modern circumstances and used 'revolutionary methods' to exploit the full potential of recent technological developments on the battlefield.[5] The particularities of invading the Soviet Union, however, threatened each of the army's strengths. These obstacles need to be considered when evaluating the German army on the eve of the campaign. By 1941, however, the German 'way of war' encompassed far more than mere combat operations, and the army's understanding of modern, industrial war, radicalised by the Nazi regime, led it to wage a war of annihilation against the Soviet Union.

On the eve of the invasion, the German army's supreme leadership remained a mixed bag. The *Oberkommando des Heeres* (Army High Command), headed by Field Marshal Walther von Brauchitsch, commander-in-chief of the German army, and Colonel-General Franz Halder, the chief of the German General Staff, had successfully executed the victorious campaigns of the first two years of war and planned Operation Barbarossa with an arrogance based on their previous performance. The army's traditional power within the German state was challenged by the *Oberkommando der Wehrmacht* (Armed Forces High Command), which while designed as a centralised armed forces command to coordinate army, air force, and naval matters, quickly degenerated into a personal military command staff for Adolf Hitler. Headed by its chief of staff Field Marshal Wilhelm Keitel and operations officer Colonel-General Alfred Jodl, it controlled troops in all other theatres of war except for the Soviet Union. This bifurcated leadership structure proved increasingly unwieldy when the war turned against the army, and the December 1941 defeat in front of Moscow resulted in Brauchitsch's ouster and his replacement as the commander of the army by Hitler himself. Halder was sacked by Hitler in September 1942 when Operation Blue bogged down in the mountains of the Caucasus and the suburbs of Stalingrad, replaced by Colonel-General Kurt Zeitler.[6]

Zeitler's ascension as Chief of Staff symbolized a shift in German officer policy. The *Bildung*, or education, deemed so important for officers dating back to the War of Liberation against Napoleon in the early nineteenth century, was now replaced by an emphasis on battlefield leadership and exploits, as well as an affinity for Nazism.[7] Ferdinand Schörner personified this transformation of the German officer corps. A January 1942 appraisal of the then Major General commanding a division described him as a 'very efficient, energetic division commander … who proved himself to be

Figure 4.1 German forces during Operation Barbarossa, 26 June 1941.
Source: ullstein bild via Getty Images.

a highly qualified officer'. Fourteen months later, the then corps commander was assessed as a 'fearless, brave soldier at the front . . . . Convinced believer in national socialist doctrines. Physical endurance and agile.'[8] As these two selections illustrate, the criteria for a German officer shifted over the course of the war; Schönerer, who ended the war as a field marshal commanding an army group, became the model officer in the increasingly Nazified army. Hitler's growing interventions into operational and even tactical matters exacerbated this situation. In combination, these developments diminished the army's combat effectiveness.

At the outset of the campaign, German leadership in the field proved both more effective and cohesive than that at the very top. Not only did the majority of German field marshals and generals have experience from the First World War, they also had commanded large formations in battle during the previous two years, providing them with a wealth of knowledge and experience. Men such as Colonel-Generals Heinz Guderian, Hermann Hoth, Erich Hoepner, and Ewald von Kleist proved themselves as panzer commanders during the invasion of France, and all received command of a panzer group for the invasion of the Soviet Union. Older or more militarily conservative officers, however, clashed with the impetuous panzer commanders during the opening stages of Operation Barbarossa. The differing conceptions of how panzer divisions could be used, as well as the outsized expectations of their potential held by some commanders, played an important role in German defeat during the three great German eastern offensives.

A shared ideological outlook also contributed to cohesion within the German officer corps. For many German officers, the immediate post–First World War era's revolutionary disturbances at home and seemingly existential fighting against nationalists and Communists on Germany's eastern frontier hardened an already staunchly anti-Bolshevik attitude. Considering the Soviet Union's Bolshevism as the greatest threat to European civilisation, they viewed the war as a true reckoning for Europe's future. This anti-Bolshevism complemented the Third Reich's radical anti-Semitism. The 'polite' anti-Semitism that had traditionally animated the German officer corps evolved into a much more venomous version – one that linked Jews with the Soviet leadership. A war against 'Judeo-Bolshevism' thus gained currency among the German military leadership. A belief that the individual German soldier was superior to his 'Asiatic Russian' counterpart was a long-standing belief in Germany, though the racial policies of the Nazi state undoubtedly intensified this belief among the officer corps. As a result of these beliefs, as well as poor showings by the Red Army in the invasions of eastern Poland and Finland, the German officer corps approached the war against the Soviet Union confidently.[9]

This ideological congruence between the army's leadership and the Nazi regime was one cause of the army's radically violent planning for war against the Soviet Union. The other was its understanding of total war. The Prusso-German army's traditional approach to war centred on the concept of military necessity. Believing that war transcended the boundaries of law, the army concluded that the need to achieve victory legitimised any and all means to do so, no matter the ethical or moral cost. With the British Empire still resisting, supported by an increasingly antagonistic United States, Germany's strategic situation in summer 1941 demanded a quick and decisive victory over the Soviet Union. Pragmatic considerations thus also lay behind the army's adoption of the Criminal Orders, decreeing the murder of commissars seen as the core of the Red Army's effectiveness. The army also adopted ferocious pacification policies designed to terrorise the population into acquiescence and lived off the land to ensure troops consumed enough food to power the advance; these strategies were all seen as vital to German victory. The Reich's desire to exploit Soviet resources for its own benefit took on even more importance over the course of the war, as the army extracted as much food and labour as possible to fuel its own war effort.[10]

An experienced and able officer corps was necessary for the German approach to the battlefield. German operations rested on achieving quick, decisive victories using speed, surprise, and shock to defeat its opponent. Eschewing frontal attacks into the teeth of the enemy defence, German practice probed the flanks for weak spots, pierced the front, and then drove as quickly and deeply as possible into the rear. By disrupting communications and preventing the construction of new defensive lines, German forces aimed to carry out large-scale encirclement battles of dislocated and rattled enemy forces.[11] Officers' training, which initially lasted for four years, instilled these principles.[12]

German leadership accepted that such mobile campaigns and battles could not be scripted or tightly controlled from headquarters. Realising that commanders in the field were best positioned to make decisions in response to a rapidly changing situation, the army leadership empowered its commanders at every level to take the initiative on the battlefield. Dubbed in the post-war era as *Auftragstaktik* – loosely translated as 'mission tactics' – the German approach focussed on creating soldiers who could operate independently on the battlefield, in service of an overall objective.[13] Such principles animated the army throughout the war; even in 1943, the army demanded that 'resolute decision-making and independent action is to be fostered above all'. Its men required 'the necessary self-confidence to act as leader and example' as victory was 'dependent on [the individual's] willingness and decisiveness in making a decision'.[14]

This did not mean, however, that commanders could do as they pleased; rather, they were to operate within the context of orders and a set objective. The tension inherent in modern military operations between central direction and individual initiative resulted in various clashes within the German leadership, most notably during the French and Barbarossa campaigns. Despite this friction, the ability of German forces to improvise in the rapidly changing conditions of mobile warfare to a far greater extent than their more slowly reacting enemies resulted in astonishing battlefield success.

The concepts behind this approach to war were then transmitted to the rank and file. Even before they entered the army, many young men had already spent time in organisations that helped prepare them for military service. These included the Hitler Youth and the *Reichsarbeitsdienst*, or RAD, a make-work program, both of which emphasised physical fitness, camaraderie, and Nazi values. German men were called up in successive draft waves, which would reach a total of thirty-five by the end of the war. Members of the earlier waves tended to be relatively fit men in their twenties. Later waves consisted of teenagers, old men, or those who had previously been deemed unfit for duty. Recruits drafted in the late 1930s underwent sixteen weeks of basic training, a gruelling ordeal that emphasised physical fitness, weapons mastery, and squad-level tactics. This was followed in some cases by more specialised training.[15]

Draftees of the lower ranks came from all walks of life and reflected all social and economic strata of the country, from farmers and craftsmen to lawyers and businessmen. Most were Protestants, with Catholics forming a sizeable minority. They were relatively well educated, having attended elementary school, sometimes high school, and in rarer cases university. One group that was exempt from service were skilled workers who were considered critical for the war economy. Throughout the war, the country would struggle with manpower shortages as it attempted to fill the army's ranks while also maintaining adequate production levels. When the invasion of the Soviet Union began in 1941, this problem was already acute, since most fit men in their twenties had already been called up and the Wehrmacht maintained only a small reserve.[16]

While experienced and well-trained officers, NCOs, and soldiers contributed to German success in the pre-Barbarossa phase of the war, so too did the German exploitation of the tank. In the mobile war desired by the army, the tank's speed became its most important attribute and the army constructed a new formation around this characteristic. The panzer division initially consisted of two tank regiments, supported by motorised infantry, artillery, supply, and other support units, ensuring that everything the tanks needed could move at their speed; in other words, the Germans focussed on creating combined

Figure 4.2 A German Christmas Eve celebration in the shelter of a command post on the Eastern Front, 24 December 1941. Source: ullstein bild via Getty Images.

arms units that could fight on their own at an accelerated tempo. This organisational structure proved vital to German battlefield success during the war.[17]

A robust structure was necessary to offset the weakness of its tank park. At the outbreak of Operation Barbarossa, the German eastern army possessed 3,255 tanks. The majority of these were obsolete. A total 1,832 tanks were split into four models – the German Mark I and II and the Czech 35 (t) and 38 (t). All four were severely under-armoured and under-gunned, with armour reaching a maximum of 25mm and the heaviest cannon at 37mm. These tanks were outdated before the campaign even began and stood no chance against the Soviet medium T-34 and the heavy KV-1 tank models.

Two newer panzers appeared during the 1939 Polish campaign, and their numbers increased in the lead up to Operation Barbarossa. A total of 979 Mark III tanks, armed with 37mm or 50mm guns and protected by 30mm of armour, and 444 Mark IV tanks, equipped with a 75mm gun and 30mm of armour, participated in the invasion of the Soviet Union. While they proved superior on the battlefield to the lighter tanks that constituted the bulk of the Soviet arsenal, they nonetheless remained inferior to the Red Army's T-34 and KV-1 in 1941.[18] German tanks only gained battlefield superiority with the introduction of the heavy Tiger tank in late 1942 and the medium Panther model in mid-1943. Armed with 88mm and 75mm cannons, respectively, they also carried far stronger armour than their predecessors, with the heavy tank protected by up to 120mm and the medium tank carrying a maximum of 100mm. They were never produced in enough numbers to change the course of the war, however, and suffered from a series of technical problems. The real strength of the German panzer force, however, was found in its personnel. Competent command and well-trained crews would make good German numerical inferiority through-out the majority of the war.

Between the fall of France in June 1940 and the invasion of the Soviet Union in June 1941, the number of panzer divisions doubled from ten to twenty in recognition of their combat effectiveness. Instead of creating these units from scratch, the army took one panzer regiment from an existing panzer division and then constructed a new unit around it. This 'principle of organisational cell division' carried both plusses and minuses. On the one hand, similar practices were used for the infantry regiments, as well as other units within the panzer division, giving the newly raised panzer divisions a core of veteran soldiers. On the other hand, the main striking power of a panzer division fell by half. While the continual replacement of obsolete tank models by superior vehicles balanced this loss of an entire regiment to some extent, the panzer divisions that invaded the Soviet Union simply lacked the numerical punch of those that fought in France in 1940.

Two other weapon systems proved vital to the army's battlefield performance over the course of the war. On the positive side, the army developed a tracked assault gun, the *Sturmgeschutz III*, or Stug III, which consisted of a 75mm cannon on top of a Mark III tank chassis. Cheaper to produce than a tank, some 250 of these took part in the initial invasion. Germany produced more Stug IIIs than any other fully tracked armoured vehicle, later upgrading it to a Stug IV, which func-tioned primarily in an anti-tank role. This was a necessary solution to one of the army's most debilitating deficiencies: the lack of an effective anti-tank gun. The German army's primary anti-tank guns in 1941 were 3.7cm and 5cm cannons. The troops referred to the former as the 'doorknocker' for the sound its shells made when they bounced off Soviet armour, and the latter, while effective against the bulk of Soviet armour, struggled to stop heavier Soviet tanks. In order to defend against Soviet armour, the Germans employed captured Red Army 7.62mm guns and their own 88mm anti-aircraft guns, which were effectively pressed into anti-tank roles in crisis situations. One of the German army's real weaknesses during the eastern campaign was its inability to provide its men with a mobile yet powerful anti-tank weapon.[19]

The Kar 98 k served as the standard German rifle during the war, supplemented by the MP40 submachine gun. By 1943, the latter was being replaced by a new assault rifle, the *Sturmgewehr 44*, that provided German soldiers with the necessary firepower to contend with Soviet small arms. German infantry units, however, centred on the machine gun. By 1941 the MG 34 furnished German units with meaningful firepower, and this only increased in 1942 with the introduction of the more robust MG 42 that could fire a withering 1,200 rounds per minute.[20]

The increase in the number of panzer divisions that occurred between the French and Soviet campaigns mirrored a general expansion of the army. When the French campaign concluded, the army consisted of 143 divisions. German planners settled on a 180-division force to defeat the much larger Soviet Union. During this expansion, the army encountered numerous problems. The first centred on leadership. As noted previously, the German approach to the battlefield relied heavily on experienced and trained leaders at all levels. The growing need for officers led to truncated training programs, as well as an influx of NCOs into the officer corps, resulting in its dilution, especially at the lower level. This had the secondary effect of weakening the ranks of the NCOs, which proved equally damaging to German operations. The promotion of individuals not necessarily ready for the next step thus rippled throughout the army, as both pre-existing and newly established units had to integrate and train their new recruits, while simultaneously trying to create the unit cohesion deemed so important for combat effectiveness. Specialists also proved to be in short supply, especially in panzer and motorised units that demanded skilled men to operate and repair their machines.[21]

Just as important to the German way of war was speed, with vehicles proving vital to Germany's chances of victory. Unfortunately for the army, it faced shortages before its hasty expansion that only exacerbated the problem. Not only did it have to find tanks, trucks, and half-tracks for the newly created panzer and motorised divisions; it needed to produce enough trucks to serve the supply needs of the recently raised divisions. The strain of outfitting so many new units with vehicles led one command to simply tell its subordinate units that 'the renewal of your request [for more vehicles] is, at this point in time, pointless'.[22] With German factories unable to produce enough vehicles, the army scavenged across the continent for equipment. The 167th Infantry Division, for example, was dependent on vehicles it procured in France and Belgium for the invasion of the Soviet Union.[23] Spare parts for such a wide range of foreign manufactured vehicles were nearly impossible to find, resulting in an ever-shrinking number of operational vehicles. And of course, vehicles manufactured for the consumer market in western Europe were ill-prepared to handle the rigors of cross-country movement on the primitive Soviet road network. As a result of this haphazard integration of vehicles and equipment from the entirety of the continent, the German army that invaded the Soviet Union resembled 'a European military museum'.[24]

The shortage of vehicles for the army meant it was essentially split into two tiers. The first consisted of the twenty panzer divisions – eighteen of which were used in the initial invasion of the Soviet Union – and fourteen motorised divisions that could match the speed if not the punch of the tank units. These thirty-four divisions formed the mobile spearhead of the German army, and it was their performance upon which hopes of victory rested. The second tier consisted of the overwhelming bulk of the army. These infantry divisions moved at the same rate of speed as those from 'the times of Prince Eugen, Max Emanuel, and Frederick the Great', constituting an 'undesirable constraint' on the 'thoughts of the High Command' whose campaigns were planned on 'the speed of the vehicle and airplane'.[25] The biggest obstacle facing the German army was ensuring that the marching divisions maintained the speed necessary to support the mobile units as they plunged deep into the Soviet interior. In the earlier and much more geographically constricted campaigns, the differing rates of speed caused problems but were eventually mastered. In the much larger Soviet Union, the increasing distances between the mobile and marching troops proved impossible to overcome.

Just as the bulk of the army marched, so too was it dependent on horses for moving heavy weapons and equipment to the battlefield and for transporting food, ammunition, and other supplies to the front. More than 600,000 horses accompanied the German army into battle in June 1941, stark evidence of an army whose ambitious operational goals far outstripped its capabilities. Divisional artillery was generally towed by horse teams, and expecting these beasts of burden to maintain the pace of the mobile units in the summer heat led to the deaths of thousands of horses from overwork, immobilising various units' artillery. The reliance on horse-drawn wagons to deliver supplies to the front, however, pointed to the army's greatest weakness as it prepared for Operation Barbarossa: logistics.

In a post-war interview, Halder remarked that 'according to our opinion, the material has to serve the spiritual. Accordingly, our quartermaster service may never hamper the operational concept'.[26] In other words, German operational plans were not constructed around the reality of logistics but rather logistics had to conform to operations. Horse-drawn wagon trains were clearly unsuited to maintain the rate of advance demanded by the army leadership, so the mobile divisions would be reliant on both railroads and trucks to feed the attack. While German trains would suffice to the border, the different gauge of Soviet tracks meant that the time-consuming conversion of track would have to occur before Soviet lines could be used. The scarcity of vehicles meant that available trucks were in no way sufficient to adequately supply the mobile units hundreds of miles to the front, and the wear and tear of continual driving them over rough Soviet terrain ensured that their numbers precipitously declined during the campaign.[27] The two-tier structure of the army promised that German victory over the Soviet Union would be difficult even in the most favourable scenarios; its rickety logistics system, however, ensured the campaign's failure.

While the German army retained a qualitative edge at the tactical level for much of the war, the extremely costly fighting in the east slowly ground away the army's officer and NCO corps. Less experienced and more Nazified officers filled the breech, and this problem was exacerbated by the so-called infantry crisis that fully emerged by 1943: an increasingly immobile and under-gunned infantry proved nearly impotent in the face of the Red Army's growing mechanisation and skill. Germany's armour situation proved no better. During the 1943 Battle of Kursk, the Germans deployed 2,699 of their 3,524 panzers and assault guns on the eastern front; they were opposed by 8,200 Soviet armoured vehicles in the region. One year later, the Soviets launched 5,818 Soviet tanks and assault guns in Operation Bagration against German formations that could muster a mere 570 German in response.[28]

The burden of overcoming the army's institutional failures fell on the shoulders of the men in the ranks. Perhaps more than any other single factor, the war's outcome depended on the willingness of average German soldiers to put their lives on the line to achieve Hitler's goals.[29] They would endure ferocious fighting, high casualties, an extreme climate, and a ramshackle supply system that frequently resulted in hunger, sickness, and countless other deprivations. Prospects of victory would fade over time as the Red Army grew stronger and the Wehrmacht became a shadow of its former self. Despite all this, very few German soldiers ever deserted their posts in Russia.[30] Instead, the vast majority obeyed orders and fought with skill and determination. They did so not simply out of fear of punishment but because they were convinced of the war's necessity and maintained the hope, however illusory, that victory could still be achieved.

Morale was high at the start of the campaign. Having recently achieved major victories in Poland, France, and the Balkans, the Wehrmacht appeared invincible in the eyes of its own personnel, as well as the wider world. Most soldiers assumed that Operation Barbarossa would result in yet another triumph and expected to return home before the onset of winter. Confidence in their training, equipment, comrades, and military leadership all contributed to this belief. Faith in Hitler also played a role. Many troops considered him the saviour of the nation and a once-in-a-generation strategist.

Even as the army assembled in the spring of 1941, rumours swirled that the deployment was a diversion to support the invasion of Britain or a means to extract more concessions from Stalin, with whom Germany had signed a non-aggression pact in 1939. Whether they expected it or not, troops found themselves reflecting on the meaning behind the conflict in their letters and diaries. They developed a wide range of justifications for their participation, sometimes drawing directly from Wehrmacht or regime propaganda and sometimes deviating from the official line.

One of the most common rationales favoured by the rank and file was the false notion that the invasion constituted a pre-emptive strike. According to this myth, heavily promoted by Wehrmacht propagandists, the USSR had secretly been planning to invade Germany, if not all of Western Europe. Operation Barbarossa was not an aggressive measure but an act of self-defence intended to stop the Soviets from using their massive military machine to wreak havoc across the continent.

For those soldiers who embraced Nazi ideology, the invasion also represented an existential conflict between the 'superior' German race and Jews, Slavs, and other supposedly 'inferior' ethnic groups that populated the Soviet Union. According to the Nazis, the Soviet Union was ruled by Jews who used communism as a vehicle to spread their malevolent influence across the globe. Only by destroying 'Jewish-Bolshevism', enslaving Slavic peoples, and seizing *Lebensraum* (living space) could the German people secure a brighter future. These messages were transmitted to the troops through lectures, newsletters, pamphlets, and other means, building upon the indoctrination already begun by the Propaganda Ministry, the Hitler Youth, and the Reich Labor Service.[31] Recent research indicates that likely only a minority of soldiers could be considered hardcore Nazis, but even those who did not fully imbibe Nazi ideology often agreed that the Soviet Union constituted a serious threat and believed that Germans had a right to rule over the East.[32] Such attitudes predisposed the Wehrmacht's fighters to acts of brutality and a callous disregard for the lives of Eastern Europeans.

Beyond ideology, soldiers were fuelled by a combination of nationalism and values with a long history in German society. To fight for one's country was considered the sacred duty of every upstanding

German man. Membership in the army was associated with laudable traits such as honour, bravery, sacrifice, hard work, and loyalty. As a result, most men, including both volunteers and draftees, took pride in their service and could count on the staunch support of their relatives back home.[33]

The sense of fighting for one's country or sacred values was made more concrete through the experience of 'comradeship' – the feeling of belonging to a community of warriors that took care of its own.[34] The Wehrmacht heightened such feelings by organising 'comradeship evenings' and holiday festivities, along with other communal activities, during periods of downtime. Many men came to see their unit as a kind of ersatz family, providing a space for care, warmth, and male bonding amid the horrors of war. According to the research of Felix Römer, even soldiers who had kept a distance from Nazism and militarism during peacetime tended to embrace the culture of comradeship, seeking promotions, medals, and respect from their commanding officers, as well as their fellow soldiers.[35]

The Wehrmacht's replacement system helped maintain this esprit de corps. The country was divided into twenty-one military districts, or *Wehrkreise*. At least in theory, each division incorporated men from the same district, which meant that its personnel shared regional ties. Divisions received march battalions, consisting of men from their military districts who had completed their training. These either joined a recuperating division in the rear or reinforced the unit at the front.[36] In the best-case scenario, the new recruits had the opportunity to mingle with and learn from the veterans before the unit was sent back into action. While this system faltered during the winter crisis of 1941–1942, it regained its equilibrium in spring 1942 and functioned reasonably effectively until mid-1944, constituting an important factor in maintaining the army's cohesion.[37]

Aside from the pre-emptive strike myth, ideology, nationalism, and military values, individual men developed a number of justifications for the campaign. Some, partly at the prompting of Wehrmacht chaplains, viewed themselves as crusaders setting out to destroy 'godless communism' and bring Christianity back to Russia. Others saw the Soviet Union as a ground ripe for colonial expansion, full of natural resources that could benefit the German people. Still others attempted to put a humanitarian spin on the campaign, preferring to see themselves as liberators freeing enslaved peoples from Soviet domination or bringing 'German order' to a chaotic land.[38]

Although the vast majority of Germany's soldiers proved willing to fight, the Wehrmacht also relied on coercion to ensure compliance. Men who refused their draft orders were simply executed. Those caught trying to desert were brought before the Wehrmacht's justice system, which was staffed by professional military jurists whose rulings were subject to the approval of commanding officers. About 17,000 men were executed for desertion through the end of 1944. Others were sentenced to *Strafbatallions* (penal battalions), where they were forced to conduct particularly dangerous operations. If a soldier was imprisoned or executed, his family could face severe financial penalties or even be sent to a concentration camp.[39]

Whatever their individual motivations, most soldiers appear to have successfully convinced themselves that their participation in the invasion was fully justified. They saw themselves not as monsters or criminals but ordinary, decent men doing a necessary if unpleasant job. Even as the Wehrmacht descended ever deeper into criminality, they defended their side's atrocities as morally reasonable or unavoidable.

As German troops pondered the meaning of the campaign, they also began to formulate their views of Eastern Europe. These varied from one soldier to the next, but the available evidence suggests that the majority of Wehrmacht personnel came to harbour a decidedly negative opinion of the land in which they found themselves and the peoples they encountered. Even before the invasion began, anti-communism, anti-Semitism, and anti-Slavic sentiments enjoyed widespread appeal among both the rank and file and army leadership. After observing the Soviet Union with their own eyes, many would report to their relatives that the East was poverty-stricken, dirty, backwards, chaotic, and uncivilised. They complained about the vast, inhospitable landscape and the harsh climate. They considered the country's inhabitants dirty, primitive, uneducated, and culturally or racially inferior to the occupiers. These views would only harden over time.

For many, their first impressions of the Soviet Union were coloured by their experiences in combat against the Red Army. Although they voiced their confidence in German arms and commented enthusiastically on the swift progress the Wehrmacht made in the USSR's western border regions, troops were forced to admit that the Soviet enemy was by far the most tenacious they had ever encountered. They were surprised at the level of resistance the Red Army mounted, pointing in their letters home to both the skill of the individual Soviet fighter and the sheer quantity of men and material that faced them on the battlefield. Gunner Hans Simon wrote his parents, 'The Russians are very tough. They defend themselves to the last drop of blood. One must pry every single one of them out of his [fox] hole.'[40] The sense of being overwhelmed by an enemy with seemingly limitless manpower and resources would only increase as the war went on.

Grudging respect was combined with a growing hatred of the Soviet opponent, fuelled by the brutality of the fighting and racist stereotypes. German soldiers complained bitterly about atrocities the other side committed, whether real or imagined. They accused Soviet defenders of firing on medics, murdering wounded POWs, and using irregular tactics the Wehrmacht considered dishonourable. Echoing Nazi propaganda, many depicted Red soldiers as 'animals' who did not deserve the protections accorded by international law. Instead, they were a soulless 'horde' made up of a mix of 'Asiatics' and other inferior races, fighting not out of conviction but because they were driven forward by their Jewish-Bolshevik masters. Special hatred was directed against the commissars – Soviet political functionaries embedded in the Red Army. German troops accused them of fanatical resistance and contempt for the lives of their own men.

The Red Army was not the only enemy the men of the Wehrmacht faced. The land itself seemed to oppose them at every turn. The summer months were marked by dust and scorching heat. Autumn rains soaked soldiers to the bone and turned the Soviet Union's primitive dirt roads into a muddy quagmire. Bitterly cold winters – for which the Wehrmacht was wholly unprepared – caused numerous cases of frostbite and breakdowns of gear and vehicles. German troops were plagued by lice, insects, and diseases like typhus and dysentery. They remarked on the vast land area of the Soviet Union, which kept units stretched thin, as well as the dense woods and swamps that formed a perfect hiding place for partisans.

As they struggled with the inhospitable climate and landscape, troops frequently commented on what they considered the Soviet Union's appalling economic conditions. In the countryside, they described villages consisting of ramshackle one-room huts where human and animals lived side by side. In the cities, modern conveniences were few and far between. A month into the invasion, Johannes Hagemann wrote:

> The Russians are a poor people. Whereas at home in Germany every house has wallpaper, the Russian makes do with old newspapers that he sticks to the walls. I have not yet seen curtains or flowers in the windows. I haven't yet seen a baker, butcher, or other craftsman. Here stand only small poor wooden houses, in which the people truly do everything themselves.[41]

Some blamed the communist system and its rulers for the state of the country. Others attributed what they saw to 'Slavic inferiority', whether this was conceived of in racial or cultural terms. Almost all agreed that the Soviet Union was an economic backwater that fell far below German standards.

If their opinion of their Red Army opponents and the land as a whole was decidedly negative, the invaders' assessment of the civilians they encountered was more complex and varied. Many soldiers expressed racist sentiments and feelings of cultural superiority towards men and women they considered dirty and primitive. Others voiced sympathy and curiosity, and recognised similarities as well as differences between themselves and the locals. Although commanders discouraged close contact with civilians, trading was common and many soldiers would spend their winters quartering in local houses. Relations tended to be relatively amicable at first, since many civilians were glad to be rid of Soviet rule. However, they quickly deteriorated as theft, rape, forced labour, and terror emerged as the hallmarks of the Wehrmacht's occupation. More and more locals joined the ranks of the partisans, and the army's brutal response would engender hatred and mistrust on both sides that continued until the end of the war.

In the vast, multi-ethnic USSR, soldiers tended to lump all civilians together under the category of 'Russians'. One major exception were Jews, whom soldiers often saw through the lens of negative stereotypes, describing them as particularly strange in garb and appearance, lazy, greedy, and dirty. Many associated them with Bolshevik rule and blamed them for partisan attacks or atrocities. These views owed much to Nazi propaganda, as well as centuries-old anti-Semitism.

Despite fierce fighting and scorching heat, morale remained high in the summer and into the fall of 1941, buoyed by the seemingly inexorable advance and news of major victories. Troops boasted of the POWs they took, who numbered in the hundreds of thousands. Many predicted the USSR would soon collapse. By late summer, however, exhaustion had already begun to set in. Racing ahead, the panzer troops encircled large pockets of enemy troops but faced constant counter-attacks and over-stretched supply lines. Struggling to keep up, the largely unmotorised infantry divisions conducted marches sometimes exceeding fifty kilometres per day while contending with enemy forces that had been bypassed by the panzers.[42] Casualties mounted,[43] and vehicles broke down or were lost to enemy action.[44] Over the course of the campaign, the Wehrmacht's logistical apparatus, unable to master the immense distances and primitive infrastructure of the Soviet theatre, predictably struggled to bring food, fuel, and supplies to the front to the point that some soldiers reported suffering hunger and malnutrition. The weather turned from hot and dusty to rainy and muddy, and by November to a cold for which soldiers were not properly equipped. They asked their relatives to send foodstuffs, gloves, and other items to supplement their meagre supplies, or stole these at gunpoint from the local population.

Morale plummeted as winter deepened and the strategic situation became increasingly critical. The tone of soldiers' writings changed. Marked above all by the bitter realisation that the war would not in fact be over by Christmas, they no longer conveyed breezy optimism but desperation. 'We are currently located in a defensive position around 80 kilometres north of Moscow', wrote a non-commissioned officer in Army Group Centre. 'I am writing this letter in a foxhole, which is particularly unpleasant now in winter. My feet are already half frozen. We few remaining soldiers of our division crave so badly the forlorn hope of replacement.'[45] By early December, the drive on Moscow had ground to a halt. Neither soldiers nor generals were prepared for what came next: a devastating counteroffensive by Russian forces that forced the invaders back from the city.

It was not only the disaster outside Moscow and the frigid weather that dealt a blow to morale; soldiers also began to recognise the enormity of their side's losses. Indeed, by late March 1942, Germany's eastern army had suffered over a million killed, wounded, and missing – about a third of its initial manpower. Among these were at least 15,000 dead officers. Despite scraping together as many men as it could from reserve units and formations not intended for combat, the Wehrmacht was never able to sufficiently make up its losses. Many divisions would remain under-strength for the duration of the war.[46] More recruits were called up. Their quality decreased dramatically over time, however, and training on the home front became shorter and less comprehensive.[47] In an effort to offset this in 1942 and 1943, German combat units carried out two-to-three-week training courses at the front to educate their newly arrived replacements in the realities of war in the east.[48]

In 1943 and 1944, as the Wehrmacht was driven from Soviet territory, German soldiers fought on despite massive casualties, including a major defeat in the Battle of Kursk. Motivations shifted towards mere survival and the determination to keep the Red Army from reaching the German homeland. Their writings indicate that servicemen were aware of the crumbling strategic situation; neverthe-less, many continued to hope for a miracle – whether in the form of new weapons technologies or a rift among the Allies – that would somehow turn the tide in their favour.[49] Faith in Hitler's leadership remained strong, as indicated by the reports of the army's censors. 'The war, that now daily increases in intensity', one soldier wrote in September 1944, 'has slowly reached its high point. May the Lord God be with us and stand at our side in the last struggle. We have complete trust in our Führer. He who led us victoriously into great battles will also lead us to victory in the final decisive battle.'[50]

In the summer of 1942, the 7th Infantry Division's commander wrote, 'the winter of 1941/42 cost the blood of the German infantry', bemoaning that 'the present infantry is no longer that of 1941'.[51] The tremendous casualties suffered in the fighting of 1941 and early 1942 could never be made good, and war against the western Allies in North Africa, Italy, and finally Northwest Europe ensured that the *Ostheer* never regained its 1941 potency. The decline in the quality of its commanders, the numerical strength of its divisions, the training of its soldiers, and the quantity of vehicles deployed to the battlefield was mirrored by an increasingly com-petent and powerful Red Army that bristled with modern weapons. While morale remained sufficient to keep the German army in the field, it was one born of desperation to save the German population from suffering the same fate as the Soviet people under German occupation. 'The soldier from 22.6.1941 [who] went with a feeling of towering superiority over every opponent in battle [and was] the enthusiastic bearer of the political will of the nation' no longer existed by 1945 as the German army was bludgeoned into submission by its Soviet opponent.[52]

Notes

1 Rolf-Dieter Müller, *Hitler's Wehrmacht: 1935–1945*, trans. Janice W. Ancker (Lexington: University Press of Kentucky, 2016), p. 175.

2 David Stahel, 'Introduction', in *Joining Hitler's Crusade: European Nations and the Invasion of the Soviet Union, 1941*, ed. David Stahel (Cambridge: Cambridge University Press, 2017), p. 11.

3 Wolfram Wette, *The Wehrmacht: History, Myth, Reality*, trans. Deborah Lucas Schneider (Cambridge, MA: Harvard University Press, 2006), p. 77; Ben Shepherd, *Hitler's Soldiers: The German Army in the Third Reich* (New Haven and London: Yale University Press, 2016), p. 148.

4 Rüdiger Overmans, *Deutsche militärische Verluste im Zweiten Weltkrieg* (München: Oldenbourg, 2000), p. 282.

5 On the 'German way of war,' see Robert Citino, *The German Way of War: From the Thirty Years' War to the Third Reich* (Lawrence: University Press of Kansas, 2005); on the 'revolutionary methods' used in France, see Karl-Heinz Frieser, *The Blitzkrieg Legend: The 1940 Campaign in the West* (Annapolis, MD: Naval Institute Press, 2013), p. 100.

6 On the German command system, see Geoff Megargee, *Inside Hitler's High Command* (Lawrence: University Press of Kansas, 2000).

7 MacGregor Knox, *Common Destiny: Dictatorship, Foreign Policy, and War in Fascist Italy and Nazi Germany* (Cambridge: Cambridge University Press, 2000).

8 Ferdinand Schörner Personnel File, F8105693, RG 319, NARA.

9 Johannes Hürter, *Hitlers Heerführer: Die deutschen Oberbefehlshaber im Krieg gegen die Sowjetunion 1941/42* (Munih: Oldenbourg, 2006), pp. 86–96, 206–222.

10 See Chapter 13.

11 Citino, *The German Way of War*, and Gerhard Groß, *The Myth and Reality of German Operational Warfare: From Moltke to Heusinger* (Lexington: University Press of Kentucky, 2016).

12 Shepherd, *Hitler's Soldiers*, pp. 15–17; Müller, *Hitler's Wehrmacht*, pp. 97–101.

13 Marco Sigg, *Der Unterführer als Feldherr im Taschenformat: Theorie und Praxis der Auftragstaktik im deutschen Heer 1869 bis 1945* (Paderborn: Ferdinand Schöningh, 2014).

14 Generalkommando XXXXVI Pz.Korps Der Kommandierende General, Ia Nr. 315/43 g. Kdos., 10.4.43, Betr.: Ausbildung, National Archives and Record Association (hereafter NARA), T-315, Roll 389.

15 Shepherd, *Hitler's Soldiers*, pp. 15–17; Müller, *Hitler's Wehrmacht*, pp. 93–97. On the various formations of the Wehrmacht and the dates they were created, see Georg Tessin, *Die Waffengattungen – Gesamtübersicht. Verbände und Truppen der deutschen Wehrmacht und Waffen-SS im Zweiten Weltkrieg 1939–1945*, vol. 1 (Osnabrück: Biblio Verlag, 1977).

16 Adam Tooze, *The Wages of Destruction: The Making and Breaking of the Nazi Economy* (New York: Penguin Books, 2008), p. 437.

17 R. L. Dinardo, *Germany's Panzer Arm in WWII* (Mechanicsburg, PA: Stackpole Books, 2006).

18 Rolf-Dieter Müller, 'From Economic Alliance to Colonial Exploitation', in *The Attack on the Soviet Union*, Vol. IV: *Germany and the Second World War*, ed. Horst Boog (Oxford: Oxford University Press, 2015), p. 219.

19 Chris McNab, *Hitler's Armies: A History of the German War Machine, 1939–1945* (Oxford: Osprey, 2011), pp. 124–125, 218.

20 Ibid., pp. 43–46, 203, 309.

21 Bernhard R. Kroener, 'The Manpower Resources of the Third Reich in the Area of Conflict between Wehrmacht, Bureaucracy, and War Economy', in *Organization and Mobilization of the German Sphere of Power: Wartime Administration, Economy, and Manpower Resources, 1939–1941*, Vol. V/IB: *Germany and the Second World War*, ed. Bernhard R. Kroener, Rolf-Dieter Müller, and Hans Umbreir (Oxford: Oxford University Press, 2015), pp. 971–972.

22 Generalkommando XVIII. Armeekorps, Abt. Ia Nr.3276/40 geh., Betr. Umgliederung der Radf.Schwadronen der Geb.Aufkl.Abt. zu Kradsch. Schwadronen u.Aufstellung eines Pi.Zuges (mot) bei der Geb.Aufkl. Abt., 18.11.40, Bundesarchiv Militärarchiv (hereafter BAMA) RH 28/4-2.

23 167. Infanterie Division, Abt. Ia, An Gen. Kdo. XII. A.K., 25.8.41, BAMA, RH 26-167/13.

24 Rolf-Dieter Müller, *Der letzte deutsche Krieg 1939–1945* (Klett-Cotta: Stuttgart, 2005), p. 84.

25 4. Gebirgs-Division, KTB Ia, 18.8.42, BAMA RH 28-4/26.

26 Paul Egon Heinrich Lüth, ed., *Gespräche mit Halder* (Wiesbaden: Limes Verlag, 1950), p. 86.

27 David Stahel, *Operation Barbarossa and Germany's Defeat in the East* (Cambridge: Cambridge University Press, 2009), pp. 119–138.

28 Karl-Heinz Frieser, ed., *The Eastern Front 1943–1944: The War in the East and on the Neighbouring Fronts*, Vol. VIII: *Germany and the Second World War* (Oxford: Oxford University Press, 2017), pp. 84, 101, 528, 526.

29 On the experience of German soldiers on the Eastern Front, see especially Stephen Fritz, *Frontsoldaten: The German Soldier in World War II* (Lexington: University Press of Kentucky, 1995); David Harrisville, *The Virtuous Wehrmacht: Crafting the Myth of the German Soldier on the Eastern Front, 1941–1944* (Ithaca and London: Cornell University Press, 2021).

30 For the latest research on desertion in the Wehrmacht, see Stefan Kurt Treiber, *Helden Oder Feiglinge? Deserteure Der Wehrmacht Im Zweiten Weltkrieg* (Frankfurt am Main: Campus Verlag, 2021).

31 On the influence of Nazi ideology in the Wehrmacht, see Omer Bartov, *Hitler's Army: Soldiers, Nazis, and War in the Third Reich* (New York: Oxford University Press, 1991); Fritz, *Frontsoldaten*; Bryce Sait, *The Indoctrination of the Wehrmacht: Nazi Ideology and the War Crimes of the German Military* (New York and Oxford: Berghahn Books, 2019).

32 See especially Klaus Latzel, *Deutsche Soldaten – nationalsozialistsicher Krieg? Kriegserlebnis – Kriegserfahrung 1939–1945* (Paderborn: Ferdinand Schöningh, 1998); Sönke Neitzel and Harald Welzer, *Soldaten. Protokolle vom Kämpfen, Töten und Sterben* (Frankfurt am Main: S. Fischer, 2011); Michaela Kipp, *'Großreinmachen im Osten': Feindbilder in Deutschen Feldpostbriefen im Zweiten Weltkrieg* (Frankfurt am Main: Campus Verlag, 2014).

33 See Felix Römer, *Kameraden. Die Wehrmacht von Innen* (München: Piper, 2012), pp. 111–157.

34 See Thomas Kühne, *Kameradschaft. Die Soldaten des nationalsozialistischen Krieges und das 20. Jahrhundert* (Göttingen: Vandenhoeck & Ruprecht, 2006).

35 Felix Römer, 'Milieus in the Military: Soldierly Ethos, Nationalism and Conformism among Workers in the Wehrmacht', *Journal of Contemporary History* 48, 1 (2013), pp. 125–149; Christoph Rass, *'Menschenmaterial': Deutsche Soldaten an der Ostfront. Innenansichten einer Infanteriedivision 1939–1945* (Paderborn: Ferdinand Schöningh, 2003), pp. 238–263.

36 See Shepherd, *Hitler's Soldiers*, p. 15.

37 For various perspectives on this issue, see Edward Shils and Morris Janowitz, 'Cohesion and Disintegration in the Wehrmacht in World War II', *Public Opinion Quarterly* 12, 2 (1948), pp. 280–315; Bartov, *Hitler's Army*; and Jeff Rutherford, *Combat and Genocide on the Eastern Front: The German Infantry's War, 1941–1944* (Cambridge: Cambridge University Press, 2014), pp. 271–279.

38 Harrisville, *Virtuous Wehrmacht*.

39 See Treiber, *Helden Oder Feiglinge?*; Robert Loeffel, 'Soldiers and Terror: Re-evaluating the Complicity of the Wehrmacht in Nazi Germany', *German History* 27, 4 (2009), pp. 514–530.

40 Hans Simon to parents, 15.7.1941, Museumstiftung Post und Telekommunikation (hereafter: MSPT) 3.2002.1288.

41 Johannes Hagemann to parents, 12.7.1941, MSPT 3.2002.7169.

42 Richard J. Evans, *The Third Reich at War 1939–1945* (New York: Penguin Books, 2010), p. 179.

43 Ibid., 199. According to Evans, around 10 per cent of the army's personnel were dead, wounded, or missing a little over a month into the invasion.

44 The 18th Panzer Division, for example, started with more than 200 tanks and was reduced to 12 tanks after a month of fighting. Bartov, *Hitler's Army*, p. 20.

45 Non-commissioned officer E.K., 21.11.1941, quoted in Craig Luther and David Stahel, eds., *Soldiers of Barbarossa: Combat, Genocide, and Everyday Experiences on the Eastern Front, June-December 1941* (Guilford, CT: Stackpole Books, 2020), p. 252.

46 Bartov, *Hitler's Army*, pp. 36–39.

47 Shepherd, *Hitler's Soldiers*, pp. 384–385.

48 Jeff Rutherford and Adrian Wettstein, *The German Army on the Eastern Front: An Inner View of the Ostheer's Experiences of War* (Barnsley, UK: Pen and Sword, 2018), pp. 148–168.

49 See Shepherd, *Hitler's Soldiers*, pp. 476–478.

50 Letter by Dickgreber, 12 September 1944, in Chef der Generalstab, Feldpostprüfberichte, September 1944, BA-MA RH 13/49.

51 7. Infanterie Division Kommandeur, Nr. 01010/42 geh., 4. August 1942, Generalkommando IX Armeekorps, NARA T-315, Roll 379.

52 101. Jäger Division, Kommandeur, Nr. 312/43 g.Kdos, 10.12.43, BAMA RH 24-44/176.

5
______

The Red Army: Leadership and Command

The Red Army started the Great Patriotic War against Germany and her allies with a strength of around 5,707,116 personnel, thanks in part to a partial mobilisation during the spring before a full Soviet mobilisation was declared on 22 June 1941.[1] Nonetheless, despite its initial size, Axis forces had a short-term superiority over the Red Army in the immediate Western border region on 22 June. Much of the Red Army's strength was at this time spread across the Soviet Union, whereas the German armed forces participating in Operation Barbarossa had a nominal strength at the start of the campaign of around 3.35 million, which was very much concentrated for the initial attack. However, in terms of numbers of tanks and combat aircraft, the Red Army had a numerical superiority on Germany's Eastern Front from the outset and even in the Western border regions, but was unable to exploit those superiorities due in part due to poor states of readiness, absurd initial orders to counterattack regardless of their circumstances, and weak command and control. Indeed, if taking just tanks, in the Western border regions as of 1 June 1941 there were around 10,540 tanks in the two highest serviceability categories for Soviet armour – categorisation that in principle meant that any repairs required for these vehicles were relatively light and could be handled by the units themselves.[2] This compared to a nominal German strength in the East at the start of Operation Barbarossa of 3,648 tanks – an incomplete figure that (even with vehicles not included in this count) does not take the armoured strength of the Wehrmacht in the Western part of the Soviet Union anywhere near the Soviet total.

Despite horrendous losses during the first weeks and months of the war, after a full mobilisation had been declared on 22 June 1941, the Red Army would soon significantly outnumber Axis forces on Germany's Eastern Front according to all key indicators. By 1 July 1941, there were around 9,638,000 personnel in the Soviet armed forces, including 3,533,000 in the field forces (and 532,000 in the navy, where a significant number of those sailors would ultimately end up fighting on land). This was a numerical superiority that would be sustained throughout the remainder of the war despite the horrendous losses the Red Army would suffer during the summer and early autumn of 1941, in particular. By the end of September 1941, the Red Army had already lost more than two million personnel through various causes – many taken prisoner – and yet Red Army strength still consisted of 3,627,000 personnel with active fronts and formations as of 10 September 1941 out of a total strength of around 8 million. By the second quarter of 1942, Red Army field strength had risen to a monthly average of 4,186,000 for the first quarter and 5,060,300 for the second quarter of 1942. This compared to a German army in the East that had a strength of around 3.2 million at the end of 1941. It was something of an economic miracle – and a testimony to long-term Soviet preparations for war – that despite the loss of thousands of tanks during the summer of 1941 the Red Army could continue to field more and often more effective tanks in late 1941 and early 1942 than its opponent, despite the fact that production in evacuated industrial plant to the east had yet to fully resume. Small inputs of Allied, and particularly British, equipment arrived in late 1941 and early 1942 at an opportune moment to help tide the Red Army over before new and increased Soviet production of key weapons systems could come online.

In order to maintain numerical superiority in terms of personnel, the Red Army had to draw on not only increasingly younger and older men from the full range of nationalities of the Soviet Union but also women. At the beginning of the war there was a reticence to mobilise some nationalities of the Soviet Union into combat units either because their loyalties were questioned or because language issues in integrating them into mixed nationality units were seen as insurmountable. During the early war period the Soviet leadership vacillated over the formation of units made up of specific nationalities, although in November 1941 the

Figure 5.1 Soviet cavalry parade through Red Square on their way to the front, 7 November 1941. Source: The Dmitri Baltermants Collection/CORBIS/Corbis via Getty Images.

formation of a large number of units specifically from the populations of Central Asia and the Caucasus was ordered – with their numbers to be topped up with Russians as required. Ultimately, as pressure mounted to mobilise ever wider elements of the population, the decision was taken to incorporate Slavic and non-Slavic nationalities into the same combat units. Nonetheless, the fact that many units were initially mobilised from a particular part of the Soviet Union meant that they had very strong representations of particular national groups in them, even if as time went those concentrations were often diluted as units were reinforced with march battalions and other replacements from different parts of the country.[3]

At the beginning of the Great Patriotic War, there was Soviet reticence to use women in combat roles, although large numbers of women were employed in the medical services behind the front lines. However, by the spring of 1942 – after the full scale of the horrendous losses suffered by the Red Army since the beginning of the war had become apparent – large numbers of women either volunteered or were conscripted into the Red Army. According to figures provided by a collective led by Russian historian G. F. Krivosheev, of the 490,235

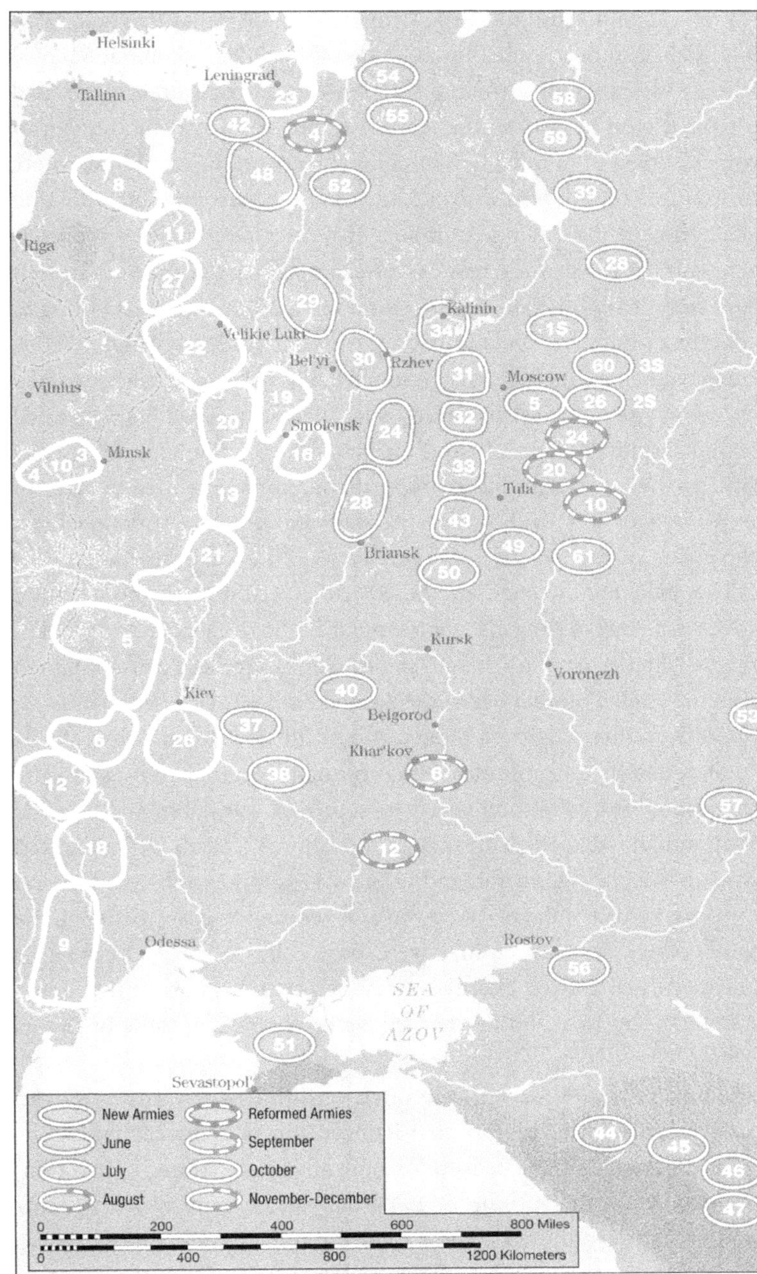

Map 1 Soviet dispositions (31 July 1941) and reinforcements
(to 31 December 1941).

women called up into the Red Army during the Great Patriotic War, only 5,594 had been called up in 1941. Of this 490,235, about 318,980 served with front-line formations. In most instances, women were used to replace men in roles in the rear areas, but an increasing number of women served in nominally non-combat roles on the front line, where for example they served as front-line medical personnel or radio and telephone operators. Large numbers of women would also serve in de facto combat roles in the rear as, for example, part of the anti-aircraft defence system of the air defences forces (PVO; for which according to a decree of the State Defence Committee of 25 March 1942, 100,000 young women aged 19–25 were to be called up). The number of women serving in front-line combat roles, such as snipers or pilots, remained limited despite the regular use of images of their activities in the media. Perhaps the most significant proportional employment of women in combat roles was within the partisan movement, where at least 10 per cent of participants were women over the war as a whole.[4]

The men and women of the Soviet armed forces and partisan movement were ultimately commanded by Soviet leader Iosif Stalin, who as Chairman of the State Defence Committee and self-appointed Supreme High Commander of the Armed Forces took a very hands-on approach to directing the military side of the Soviet war effort. While the State Defence Committee – that brought together party and state institutions into what amounted to a sort of war cabinet – handled many military-related matters such as resource allocation for the Red Army, it was the high command or Stavka – supported by the General Staff – that directed the Red Army in an operational sense. Although the memberships of these entities were nominally supposed to meet as collectives, Stalin often chose to meet their members on an individual or small group basis, rather than convene meetings of these bodies as a whole.[5]

Members of the Stavka were often sent out to the various Soviet fronts in order to make sure that its orders were being carried out as intended. After the aborted use of multi-front or 'strategic direction' commanders in the autumn of 1941, the role of multi-front coordination on behalf of the Stavka was carried out by Stavka representatives who were part of a machinery that both informed Stalin about what was going on at the front and ensured that what had been decided upon centrally was being carried out. This apparatus relied not only on the big-name Stavka representatives to fronts or groups of fronts (with Marshal Georgii Zhukov frequently leaving Moscow to carry out such a role) but also lesser representatives of the General Staff – the so-called Officers of the General Staff posted down as low as divisional level as required.[6]

At the beginning of the Great Patriotic War, the Red Army's senior leadership still suffered from the tendency for political reliability and cronyism to be reflected in senior appointments more than ability. While relatively capable commanders such as Zhukov had risen to senior leadership positions – in Zhukov's case where he was Chief of the General Staff at the outbreak of war – close confidants of Stalin such as Kliment Voroshilov, Semen Budennii, and to a lesser extent Grigorii Kulik still held prominent positions in the military and military-political hierarchies. Indeed, Voroshilov, Budennii, and Kulik were the only three Marshals of the Soviet Union at the outbreak of war. They were joined in terms of influence by obvious 'politicals' such as Lev Mekhlis in bringing low levels of military education to the Soviet high command, where any practical military experience they possessed was largely from the period of the Russian Civil War. As the war progressed, the likes of Georgii Zhukov, Aleksandr Vasilevskii, Aleksei Antonov, and Konstantin Rokossovksii eclipsed the 'cronies' and 'politicals' and brought greater ability combined with the necessary ruthlessness to the senior command of the Red Army.

The Red Army that they led had a conventional military structure, although its rifle divisions were at times significantly smaller than those of its opponents and armoured formations significantly larger. At the beginning of the war the Red Army had a tendency towards gigantism in its creation of mechanised formations that were inspired in part by the large German panzer divisions employed in 1939–1940, but where it soon became clear that its capacity to actually direct such large and cumbersome formations in a meaningful way was woefully lacking. As a result of this realisation and heavy losses during the first weeks and months of the war, the Red Army was to some extent forced to build up replacement formations from the most basic elements being created – the battalion and regiment. During late 1941 and into 1942, many armoured battalions in particular fought essentially not as organic parts of larger formations such as divisions, corps, and armies, but as distinct battalion-sized units that were often attached to rifle regiments and divisions. As the war progressed, these battalions were increasingly incorporated into mechanised or tank brigades, divisions, corps, and armies as Red Army experience in coordinating the activities of multiple units within an organic formation increased. Nonetheless, throughout the war a shortage of experienced staff officers hampered the activities of formations at the corps level in particular. As time went on, increasingly large units and formations, including of artillery and airpower, were held by the Stavka for deployment to particular sectors of the front for particular operations.

The Red Army was significantly different from the armies of its opponents and indeed allies in having a political structure that early in the war shared responsibility for all command decisions up to Front level, just before the start of the successful counteroffensive near Stalingrad. Political commissars had been introduced during the Russian Civil War as a way of supervising the activities of former Tsarist officers whose political allegiances were sometimes in doubt. Their dual command function had gradually been disbanded during the 1920s and early 1930s, only to be reintroduced during the Great Purges of 1936–1938, disbanded again after the war with Finland of 1939–1940, and reintroduced again in July 1941. In principle Stalin and other senior military figures acknowledged that in an ideal world there would be unitary command in military units, but Stalin's suspicion of military commanders during times of crisis led to the reintroduction of dual command both during the Great Purges and first weeks of the Great Patriotic War.[7] By October 1942, Stalin seems to have been sufficiently confident in the Red Army's command elements not only to abolish dual command in military units but to reward commanders with the pre-Soviet officer designations that had been abolished after the October Revolution.

The Red Army had started preparations for a large-scale future war well before its principal opponent, Germany – even if when those preparations had begun in the late 1920s and early 1930s the Soviet leadership didn't have a particular threat in mind. Although in many spheres German forces had a technological edge over the Red Army in terms of equipment throughout the war, overall the Red Army was provided with weapons and equipment that made up for any technological deficiencies through being robust and fit for purpose – and of course ultimately being available in large numbers, thanks to large pre-war stocks and a ruthless focus on military production during the war itself.

Regarding infantry weapons, at the beginning of the Great Patriotic War the Red Army was starting to introduce the PPSh sub-machine gun into infantry units – a weapon that would become almost as ubiquitous for the Red Army as the T-34 tank as the war progressed. The PPSh sub-machine gun was introduced to a large extent in the face of experience of the Finnish use of the Suomi KP-31 sub-machine gun in 1939–1940. Simple to maintain and use, and with a sizeable magazine, the PPSh weapon was rugged and relatively simple to manufacture but effective. While the PPS sub-machine gun was introduced as the war progressed as an easier-to-manufacture alternative to the PPSh, the latter was produced in far larger numbers. Many infantrymen nonetheless continued to use weapons that were essentially of First World War vintage, such as the Mosin Nagant rifle stemming from the initial 1891 variant, although this rifle was supplemented with Tokarev SVT automatic rifles originating from the immediate pre-war period. The Red Army's penchant for the mortar developed during the period immediately prior to and at the beginning of the Great Patriotic War, where once again it was the war in Finland that highlighted the weaknesses of the Red Army's indirect fire capabilities with conventional artillery and the value of the mortar in a wooded environment. Such experience prompted the rapid adoption of mortars from 60mm to the ubiquitous 120mm models that were subsequently copied by Germany. That Soviet infantry also used the 76mm M1927 regimental field gun from the beginning of the war – a light artillery piece later replaced with the M1943 variant on a different and even lighter carriage – which highlighted the continued Soviet desire to provide artillery for direct fire use by the infantry at the regimental level and below.

The Soviet tank park at the beginning of the war was dominated by models that had been developed during the early 1930s and subsequently produced in very large numbers, such that at the beginning of the Great Patriotic War it numbered more than 20,000 in total. While the Soviet conceptions of 'Deep Battle' and 'Deep Operations' of the 1930s envisioned different types of tanks performing different roles on the battlefield in a manner not dissimilar to conceptions held by the British during the same period (e.g., with the T-26 performing more of an infantry tank role than the BT-series 'cruiser' tanks tasked with the exploitation role), by the beginning of the Great Patriotic War the Soviet Union had clearly adopted a schema that divided tank into light, medium, and heavy variants.[8] Although light tanks continued to be used by the Red Army until late in the war, as the war progressed the tank dichotomy in the Red Army was further simplified with the core divide being between the maid of all work T-34 and the heavy IS-2 tank in the breakthrough role, where the latter was the successor to the early-war KV-series tanks that on occasion had provided so much consternation to German forces.

While the Soviet tanks available in large numbers at the beginning of the war were increasingly looking outdated on the modern battlefield, and in particular in terms of the lack of widespread provision of radios to facilitate their command and control, the basic designs still had utility against the German tanks fielded in 1941. The Soviet medium (T-34 series) and heavy tanks (KV- and IS-series) produced from 1940 onwards, which were available in increasing numbers as the war progressed, were characterised by relatively strong armament and armour and good speed for their armament and armour – as well as rugged construction. What they lacked in terms of refinements such as optics was in many ways compensated for with their other characteristics and availability in increasingly large numbers. As the war progressed, the Red Army's tank pool was augmented by large numbers of specialist tank destroyers used either in breakthrough or anti-tank roles and Lend-Lease vehicles.

Artillery was widely considered a strength of the Red Army, not because it was particularly well directed in an indirect fire role but more when it was used either *en masse* or in a direct fire role. The Red Army began the war with a mix of First World War vintage guns, along with models developed during the 1930s that continued to serve throughout the war, such as the 122mm M1938 howitzer. Of particular note was the Red Army's increasing use of large numbers of rockets that could be particularly effective when used in large numbers where their poor accuracy was compensated for by weight of fire. Although the 'Katiusha' is another weapon that has become synonymous with the Red Army of the Great Patriotic War, the Red Army employed several rocket types collectively described as the 'Katiusha', with calibres ranging from 82mm up to 300mm.

Like the German Luftwaffe, the Soviet air forces were developed to a considerable extent with support for the Red Army in mind. As such, in addition to fighter aircraft such as the I-16 being used in a close support role, the war saw the development of the 'flying tank' concept that led to the mass production and use of the Il-2 '*Sturmovik*'. Despite relatively heavy armour limiting speed and the fact that airpower had less of an impact on fighting across the vast expanses of the European part of the Soviet Union than it did in the West, when used in large numbers the '*Sturmovik*' further contributed to the Red Army's ability to deliver considerable firepower on enemy targets at the outset of operations. Although air-ground coordination improved as the war progressed, the effectiveness of this air support for dynamic operations in progress remained relatively low compared to similar air support provided by the German Luftwaffe to the Wehrmacht early in the war.[9]

Among the principal armies beginning their participation in the Second World War, the Red Army was unusual in having both large airborne forces and a considerable cavalry component. While other armies such as those of the US and UK developed their airborne forces as the war progressed and indeed used them *en masse*, the Soviet experience was the inverse in part due to an absence of large numbers of transport aircraft. Meaningful use of airborne forces was made, however, during the counterattacks near Moscow of the winter of 1941–1942 and during operations to cross the Dnepr River in late 1943.

The Red Army made considerable use of cavalry units and indeed formations during the Great Patriotic War. Such cavalry formations provided excellent mobility in the context of those many parts of the Soviet Union lacking good road networks, although their misuse early in the war led to heavy casualties. Once it had been accepted that in modern warfare the cavalry charge was essentially a thing of the past and that cavalry were best considered as being horse-mobile infantry, then they remained an asset for much of the war.

For the Red Army at the beginning of the Great Patriotic War, the Achilles' heel in terms of equipment was undoubtedly transport – both armoured and otherwise – and communications equipment. While the Red Army had aspirations towards considerable mechanisation, at the beginning of the war it remained reliant on the horse to a considerable extent – much of course like its German opponent. Considerable losses

Figure 5.2 Soviet infantrymen mounting an attack supported by a 45mm gun, 1943. Source: Alexander Ustinov/Slava Katamidze Collection/Getty Images.

of wheeled vehicles during the first weeks and months of the war contributed to transport issues from railheads to the front line that, although not critical when the Red Army was falling back on those railheads, became a significant problem on the advance. By the mid-war period, considerable numbers of powerful US-manufactured trucks were being provided to the Soviet Union under Lend-Lease, which would greatly ease the Red Army's transport and resupply issues as the war progressed.[10] Throughout the war, the Red Army also lacked significant numbers of armoured personnel carriers to provide a degree of protection for infantry accompanying tanks and self-propelled guns on the advance. Small numbers of US-supplied vehicles gave Soviet reconnaissance forces some armoured protection, but the practice of Soviet infantry riding on tanks into combat continued throughout the war, with the heavy losses such a practice often entailed.

It has already been noted how Soviet tanks of the early war period in particular lacked communications equipment – a problem that afflicted the Red Army as a whole when compared to its German opponent. This relative lack of communications equipment greatly impeded the command and control of forces, particularly in dynamic situations. To some extent this situation was ameliorated as the war progressed through Lend-Lease deliveries from the United States and United Kingdom.

In the main, the Red Army was relatively well equipped for war both in June 1941 and as the war progressed, where deficiencies particularly in higher technologies (e.g., in terms of communications equipment and optics) were to some extent compensated for by the soundness of basic designs and ruggedness of Soviet equipment – along with numbers available. It was one thing, however, to have suitable equipment but of course another to use it effectively. Pre-war inadequacies in training had been laid bare by the debacle of the war in Finland in 1939–1940, and some steps had been taken prior to the Great Patriotic War to provide Red Army troops with more resources and more realistic training.[11] During the war itself, efforts were made to develop materials on best practice and disseminate those ideas – even if the exigencies of crises sometimes hampered this process. Certainly, the exigencies of the early years of the war in particular and need to replace horrendous losses often led to truncated training regimes and contributed to further high loss rates, although as the war progressed there were signs that for all branches, with the exception of the infantry, substantially more care was being taken to train replacements. Even late in the war, in the case of the infantry, there is some evidence that soldiers ended up on the front line with relatively little training, given the acute shortages being felt in front-line infantry units, and where the partisans and the members of the male populations of previously occupied territory were sometimes drafted into the infantry at the front immediately on liberation of territory, rather than being sent to the rear for more substantive training.

In addition to a growing pre-war awareness of the need for more and realistic training, there was also a growing awareness of the need for greater decentralisation of decision-making – at least by Red Army standards. While the Red Army would never get anywhere near to the much-vaunted *Auftragstaktik* of the Wehrmacht, by the end of the war there were signs that in the conduct of reconnaissance and small unit tactics in urban areas, for instance, the Red Army had made considerable progress in allowing lower-level initiative to play a part in making outcomes more successful and less costly.

At a higher level, considerable efforts were expended within the Red Army to try to learn from war experience and apply that experience, but in some ways hard-learnt lessons were undermined by Stalin's continued tendency to bludgeon commanders to push their troops forward without the necessary preparations in order to secure objectives more quickly. In some ways this tendency on the part of Stalin fed into tendencies that had already developed within the Red Army to launch troops forward with relatively reckless abandon as a response to difficult or unachievable objectives set from on high – itself drawing on a wider cultural disposition towards acting *na avos'* (in a spur-of-the-moment manner without due forethought and planning). Symptomatic of these tendencies was the propensity for Soviet reconnaissance forces to conduct reconnaissance 'by battle' rather than 'by stealth' – often successfully revealing German positions but at considerable cost in human life.

Notes

1 Unless otherwise stated, the source for material in this chapter is Alexander Hill, *The Red Army and the Second World War* (Cambridge: Cambridge University Press, 2017). Other useful works in English that also encompass material considered in this chapter include Chris Bellamy, *Absolute War: Soviet Russia in the Second World War* (New York: Alfred Knopf, 2007); John Erickson, *The Road to Stalingrad* (London: Weidenfeld & Nicolson, 1977) and *The Road to Berlin* (London: Weidenfeld & Nicolson, 1983) and many later editions; David Glantz, *Stumbling Colossus: The Red Army on the Eve of World War* (Lawrence: University Press of Kansas, 1998) and *Colossus Reborn: The Red Army at War* (Lawrence: University Press of Kansas, 2005); and Evan Mawdsley, *Thunder in the East: The Nazi-Soviet War 1941–1945*, 2nd ed. (London: Bloomsbury, 2016).

2 This data is available in a table in Alexander Hill, *The Red Army and the Second World War*, appendix 2, p. 691.

3 On nationality and the Red Army during the war, what should become a 'standard work' on the subject, although currently only available in Russian, is Aleksei Bezugol'nyi, *Natsional'nyi sostav Krasnoi armii. 1918–1945* (Moscow: Tsentrpoligraf, 2021).

4 See Jennifer G. Mathers with Alexander Hill, 'Women in the Russian and Soviet Armed Forces', in *The Routledge Handbook on Soviet and Russian Military Studies*, ed. Alexander Hill (Abingdon: Routledge, 2025), pp. 419–432.

5 On the roles and functions of the Stavka and State Defence Committee, see both Sergei Kudriashov, 'Stalin's War: Soviet Command and Control during the Great Patriotic War' in *The Routledge Handbook on Soviet and Russian Military Studies*, ed. Alexander Hill (Abingdon: Routledge, 2025), pp.

145–159, and Alexander Hill, 'Stalin and the Stavka: Formulating Soviet Strategy During the Great Patriotic War', in *Supreme Leadership in Modern War: Civil Military Relations During Competition and War*, ed. James Lacey and Williamson Murray (New York: Routledge, 2024), pp. 145–169.

6 For an excellent biography of Zhukov in English, see Geoffrey Roberts, *Stalin's General: The Life of Georgy Zhukov* (New York: Random House, 2012).

7 For some indication of the impact of the Great Purges on the Red Army, see Hill, *The Red Army and the Second World War*, chapter 3 and appendix 1, p. 690.

8 For a concise consideration of the development of Soviet military theory during the interwar period, see David Stone, 'The Interwar Development of Soviet Military Theory', in *The Routledge Handbook on Soviet and Russian Military Studies*, ed. Alexander Hill (Abingdon: Routledge, 2025), pp. 98–107.

9 On Soviet airpower during the war, see one of the few books in English to cover the topic as a whole: Von Hardesty and Ilya Grinberg, *Red Phoenix Rising: The Soviet Air Force in World War II* (Lawrence: University Press of Kansas, 2012).

10 On Lend-Lease and the Soviet war effort, see Alexander Hill, ed., *The Great Patriotic War of the Soviet Union, 1941–1945: A Documentary Reader* (Abingdon: Routledge, 2009), chapter 8.

11 On education, training, and the use of war experience in the Red Army, see Alexander Hill, '"Sadder – but Wiser" ("Ubitok – umu pribitok"): Learning from Experience in the Red Army, 1928–1945', in *The Skill of Adaptability: The Learning Curve in Combat* (2017 Chief of Army History Conference), ed. Peter Dennis (Canberra: Big Sky Publishing, 2018), pp. 135–153.

6

The Red Army: Motivation and Experience

Mass rather than skill formed the basis of the Red Army's military effectiveness, primarily due to inadequate training and weak motivation of the front-line officers and men. Weak motivation and low morale plagued the army for the duration of the war. Often poorly led, inadequately fed, ill-trained, and under-supplied, Red Army soldiers faced daunting prospects just to survive let alone fight. Besides these difficulties, low motivation and morale was rooted in pre-war dissatisfaction with the Soviet regime stemming from the forced collectivisation of agriculture, the terror purges, low material quality of life, and discrimination against national minorities. Excessive casualties also became an important factor. Between September 1939 and September 1945, of the thirty-eight million men and women who served in the armed forces, it is likely that more than fourteen million were killed or captured and more than thirteen million were wounded.[1] Consequently, the dire need for replacements led to abbreviated training, and troops were thrown into battle with little preparation. Thus combat effectiveness suffered; fearful and feeling unprepared, soldiers deserted, shirked, straggled, and showed cowardice. They committed many acts of indiscipline, crimes, and violations of regulations on a wide scale. Such unheroic behaviour of Red Army soldiers preceded the German invasion; it manifested in 1939 and continued throughout the war, challenging the ability of officers to manage, train, and lead both the willing and unwilling in combat.

Discipline problems in the Red Army first manifested during the invasion of Poland and the Russo-Finnish 'Winter War.' During the two-week invasion of Poland in September 1939, the Red Army arrested 700 soldiers for shirking, going absent without leave (AWOL), deserting, looting, and mistreating the civilian population. During the bloody four-month-long Russo-Finnish Winter War, soldiers, non-commissioned officers (NCOs), and junior officers deserted by the thousands. Thousands more shirked, fled the front lines, or intentionally wounded themselves. Soldiers murdered incompetent or hated officers. In response, division commanders, on their initiative, created blocking detachments and penal battalions. Some generals summarily executed non-compliant soldiers.[2] Adding to the problem, the Soviet government relied on partial mobilisations of hundreds of thousands of reservists in their late twenties and thirties who had no desire to go to war to bolster the strength of the forces invading Poland and Finland.

Discipline problems persisted in the immediate aftermath of the Winter War as the army continued to expand with large contingents of draftees and reservists joining the active army. Poor discipline was characterised by malingering, drunkenness, going AWOL from garrisons, desertion, and feigning illness to avoid training. The already serious problem with alcohol abuse increased. The number of rapes and assaults rose substantially in garrison towns. With weak oversight by overburdened, inexperienced, and under-trained junior officers, soldiers wandered off post to sell stolen government property in the local markets. In response to this indiscipline, the Commissariat of Defence, on 8 July 1940, issued an order titled 'On Criminal Liability for Unauthorised Absences and Desertion'. This order authorised military district commanders to organise disciplinary battalions (*disbats*) to which soldiers could be sentenced for up to two years. These measures had almost no effect on discipline. Recognising that its first attempt to tighten up on discipline had failed, in October, the Commissar of Defence, Marshal Semen Timoshenko, issued NKO Order No. 356, which allowed officers to use physical force and even weapons to punish disobedience. Furthermore, officers who were slack in maintaining discipline could be charged with dereliction of duty. Soldiers saw the order as a return to the abusive days of the tsarist army.

Between January 1939 and June 1941, the army expanded from 1.9 to 4.5 million men and from 140 to 303 infantry and armour divisions but failed to recruit and train enough willing and capable leaders in a timely fashion to make most of them combat-ready by the time of the German invasion. The resultant dearth of experienced competent officers contributed to low motivation and morale and weak discipline. The Communist Party and the Communist Youth League (Komsomol) compelled their soldier and civilian members to serve as officers. That, and reducing training time from four years to three months, still did not produce enough officers, so the army lowered its educational standards and promoted men from the ranks – willing or not. The army went to war in 1941 with around 67,000 officer vacancies unfilled and many others held by NCOs and ordinary soldiers. There followed massive and continuous casualties. The tens of thousands of officers lost in 1941 were replaced by hastily trained men, many of whom were reluctant to assume leadership responsibility. This led to a fraught command climate in which many poorly trained, unmotivated officers with a short life expectancy led poorly trained and unmotivated conscripts.[3]

The use of armour and massive amounts of artillery would prove to be the key to victory, yet in 1941 the armoured forces were the least prepared to confront the Axis invaders. Although the Red Army had developed a dynamic doctrine for mechanised warfare, the decision to disband the few division-sized and larger mechanised units in 1939 set back the training that would be so necessary in 1941. Only with the fall of France in June 1940 did the high command reconsider the utility of armoured divisions. Once the decision was made to create huge mechanised corps and dozens of new armoured divisions, the army had less than a year to stand them up. The new armoured brigade and division commanders and their staffs had little or no experience commanding units of those sizes. It is unclear how well versed they were in armoured warfare, but it is clear that their time to learn and practice maneuvering their units was short and often delayed by late delivery of tanks and other vehicles.

6.1   The First Six Months of 1941

The first six months of 1941 were traumatic for the Red Army. Soldiers' motivation and ability to fight were often found wanting. The Axis forces punched and pummelled their way eastward, encircling hundreds of thousands of Soviet soldiers at a time, killing, wounding, and capturing nearly five million by mid-December. The loss of men and territory convinced many that the war would soon be lost and that the days of Stalin and the Communist Party were numbered. Of the various factors affecting morale, the lack of confidence in victory was the most serious in 1941.

Making matters worse, soldiers and officers suffered from a lack of self-confidence. A sense of helplessness pervaded the ranks due to inadequate training and inferior equipment. Training had suffered in 1939–1941 because of a dearth of qualified, prepared, and motivated officers and non-commissioned officers to man the existing and newly created units. The army expanded faster than it could produce leaders capable of training men above the level of basic skills. Small- and large-unit training was not conducted consistently enough to build cohesion and impart sufficient experience to prepare men to react properly under the stress of combat. Most of the year, soldiers engaged in individual and company-level training; it was only during the summer that regiments and larger units trained together. So, while company and battalion commanders had time to get to know their men and their duties (unless reassigned), commanders and staffs of regiments and higher only practiced their skills at maneuvering two or three months each year.

The continual process of creating new units entailed the frequent break up of existing units and transfers and promotions of officers to duties for which they were unprepared. All of this was made worse in spring 1941 when Stalin ordered the army to call up 800,000 reservists to augment the draft cohort of 1941. The influx of new men degraded what little cohesion and unit identity had been created and reduced combat readiness. This was compounded by the army's failure to acquire sufficient weapons and equipment for the new men in a timely manner. In the first half of 1941, conscripts and reservists sat idle for weeks, waiting for simple things like boots, uniforms, and rifles. Artillery units were formed weeks or months before their guns were delivered. Because few operable tanks were on hand, drivers might have only one or two hours of driving time before the war started.

Soldiers' confidence in their leaders would be a long time coming. At the onset of the German invasion, the army afforded an early graduation to most of the officers in training units, and then hastily trained and threw into combat an additional 80,000 new officers to replace casualties and serve as cadre for newly created divisions. Thousands of sergeants and soldiers were given battlefield promotions to plug the gap in officer casualties. Only when the units were pulled from the front to rest and refit did these new junior officers receive abbreviated training for their leadership responsibilities. Senior officers slated to lead regiments and higher were sent to the rear for four to six months of advanced training before assuming command. Such shortened training could only give officers a shallow grasp of the doctrine and tactics the army hoped to employ; much would have to be learned on the job.

Morale also faltered because soldiers felt they were not being taken care of. For a variety of reasons, including combat action and historical ineptness with logistics, soldiers often went hungry. Damaged or lost weapons, uniforms, and equipment were slow to be replaced or repaired. A perceived German technological superiority in tanks and aircraft, and their ability to provide good food and equipment to their soldiers, also depressed morale. The pervasive lack of self-confidence based on inadequate training and ineffective leadership led soldiers to feel let down or betrayed. Drunkenness among officers increased with the start of the war and further demoralised the men.

The same problems associated with motivation and morale seen during the Winter War manifested again during the fight with the Axis but on a larger scale. Desertions skyrocketed; during the war, there were nearly three million instances of desertion and draft evasion. Hundreds of thousands of soldiers intentionally missed movement when their units entrained for the front. Straggling was endemic as units marched to the front. Shirking during an attack and melting away from the front lines were commonplace. Army doctors diagnosed self-inflicted wounds by the tens of thousands. Most troubling for the Soviet leadership were the soldiers who, primarily during the first year of war, went willingly and eagerly into captivity, along with the hundreds of thousands who crossed over to the German lines to give themselves up.[4]

To bolster discipline at the front, Stalin, on 17 July 1941, signed an order authorising the secret police (NKVD) detachments in the army to shoot non-compliant men on the spot. He followed that up with NKO Order No. 270 on 16 August 1941, which reiterated the provisions of 1940's NKO Order No. 356, reminding officers of their right and duty to shoot subordinates who failed in their duties through irresponsibility, neglect, or disobedience. It instructed division commanders to relieve any officers they deemed not up to their tasks and, if necessary, to shoot them.

A veritable fratricidal conflict began in the front-line units. Commanders and commissars shot disobedient, hesitant, and recalcitrant soldiers by the thousands and were in turn murdered by soldiers. The situation got so out of hand that the generals begged Stalin to countermand the order. Stalin did not withdraw it but did issue Order No. 391 one month later, ordering commanders and commissars to use restraint in applying deadly force in the interest of discipline. The shooting of soldiers by officers subsided, however; field courts-martial and the NKVD regularly imposed the death penalty for acts of cowardice, desertion, and treason.

In contrast to those reluctant to serve, nearly four million men and women eagerly volunteered for the Red Army and the citizens volunteer units (*opolchenie*) in 1941. These volunteers came from all walks of life but were mostly in the ages of eighteen to thirty from urban and industrial areas of the country. Unlike draftees, the volunteers tended to accept the shortages of arms and equipment and their rushed training with good humour. They were motivated by faith in the socialist society they were helping build and usually had a positive outlook regarding the Communist Party and Stalin. Others were motivated by an instinctive patriotism to defend their homeland against an invader. These volunteers, and the conscripts and reservists who shared their world-view, fought as hard and as well as they could under the circumstances. They tried to boost their fellow soldiers' willingness to fight with encouraging words and heroic deeds and denounced malcontents and defeatists to the secret police. Although their morale would also flag in the face of battlefield disasters – most *opolchenie* units were annihilated in their first combats – their motivation to defend the country and oust the invaders held firm.[5]

When given the right equipment and weaponry, properly trained to use it, and provided competent leaders, most soldiers fought well and with determination. These conditions, however, did not present themselves very often until mid-1943. Between the outbreak of war and the end of 1941, the Red Army created another 194 infantry and armour divisions and eighty-four infantry and armour brigades, along with scores of artillery brigades, from the ground up. Leaders in these new and existing units, often in positions for which they were unprepared, led their semi- or untrained men into costly failed attacks or instigated panicked retreats. Poorly trained and inept infantry commanders often did not coordinate artillery fire or tank support. They did not maintain contact with their higher headquarters or neighbouring units, making their units susceptible to being outflanked or surrounded. They routinely, through inexperience, put their men in the wrong place, at the wrong time, without adequate means to fight or maneuver against the enemy. Tank units deployed in small groups rather than in mass, also without proper coordination with infantry and artillery. Poor leadership dismayed even eager and willing troops. Still, most Soviet soldiers, despite the setbacks and betrayal by unmotivated, unpatriotic, and disloyal comrades, stayed in the fight, buying time for Stalin and his generals to turn things around.

Under the able direction of General Georgi Zhukov, the Red Army stopped the Germans and then counterattacked in the last week of December, pushing them back a safe distance from the capital. Hailed as a great victory, a close look at discipline during the battle reveals that the Red Army was still on shaky ground. The ranks were rife with defeatist attitudes; many soldiers, convinced that Moscow would fall and that the Germans would push beyond the city, sought to save themselves rather than fight. Between 19 October and 13 December 1941, Moscow authorities detained 123,423 people for straggling, deserting, evading conscription, and various infringements of military regulations. Most soldiers were sent back to their units under guard or were reassigned; 357 were executed.[6] Fully 10 per cent of the manpower allocated to defend Moscow was absent from the front due to malingering, AWOL, and desertion.

6.2   1942

The Germans launched a hugely successful spring offensive in 1942, taking them all the way to the Volga River and Stalingrad and then southward into the Caucasus. Stalin, unnerved by indications that many soldiers did not want to fight – from the beginning of the war to 1 April 1942, the NKVD and police had detained nearly 700,000 soldiers who had deserted, straggled, and avoided the draft – issued his infamous 'Not one step back' order through the GKO (*Gosudarstvennii Komitet Oboroni*) State Defence Committee, GKO Order No. 227, on 28 July.[7] This order forbade unauthorised retreat and most importantly ordered the creation of combat penal (*shtrafnyi*) battalions and blocking detachments. Order No. 227 stipulated that soldiers and officers who committed serious infractions, short of treason, were instead to be sentenced to serve up to three months in a *shtrafnyi* battalion and then be returned to their units. These units served as ordinary infantry battalions that were deployed at the discretion of the army group headquarters. In the ten weeks following the announcement of Order No. 227, blocking detachments apprehended 140,755 servicemen away from their units. Fewer than 1 per cent of those detained were executed, a number that certainly would have been higher without Order No. 227. Head of the secret police, Lavrentii Beria, reported to Stalin on 11 October 1942 that since January, the NKVD had dealt with 1,187,747 men who had gone AWOL, deserted, or were caught attempting to evade the draft. It seems, then, that the victory at Moscow had not turned the tide of troop morale, nor had the threat of a stint in a *shtrafnyi* battalion or execution stiffened the resolve of a great many men.[8]

Still, desertion continued to plague the army. In October, the military procuracy, at the urging of the GKO, issued an order that any deserted soldier who resorted to armed banditry or other criminal activity was to be considered a counter-revolutionary and charged under article 58 of the criminal code – the article infamously used to imprison and execute millions during the purges of the late 1930s. Not only were soldiers subject to the death penalty; their families were to be punished as traitors. Despite the potentially fatal consequences, deserters continued to run amok in the rear areas until the end of the war.[9]

Officer leadership still showed major deficiencies, though fewer than in 1941. The encirclements the Germans were able to achieve were smaller due to better communication and more nimble maneuvering by senior commanders. Officer casualties continued to be frightfully high, necessitating replacing losses with hastily trained men. During the year, the army trained or promoted 420,000 officers to replace combat losses – 135,000 were new lieutenants and about 20,000 were political workers who had been granted commissions.

The other 265,000 were officers given instruction to prepare them for the next higher level of command.

New soldiers were better trained in 1942 than in 1941. The army created fifty new divisions and gave them from three to six months to train before being thrown into combat. Replacement soldiers for existing divisions were also given at least three months training before being sent to units. Rather than being fed into units that were in combat, Stalin, in hopes of increasing life expectancy and unit cohesion, decreed that all infantry replacements, delivered as march companies, be integrated into their new regiments only in the rear.

6.3   1943–1945

The victory at Stalingrad still left many Red Army soldiers skeptical that the Soviet Union would prevail. They looked with trepidation on the coming summer, fully expecting the Germans to regroup and launch another successful offensive. It was the Soviet victory at the Battle of Kursk in July 1943 that finally convinced most soldiers that the war had turned in their favour. At the start of the battle, motivation and morale were still fragile; in just one week, blocking detachments picked up 7,000 men who had abandoned their units. One division lost 10 per cent of its men to battlefield desertion.[10] Subsequently, liberating conquered territory boosted soldiers' spirits and resolve. The Red Army's advance westward allowed the army to replace its horrendous losses with 940,000 men found to have avoided returning to Soviet lines after escaping or evading German capture in 1941. Between the summer of 1941 and the end of 1943, to replace casualties, the NKVD transferred, by both consent and compulsion, 975,000 convicts from the Gulag to the army. Lacking commitment to the state, ideologically indifferent, and weak on self-discipline, the former convicts proved to be troublesome.

The spectacularly successful Operation Bagration in the summer of 1944, which destroyed Germany's Army Group Centre and took the Red Army to the gates of Warsaw, shows that properly trained, abundantly supplied, and competently led soldiers could perform well. Stalin's determination to fight the war on a broad front which spread the army's resources thin, however, prevented the Red Army from repeating this success. Despite costly battlefield victories, the persistent poor quality of life and weak troop-level leadership continued to challenge morale and discipline. Chronic supply problems hurt morale and caused soldiers to question their leaders' commitment to their well-being.[11]

Discipline was also poor away from the fighting. Soldiers in the rear areas who were recuperating in hospitals or were assigned to support or training units habitually left their posts without authorisation to go into the nearby towns, villages, or collective farms. There they bartered or sold stolen government property for vodka and food. In cases where soldiers lacked money or items to sell or trade, they simply stole what they wanted – usually food. They also sought out prostitutes or other women to seduce or rape. There were even cases of officers getting drunk and shooting up the streets and hitting civilians.

During the campaign in the Balkans, the NKVD detachments that followed behind the Second and Third Ukrainian Fronts to police the rear areas detained about 172,000 soldiers for either being illegally away from their units or committing crimes, or both – 48,300 from late August to mid-October 1944, and 123,700 between mid-October and June 1945. Those caught away from their units were charged with desertion, straggling, or not having valid documents approving their absences from the front. Most criminal charges were those of drunkenness, rape, robbery, banditry, marauding, treason, and other serious infractions committed in the rear areas. The areas immediately behind the front were veritable crime zones. Officers occupied themselves with prostitutes, drink, and fighting among themselves, much as they had before the war while soldiers, drunk on 'liberated' alcohol, drifted away from their units for days at a time to avoid combat. Venereal diseases spread widely among officers and men. The behaviour of the soldiers of these two fronts in 1944 and 1945 was representative of the whole advancing Red Army.

Even though the Soviets were on the path to victory and the end of the war was in sight, the Red Army still struggled with motivation- and morale-based discipline problems. During the last year of the war, from mid-1944 to May 1945, more than two-thirds of the soldiers had only been in the army for a short time and the majority of them were peasants conscripted from the recently liberated areas of southwestern Russia and Ukraine. Most had come of age under German occupation or shortly thereafter. Many others were liberated Red Army prisoners of war and

Figure 6.1 Soviet soldiers waving from onboard a train, 1944. Source: Culture Club/Getty Images.

Soviet citizens working as forced labourers in Romania and Hungary in ill health and untrusted by their officers.

Creating solid discipline and high morale was difficult because casualties remained heavy until the end of the war. Soldiers were correct that senior officers were callous to the men's suffering and would not hesitate to recklessly expend lives to achieve objectives. The continual infusion of hundreds of thousands of new, inexperienced lieutenants as replacements (with the Red Army suffering nearly one million officer casualties during the war) meant leadership proficiency remained low and casualties high.

6.4 Conclusion

When given the right equipment and weaponry (and properly trained to use it), and led by trained and knowledgeable leaders, most soldiers fought well and with determination. These conditions, however, did not present themselves very often in 1941 or 1942 and irregularly thereafter. Leaders, often in positions for which they were unprepared, led their men into costly failed attacks or themselves instigated panicked retreats. Still, most Soviet soldiers, despite the difficult living conditions, battle-field setbacks, and betrayal by disloyal comrades, stayed in the fight. The ability of the Red Army to fight well improved dramatically in 1943, with defence production back to full capacity and expanding and American Lend-Lease delivering vital supplies. Mid-grade and senior officers were more experienced. After the Battle of Kursk, soldier motivation and morale improved, and the army devoted more time to training, which paid dividends in the last two years of the war.

Notes

1 The casualty figure officially accepted by the Russian army, established by an army commission headed by G. F. Krivosheev and published in his *Grif Sekretnosti Sniat* (Moscow: Voenizdat, 1993) is 8.6 million killed. However, Lev Lopukhovsky and Boris Kavalerchik make a compelling case for the larger figure of 14.6 million in their book *The Price of Victory: The Red Army's Casualties in the Great Patriotic War* (Barnsley: Pen and Sword, 2017).

2 R. Reese, 'Lessons of the Winter War: A Study in the Military Effectiveness of the Red Army, 1939–1940', *Journal of Military History* 72, 3 (July 2008), pp. 846–848.

3 R. Reese, *Stalin's Reluctant Soldier: A Social History of the Red Army, 1925–1941* (Lawrence: University Press of Kansas, 1996), pp. 148–151.

4 M. Edele, *Stalin's Defectors: How Red Army Soldiers Became Hitler's Collaborators, 1941–1945* (Oxford: Oxford University Press, 2017), pp. 1–18; Grigorii F. Krivosheev, 'O dezertirstve v Krasnoi Armii', *Voenno-istoricheskii zhurnal* 6 (2001), p. 94.

5 R. Reese, *Why Stalin's Soldiers Fought* (Lawrence: University Press of Kansas, 2011), pp. 104–129.

6 'O proisshestviiakh po gorodu Moskve i merakh bor'by s pravonarushiteliami za vremia s 20.10 po 13.12.1941 goda', *Izvestiia TsK KPSS* 4 (1991), p. 210.

7 'Dokladnaia zapiska NKVD SSSR no. 743/B v GKO ob itogakh deiatel'nosti voisk NKVD po okhrane tyla Deistvuiushchei Krasnoi Armii po sostoianiiu na 1 aprelia 1942 g. i peropriiatiiakh po uluchsheniiu organizatsii i okhrany voiskovogo tyla', in Nikolai P. Patrushev, ed., *Organy gosudarstvennoi bezopasnosti SSSR v Velikoi Otechestvennoi voine: Sbornik dokumentov vol. 1: Krushenie 'Blitskriga" 1 ianvaria – 30 iiunia 1941 goda* (Moscow: Rus', 2003), p. 383.

8 V. S. Khristoforov, *Organy gosbezopasnosti SSSR v 1941–1945 gg* (Moscow: Glavnogo arkhivnogo upravleniia goroda Moskva, 2011), p. 175.

9 'Direktiva Prokurora SSSR no. 13/18580s o kvalifikatsii dezertirstva, sviazannogo s banditizmom', in Patrushev, *Organy gosudarstvennoi bezopasnosti SSSR v Velikoi Otechestvennoi voine: Sbornik dokumentov,* vol. 1, p. 352.

10 Reese, *Why Stalin's Soldiers Fought,* p. 173.

11 ' Prikaz o nedostatkakh v material'no-bytovom obsluzhivanii boitsov na fronte i v zapasnykh chastiakh', in Vladimir A. Zolotarev, ed., *Russkii arkhiv: Velikaia Otechestvennaia 2(3)* (Moscow: Terra, 1997), pp. 36–38.

Part III

Campaigns

DAVID STAHEL

7

Operation Barbarossa, 1941

After almost a year of strategic planning and political preparations, Hitler launched Operation Barbarossa on 22 June 1941. The Wehrmacht's *Ostheer* (Eastern Army) counted more than 3 million men, 3,350 tanks, 2,770 aircraft, 600,000 motor vehicles, and 625,000 horses, making it the largest military operation in history. The German invasion was be supported by Finland and Romania, who each fought parallel wars against the Soviet Union, providing hundreds of thousands of additional troops. Fascist regimes in Italy, Hungary, Slovakia, and Spain sent tens of thousands of soldiers each, while additional thousands of volunteers from across German-occupied Europe were allowed to enlist in Hitler's 'Crusade against Bolshevism'.[1]

Facing the onslaught was the Soviet Red Army, which on paper was an even larger force, but not all of it was concentrated in the Western Military Districts and the general state of readiness was low. Compounding the problem, Soviet military doctrine, training as well as command and control, were hopelessly outclassed by the fast-moving Wehrmacht, which paralysed and confused the Soviet response in the initial period following the invasion. The only silver lining was that the Stalinist regime quickly instituted a host of radical measures to mobilise millions of men as well as the economic resources of the country. These measures saw the Red Army grow rapidly in size, while industrial conversion to armament production transformed civilian life almost overnight. Yet these responses would only provide benefits in the medium term and only if Soviet resistance endured beyond the summer period.[2]

The German plan for Barbarossa was predicated upon a short, decisive campaign to overwhelm and defeat the Soviet Union before the autumn weather could impact their operations. To this end, the German panzer groups were the essential ingredient because, despite being only a small part of the *Ostheer*, they were the only fully motorised element capable of propelling the Wehrmacht forward. The remainder of the *Ostheer*, some 80 per cent, consisted of infantry divisions with foot-marching infantry and horse-drawn guns and supplies. Consequently, the *Ostheer* moved at two different speeds, which meant the limited motorised forces were left to fight their forward engagements alone and unsupported. This did not stop them from dictating the terms of battles as whole Soviet armies were encircled and vital economic and industrial regions were captured, but in doing so the losses Germany sustained were overwhelmingly concentrated in their vital panzer divisions.[3]

Soviet resistance in the initial weeks of the invasion was disproportionally aided by the country's poor infrastructure and forbidding landscape, which alternated between dense forests and swampy marchlands in the north and centre, while open plains dominated much of Ukraine in the south. Intersecting these were only a limited number of west-east roads, which were typically unsealed, narrow, and in places badly potholed. The damage this inflicted on heavily loaded German trucks compromised the continued mobility of German operations to a far greater extent than anything the Red Army could muster. At the same time, the spartan Soviet rail network, with a gauge too wide to accommodate European locomotives or rolling stock, meant a conversion process first had to be undertaken in order for the bulk of German supplies to flow eastward. Moreover, the retreating Soviet forces waged an effective 'scorched earth' campaign against their own infrastructure to complicate this process and, given the importance of rail-borne logistics to an army the size of the *Ostheer*, significantly slowed the rate of German advance.[4]

Operation Barbarossa proceeded across a broad front spanning the Baltic to the Black Sea, a linear distance of some 1,250 kilometres, but importantly, Soviet geography expands like a funnel, meaning that German strength would be increasingly dissipated the further it advanced to the east.[5] The *Ostheer* was divided into three 'army groups' identified by their geographic location. *Generalfeldmarschall* Wilhelm Ritter von Leeb's Army Group North was to advance northeast towards Leningrad,

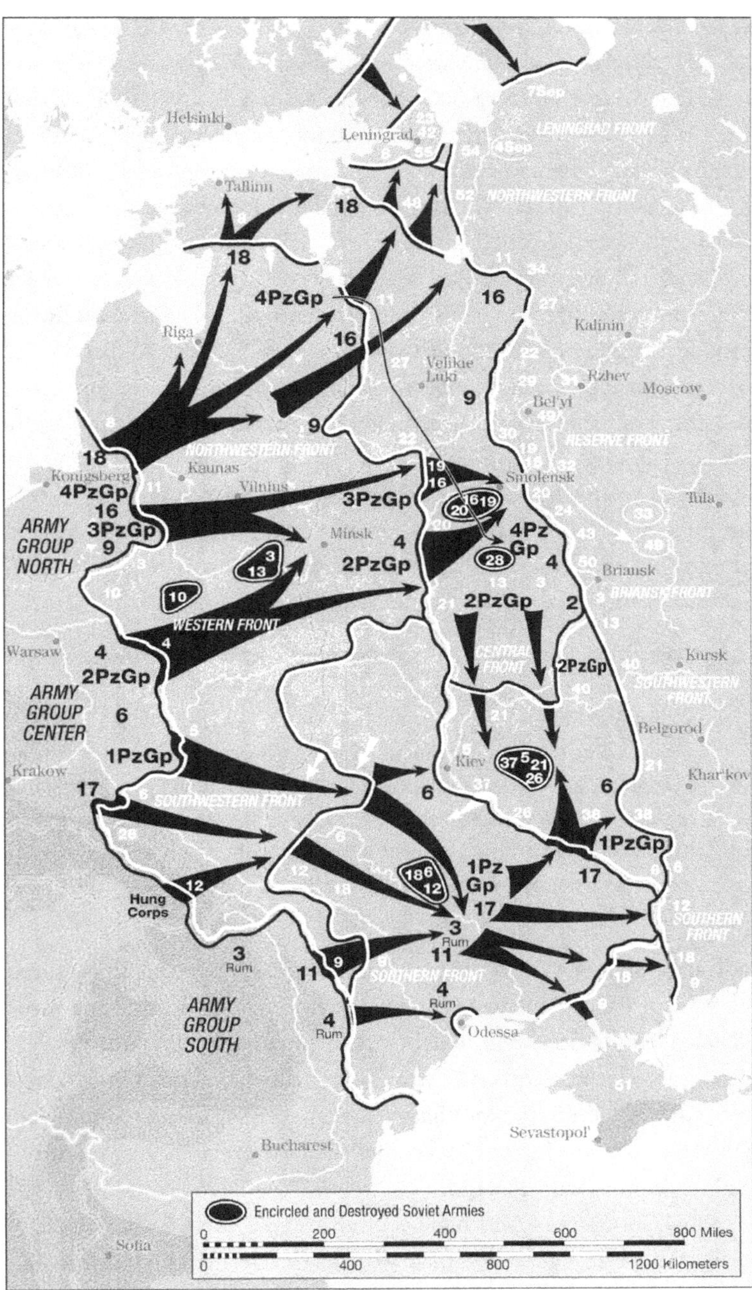

Map 2 Summer–autumn campaign (22 June–30 September 1941).

Generalfeldmarschall Fedor von Bock's Army Group Centre was to drive due east in the direction of Moscow, and *Generalfeldmarschall* Gerd von Rundstedt's Army Group South was directed mainly towards Kiev with a secondary drive, aided by Romanian forces, pushing into southern Ukraine. In total there were four of the German panzer groups spearheading the advance – one each in the northern and southern army groups and two slightly stronger panzer groups in the centre. Not surprisingly therefore, Bock's army group enjoyed the most success early on with two major encirclements centred on Minsk and Smolensk that shattered the Soviet front and together captured well over half a million Soviet soldiers.[6]

A month into the invasion, the German command was convinced that the campaign was proceeding in their favour and confidently foresaw an end to the campaign. Army Group Centre was at Smolensk, two-thirds of the way to Moscow, and it was believed that the bulk of the Red Army had already collapsed and could not be rebuilt. As early as 3 July, the chief of the Army General Staff, *Generaloberst* Franz Halder, wrote in his diary:

> Overall, one can already now say that the objective to destroy the mass of the Russian army in front of the Dvina and Dnepr [Rivers] has been accomplished. I do not doubt . . . that eastwards of the Dvina and Dnepr we would only have to contend with partial enemy forces, not strong enough to hinder realisation of the German operational plan. Thus, it is probably not too much to say, when I claim that the campaign against Russia was won within fourteen days. Naturally it is not yet over. The wide-open spaces and the stubborn resistance, conducted with all means, will still claim our efforts for many more weeks to come.[7]

Indicative of Soviet fortunes, on 18 July Stalin's own son was captured (he was an officer in the 14th Tank Division), and around the same time, executions for defeated Soviet commanders, like the hapless Lieutenant-General Dmitri Pavlov, were being authorised. The suspicion towards military commanders also saw political commissars reinstated, after having only been abolished the previous year following the Winter War with Finland.[8]

While German progress had been remarkable, the toll this had taken on the panzer groups should have worried the German high command. Panzer Group 2, operating in Army Group Centre, reported a severe

Figure 7.1 Serving as an artillery officer in the 14th Tank Division, Jacob Dzhugashvili, Stalin's eldest son, was captured during the Battle of Smolensk, July 1941. Source: Bettmann/Getty Images.

decline in the number of serviceable tanks. On 22 June 1941, the panzer group had fielded 953 tanks of all models, but by 29 July this total had sunk to 286 operational tanks – only 30 per cent of the original strength. As the panzer group's war diary noted, 'this figure is *exceedingly low*'. More worrying still, no less than 132 of the remaining tanks were outdated models (Mark Is and Mark IIs), leaving the panzer group with just 135 advanced tanks (Mark IIIs and Mark IVs). The figures for Army Group Centre's second panzer group, Panzer Group 3, were scarcely better with one panzer corps at 40 per cent strength and the other at just 30 per cent.[9] Wheeled transport was also suffering dangerous fallout rates, which threatened the mobility and striking power of the panzer groups out of all proportion to other losses, yet this disturbing reality garnered remarkably little attention from the German generals.

The main concern for the German high command was the strategic question of how best to continue the offensive. The rapid breakthrough in the centre had been anticipated, and having defeated Soviet forces on the road to Moscow, Hitler intended to turn Panzer Group 3 north and Panzer Group 2 south to assist the German advance on the wings. Yet the high command of the army, who were nominally responsible for conducting the war in the east, strongly disagreed. In their conception, Army Group Centre should continue pressing east to seize Moscow. The dispute proved fractious and reinforced Hitler's mistrust of his generals. To win support, Hitler flew to Army Groups Centre and South to secure backing for his preference. The response, *Generalfeldmarschall* Wilhelm Keitel later contemptuously noted, was a united front against Hitler orchestrated by the army high command.[10]

Leading the army's opposition was Halder, who believed Hitler's ardent determination to avoid taking the road to Moscow stemmed from an unwarranted fear of treading the same path as Napoleon. For Halder, and many of the generals, the fall of Moscow was seen to be the decisive move in ending Soviet resistance. Hitler, on the other hand, emphasised Leningrad's importance as 'the cradle of Bolshevism', while in the south he argued that seizing raw materials from resource-rich eastern Ukraine would boost Germany's war effort as much as it would damage the Soviet economy. Throughout late July and early August, the respective positions proved intractable and the rancour was further inflamed by the slowing momentum of German attacks as positional warfare bogged down increasing stretches of the front.[11]

The dawning realisation that Barbarossa was not meeting expectations was first grasped by the German propaganda minister, Joseph Goebbels, who at the end of July sought to rein in public expectations of a rapid victory. Writing in his diary, Goebbels declared, 'We must no longer promise so much.' He then signalled a new direction for propaganda: 'It is therefore correct, when we very explicitly inform the German people of the harshness of the battles playing out in the east. One must tell the nation that this operation is very difficult, but that we can overcome it and also will overcome it.'[12] Yet by the second week of August German intelligence was telling a very different story, with new reports pointing to the frightening scale of Soviet mobilisation, which surpassed anything the Germans had considered possible. Halder wrote in his diary on 11 August:

> Regarding the general situation, it stands out more and more clearly that we underestimated the Russian colossus .... This statement refers just as much to organizational as to economic strengths, to traffic management, above all to pure military potential. At the start of the war we reckoned with 200 enemy divisions. Now we already count 360. These divisions are not armed and equipped in our sense, and tactically they are inadequately led in many ways. But they are there and when we destroy a dozen of them, then the Russians put another dozen in their place. The time factor favours them, as they are near to their own centres of power, while we are always moving further away from ours.[13]

While the German command was only just beginning to comprehend the scale and cost of the new war in the east, any illusions held by the Soviet populace about the 'invincibility' of the Red Army were quickly dispelled in the opening days of the war. With the exception of the Soviet territories recently incorporated into the USSR and certain regions of the Ukraine, the popular mood can generally be characterised as one of defiance and nationalistic zeal. Although Soviet post-war histories went to great lengths to demonstrate the absolute unity of the Soviet population, in truth of course there were exceptions. Yet much evidence still points to widespread support for the Soviet Union's war effort, indicating that the war evoked a passion beyond a simple adherence to the Soviet state or Stalin. Many people did fight for socialism, although not always Stalin's particular brand of it, while others fought, in spite of the Soviet system, for their homeland. Some supported the Soviet war effort to forestall the advent of Nazi rule, which they wisely feared. Of course, there were also many who were simply given no choice, being drafted to the army or into the factories where draconian discipline enforced loyalty.[14]

In the rush to defend the state, past mistakes of the political leadership were soon forgotten. Stalin shrewdly exploited this by enacting a quiet revolution in state freedoms which was previously unthinkable. Anti-religious propaganda was soon halted, and past national heroes, forgotten in favour of new socialist idols, were resurrected as symbols of former national glories. *Pravda*, the Soviet daily newspaper, dropped its weary peacetime slogan 'Proletarians of all lands, unite!' Instead, the new message was simple and direct: 'Death to the German invaders!' The war was soon being portrayed as 'a great patriotic war' to evoke comparisons with the victorious ejection of Napoleon's invading army by Tsar Alexander I. Some 600,000 people were freed from labour camps, 175,000 of whom were then mobilised. It was a new Stalinist state with a slightly more compassionate face, designed to bleed every last drop of popular fervour from its inhabitants while retaining an iron-fisted grip on power.[15]

On the eve of the German invasion, the Red Army possessed a mobilization base of some 14 million men. Only a week into the war some 5.3 million Soviet reservists had been called up, with further mobilizations following in succession. By July 1941, no less than thirteen new field armies appeared, and in August another nineteen came into service.[16] While there can be no doubt that the Red Army was suffering appalling casualties, as Halder noted in his diary the Soviet Union's force generation scheme was not merely replacing these losses; it was dramatically expanding the size of the Red Army. On 22 June the Red Army numbered 5,373,000 men. By 31 August, in spite of its losses, it had grown to 6,889,000 men, and by the end of 1941 the Red Army had reached an estimated 8 million men.[17]

Just as important as manpower, the Red Army needed equipment and vehicles to sustain itself and cover the staggering losses at the front. Given that the heavy concentration of industrial enterprises in the western parts of the country were in danger of being overrun by the German advance, an unprecedented evacuation of Soviet industry was deemed indispensable to ensuring the economic durability of the Soviet war effort. Accomplished in extraordinary time and under the most adverse circumstances, between July and December, 1,910 industrial enterprises were moved to the Volga region, Siberia or Central Asia, amounting in total to some 300,000 trains with 1.5 million railway wagon-loads.[18] Even more remarkable, the production of vital weapons actually increased in the second half of 1941, with official production quotes in some cases being exceeded. Indeed, the Soviet Union produced more tanks in 1941 than Germany, and 66 per cent of these were of the newer T-34 and KV-1 variety. Soviet industry also turned out more aircraft and a great deal more artillery pieces than Germany, helping meet the most immediate needs of the army.[19]

As the German command debated its strategic options for the next phase of the campaign, a parallel dispute over Stalin's insistence to hold

Kiev gripped the Soviet command. Like Hitler in future years, Stalin typically refused to countenance withdrawals no matter how much strategic sense they might make. Army Group Centre's deep advance had proceeded well to the east of Kiev in the north and posed a serious threat if it turned south and attacked the overextended Soviet forces, covering the long and exposed northern flank of Ukraine. In July the chief of the Soviet General Staff, Marshal Georgi Zhukov, pressed for withdrawal, but Stalin promptly fired him for daring to suggest that Kiev be surrendered. Remarkably, the profound danger that Zhukov and many of his subordinates identified were not shared by Halder and most of the generals in Army Group Centre who remained fixated on Moscow. Accordingly, when in late August Hitler finally imposed his will on the army and insisted upon diverting Guderian's panzer forces into Ukraine, it became the greatest German encirclement of 1941, which ironically much of the army had argued to avoid. By the end of September Kiev was in German hands and the triumph netted some 650,000 Soviet POWs.[20] The scale of the success was much more a product of Stalin's disastrous leadership, rather than the strength of German arms, but it renewed hope that the *Ostheer* might still force an end to the conflict in 1941.

Although Hitler had previously opposed the army's desire to drive on Moscow, the September advance into Ukraine, along with the investment of Leningrad in the north, gave the dictator confidence to authorise planning for a new offensive in the centre. Codenamed 'Typhoon', the new operation sought to compensate for Army Group Centre's dwindling offensive strength by concentrating almost every tank in Bock's army group. In addition to Panzer Groups 2 and 3, Panzer Group 4 was transferred south and an additional panzer corps was sent north from Panzer Group 1 in the Ukraine. Moreover, two newly refitted panzer divisions that had seen service in the previous Balkan campaign were sent to Army Group Centre, along with some 300 new tanks from German production. Bock's infantry forces also received reinforcements, giving Bock the distinction of commanding the most potent military force Nazi Germany would ever assemble under a single commander.[21]

While the German command focused on Typhoon's firepower, the offensive's Achilles' heel was its poor logistics. Although precise figures for overall truck losses are not available, Panzer Group 2 reported a loss of 30 to 40 per cent of its wheeled transport by 20 September. If that figure may be extrapolated to the whole *Ostheer*, then anywhere between 180,000 and 240,000 vehicles had been written off during the summer campaign, and a sizable number of those remaining could be considered serviceable but in a highly provisional state of repair. To illustrate the problem, one panzer division recorded the distances its vehicles travelled to secure supplies. In total, 303,982 kilometres were covered hauling ammunition, another 199,385 kilometres were driven transporting fuel, and 63,073 kilometres were travelled carrying spare parts. Considering the corrosive effects of moving such enormous distances on Soviet roads, with their notoriously uneven surfaces as well as the all-pervasive clouds of dust that overwhelmed air filters and ruined engines, it is not surprising that the *Ostheer's* truck fleet had declined so sharply. Trucks had to bridge the distances between the railheads and the front, which could only be shortened by the rapid eastward extension of the German railroad network. Yet Army Quartermaster-General *Generalmajor* Eduard Wagner, in spite of being repeatedly called out for his failed promises, retained a seemingly unrestrained optimism and continued with his confident predictions, especially in rail transport. On 11 September, he assured Halder that twenty-seven fuel trains a day would be supplied to support the build-up for Typhoon. Nothing of the sort was achieved, and by 22 September Halder complained that a minimum of at least nineteen fuel trains a day was necessary.[22] The amounts of fuel being delivered were barely enough to meet the daily requirements of army group, so that stockpiling for the coming operation was in no way sufficient.

Operation Typhoon began on 2 October and enjoyed immediate success. Soviet forces were tightly packed along hundreds of kilometres of front, which for fast-moving panzer groups concentrated on narrow sectors to facilitate rapid breakthroughs. Two days into the offensive Halder noted in his diary, 'Operation Typhoon is developing on a truly classic course . . . . The enemy is holding all parts of the front not under attack, which bodes well for the establishment of pockets.'[23] This is exactly what transpired. The Soviet command's rigid determination to defend forward, as opposed to building defences in depth with reserves for counterattacks against identified German penetrations, doomed

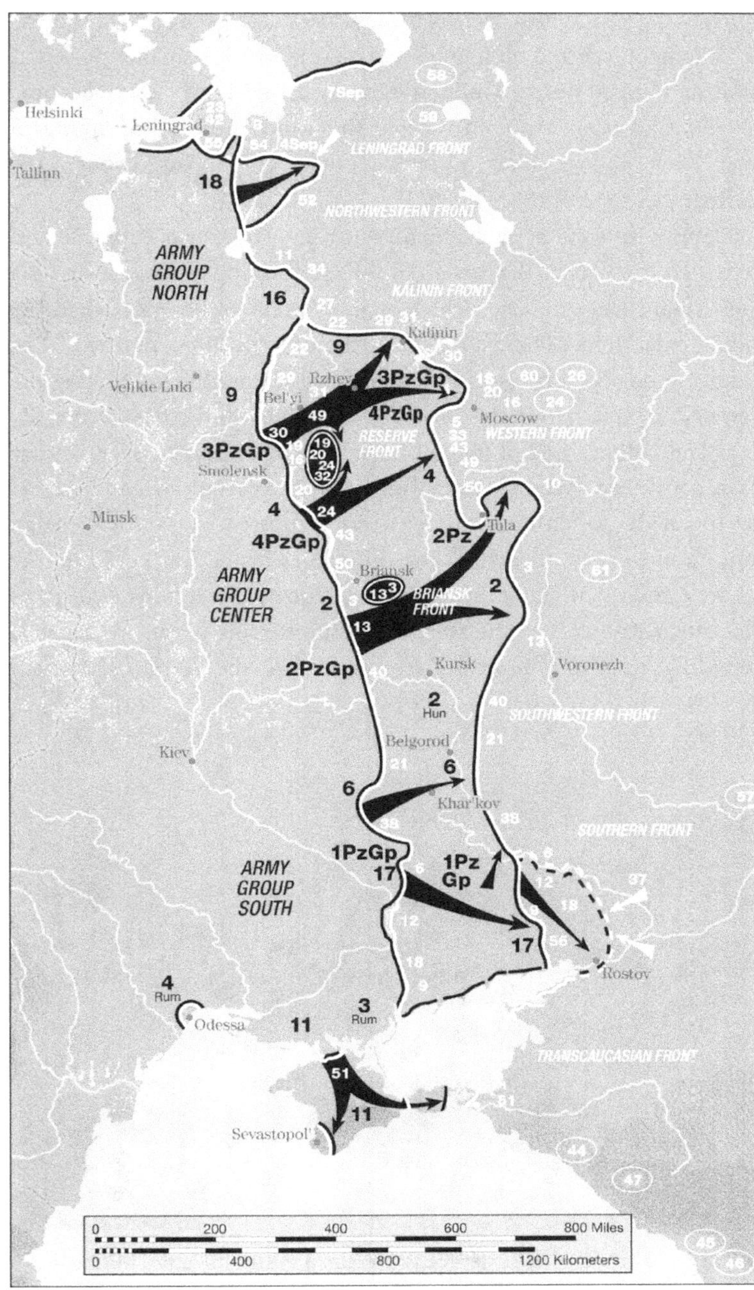

Map 3 Autumn–winter campaign (2 October–5 December 1941).

much of the Red Army covering the approach to Moscow. The resulting encirclement, centred on the town of Viaz'ma with a smaller pocket at Briansk, trapped nearly a million men. By the middle of October some 600,000 had been captured, untold thousands were killed trying to break out, and a small minority fought or slipped through the German net to temporary safety.

Coming so soon after the victory at Kiev, Hitler was euphoric and predicted the end of the Soviet Union. He even instructed his media spokesman, Dr Otto Dietrich, to hold a press conference where he publicly declared, 'The campaign in the east has been decided.' The following day Nazi newspapers carried banner headlines extolling the news: 'The Great Hour Has Struck!', 'Campaign in the East Decided!', and 'The Military End of the Bolsheviks'.[24] Goebbels, however, was far from convinced and justifiably worried that expectations had been set far too high. A similar sentiment was expressed by senior German officers in the east for whom the difficulties of the war could not be ignored. Indeed, in the second week of October, as Germany rejoiced at the anticipated end of the war, the autumn rains began in the east, heralding what the Russians referred to as the *rasputitsa*, which

Figure 7.2 The unsealed Soviet roads presented great difficulties for the Germans in sustaining their advance during Operation Barbarossa, 1 August 1941. Source: ullstein bild via Getty Images.

translates as 'quagmire season'. At almost the same time, Bock's panzer groups sought to exploit their success by driving on Moscow, but the available fuel supplies had been largely exhausted in the battles at Viaz'ma and Briansk. Thus, as the eastern roads quickly disappeared into a morass of endless mud, the already fragile logistics system finally broke down, leaving Bock's panzer forces largely immobile.

The Soviets used the enforced pause to hastily bring up reserve armies, which benefited from Moscow's highly developed railway connections. From October to December some seventy-five Soviet divisions were deployed to the capital. In addition, the city's population was mobilised for the construction of an outer defensive ring which involved some 100,000 workers (mostly women) building 1,428 artillery emplacements, 160 kilometres of anti-tank ditches, 120 kilometres of barbed-wire entanglements, and numerous other fortifications and obstacles. In Moscow itself, the city council directed a network of urban defensives; roads were heavily barricaded with steel 'hedgehogs', barbed-wire entanglements, reinforced concrete pillboxes, and fortified gun emplacements. Narrow gaps allowed vehicles to pass, while all movement was observed from the surrounding buildings, which were transformed into strong points with bricked-up windows and fortified balconies.

During this same period the Soviet effort was being tangibly reinforced by newly arrived western war material under the terms of the Lend-Lease aid program. Before the end of 1941 some 466 British tanks had been delivered, along with 699 British and American planes. While their military value was limited, the psychological impact was profound. As one Soviet admiral later recalled, 'I can still remember with what close attention we followed the progress of the first convoys in the late autumn of 1941, with what speed and energy they were unloaded in Archangel and Murmansk.' Conversely, the appearance of British tanks on the Moscow front proved a nasty surprise for Germans, which was noted in official reports as well as the letters of soldiers.[25]

From mid-October to mid-November Operation Typhoon was essentially halted until the cold weather sufficiently froze the ground to again allow movement. It was in this late-autumn period, before the onset of the fierce Russian winter, that the German high command still hoped to seize Moscow. The resumption of the offensive, however, achieved no rapid breakthrough and only gained ground slowly in increasingly difficult conditions. Having neglected any prospect of a winter campaign, German planning included no provision for the adequate supply of winter clothing and equipment, meaning that already in November their troops were freezing at night. By 5 December, Typhoon had slowed to a crawl, and with only a handful of Bock's forces reporting any combat readiness, the decision was finally taken to end the German offensive for 1941. Despite how some historians have characterised it, the battle for Moscow was not a close-run affair – the Germans never had the strength to seize the city. Typhoon, therefore, replicated Barbarossa by gaining a lot of ground and inflicting staggering losses on the Red Army but never achieving its strategic goal of ending the campaign.

Clearly the German high command had overestimated their offensive power, but more worryingly they had again underestimated Soviet strength. No less than five new Soviet armies had been held back from the final phase of the German offensive, and in late November Zhukov finalised plans to use them in a winter offensive against Army Group Centre. He telephoned Stalin and asked for permission to proceed. 'Are you sure that the enemy has reached a critical point and is in no position to bring some new large force into action?', Stalin asked. 'The enemy has been bled white', Zhukov assured him.[26] Accordingly, on 6 December, the day after Army Group Centre had halted it attack, Bock's exhausted and overextended forces north and south of Moscow came under attack. At first these were thought to be nothing more than local attacks, but as the days passed and the intensity of the fighting grew, it became apparent that Army Group Centre was facing an unexpected winter offensive.

The German retreat from Moscow was conducted under pressure, which at times led to chaos, but that was the exception rather than the rule. For the most part units withdrew in orderly, if hasty organised, marches. A large share of irreplaceable equipment, especially vehicles, was lost, but a good percentage of this material was so worn out as to have had a limited practical value anyway. Two weeks into the retreat Hitler refused to countenance any further loss of ground and ordered a halt. This denied German commanders, up and down the chain of command, the flexibility and freedom of action to respond to events, but recent

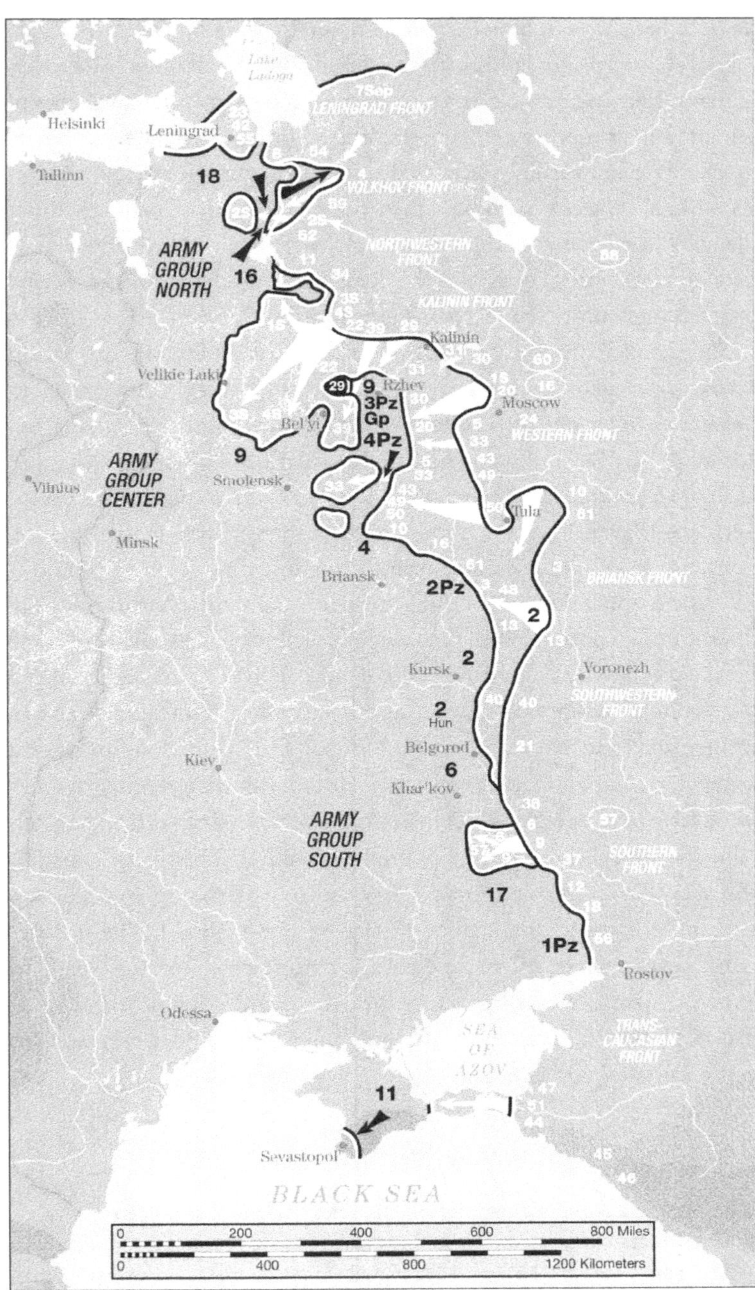

Map 4 Winter–spring campaign (6 December 1941–April 1942).

research has shown that in their desperation they manipulated, deceived, selectively interpreted, and outright refused Hitler's halt order. Moreover, as the Soviets began to seize ground Stalin repeated Hitler's mistake of demanding far more than his overstretched forces could achieve. Soviet attacks were increasingly dispersed rather than concentrated, and rigid operational objectives meant men were flung into battle without adequate intelligence, planning, or heavy weapons support. The results were horrendously costly for the Red Army, and the winter period claimed many times the losses sustained by the Germans.[27]

Far from achieving the demise of the Soviet Union, Operation Barbarossa began a war that, more than any other, contributed to Germany's own defeat. While in 1941 no one could yet predict the Red Army in Berlin, Stalin had the population, industrial base, and access to resources to wage a victorious war of attrition against Nazi Germany. Barbarossa was not defeated in the classical sense – in fact, Germany won every major battle throughout the summer period – but the implications of failing to end the war were profound. Operation Typhoon was the stopgap solution designed to deal a decisive blow at Moscow, and it too delivered crushing initial success but floundered on account of Germany's dwindling offensive momentum and the autumn *rasputitsa*. Determined to press the issue, Germany entered the Russian winter with dangerously overextended forces, operating on a logistical shoestring and exhausted from five-and-a-half months of offensive action. Their only consolation was that things had to be worse on the Soviet side, but that too only underlined the deficiency of German intelligence. The unforeseen Soviet winter offensive proved a microcosm of the years to come – Germany traded space for time and fought a battle of resources that Hitler tended to dominate but could never sustain to the same extent as Stalin.

Notes

1 For why each of these nations joined Hitler's war in the East, see David Stahel, ed., *Joining Hitler's Crusade: European Nations and the Invasion of the Soviet Union, 1941* (Cambridge: Cambridge University Press, 2017).

2 For a first-rate overview of the Soviet war effort, see Alexander Hill, *The Red Army and the Second World War* (Cambridge: Cambridge University Press, 2017).

3 For a detailed study of Germany's initial period of warfare in the East, see David Stahel, *Operation Barbarossa and Germany's Defeat in the East* (Cambridge: Cambridge University Press, 2009).

4 Martin van Creveld, *Supplying War: Logistics from Wallenstein to Patton* (Cambridge: Cambridge University Press, 1984), chapter 5, 'Russian Roulette'; Geoffrey Megargee, *Inside Hitler's High Command* (Lawrence: University Press of Kansas, 2000), chapter 7, 'Logistics, Personnel, and Barbarossa'.

5 Finland's parallel invasion, with some supporting German units, extended the front another 900 kilometres north to the Barents Sea.

6 Stahel, *Operation Barbarossa and Germany's Defeat in the East*, chapters 5–8.

7 Franz Halder, *Kriegstagebuch: Tägliche Aufzeichnungen des Chefs des Generalstabes des Heeres 1939–1942. Band III, Der Russlandfeldzug bis zum Marsch auf Stalingrad (22.6.1941–24.9.1942)*, ed. Hans-Adolf Jacobsen and Alfred Philippi (Stuttgart: Kohlhammer, 1964), pp. 38–39 (3 July 1941).

8 Evan Mawdsley, *Thunder in the East: The Nazi-Soviet War 1941–1945* (London: Bloomsbury, 2016), p. 63.

9 Stahel, *Operation Barbarossa and Germany's Defeat in the East*, pp. 315–317.

10 Walter Gorlitz, ed., *The Memoirs of Field-Marshal Keitel: Chief of the German High Command, 1938–1945* (New York: Stein and Day, 1966), pp. 150–151.

11 Ernst Klink, 'The Conduct of Operations', in *Militärgeschichtliches Forschungsamt, Germany and the Second World War. Volume IV, The Attack on the Soviet Union*, ed. Militärgeschichtliches Forschungsamt (Oxford: Clarendon Press, 1998), pp. 569–581.

12 Elke Fröhlich, ed., *Die Tagebücher von Joseph Goebbels Teil II Diktate 1941–1945 Band 1 Juli-September 1941* (Munich: De Gruyter, 1996), pp. 115–116 (24 July 1941).

13 Halder, *Kriegstagebuch*, p. 170 (11 August 1941).

14 For an insightful perspective on Soviet motivations, see Roger R. Reese, *Why Stalin's Soldiers Fought: The Red Army's Military Effectiveness in World War II* (Lawrence: University Press of Kansas, 2011).

15 For the best studies of the Soviet home front, see John Barber and Mark Harrison, *The Soviet Home Front 1941–1945: A Social and Economic History of the USSR in World War II* (London: Longman, 1991); Wendy Z. Goldman and Donald Filtzer, *Fortress Dark and Stern: The Soviet Home Front during World War II* (Oxford: Oxford University Press, 2021).

16 David M. Glantz and Jonathan House, *When Titans Clashed: How the Red Army Stopped Hitler* (Lawrence: University Press of Kansas, 2015), pp. 79–81.

17 David M. Glantz, *Barbarossa: Hitler's Invasion of Russia 1941* (Stroud: Tempus, 2001), p. 68.

18 Glantz and House, *When Titans Clashed*, p. 83.

19 M. R. D. Foot, 'USSR', in *The Oxford Companion of the Second World War*, ed. I. C. B. Dear and M. R. D. Foot (Oxford: Oxford University Press, 1995), cf. German and Soviet weapons production, pp. 459 and 1231.

20 For a detailed study of the battle, see David Stahel, *Kiev 1941: Hitler's Battle for Supremacy in the East* (Cambridge: Cambridge University Press, 2012).

21 David Stahel, *Operation Typhoon: Hitler's March on Moscow, October 1941* (Cambridge: Cambridge University Press, 2013), p. 8.

22 Halder, *Kriegstagebuch*, p. 245 (22 September 1941).

23 Halder, *Kriegstagebuch*, p. 267 (4 October 1941).

24 Janusz Piekalkiewicz, *Moscow 1941: The Frozen Offensive* (London: Arms and Armour Press, 1985), p. 113.

25 Alexander Hill and David Stahel, 'British "Lend-Lease" Aid to the USSR and the Battle of Moscow in the Light of Soviet and German Sources', *Journal of Slavic Military Studies*, 34, 2021, pp. 537–557; David Stahel, *The Battle for Moscow* (Cambridge: Cambridge University Press, 2015), pp. 176–178, 250–251.

26 G. K. Zhukov, *The Memoirs of Marshal Zhukov* (New York: Delacorte Press, 1971), pp. 347–448.

27 For much of this research, see David Stahel, *Retreat from Moscow: A New History of Germany's Winter Campaign, 1941–1942* (New York: Farrar, Straus and Giroux, 2019).

ADRIAN E. WETTSTEIN

8

Stalingrad and the Eastern Front, 1942

8.1 Plans, Forces, and Preliminary Operations

The failure to defeat the Soviet Union in 1941, the Red Army's counter-offensive in winter 1941–1942, and Hitler's declaration of war against the United States of America (11 December 1941) created a new strategic situation for the Third Reich.[1] It was now facing a combined alliance of Great Britain, the United States, and the Soviet Union, which could simply overwhelm the Axis powers through its far superior potential. Therefore, Hitler and the German military leadership agreed, from early 1942 on, that Germany should focus on a second campaign in the east to decide the war against the Soviet Union. The German leadership hoped to eliminate one enemy while at the same time gaining a resource base that would allow it to compete with Anglo-American powers. Lacking the forces for an attack along the whole front, Hitler chose the Caucasian oil fields as the primary objective. Achieving this goal sought to make Germany self-sufficient in terms of its oil supply, while at the same time depriving the Soviet Union of some 85 per cent of its oil production.[2]

On 5 April 1942, Hitler issued Führer Directive No. 41, which defined the strategic framework for 1942. The planned operations in the east should try 'to wipe out irrevocably the defence potential remaining to the Soviets, and to deprive them, as far as possible, of their most important centres of wartime economy'.[3] For this purpose, the German southern wing was intended to assault the Caucasian region, while the northern wing was tasked with taking Leningrad. The German centre would remain on the defensive. Preliminary operations aimed to clear the

Crimea and the Soviet bulge at Izjum.[4] An additional implication of the German plan was to sever Allied Lend-Lease supply routes, both in the south (through Persia and the Caucasus) as well as the north (via the Murman railway). The latter route was to be attacked after the fall of Leningrad in a combined Finnish-German offensive.[5]

The first stage of the main operation in the south, codenamed Blau, had to be split into phases, as fresh Axis forces would inevitably arrive in echelons due to limited transport capabilities. In three successive encirclement operations that ran from north to south, Axis armies were to destroy Soviet forces west of the Don River. 'In any event', the war directive continued, 'it must be attempted to reach Stalingrad itself, or at least to bring it within range of our heavy weapons so that it ceases its function as a further industrial or communications centre.'[6] With that achieved, Axis troops should then turn southward to seize the oilfields of Maykop, Grozny, and Baku.

Conquering this enormous area – with the distance between Baku and the German front line amounting to a staggering 1,400 kilometres – required large forces. However, due to the loss of one million men up to 20 March 1942, the German *Ostheer* was severely weakened, especially as reinforcements were quantitatively as well as qualitatively insufficient.[7] Therefore, the Axis allies had to send more forces, finally encompassing four armies with roughly thirty-five divisions. Yet these units were not comparable to average German ones, lacking adequate anti-tank and anti-aircraft weapons, but also proper training and command.

The logistics would prove to be even more challenging, a problem said to be the Achilles' heel of the German war in the east. A lack of transportation means, poor roads and rail infrastructure, demanding weather, and institutional problems plagued the Wehrmacht's supply system since the first days of Operation Barbarossa. But the problems multiplied in the areas south and east of the Don, as the Wehrmacht encountered infrastructure that was rudimentary at best. At the same time, fighting in the sparsely wooded steppe regions would demand additional supplies: there was no wood for construction or firewood, there was no fodder for the tens of thousands of horses needed to haul guns and wagons, and even water was sometimes lacking. Food became a problem, too, as the steppe could not sustain the large number of Axis soldiers. This led to more supplies having to be transported over longer distances with less means.[8]

The Red Army had suffered some five million casualties up to April 1942, yet its overall field strength had risen. And despite further evacuations of entire manufacturing plants, the Soviet arms industry produced new equipment in impressive numbers in 1942. This included nearly 25,000 tanks, far surpassing the German output of a mere 5,500 new tanks. This coincided with increased Allied material support for the Soviet Union, which included, for example, more than 5,000 tanks in 1942. On the other hand, the Red Army's weaknesses in tactical and operational leadership proved persistent, as it again incurred heavy losses in 1942. Expecting a renewed German offensive against Moscow, Stalin temporarily opted for a strategic defence. The one exception was to allow Timoshenko's Southwestern Front to conduct an offensive to take Kharkov, beginning on 12 May 1942. While seemingly promising at the outset, a mixture of Soviet errors in command and German air superiority brought the attack to a halt. Germany's Army Group South (under the command of *Generalfeldmarschall* Fedor von Bock) launched a counterattack to encircle and then destroy the Soviet forces east of the Donets River. By 28 May some 235,000 prisoners had been taken. Following this impressive victory, Army Group South seized upon its advantage with two follow-up operations. In Operation Wilhelm (10–15 June) the Soviet bridgehead east of Kharkov was eliminated, while the mass of the Soviet Twenty-Eighth Army escaped encirclement. Operation Fridericus II (22–26 June) saw a similar outcome, ensuring that no more than a combined 50,000 Soviet prisoners were taken. This Soviet shift to an elastic defence that avoided sacrificing forces in untenable positions, as it had in the summer and autumn of 1941, should have served – but failed – to alarm the German leadership.[9]

At the same time, the German Eleventh Army under *Generaloberst* Erich von Manstein cleared the Crimea. In Operation Trappenjagd (8–21 May 1942), the Eleventh Army reconquered most of the Kerch peninsula and took 170,000 Soviet war prisoners. This swift success can be explained by both excellent German as well as abysmal Soviet leadership.[10] Next was Operation Störfang (2 June–5 July 1942), the attack on Sevastopol. The defending Soviet Separate Coastal Army (Major-General Ivan Petrov) had used the five-month-long siege to

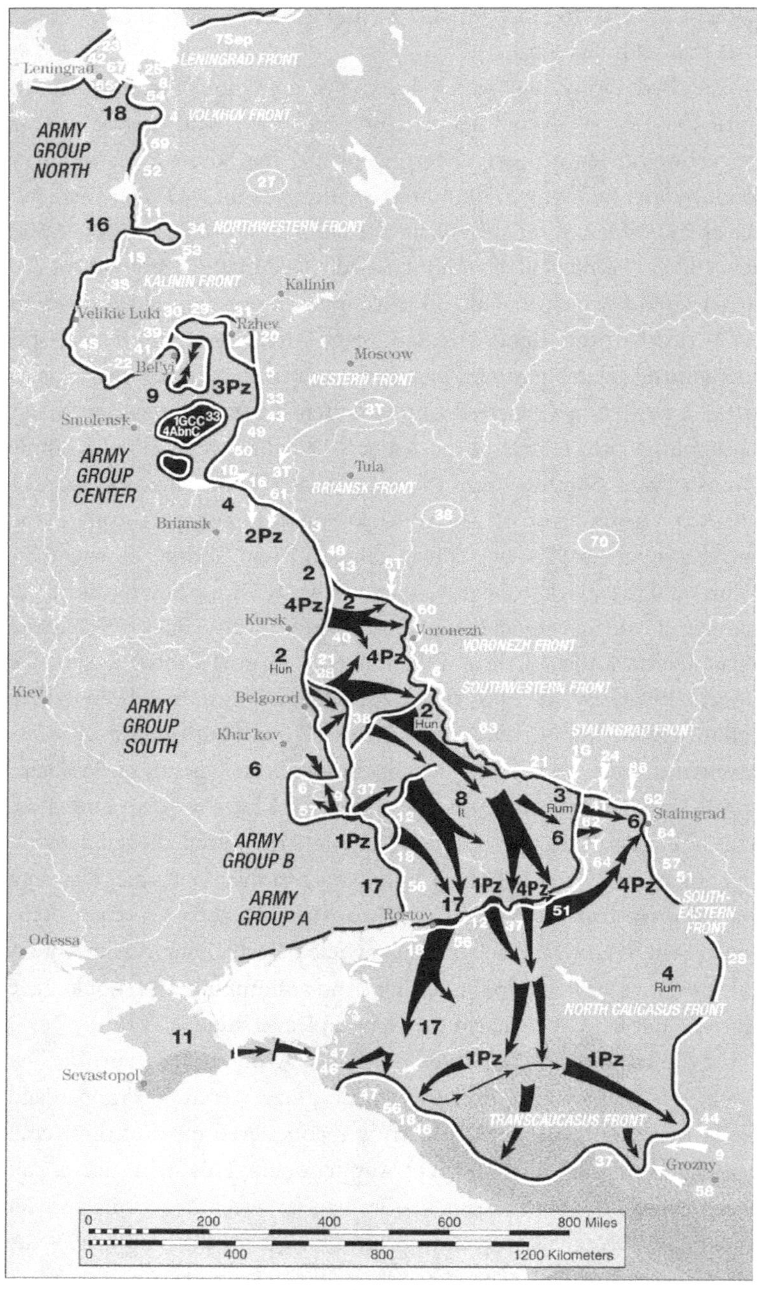

Map 5 Spring–autumn campaign (May–October 1942).

create three well-entrenched defensive lines, backed by massive coastal batteries. To crack this fortress, the Germans concentrated their heaviest artillery, expending 26,281 tons of artillery shells as well 20,529 tons of bombs dropped by the Luftwaffe. Nevertheless, the tenacious Soviet defence cost the Axis 35,000 casualties and postponed the use of the Eleventh Army's forces. While the fall of Sevastopol – together with that of Tobruk in North Africa (21 June 1942) – was exploited for propaganda, already at the time, the military wisdom of the resource-intensive operation was debated.[11]

8.2 Operation Blau Unleashed

On 28 June 1942, Operation Blau was launched. The German Fourth Panzer Army, starting from the Kursk area, crossed the Don River on 4 July. Instead of racing southward along the Don, it got entangled in the Voronezh area. This circumstance, combined with a lack of fuel and a timely Soviet retreat prevented any larger encirclement of Soviet forces in the initial phase of Operation Blau. While German forces pushed in a southeastern direction, the Second Hungarian and Eighth Italian Armies were introduced to protect the Don line.

On 7 July, Army Group South was divided into Army Group B and A, thus beginning the process of diverging German forces towards Stalingrad and the Caucasus at the same time. The newly formed Army Group A initialized the second phase of Operation Blau on 9 July and immediately endured three sobering weeks of battle, as all major attempts at encirclement failed, which cost von Bock his position as commander-in-chief of Army Group B.

Nevertheless, the Axis forces advanced rapidly and Hitler became overly optimistic, misjudging the Red Army's retreats as a sign of weakening enemy strength. On 23 July, he declared in his Directive No. 45 that 'the goals set [are] essentially achieved [and] only weaker enemy forces' had escaped.[12] Therefore, Hitler refashioned the original plan of serial offensives into one of parallel operations. Army Group B would now conquer Stalingrad and secure the flank of Army Group A's simultaneous offensive to the Caucasian oilfields (Operation Edelweiss). Furthermore, Hitler detached the Eleventh Army to the Leningrad area, further weakening his offensive forces in the south.

None of the Army Groups were strong enough to achieve their objectives, and mutual support was not possible due to the diverging axes of their attacks. Thus it can be concluded that Directive No. 45 marked the beginning of the disaster at Stalingrad, driven by a fatal underestimation of Soviet will and strength, as well as an overestimation of Germans means.[13]

A mere week later, Hitler changed his mind again and turned the Fourth Panzer Army towards Stalingrad, postulating, 'The fate of the Caucasus is to be decided at Stalingrad.'[14] The former secondary objective Stalingrad had now become the main objective, and the city was to be conquered – something that had never been a part of German planning. However, the window for a surprise attack had already closed, as the Red Army had bolstered Stalingrad's defences with massive reinforcements.

On the other side, Stalin had also changed his mind. Never having been convinced of the logic behind an elastic defence, he issued his famous Order No. 227 on 28 July 1942. 'Not one step back' became the main slogan, infusing Soviet soldiers with new combat motivation – motivation that, as soon became clear, required backing by disciplinary measures such as blocking detachments and penal battalions.[15] These changes in the Soviet operational mode meant that the campaign would develop from one of movement to one of attrition, as dogged German attacks would soon exhaust themselves on desperate Soviet defences. The first larger encounter was the battle for Kalatch (25 July–11 August 1942), in which the German Sixth Army (under the command of *Generaloberst* Friedrich Paulus) destroyed some 1,000 Soviet tanks and took 57,000 prisoners, but lost precious time that was used by the Red Army to further strengthen Stalingrad's defence.

8.3   The German Attack on Stalingrad

The German assault on Stalingrad began on 23 August 1942, when the Sixth Army's spearhead, the 16th Panzer Division, reached the northern suburbs of Rynok and Spartakovka, where fierce Soviet resistance put an end to any further advances. Over the next two weeks, the Sixth Army's infantry divisions reached the outskirts of Stalingrad on a broad front. The German Fourth Panzer Army, which had now turned northward, advanced no faster than the Sixth Army, as it possessed only a single panzer corps. These early September days made plain just how much German offensive power had diminished, as the few mobile offensive units were too scattered. Furthermore, many combat units were simply exhausted from constant fighting and marching for two months and had already lost 50 per cent of their regular combat strength. The supply situation proved equally dire: the Sixth Army, Fourth Panzer Army, and Romanian Third Army were mostly supplied by two single-tracked railway lines. German quartermaster staffs grasped the danger and advocated for a retreat from late September onwards, as they doubted that the Sixth Army would survive a winter on the Volga, even after taking Stalingrad.[16] Still, Hitler and the German high command pushed the troops forward. On 13 September, the LI Army Corps attacked the centre of Stalingrad, while the XXXXVIII Panzer Corps cut the southern approaches to the city and entered its southern districts. The next two weeks saw house-to-house fighting, as the attacking German forces slowly conquered those parts of Stalingrad. Alexander Rodimtsev, the 13th Guards Divisional commander, described the chaotic fighting: 'A house was held by us, then by the enemy, then again by us, so that locating the frontline exactly proved impossible.'[17]

Soviet defenders, under the equally skilled and ruthless leadership of Lieutenant-General Vasily Chuikov, had to lose territory slowly, but Red Army resistance never collapsed.[18] However, contrary to the myth of a numerically superior Wehrmacht, inexperienced and clumsy in urban warfare and defeated by superior Soviet tactics, it was in fact the Soviets who enjoyed numerical superiority at Stalingrad. The constant stream of Soviet reinforcements proved decisive. From 13 September to 3 October 1942, the Red Army transferred at least 70,000 soldiers into Stalingrad, while in the same three-week period the Wehrmacht's combat power shrank by about 5,000 men. The fact that German forces in these conditions managed to advance in difficult urban terrain and against a fiercely resisting Sixty-Second Army at all can only be explained by tactical superiority. Heavy losses notwithstanding, in 1942 German troops maintained a high standard of training, were more effective in combined-arms tactics, and – most importantly – had more professional lower-level leadership. German air superiority also was a factor but was less important than it would have been in open areas. Indeed, however effective the German Sixth Army was, the Soviet leadership achieved its goals: German strength sapped, and the advance slowed further. Time became critical, as German forces should have started with winter preparations in October. However, intensive fighting in Stalingrad severely impeded any stockpiling or forwarding of winter equipment in noteworthy quantities.[19]

Dwindling resources and manpower brought about the need for operational breaks. After the reduction of the Orlovka salient west of Stalingrad in early October, the LI Army Corps could only attack the industrial area of Stalingrad in separate thrusts over the space of several weeks. After a few days of attack, German forces needed to secure the conquered area, regrouping their units to gain renewed momentum and restock on ammunition. Those days proved of great value to the Soviet defenders in bringing in reinforcements and entrenching themselves. German gains became smaller while losses rose. The widely destroyed, sprawling industrial areas proved an especially difficult area for fighting, as a report by Engineer Battalion 179 describes:

Figure 8.1 A German machine gun crew during the battle of Stalingrad, 1942. Source: AFP via Getty Images.

Shot at by enemy snipers firing through hatches, openings and hidden nooks, the spearhead penetrated into the hall from the side. The inextricable mess of iron parts, debris from the wall, destroyed machines, twisted beams and rubble demanded the highest concentration and decisively delayed the advance. The men were dazed by the chaos before their eyes. It was impossible to take a secure step, as there was no footing in the jumble of iron pieces. Inevitably, attention was therefore kept off of the enemy. At once, concentrated enemy defensive fire from all directions opened up after the penetration. Satchel charges, hand grenades, and submachine gun salvos hindered all further advances to main hall 4.[20]

A final series of assaults from 9 November on achieved only minor gains for heavy losses, signalling to the Red Army the increasingly calamitous condition of the Sixth Army.

8.4   The German Thrust to the Caucasus and Operations in the North and the Centre

Conquering Rostov and gaining bridgeheads over the Don on 23 July 1942 marked the beginning of Operation Edelweiss. In the initial phase, German forces met only local resistance and rapidly gained ground. However, this meant lengthening supply lines and Army Group A also started to suffer from shortages. While the German Seventeenth Army managed to take Krasnodar on 9 August 1942, the battle marked the beginning of more resolute Soviet resistance. That same day, First Panzer Army conquered Maykop, the smallest Caucasian oil field. However, the extensive Soviet demolition of the site prevented any noteworthy oil production there until the German retreat in January 1943. In September 1942, the German offensive towards the Caucasus petered out. While the German V Army Corps took most of the Soviet naval base of Novorossiysk, its advance was stopped in the industrial area south of the city. Specialized Axis mountain formations as well as regular infantry fought on several axes to cross the Caucasus mountains and reach the Black Sea coast, but none of the isolated wedges succeeded. First Panzer Army passed over the Terek River, the last major obstacle in front of the Grozny oil fields, but lack of forces, supplies, and Soviet counterattacks hampered the advance.[21] As in the Stalingrad region, German troops in the Caucasus region were dangerously dispersed by September, lacking reserves as well as a stable supply base.

Army Group A's lack of forces was a consequence of two major troop shifts already mentioned, namely the dispatch of Fourth Panzer Army to Stalingrad and the Eleventh Army northward. While that army assembled south of Leningrad, the Soviet Volchov Front attacked on 27 August 1942 to break the German siege. The carefully prepared Soviet offensive proceeded despite a difficult approach march through swamps and woods dangerously close to the dominating Siniavino heights. Hitler ordered a counterattack, using the forces originally designated for the assault on Leningrad. It took the German pincers five days to advance the necessary four kilometres to encircle the Soviet attacking forces and one further week to reduce the pocket. However, in the face of 26,000 German casualties and a rapidly approaching cold season, Operation Nordlicht, the attack on Leningrad, had to be postponed to 1943. The planned Finnish-German attack to cut the Murman railway suffered the same fate.[22]

More important but less widely known are the effects of the major Soviet offensive aiming at the Rzhev salient on the central section of the Eastern Front. The Rzhev salient was a product of the failed Soviet winter offensive in the rear of Army Group Centre and blocked any further Soviet advance towards the Baltics or Army Group Centre's communication lines. On 30 July 1942, Konev's Kalinin Front attacked and came close to seizing Rzhev. Five days later, Colonel-General Georgy Zhukov's Western Front joined the offensive and threatened to take Sychyovka. German casualties amounted to around 1,000 soldiers daily, but the defence did not collapse. While not achieving the destruction of the German Ninth Army, the First Rzhev-Sychyovka Operation (as Soviet historiography calls it) tied down and further eroded German forces. However, in light of the nearly 200,000 Red Army casualties in less than a month, the Soviet price was extraordinarily high.[23]

But it was not the Red Army alone that distracted German forces from the main theatre in the south. Similar to Stalin during the winter of 1941–1942, Hitler's thinking entertained too many operational options. A telling example was the ill-fated effort to shorten the front in the Belev-Juchnov area, codenamed Whirlwind (11–22 August 1942).

Without necessity, two of the mere nine German panzer divisions fighting on the southern wing were diverted for this operation. In all, even if Soviet territorial gains in the central and northern part of the Eastern Front in 1942 were negligible, the attrition of Axis forces achieved was essential.[24]

8.5   The Soviet Counteroffensive

After the failure of its last attack, the Sixth Army scraped together reserves to strengthen its long flank. German intelligence had observed the Soviet build-up in the two Don bridgeheads of Serafimovich and Kletskaya, but had underestimated its scale. While the benefit of hindsight might lead one to blame German intelligence alone, one should not forget that no Red Army operations prior to Operation Uranus had ever been able to envelop and destroy large German forces. Moreover, there had been at least five large Soviet attacks on the Sixth Army's northern flank between August and October that had failed. Therefore, Soviet leadership chose this time to attack weaker Romanian forces.[25]

In the early morning of 19 November 1942, the Soviet Southwestern Front opened its attack with a massive artillery barrage. Around noon, Romanian resistance in the II and IV Corps sectors collapsed, while most of the V Corps was encircled. The only operational reserve, a combined German-Romanian panzer corps with obsolete tanks, utterly failed to blunt the Soviet offensive and was in the process virtually destroyed. By the end of the day there was a seventy-kilometre gap in the Axis front line and Soviet mobile forces pushed towards Kalach, spreading panic throughout the Axis rear area.[26] The following day, the Soviet Stalingrad Front attacked south of Stalingrad, again hitting Romanian troops and achieving a breakthrough on the first day. On 23 November the Soviets' pincers met near Kalach, encircling the Sixth Army, a corps of Fourth Panzer Army, and elements of several Romanian divisions – in all about 300,000 soldiers.

Hitler forbade any breakout and ordered the Sixth Army to hold Stalingrad at all costs. Furthermore, he detached Manstein and his staff to the area, forming Army Group Don with shattered Romanian forces, German rear and security units, and newly arriving reinforcements. His mission was to relieve the Sixth Army and hold Stalingrad. To keep the undersupplied and isolated Sixth Army alive, an airlift was organized.

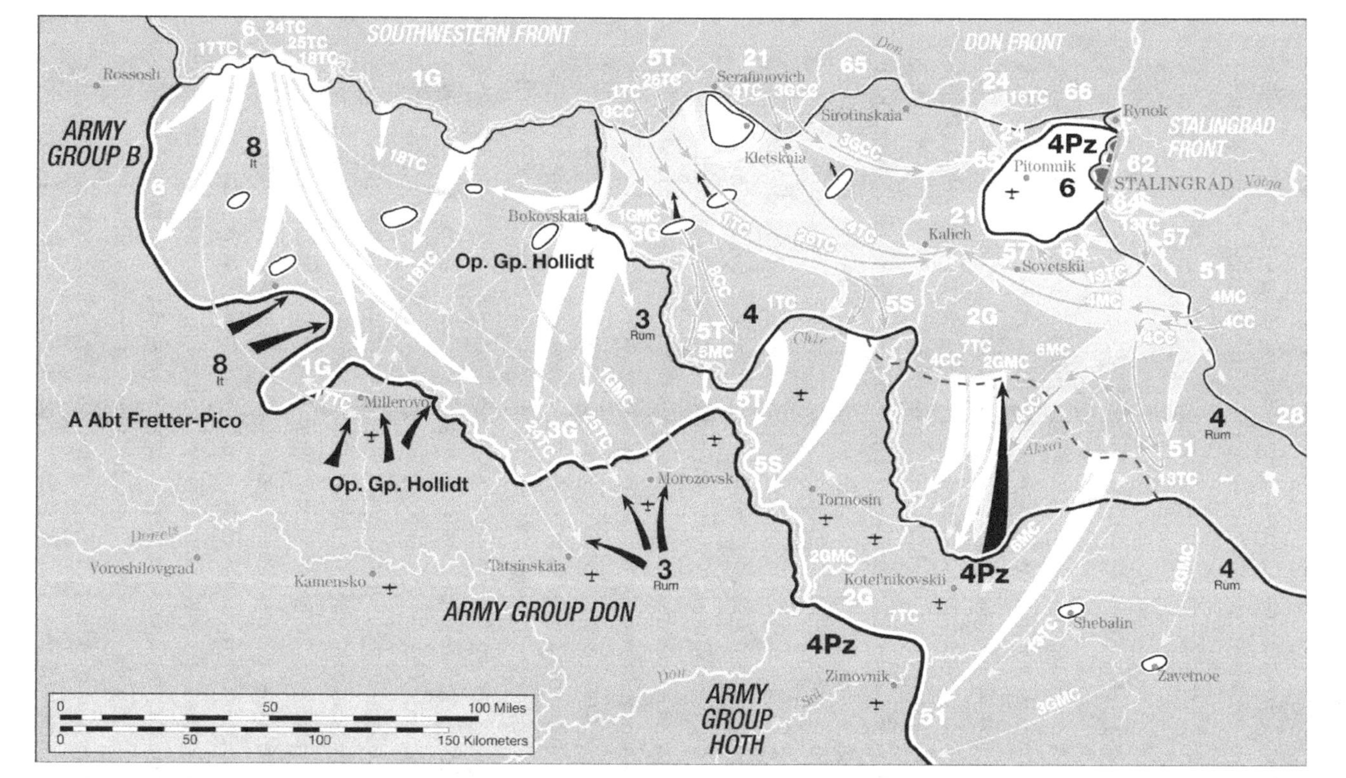

Map 6 Soviet counteroffensive at Stalingrad (November–December 1942).

Figure 8.2 Soviet troops fire on German positions in the vicinity of the Red October plant in Stalingrad, 26 November 1942. Source: Hulton Archive/Getty Images.

The Luftwaffe staff deemed a daily transport capability of 350 tons realistic, while Göring assured Hitler of the Luftwaffe's ability to fly in 500 tons, which was still less than the minimum 600 tons daily demanded by the Sixth Army. However, Luftwaffe commanders in the field considered even 350 tons to be unrealistic – and were soon proven right. They knew the destitute conditions of the airfields and the ground organization. As a result, rates of operational aircraft decreased steadily, reaching as little as 10 per cent by January 1943. In addition, bad weather and Soviet countermeasures hampered the German effort. Lacking the necessary Ju-52 transport aircraft, the Germans pressed He-111 bombers, Ju-86 training aircraft, and Fw-200 long-range recon-naissance aircraft into transport services, all less effective as transporters and unavailable for their original tasks.[27]

The Wehrmacht mobilized forces from all over Europe to stabilize the Eastern Front, but it took time to gather them. The transfer of a panzer division required some seventy trains, and in the chaotic situation of winter 1942–1943, it easily took a month until such a unit was transferred from Western Europe to the Eastern Front. Therefore, when the German relief attack for Stalingrad (Operation Wintergewitter) started on 12 December 1942, the assemble of forces was still not complete, but they caught the Soviets by surprise. However, the Soviet High Command quickly detached the Second Guards Army, which succeeded in containing the German offensive. The relief attack never came closer than forty-eight kilometres to the encircled Sixth Army, which lacked the forces for a breakout attack. A further Soviet offensive, codenamed Little Saturn, commenced on 16 December against the Italian Eighth Army, which rapidly disintegrated. This forced Manstein to halt the relief attack towards Stalingrad on 23 December and to detach forces northward to stabilize the situation, a move that ultimately doomed the encircled Sixth Army.[28]

The successful Operation Uranus was not the only Soviet offensive that sought a decisive victory. On 25 November, the Western and Kalinin Fronts launched a second major offensive, codenamed Mars, again aimed at the Rzhev salient. This operation, planned and executed under the aegis of Zhukov, had the objective of destroying the German Ninth Army. The Soviet effort encompassed some 668,000 men and almost 2,000 tanks. In scope and scale, this offensive was similar to Operation Uranus, yet it resulted in a colossal failure, which the Soviets later attempted to mask by claiming it was only a diversionary attack designed to support their operations in the south. However, as historian David Glantz asserts, if 'Mars was really a diversion, there has never been one so ambitious, so large, so clumsily executed, or so costly'.[29] And costly it was, with some 335,000 Soviet casualties (compared to 50,000 German). This was one of the bloodiest failures of the Red Army in the entire war.

8.6   The End of the Sixth Army and the Soviet Winter Offensive

Inside the Stalingrad cauldron, German troops had to defend in the open steppe in temperatures that reached forty degrees below zero, all without prepared positions or shelters, lacking firewood and warm food. While the hope of relief kept the Germans soldiers fighting, supply stocks dwindled. To allow a breakout attempt, fuel and ammunition were flown in, but the range of German tanks decreased to twenty kilometres on 21 December – not even half of the necessary distance to reach the spearhead of the relief attack.

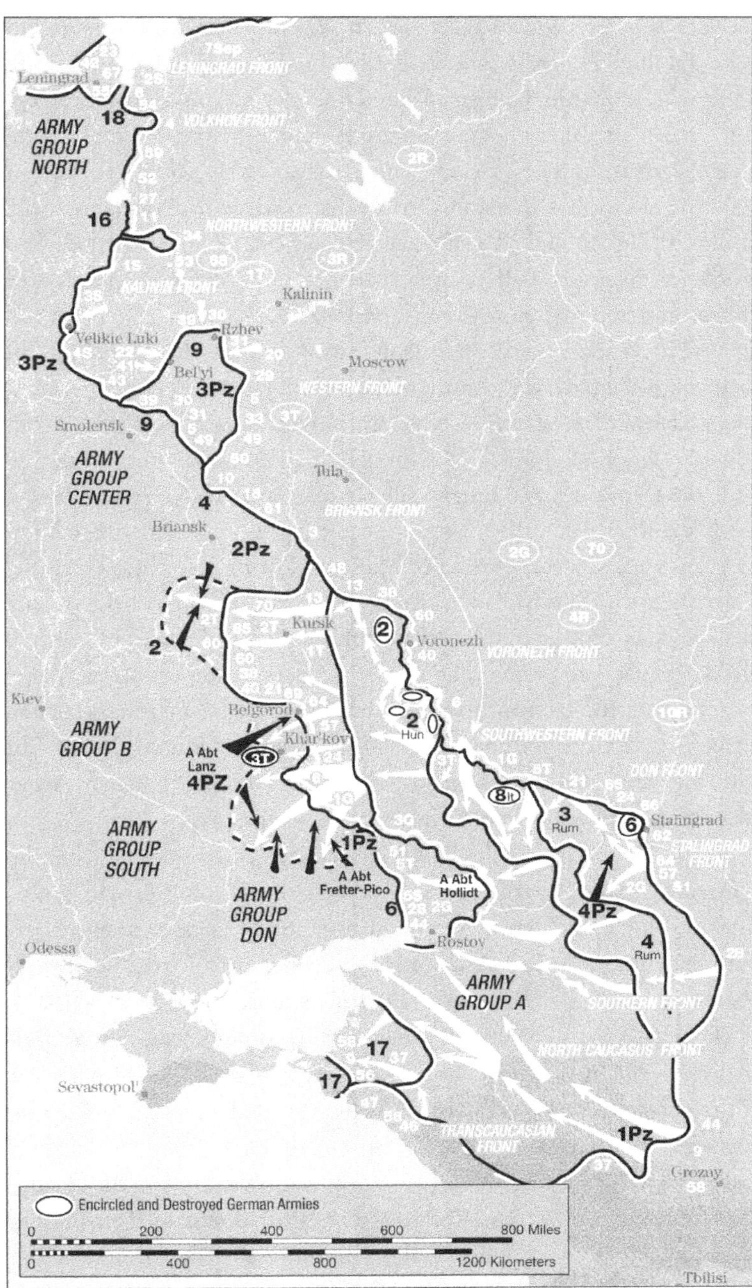

Map 7 Autumn–spring campaign (November 1942–March 1943).

After the cessation of the relief attack, the Sixth Army's situation grew rapidly desperate. Most soldiers now realized that they were fighting a lost battle. Hunger plagued them, as rations were repeatedly cut. On 21 December, the first German soldiers were reported as having died of starvation. The Luftwaffe completely failed to achieve the goal of 300 tons of supplies, demanded by the Sixth Army as an absolute daily minimum. In 4,000 flights, it delivered some 8,300 tons of goods and evacuated at least 25,000 wounded soldiers, but this came at the cost of 488 aircraft and many experienced aircrews.[30]

On 10 January 1943, the Don Front (under the command of Lieutenant-General Konstantin Rokossovsky) commenced Operation Ring. German resistance was astonishingly dogged, and the Soviet advance lagged behind Rokossovsky's expectations, but beginning with Basargino on 14 January, all German airfields were lost in the following days. From then on, supplies could only be airdropped. On 23 January, Soviet forces reached Stalingrad from the west and cut the German pocket in two. The day before, Hitler had ruled out any possibility of capitulation, even after the last cartridge had been fired. On 31 January, the remaining German forces in the southern pocket surrendered; the troops in the north followed on 2 February at nine o'clock in the morning. Some 200,000 Axis soldiers became prisoners of war, but due to their miserable condition, along with harsh Soviet treatment, only 6,000 would ever return to Germany.[31]

A few days before, Hitler had finally consented to a retreat from the Caucasus. However, strong Axis forces remained on the Taman peninsula, forming a bridgehead for an illusory future Caucasus offensive. At the same time, the Red Army advanced on a broad front westward, liberating Kursk (8 February 1943) and Belgorod (9 February 1943). Their pressure on Kharkov threatened German forces there with encirclement. In this dangerous situation, Paul Hausser, commander of the newly arrived II SS Panzer Corps, obviated a second Stalingrad, defying Hitler's direct order as he pulled back from the city on 15 February 1943. Kharkov was a Soviet prestige victory, but the balance of forces was shifting. The Red Army's units had outrun their lines of communication, were exhausted from the ceaseless advance under difficult winter conditions, and consequently were dangerously exposed. On the German side, command was unified in a newly formed

Army Group South under Manstein. The retreat from the Caucasus as well as the final destruction of the Sixth Army at Stalingrad allowed Manstein greater flexibility, as he could now pull back from exposed positions that previously had to be held for the Caucasus retreat or the Stalingrad relief. Furthermore, reinforcements gave Manstein the necessary strength to regain the initiative. In a textbook operation, he struck at the Red Army, reconquering Kharkov (16 March 1943) and Belgorod (18 March 1943). However, the beginning of the mud season prevented his forces from eliminating the Kursk bulge, the region that would become the focus of operations in the summer of 1943.[32]

The German summer offensive in 1942 began with a strategic rationale, but according to Arthur F. Lykke's conception, Hitler and the German military leadership set their 'end' too high, refused outrightly to concentrate their 'means', and (more than once) strayed from the chosen 'ways'.[33] Furthermore, as in 1941, they recklessly underestimated Soviet resources and the Red Army's will to fight. Stalingrad became the operational dead end of an increasingly confused campaign, where understrength and undersupplied German forces had to frontally attack a city defended by a well-entrenched, determined, and numerically superior Soviet Sixty-Second Army that received steady reinforcements. Superior lower-level leadership, training, and tactics allowed German forces to conquer nine-tenths of Stalingrad against all odds, but their sacrifices served no operational, let alone strategic, purpose. The Red Army, conducting a battle of attrition, created the conditions for its first successful encirclement operation, which in turn created the conditions for a series of offensives that drove the Axis forces back to where they started in the summer of 1942. Together with comparable Allied victories at Midway, El Alamein, and Guadalcanal, Stalingrad is part of a larger turn of the tide in the Second World War.

Notes

1 While the literature on Stalingrad has become legion, a serious study of the campaign must take into consideration the following three major studies with a dense source base: Bernd Wegner, 'Der Krieg gegen die Sowjetunion 1942/43', in *Das Deutsche Reich und der Zweite Weltkrieg, Vol. 6: Der globale Krieg. Die Ausweitung zum Weltkrieg und der Wechsel der Initiative, 1941–1943*, ed. Militärgeschichtliches Forschungsamt (Stuttgart: Deutsche

Verlags-Anstalt, 1990), pp. 761–1102, David Glantz and Jonathan M. House, *The Stalingrad Trilogy* (Lawrence: University Press of Kansas, 2009–2014), and Manfred Kehrig, *Stalingrad: Analyse und Dokumentation einer Schlacht* (Stuttgart: Deutsche Verlags-Anstalt, 1974).

2 Wegner, 'Der Krieg gegen die Sowjetunion 1942/43', pp. 807–810.

3 *Hitlers Weisungen für die Kriegführung 1939–1945: Dokumente des Oberkommandos der Wehrmacht* (Bernhard und Graefe: Frankfurt am Main, 1962), p. 184.

4 Kehrig, *Stalingrad*, p. 25.

5 Andreas Hillgruber, '"Nordlicht" – Die Deutschen Pläne zur Eroberung Leningrads im Jahre 1942', in *Festschrift Percy Ernst Schramm zu seinem Siebzigsten Geburtstag von Schülern und Freunden zugeeignet*, vol. 2, ed. Peter Classen and Peter Scheibert (Wiesbaden: Franz Steiner Verlag GmbH, 1964), pp. 269–287, here p. 270f.

6 *Hitlers Weisungen*, p. 186.

7 Wegner, 'Der Krieg gegen die Sowjetunion 1942/43', pp. 787 and 791.

8 Kehrig, *Stalingrad*, pp. 69–78.

9 Wegner, 'Der Krieg gegen die Sowjetunion 1942/43', pp. 856–864.

10 Alexander Hill, *The Red Army and the Second World War* (Cambridge: Cambridge University Press, 2017), pp. 361–374.

11 Wegner, 'Der Krieg gegen die Sowjetunion 1942/43', pp. 845–852.

12 *Hitlers Weisungen*, p. 196.

13 David M. Glantz and Jonathan House, *When Titans Clashed: How the Red Army Stopped Hitler* (Lawrence: University Press of Kansas, 2015), p. 120.

14 Franz Halder, *Kriegstagebuch: Tägliche Aufzeichnungen des Chefs des Generalstabes des Heeres 1939–1942. Band III, Der Russlandfeldzug bis zum Marsch auf Stalingrad (22.6.1941–24.9.1942)*, ed. Hans-Adolf Jacobsen and Alfred Philippi (Stuttgart: Kohlhammer, 1964), p. 494 (30 July 1942).

15 Hill, *Red Army*, pp. 353–359.

16 Wegner, 'Der Krieg gegen die Sowjetunion 1942/43', pp. 988–993.

17 Jochen Hellbeck, *Die Stalingrad-Protokolle: Sowjetische Augenzeugen berichten aus der Schlacht* (Frankfurt am Main: S. Fischer, 2013), p. 361.

18 The operational and tactical level, mostly from a Soviet perspective, is described in D. Glantz and J. M. House, *Armageddon in Stalingrad: September–November 1942, Vol. II* (Lawrence: University Press of Kansas, 2009).

19 See the detailed analysis of German numbers, operational approach, tactics, leadership, and logistics in Adrian Wettstein, *Die Wehrmacht im Stadtkampf, 1939–1942* (Paderborn: Schöningh, 2014), pp. 268–349.

20 Federal Military Archives, Freiburg i.Br. (BA-MA), RH 26-79/61, Engineer Battalion 179, Attack on the North Western Part of Red October's *Martinofenhalle* (Hall 4) on 11 November 1942, 12.11.42.

21 Wegner, 'Der Krieg gegen die Sowjetunion 1942/43', pp. 927–951.

22 Hillgruber, 'Nordlicht', p. 283f.

23 Svetlana Gerasimova, *The Rzhev Slaughterhouse: The Red Army's Forgotten 15-Month Campaign against Army Group Center, 1942–1943* (Solihull: Helion, 2013), pp. 74–100.

24 Wegner, 'Der Krieg gegen die Sowjetunion 1942/43', pp. 908–910.

25 See a detailed discussion on the planning process in David M. Glantz and Jonathan M. House, *Endgame at Stalingrad. Vol. III, Book One: November 1942* (Lawrence: University Press of Kansas, 2014), pp. 20–52.

26 Kehrig, *Stalingrad*, pp. 131–217.

27 Johannes Fischer, 'Über den Entschluss zur Luftversorgung Stalingrads. Ein Beitrag zur militärischen Führung im Dritten Reich', *Militärgeschichtliche Mitteilungen* 6 (1969), pp. 7–67.

28 Kehrig, *Stalingrad*, pp. 307–454.

29 David M. Glantz, *Zhukov's Greatest Defeat: The Red Army's Epic Disaster in Operation Mars, 1942* (Lawrence: University Press of Kansas, 1999), p. 320.

30 Joel S. A. Hayward, *Stopped at Stalingrad: The Luftwaffe and Hitler's Defeat in the East, 1942–1943* (Lawrence: University Press of Kansas, 1998), p. 330.

31 David M. Glantz and Jonathan M. House, *Endgame at Stalingrad. Vol. III, Book Two: December 1942–February 1943* (Lawrence: University Press of Kansas, 2014), pp. 20–52.

32 For a detailed analysis of this campaign, see Eberhard Schwarz, *Die Stabilisierung der Ostfront nach Stalingrad: Mansteins Gegenschlag zwischen Donez und Dnjepr im Frühjahr 1943* (Göttingen: Muster-Schmidt-Verlag, 1985), and David Glantz, *From the Don to the Dnepr: Soviet Offensive Operations, December 1942–August 1943* (London: Frank Cass, 1991), pp. 433–571.

33 Arthur F. Lykke understood strategy as a process to identify and balance ends, ways, and means. Ends are the goal of the strategy – the desired end state. Ways are the actions taken, whereas means are the resources required to achieve this end state. Arthur F. Lykke Jr., 'Toward an Understanding of Military Strategy', in *Military Strategy: Theory and Application*, ed. Arthur F. Lykke (Carlisle Barracks: US Army War College, 1989), pp. 3–8.

9

The Battle of Kursk, 1943

During the autumn and winter of 1942–1943, the last strategic major offensive of the Wehrmacht in the Caucasus and at Stalingrad had failed. Following this defeat, Adolf Hitler recognised that the Wehrmacht could not militarily overcome the Soviet Union as long as the German Reich was engaged in a war on multiple fronts. Consequently, the High Command of the army planned no offensives with ambitious objectives on the Eastern Front for 1943. On 18 February 1943, Hitler stated during a situation briefing in Zaporozhye, 'We cannot undertake any large-scale operations this year. We must avoid all risk. I envision that we will only make small maneuvers.'[1]

Within a limited space, the Red Army was to be drawn into a war of attrition, thereby weakened to such an extent that they would not initiate any further attacks in 1943. Hitler and his High Command intended to use the anticipated respite along the German-Soviet front to relocate the most combat-ready units of the Wehrmacht and Waffen-SS to the west. There they were to repel the expected Anglo-American landings, thus crushing the Western powers' hope for victory and compelling them to exit the war.[2]

9.1 Planning and Preparation

The German army's planning process for the assault rested on a fatal underestimation of Soviet forces. German intelligence was, on one hand, unable to realistically assess the resources of the Soviet Union, and on the other hand, it overlooked a large portion of the massive reserves that the Red Army had prepared for its own attacks in the spring of 1943. The Soviet General Staff planned several extensive operations for the summer of 1943. The principal offensive was to commence in the Belgorod-Kharkov region and initially be aimed at the Dnieper River, with the objective of cutting off the German Army Group South's retreat to the west. As a foundation for this operation, which was codenamed *Field Marshal Rumyantsev*, the substantial Soviet salient around the city of Kursk presented itself. This bulge had formed at the conclusion of the winter battles of 1942–1943. In the spring of 1943, the Red Army began to assemble significant forces in this Kursk salient.[3] This in turn appeared to provide the Wehrmacht with the opportunity for its planned battle of annihilation, intended to decisively weaken the Red Army within that year.

However, Hitler was not enthusiastic about the idea of attacking the Kursk salient. He favoured an offensive in the Donets Basin, as he deemed the Donbas, with its abundant natural resources, to be critical to the war effort. His generals nevertheless persuaded him that it would be more strategic to attack at Kursk. They believed that the Red Army would assemble a substantial portion of its entire offensive forces there. Thus, they argued, only at Kursk could a supposedly decisive defeat be inflicted upon the Soviets.[4]

Hitler found this argument persuasive and ultimately agreed. As the Wehrmacht subsequently began to assemble formidable attack forces at the Kursk salient, Soviet leadership quickly discerned that the next major battle would occur there. However, the Soviet High Command greatly overestimated German potential, believing that Hitler intended to launch another large offensive from the Kursk area, aimed ultimately at Moscow. Additionally, Soviet reconnaissance mistakenly reported that the Wehrmacht possessed hundreds of the new heavy 'Tiger' tanks, which were far superior to the Soviet tanks in one-on-one confrontations.[5] The Soviet High Command thus decided to initially take a defensive posture and transform the Kursk salient into a fortress. Through several deeply layered defence belts, fortified with all available means of defence, the Red Army was to first halt the German offensive and especially debilitate the Wehrmacht's armoured units. Only thereafter would the Soviet forces, including multiple tank armies, commence their counteroffensive.[6]

Both the Germans and Soviets initially anticipated that the Battle of Kursk would begin in early May 1943. Yet several events compelled Hitler to repeatedly delay the offensive. At the end of April, Colonel-General Walter Model, the commander of the Ninth Army, informed Hitler that his forces were still too weak to achieve a rapid victory at Kursk. Hitler thus decided to postpone the attack to allow time to equip Model's army with more tanks and assault guns. Furthermore, on 13 May, the last German-Italian forces in North Africa capitulated. Hitler feared that Italy might soon withdraw from the Tripartite Pact with Germany and Japan. Additionally, the dictator believed the Allies would soon land in Italy or Greece. Should this occur, he would likely have to withdraw units from the Eastern Front, and under no circumstances could those units be engaged in offensive battles at Kursk.

In the latter half of May 1943 weather conditions rendered the offensive impossible. Within the region of Oryol under Army Group Centre, rain fell almost without end, transforming roads and paths into quagmires that had to be temporarily closed to all traffic.

By June 1943, the situation in Southern Europe had stabilised and the weather on the Eastern Front had improved. However, Hitler had grown skeptical about whether an offensive at Kursk still made sense. Both the commander-in-chief of Army Group South, Field Marshal Erich von Manstein, and the chief of the Army General Staff, General of Infantry Kurt Zeitzler, had unnerved Hitler. They repeatedly emphasised that the Red Army was growing in strength much more rapidly than anticipated and far outmatched the Wehrmacht's forces. The longer the offensive was delayed, the greater the risk that the Soviets could not be decisively defeated. Hitler thus preferred to wait for the Red Army to initiate an attack first. Yet, by the end of June, Field Marshal Günther von Kluge, the commander-in-chief of Army Group Centre, convinced Hitler that it would be better to attack first and to do so as rapidly as possible. Consequently, the dictator fixed the date for the attack as 5 July 1943.[7]

In early July 1943 the Wehrmacht had amassed approximately 780,000 soldiers, 3,400 tanks and self-propelled guns, 1,800 aircraft, and 7,400 artillery pieces and mortars at the Kursk salient. In comparison, the Red Army had more than 1.9 million soldiers, 5,600 tanks and self-propelled guns, 3,600 aircraft, and 31,400 artillery pieces and mortars available for defending Kursk. Although the German High

Command was unaware of these precise figures, they were conscious that the Red Army held numerical superiority at Kursk. Nevertheless, both Hitler and the German General Staff were confident that the qualitative superiority of German weapons, training, and the Wehrmacht's tactical leadership principles would more than counterbalance the Soviets' quantitative advantage.

9.2 Operation Citadel: The German Attack on Kursk

On 5 July 1943, German forces initiated their attack on Kursk, in an operation codenamed *Citadel*. This marked the last major German summer offensive of the war. Attempting to advance on Kursk through a pincer movement from both north and south, three German armies aimed to cut off the salient and encircle the Soviet forces assembled there. From the north, within the area controlled by Army Group Centre, the Ninth Army under Colonel-General Model launched an assault with seventeen divisions, comprising ten infantry divisions, one armoured infantry division, and six panzer divisions. Model's forces were further reinforced by a heavy tank battalion equipped with Tigers and two tank destroyer battalions armed with the new heavy assault gun Ferdinand. This formidable weaponry, with its powerful armour, armament, and the deafening noise produced by its drive system, instilled terror in Soviet soldiers, sometimes escalating into panic.

Model's army faced the Soviet Central Front under Army General Konstantin K. Rokossovsky. This front was supported by six subordinate armies (along with its own air force), three of which were engaged in the defensive battle against Model's Ninth Army. The Soviet defence relied heavily on its vast numerical superiority in terms of artillery and mines, 400,000 of which had been laid in the Central Front's sector alone. The southern sector of the Kursk salient was guarded by the Voronezh Front under Army General Nikolai F. Vatutin. In addition to an air army, Vatutin commanded six ground armies, five of which participated in the defence against the German offensive Operation Citadel. In the southern part of the Kursk salient, the Red Army had laid an impressive 600,000 mines. However, the Soviets' density of artillery was not as high as it was when facing Model's Ninth Army, where Soviet leadership mistakenly anticipated the main German attack.[8]

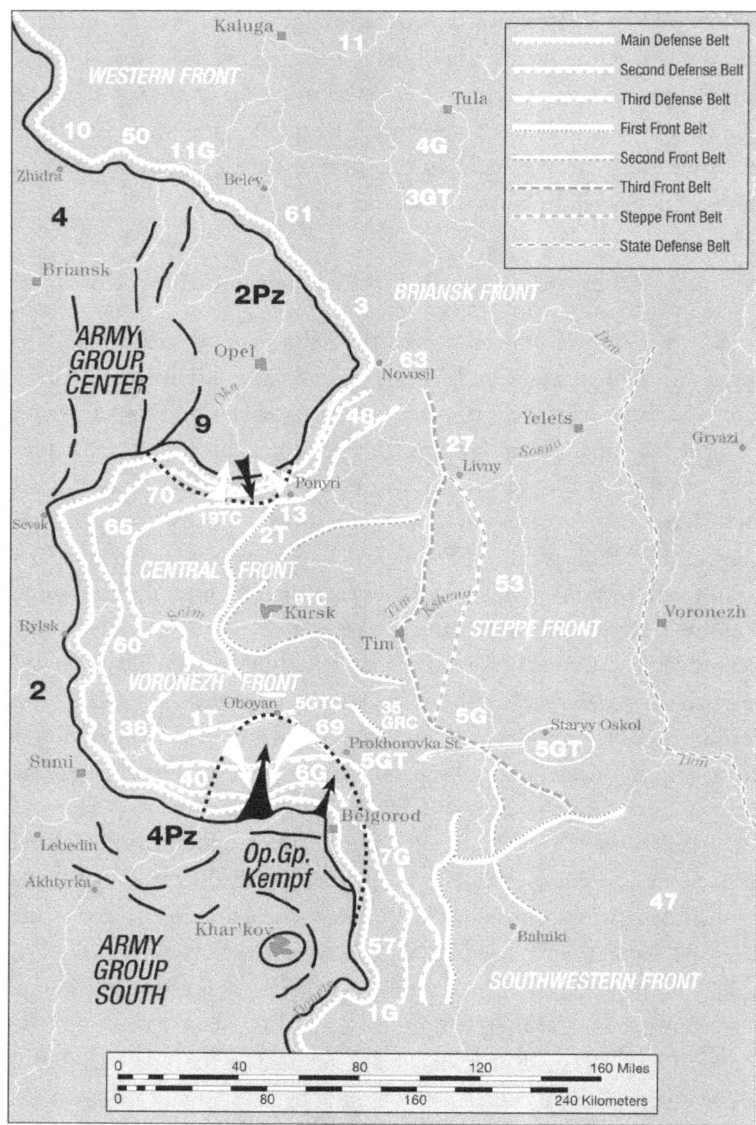

Map 8 German Kursk offensive (5–16 July 1943).

In preparation of launching the counteroffensive *Field Marshal Rumyantsev* with fresh forces immediately following the defensive phase, the Soviet command assembled a complete reserve army group

Figure 9.1 German offensive in the Orel region, July 1943. Source: ullstein bild via Getty Images.

outside the Kursk salient. Initially designated the Steppe Military District, it was renamed the Steppe Front from 9 July 1943 onward. Under its commander, Colonel-General Ivan S. Konev, were an air army and six ground armies. This substantial concentration of forces remained entirely undetected by German intelligence.[9]

Contrary to what was planned by the Soviet leadership, large portions of the Steppe Front had to be engaged early in July to halt the advances of two German armies in the southern sector of the Kursk salient. These were the Fourth Panzer Army, commanded by Colonel-General Hermann Hoth, and Army Detachment Kempf, commanded by General of Panzer Troops Werner Kempf.

Hoth's Fourth Panzer Army was designated to lead the primary assault on Kursk, while Army Detachment Kempf was tasked with offensively shielding its eastern flank. Both armies were part of Army Group South under Field Marshal von Manstein. In Operation Citadel, they deployed a total of sixteen divisions, including nine armoured and seven infantry divisions. The low number of infantry divisions emerged as a significant deficiency for the Wehrmacht. Time and again, the tank units had to halt due to a lack of infantry to secure their flanks or hold captured territory. Although Manstein had identified this weakness in the spring, the manpower resources of the Eastern Army could not facilitate greater troop concentration. Hitler also believed that more tanks could replace infantry.

On the eve of the offensive, elements of the Fourth Panzer Army conducted limited advances to enhance their starting positions. German defectors had also disclosed that the main attack would occur on the morning of 5 July.[10] Soviet leadership intended to capitalise on this information and pre-empt the Germans. Just before the German assault, Soviet artillery planned to bombard the enemy's staging areas. In addition, hundreds of Soviet planes were launched to attack enemy airfields at dawn and crush the German Air Force on the ground. However, the artillery barrage largely missed its mark, and when Soviet pilots appeared over the front, they discovered that the German fighter planes had already ascended to intercept them. Consequently, the Battle of Kursk began with an intense aerial dogfight, during which Soviet air regiments sustained heavy damages, losing more than 300 aircraft that day.[11]

Despite being significantly outnumbered, the German Air Force achieved nearly 4,800 sorties against the enemy on the first day of the attack through rolling operations – a strategy where airplanes are constantly present over the battlefield, with squadrons being refuelled and re-armed immediately upon landing, ready to take off again at once. This was approximately 1,400 more sorties than the Soviets conducted. Due in no small part to this remarkable air support, the German assault was initially successful at key points. On the very first day of the attack, the Germans managed to penetrate the particularly well-fortified first line of defence of the Red Army, both in the north and south of Kursk.[12] By the next day, the second defensive line was also overcome. The Soviet side was stunned, as during the months-long preparation for the German assault, they had particularly fortified these first two defensive belts. In a hasty and rushed response, both the Central Front and the Voronezh Front deployed their operational reserves to repel the attackers and push them back to their initial positions.

In the north, on 6 July, the Soviet Second Tank Army, commanded by Lieutenant-General Alexey G. Rodin, attacked the German XXXXVII Panzer Corps, constituting the centrepiece of Model's assault forces. The Soviet counterattack, however, quickly faltered, suffering heavy losses.[13]

In the south, Lieutenant-General Mikhail Y. Katukov's First Tank Army engaged the German Fourth Panzer Army on 7 July. The following day, the tank battle in the southern sector reached its initial peak when three Soviet tank corps attempted to encircle the II SS Panzer Corps. As already seen in the north, the distinct inferiority of the Soviet tanks in direct engagements with German armoured vehicles was evident in the south. On 8 July alone, the Red Army lost 343 tanks and self-propelled guns in the southern sector of Kursk, with about two-thirds considered total losses. In contrast, the losses of Hoth's Fourth Panzer Army amounted to only around 20 tanks and self-propelled guns. Furthermore, the Soviets had sacrificed portions of their operational reserves without successfully pushing the enemy back as planned, allowing German units to continue their advance.[14]

9.3 The Soviet Counteroffensives

Despite initial success, Model's assault became bogged down in the third Soviet defensive belt from 7 July onward. Many of the heavy tanks and assault guns fell victim to mines, and the relentless Soviet artillery fire rendered any further progress impossible for the grenadiers.[15] Field Marshal von Kluge, the commander-in-chief of Army Group Centre, was indeed correct when he noted on 11 July that the failure of the Ninth Army's attack was 'solely attributable to the effects of the enemy's artillery, rocket launchers, and mortar fire'.[16] He retained hope that the offensive might be resumed after a realignment of his forces. However, on the following day, the Red Army initiated its first major counteroffensive, known as *Operation Kutuzov*. Two army groups, the Western Front under Colonel-General Vasily D. Sokolovsky and the Bryansk Front under Colonel-General Markian M. Popov, assaulted the German bulge around the city of Oryol. Sokolovsky and Popov's combined forces consisted of 720,000 soldiers, almost 3,300 tanks and self-propelled guns, and 16,000 artillery pieces and mortars. They were opposed by only the German Second Panzer Army, with 120,000 men, 550 tanks and self-propelled guns, and 940 artillery pieces and mortars. With these limited forces, the Wehrmacht was unable to prevent Soviet break-throughs. Consequently, units of the Ninth Army had to be rapidly withdrawn from the Kursk salient and redeployed to defend the sector of the Second Panzer Army.[17] Operation Citadel had failed. A continuation of the attack on Kursk by the Ninth Army was now out of the question, and the forces of Army Group South alone were too feeble to encircle the Soviet armies in the Kursk bulge. As Field Marshal von Manstein himself stated on 13 July, the striking power of his attacking forces 'reached at best to the section south of Kursk'.[18]

In contrast to Model's Ninth Army, the Fourth Panzer Army and Army Detachment Kempf in the southern sector of the Kursk bulge had made further gains in the preceding days, and on 11 July, they even broke through the third Soviet defence belt.[19] To finally halt the attackers and launch an offensive south of Kursk, the Soviet High Command planned a significant counterstrike for 12 July. Several Soviet armies were to attack the German offensive wedge in a concentrated manner and shatter the German Fourth Panzer Army. The primary roles were assigned to two large, fresh formations acquired from the 'strategic reserve' of the Steppe Front: the Fifth Guards Army and the Fifth Guards Tank Army. The latter, commanded by Lieutenant-General Pavel A. Rotmistrov, possessed more than 900 tanks and self-propelled guns as of 12 July. Rotmistrov's army aimed to annihilate German tank forces south-west of the village of Prokhorovka, breach the German lines, and advance thirty kilometres south-west.[20] To coordinate the assault, Stalin personally dispatched Soviet Chief of Staff Marshal Alexander M. Vasilevsky to Prokhorovka. Vasilevsky panicked, however, when he found that German spearheads had penetrated much further than anticipated, leading him to hastily initiate a counterattack on the morning of 12 July, without adequate preparation or terrain analysis.

The main thrust of the Fifth Guards Tank Army collided south-west of Prokhorovka with the II SS Panzer Corps. German reconnaissance had failed, and the approach of fresh Soviet forces went undetected. The Waffen-SS soldiers were consequently caught entirely off guard by the Soviet onslaught. Nevertheless, they managed to repulse enemy attacks and deal a severe blow to the Fifth Guards Tank Army. Not only could the

Germans maintain their positions, but they also knocked out 382 tanks and self-propelled guns. Of those, 227 were so heavily damaged that they were written off as total losses. Soviet claims that the Germans also lost hundreds of armoured vehicles at Prokhorovka can easily be refuted. Over the entire course of Operation Citadel, the II SS Panzer Corps reported only forty-four tanks and self-propelled guns as total write-offs, including four heavily damaged vehicles which were sent back to Germany for factory maintenance.[21] Yet on the eve of the Battle of Prokhorovka, twenty-three of these vehicles had already been reported as total losses. Therefore, the II SS Panzer Corps cannot have lost more than twenty-one tanks and self-propelled guns at Prokhorovka.[22]

Manstein believed that the heavy Soviet losses signalled that the Red Army had exhausted its strength in the southern sector of the Kursk bulge. The field marshal was optimistic that Operation Citadel could be successful. However, on 13 July, Hitler summoned Manstein and Field Marshal von Kluge to a situation briefing at his headquarters. During this meeting, Kluge pointed out that his forces could not continue the attack on Kursk. The Red Army had already broken through the German lines in the Oryol salient, and he needed as many forces as possible for defence. Manstein, on the other hand, spoke out vehemently for the continuation of Operation Citadel. To avoid further discussion with the obstinate Manstein, Hitler commanded that even Army Group South should relinquish forces. Three days earlier, the Western Allies had landed in Sicily (Operation Husky). Hitler now asserted that without detachments from the Eastern Front, he could not stabilise the situation there.

This was merely an excuse, and in reality, Hitler sent not a single unit from the Eastern Front to Italy in the ten days that followed. But this pretext served its purpose: Manstein accepted the cancellation of Operation Citadel without further objection and came to terms with the failure of the once-promising summer offensive. Hitler's lie that he had to call off the attack due to the Anglo-American Operation Husky became one of the most enduring myths about the Battle of Kursk, a belief still held by many today.[23]

On 13 July, Manstein was at least able to persuade the dictator that he could still achieve a significant victory against the Red Army. Manstein believed the Soviets had already deployed all their reserves south of Kursk and were on the brink of collapse. In reality, this was not the case, as the Red Army still had a considerable number of reserves. However, German intelligence had failed to recognise this. Since Hitler was no better informed about the opposing forces than Manstein, he permitted a limited assault south of Kursk, aiming to destroy the assembled Soviet tank forces there.

The Red Army, however, foiled this plan: on 17 July, the Soviet South-western Front under Army General Rodion Y. Malinovsky and the Southern Front under Colonel-General Fyodor I. Tolbukhin launched an offensive in the Donbas with a total of nine armies. In the Donets Basin, the Germans had only two armies. Against these, the Red Army deployed more than double the number of soldiers and more than four times as many tanks and self-propelled guns. Within days, the Soviet forces achieved a significant breach in the German Sixth Army's line at the Mius River. A breakthrough to Stalino (now Donetsk), the capital of the Donets Basin, seemed imminent for the Red Army. To prevent this, Manstein had to relocate two of his tank corps from the southern sector of Kursk to the Donbas.

Manstein was also forced to transfer tank forces to Army Group Centre. In the early days of the Kutuzov offensive, the Soviet Eleventh Guards Army under Lieutenant-General Ivan Bagramyan significantly breached the German front north-west of Oryol. On 19 July, Bagramyan's leading tank units even managed to reach the Bryansk-Oryol railway line. The German Ninth Army and the Second Panzer Army, both now com-manded by Colonel-General Model, risked encirclement in the Oryol area. With assistance from the *Großdeutschland* Panzer Grenadier Division, brought up from the southern sector, Model successfully repelled Bagramyan's thrust into his lines by the end of July. As a result, the Soviet Kutuzov offensive lost substantial momentum.[24]

In the subsequent weeks, the Red Army had to laboriously advance westward near Oryol, engaged in arduous fighting and suffering heavy losses. On 5 August 1943, formations of the Bryansk Front succeeded in liberating the city of Oryol. However, Soviet forces could not prevent Model's troops from methodically retreating to new defensive positions. By the time the Germans had pulled back to the Hagen Line on 18 August, the Red Army had completed the Kutuzov offensive, securing a victory in the second phase of the Battle of Kursk. The casualties were tremendous. According to official Russian figures, the Kutuzov operation

Figure 9.2 Soviet infantry attacking German positions, July 1943. Source: Sovfoto/Universal Images Group via Getty Images.

cost the Red Army 2,586 tanks and self-propelled guns, among other losses.[25] However, the actual losses were likely higher, as official Russian numbers have often been found unreliable.

While Model had managed to orchestrate a relatively orderly withdrawal of his forces from the Oryol salient, Manstein's situation in the southern sector of the Eastern Front was more perilous. Although the Germans had succeeded in repelling the Soviet thrust towards Stalino and temporarily stabilising the situation on the Mius River in early August,[26] the Soviets had achieved a significant objective: substantially weakening the German front north of Kharkov. Only a few Wehrmacht tank forces remained there. Conversely, the Red Army had replenished its units near Kharkov and brought in fresh troops. By the beginning of August, the Voronezh Front and Steppe Front had at their disposal a total of one million soldiers, along with 2,440 tanks and self-propelled guns.

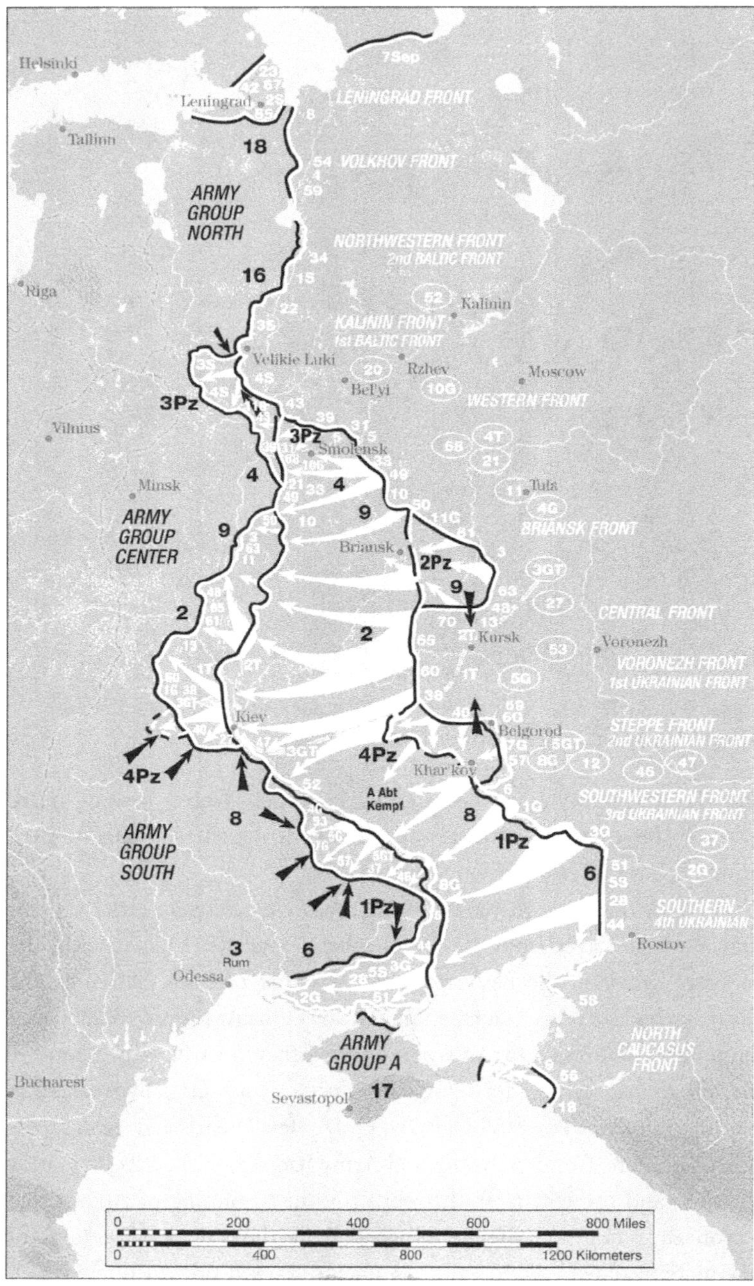

Map 9 Summer–winter campaign (June–December 1943).

On 3 August, the third and final phase of the Battle of Kursk commenced with the Soviet offensive bearing the codename *Field Marshal Rumyantsev*. Seven Soviet armies, two of them tank armies, assaulted German positions in the southern segment of the Kursk bulge, and three more armies joined in the subsequent days. The already-weakened German Fourth Panzer Army and Army Detachment Kempf could not withstand this concentrated force. On the very first day of the attack, Soviet troops broke through the German lines north of Kharkov and pushed south-west, seemingly unstoppable. To avoid being encircled and destroyed, the Germans were forced to retreat rapidly. By 5 August, the Red Army had liberated Belgorod, and two days later, the vanguards of Lieutenant-General Katukov's First Tank Army reached Bogodukhov, positioning themselves fifty kilometres west-northwest of Kharkov, nearly behind the German forces engaged near Kharkov.[27]

In a hurried response, the Germans redeployed several panzer divisions from the Donbas back to the Kharkov region. They managed to halt Katukov's advance near Bogodukhov, and in the ensuing days, both sides committed more units to the area, resulting in a tremendous tank battle. During this clash, the Voronezh Front's troops, commanded by Army General Vatutin, attempted to continue their breakthrough towards the south-west, aiming for Poltava, a vital communication and logistics hub for Army Group South. Manstein countered Vatutin's primary thrust with all the forces he could muster, striving to halt the Red Army's further advance on Poltava.[28]

For Manstein the city of Kharkov was of secondary importance – but not for Hitler. Primarily for reasons of political prestige, Hitler was determined to maintain control of the Ukrainian metropolis. He urged Manstein to retain Kharkov under any circumstance. Hitler likely had an additional motive for this order – one he concealed from the field marshal. In August 1943 the commander of the Security Police and SS Security Service in Kharkov, *SS-Sturmbannführer* Friedrich Kranebitter, was evidently attempting to eliminate traces of German crimes. In Kharkov, there were several extensive mass graves, each holding thousands of murdered Jews. Since spring 1943 the SS and police had been working to eradicate evidence of the Holocaust across the occupied territories of the Soviet Union by exhuming mass graves and incinerating the bodies. However, as with many other locations, they failed in Kharkov since the Red Army arrived before the perpetrators could complete their grim assignment.[29]

By 11 August, the Voronezh Front and Steppe Front had already committed eleven armies to battle. Yet the Red Army's strength was still not fully deployed. The next day, south-east of Kharkov, Colonel-General Vasily I. Kuznetsov's First Guards Army entered the fray as part of Malinowski's South-western Front. Its task was to encircle Kharkov from the south.[30] The situation for the units of Army Detachment Kempf, assigned to hold Kharkov, became ever more desperate as the Red Army now squeezed them from three sides. Even a change in leadership made no difference: on 15 August, General Wöhler replaced the increasingly pessimistic General Kempf, and the following day Army Detachment Kempf was re-designated the Eighth Army.[31]

While the armoured forces of Army Group South, about sixty kilometres west of Kharkov, thwarted all breakthrough attempts of the Voronezh Front towards the south-west, the units of the Steppe Front and parts of the South-western Front relentlessly advanced on Kharkov. On 18 August, unable to ignore the dire situation any longer and wanting to avoid a second Stalingrad, Hitler finally granted Manstein permission to 'abandon Kharkov in case of extreme emergency'.[32]

But it was not only Manstein who was under intense pressure; General Vatutin, the commander of the Voronezh Front, also felt the strain. On the night of 22 August, Stalin urged him to stop dispersing his attacking forces and to concentrate them near Akhtyrka.[33] That was where most of the German tank units were positioned, hindering Vatutin's troops' progression towards Poltava and the Dnieper. On the morning of 22 August, Vatutin's forces thus launched a united assault south-east of Akhtyrka. Initially, the situation seemed promising for the Soviet soldiers; it appeared they would achieve a breakthrough behind the concentrated German tank forces. However, in the afternoon, German tank units counterattacked and severed the tip of Vatutin's assault wedge. The Soviet push from Bogodukhov to Poltava was thereby definitively thwarted.

Despite this operational setback, the Red Army was able to triumph in the Battle of Kursk. On 22 August, the units of the Steppe Front had nearly encircled Kharkov. Consequently, the Germans had to withdraw from the city that night. The next day, Colonel-General Konev's troops entered Kharkov as liberators. This marked the end of the fifty-day Battle of Kursk.

9.4 Balance and Outlook

Kursk was not only the largest battle of the Second World War but also one of the bloodiest engagements in history. The losses of the Red Army are still debated; the precise numbers may never be determined. It is likely that at least 1.2 million Soviet soldiers were killed or wounded, and 7,000 tanks and self-propelled guns, as well as 3,000 aircraft, were destroyed. In contrast, the Wehrmacht suffered approximately 203,000 casualties, including killed, wounded, and missing soldiers, along with 1,200 tanks and self-propelled guns and 650 aircraft.[34]

Although the Red Army sustained disproportionately higher losses and failed to achieve its operational objectives, it nevertheless inflicted a severe defeat on the Wehrmacht at Kursk. The Germans failed to reach any of the goals they had set for their summer offensive; they could not manage to break the Soviet forces in the Kursk bulge, nor were they able to critically weaken the Red Army and strip it of its offensive capability in 1943. Furthermore, the hoped-for shortening of the front lines, and the capture of hundreds of thousands of Soviet soldiers to be used for labour in the German Reich, remained unfulfilled dreams. In reality, during Operation Citadel the Germans only managed to take 40,600 prisoners.[35]

Hitler had hoped that a German victory at Kursk would convince the world that the Wehrmacht was ultimately invincible. However, the reverse happened: for the first time, the Red Army was able to repel a German summer offensive within just a few days, and despite tremendous losses, it managed to launch counteroffensives almost everywhere along the German-Soviet front. By the end of August, the combat effectiveness of the German Eastern Army was depleted, and the losses could no longer be compensated.

By the spring of 1943 numerous Wehrmacht commanders and soldiers had sought to foster a positive relationship with the Soviet civilian population. This was driven not only by practical considerations but also by the understanding that the Soviet Union would be hard to defeat without the voluntary collaboration of the local population. However, the defeat at Kursk also triggered a transformation in this regard. As the Germans were compelled to withdraw from Ukraine once again – this time permanently – in the summer of 1943 the indigenous population in some areas was presented with the stark choice of either marching westward or being executed.[36]

Thus the Battle of Kursk marked a watershed moment in several ways. Militarily it was a clear defeat for Germany, but for the millions of Soviet people under Nazi rule, the Soviet victory marked their final liberation.

Notes

1 Federal Military Archives, Freiburg i.Br. (BA-MA), N 507/99, Estate of Erich von Manstein, Personal File February 1943, fol. 106.
2 R. Töppel, *Kursk 1943: The Greatest Battle of the Second World War* (Helion: Warwick, 2018), pp. 20–24.
3 D. M. Glantz and H. S. Orenstein, eds., *The Battle for Kursk 1943: The Soviet General Staff Study* (London: Frank Cass, 1999), pp. 1–17.
4 Töppel, *Kursk 1943*, pp. 24–30.
5 P. Samsonov, *IS-2: Development, Design and Production of Stalin's War Hammer* (London: Military History Group, 2022), pp. 32–33.
6 D. M. Glantz and J. M. House, *The Battle of Kursk* (Lawrence: University Press of Kansas, 1999), pp. 55–73.
7 Töppel, *Kursk 1943*, pp. 30–37.
8 R. W. Harrison, ed., *The Battle of Kursk: The Red Army's Defensive Operations and Counter-Offensive, July–August 1943, Soviet General Staff* (Solihull: Helion, 2016), pp. 47–75.
9 Glantz and House, *The Battle of Kursk*, p. 74.
10 V. N. Zamulin, *The Battle of Kursk: Controversial and Neglected Aspects* (Solihull: Helion, 2017), pp. 178–191.
11 Töppel, *Kursk 1943*, pp. 83–89.
12 The southern part of the Kursk salient is described in great detail in C. A. Lawrence, *Kursk: The Battle of Prokhorovka* (Sheridan: Aberdeen Books, 2015), pp. 359–429.
13 Töppel, *Kursk 1943*, pp. 102–104.
14 Lawrence, *Kursk*, pp. 601–659.
15 M. Nevshemal, *Objective Ponyri! The Defeat of XXXXI. Panzerkorps at Ponyri Train Station* (Sydney: Leaping Horseman, 2015), pp. 79–103.
16 BA-MA, RH 24–46/91, Generalkommando XXXXVI. Panzerkorps, Ia, Kriegstagebuch No. 7, 1.6–15.8.1943, fol. 90.
17 Töppel, *Kursk 1943*, pp. 136–139.
18 Private archive of the von Manstein family, Erich von Manstein estate, personal war diary No. 5, 30.3.1943–1.4.1944, entry dated 13.7.1943, unpaginated.

19 Lawrence, *Kursk*, pp. 725–760.

20 V. N. Zamulin, *Demolishing the Myth: The Tank Battle at Prokhorovka, Kursk, July 1943: An Operational Narrative* (Solihull: Helion, 2011), pp. 268–276.

21 BA-MA, RS 2-2/25, Generalkommando II. SS-Panzerkorps, KTB Nr. 6 der Abt. Qu. vom 1.6.1943–2.8.1943 mit Anlagen, fol. 109.

22 Ibid., fol. 25. For a detailed look at the German tank losses at Prokhorovka, see also R. Töppel, 'The Battle of Prokhorovka: Facts against Fables', *Journal of Slavic Military Studies*, 34 (2021), pp. 251–270.

23 See for example M. Healy, *Zitadelle: The German Offensive against the Kursk Salient 4–17 July 1943* (Stroud: The History Press, 2008), pp. 353–354; L. Clark, *Kursk: The Greatest Battle, Eastern Front 1943* (London: Headline Review, 2011), pp. 376–377; K.-H. Frieser, 'The Battle of the Kursk Salient', in *Militärgeschichtliches Forschungsamt, Potsdam, Germany. Germany and the Second World War, Vol. VIII: The Eastern Front 1943–1944: The War in the East and on the Neighbouring Fronts*, ed. Militärgeschichtliches Forschungsamt (Oxford: Clarendon Press, 2017), pp. 145–146.

24 E. E. Shchekotikhin, *Krupneyshee tankovoe srazhenie Velikoy Otechestvennoy: Bitva za Orël* (Moscow: Yauza/Eksmo, 2009), pp. 113–130.

25 G. F. Krivosheev, ed., *Soviet Casualties and Combat Losses in the Twentieth Century* (London: Greenhill/Stackpole, 1997), p. 262; Shchekotikhin, *Krupneyshee tankovoe srazhenie Velikoy Otechestvennoy*, p. 394.

26 G. M. Nipe, *Decision in the Ukraine, Summer 1943: II. SS and III. Panzerkorps* (Winnipeg: J. J. Fedorowicz, 1996), pp. 249–257.

27 D. M. Glantz, *From the Don to the Dnepr: Soviet Offensive Operations, December 1942–August 1943* (London: Frank Cass, 1991), pp. 291–293.

28 Töppel, *Kursk 1943*, pp. 147–149.

29 A. Angrick, *'Aktion 1005' – Spurenbeseitigung von NS-Massenverbrechen 1942–1945: Eine 'geheime Reichssache' im Spannungsfeld von Kriegswende und Propaganda*, vol. 1, 2nd ed. (Göttingen: Wallstein, 2019), pp. 359–360.

30 Glantz, *From the Don to the Dnepr*, p. 328.

31 Töppel, *Kursk 1943*, p. 148.

32 BA-MA, RH 2/3061, Operationsabteilung des Generalstabs des Heeres, Kriegstagebuch, vol. 7, 1.8.–8.10.1943, fol. 61.

33 Glantz, *From the Don to the Dnepr*, pp. 349–351.

34 Töppel, *Kursk 1943*, p. 154.

35 BA-MA, RH 2/2047, Generalstab des Heeres, Abteilung Fremde Heere Ost, Lageunterrichtung König Boris von Bulgarien, 19.7.1943, fol. 112-3.

36 J. Rutherford, 'Germany's Total War: Combat and Occupation around the Kursk Salient, 1943', *The Journal of Military History*, 85 (2021), pp. 954–979, here p. 977.

10

The Siege of Leningrad, 1941–1944

10.1   Background, Geography, History

The siege of Leningrad was an uncharacteristic episode in the history of the Soviet-German War and the Second World War as a whole. It does not fit into the basic strategic 'forward-and-back' narrative of the Red Army's 1941–1945 war, with Stalingrad as the midpoint; it was almost the opposite of a war of movement. And yet in terms of tragic scale and human consequences, it exceeds almost any other single wartime event. Various factors explain these anomalies; some are historical, some geographical or topographical, and some relate to developments on the Soviet-German front as a whole.

Leningrad had a pre-war population of 2,544,000 and was the fifth-largest city in Europe (after London, Paris, Berlin, and Moscow). The city, formerly known as St Petersburg, had served as the imperial capital for something like 200 years, before Lenin's government moved to the geographical safety of Moscow in 1918. It became, and remained in 1941, a centre of Russian industry, especially heavy engineering and shipbuilding. It was also the 'cradle of the revolution', and was celebrated or vilified for that.

The city always had a certain artificial quality. It was created in the nearly empty wilderness of the Neva River delta (part of what was known as Ingria) by Peter the Great.[1] The Russian ruler's objective was to give his state direct access to the open sea. The new city was some distance from the traditional heartland of central Russia. As it grew, it depended on food supplies from outside, and this would still be the case when an enemy army surrounded it in 1941. After the collapse of the Russian Empire in 1917–1918, when Estonia and Finland became independent states, Petrograd (from 1924 named Leningrad) lay exposed on the very edge of Soviet territory.

On the other hand, geography did provide certain advantages. Leningrad/St Petersburg is set on the Karelian isthmus, between the Gulf of Finland and Lake Ladoga.[2] In 1941, the two bodies of water protected the city. As far as the northern end of the isthmus was concerned, serious attack was unlikely from the north shore of the Gulf of Finland. In August and September 1941, as a co-belligerent with Germany, the Finns took back the large part of the isthmus which the Soviets had annexed after the Winter War (roughly from Vyborg to near Beloostrov). However, with their small army they made no attempt to move further towards Leningrad, and it was not practical to deploy German troops here. Meanwhile the western sea approaches to Leningrad were covered by the Gulf of Finland, in which lay the island fortress of Kronshtadt.

Some forty kilometres east of Leningrad was Lake Ladoga, from which water flowed down the Neva through Leningrad. Entering Lake Ladoga from the south was the Volkhov River. Also significant was the Svir' River, which entered Lake Ladoga from the east. It marked the extreme limit at which the Finnish Army would be prepared to operate.

Unlike Moscow or Kiev, Leningrad could be reached relatively easily. Estonia and Latvia had been annexed by the USSR in 1940, but adequate defences had not been put in place there and the population was hostile to rule from Moscow. In the summer of 1941, only ten weeks were actually required to drive from East Prussia to the outskirts of Leningrad. Once the outskirts of the city had been reached, it was relatively easy to cut Leningrad off from the Soviet 'mainland' to the south.

It was also important that the terrain of the hinterland – the Leningrad region (*oblast'*) and part of the Novgorod region – was a sparsely populated wilderness of swamps and forest. There were few paved roads, and movement was difficult for much of the year for wheeled vehicles and tanks. Once the German army was in place, especially between the Neva and the Volkhov Rivers, it proved very difficult to drive it out, even when the numerical balance of forces began to change in the Soviets' favour.

The final feature was six rail lines radiating from Leningrad to the south and southeast. The German Army would sever all these railways by early September 1941, the most important being the main line to Moscow. However, Leningrad was able to maintain a tenuous connection to the outside world, thanks to the rail line from the town of Vologda and the main Soviet network; it ran west through the town of Tikhvin to a railhead southeast of Lake Ladoga. From here, supplies and reinforcements could be sent into the city; the railway also provided a route for evacuation. Meanwhile, troops behind the Volkhov River trying to break the blockade from outside had working rail links with central Russia.

Geography was on the side of the defenders of Leningrad, despite its exposed position and the vulnerability of its supply routes. Even Stalin came to realise the defensibility of the city, as he admitted to one comrade in the middle of October: 'Moscow cannot be defended like Leningrad.'[3]

10.2   The Retreat to Leningrad, June to December 1941

The essence of the Barbarossa campaign, as laid out in Hitler's pre-war Directive No. 21 of 18 December 1940, was the rapid destruction of the Red Army in the borderlands of the USSR, west of the Dvina and Dnepr Rivers. The Wehrmacht planners expected that, having fatally crippled their Soviet opponents, a significant portion of the German forces would advance northeast through the former Baltic states: 'Only after the accomplishment of offensive operations, which must be followed by the capture of Leningrad and Kronshtadt [naval base], are further offensive operations authorised with the objective of occupying Moscow.'[4]

When war actually began in June 1941, the Wehrmacht did indeed rapidly break through the poorly prepared defences all along the long front. In mid-July, a month into the war, Hitler made a fateful decision about the deployment of his forces. Rather than concentrate for an immediate Panzer-led drive on Moscow, he would deploy mobile armoured forces on the flanks of the invasion, in the Baltic region (including Leningrad) and Ukraine. In Army Group North, General Erich Hoepner's Panzer Group 4 was reinforced in July by two panzer divisions and two motorised divisions, as well as 400 planes.

The selection of Leningrad as an objective, after the initial phase, may have been motivated by political factors for Hitler, based on the city's revolutionary past. But it was in line with his December 1940 Barbarossa directive. It also reflected the importance of the war industries of Leningrad, as well as a concern about the danger to vital German shipping from Soviet naval forces based there. By this time, mid-July 1941, Army Group North's spearheads had already reached the Luga River line, only 130 kilometres from Leningrad, so there was no doubt also an element of opportunism. In addition, the capture of the city on the Neva could be expected to bring an end to fighting in the northern theatre. Unlike the situation with Moscow and Kiev, no major population centre was located behind Leningrad and there was little threat of any attempt to reclaim the city from the east once it had fallen. As soon as Leningrad was captured, formations from Army Group North could safely be transferred to other fronts.

Army Group North, commanded by Field Marshal Wilhelm Ritter von Leeb, had cut quickly through Estonia. At the end of August 1941, a German drive through Novgorod unexpectedly cut the last two railway lines connecting Leningrad to the rest of the Soviet Union. Soviet problems of supply and troop movement were now drastically complicated. Then, on 8 September, Panzer forces driving around the southern outskirts of Leningrad captured a corridor on the southern bank of the Neva River, occupying the town of Shlissel'burg and the southwestern shore of Lake Ladoga. With this, Leningrad's last land link with the mainland (along the shore of Lake Ladoga) was broken. The 900-day 'siege' had begun.

The Soviet defence of Leningrad was not well conducted, even when the invaders reached the Luga River about 110 kilometres from the city. The retreating remnants of the border force had been shattered by weeks of retreat. Soviet leaders in Leningrad initiated the raising of People's Militia (*Narodnoe opolchenie*) formations, but these proved ineffective. The overall commander in the northern theatre, Marshal K. E. Voroshilov, was incompetent, even though he was a member of Stalin's pantheon.

Especially important was the arrival on 10 September 1941 of General G. K. Zhukov, who for some weeks was able to stiffen the defence. David Glantz properly stressed Zhukov's role,[5] effectively replacing Voroshilov. However, three weeks after his arrival, Zhukov was ordered away to deal with an even more existential crisis west of Moscow. And the local front immediately south and west of Leningrad had already stabilised. In addition, a fifty-five-kilometre-long, twenty-five-kilometre-deep coastal bridgehead (*platsdarm*) had been held west of the city around Oranienbaum, which was supported by artillery from nearby Kronshtadt. More important, in general, five days before Zhukov arrived in Leningrad, Hitler had made another vital strategic decision to begin transferring troops and aircraft away from Army Group North in preparation for the assault on Moscow; this involved the vital mobile formations of Hoepner's Panzer Group 4.

At this critical time no one could be certain whether Leningrad would remain in Soviet hands, whether like Kiev it would be abandoned, or whether it would simply be barricaded and starved. In early September 1941, Moscow despatched secret orders to prepare for the scuttling of the ships of the Baltic Fleet and the destruction of any industrial plants that could be used by the enemy. In late October, as

Figure 10.1 Women help dig Leningrad's defences, 25 October 1941.

the Germans advanced on Tikhvin, the Red Army high command ordered the Leningrad commanders to strive to establish contact with the Soviet armies operating southeast of Leningrad, lest they risk falling into captivity 'in the event of the impossibility of holding Leningrad'.[6] (The Germans began the drive towards Tikhvin in late October and captured it on 8 November.)

In truth, events for both flanks of the Barbarossa campaign were in these weeks overshadowed by developments in the centre, in particular the German advance on the Moscow axis. Operation Typhoon was specifically intended to destroy the Soviet armies defending the capital. Caught by surprise, the Red Army suffered a catastrophic defeat in the Battle of Viaz'ma-Briansk in the first half of October. The road to the capital seemed open, and partial evacuation had to be ordered; fortunately, the autumn rain and mud of the *rasputitsa* slowed the advance of the Wehrmacht.

The historic Red Army counteroffensive in front of Moscow took place in the second week of December. In late November it had seemed that Moscow was about to fall; two or three weeks later, it was abundantly clear that this was not going to happen. Soviet reserves had been thrown into the battle, and German Army Group Centre was now under a heavy counterattack and appeared to face a disaster on the scale of 1812. One result of the fighting in front of Moscow was the recapture of Kalinin (Tver'), which kept open a key supply railway from central Russia to the Soviet forces around Leningrad. Even more important from the point of view of Leningrad's defenders, the invaders were forced to give up their most advanced position on the front of Army Group North, east of Leningrad. This was at Tikhvin, which controlled the railway from the 'mainland' to Lake Ladoga – and Leningrad.

Field Marshal Leeb was replaced as commander of Army Group North by General Georg von Küchler in January. Leeb's removal was partly related to Hitler's removal in December of other senior commanders, including Brauchitsch (Army C-in-C), Bock (Army Group Centre), and Rundstedt (Army Group South). But Leeb's departure also came from his failure to take Leningrad or hold Tikhvin, along with his pessimism about keeping the Eighteenth Army and other elements of Army Group North in forward positions after the crisis at Moscow. His successor had commanded Eighteenth Army, the formation most directly involved in the fighting near Leningrad; Küchler in turn was replaced by General Georg Lindemann.

Developments in December 1941 were important in another respect for Leningrad's fate, as they deterred the Finns from any decisive involvement. Defeated in the Winter War of 1939–1940 and forced to give up substantial territory, the Finnish government had allowed Germany to base some air and ground forces on Finnish territory before the June 1941 invasion. They did not immediately declare war on the USSR on 22 June, and there was no formal alliance treaty with Germany. As soon as the Soviets attacked German bases in Finland, however, the country became involved in the so-called Continuation War. The Finnish government and Commander-in-Chief Marshal Carl Gustav Mannerheim kept their commitments vague but undertook to confine future operations against the Red Army to the far (western) side of Lake Ladoga. As already mentioned, the Finns were able to occupy the larger part of the Karelian Isthmus when the Red Army formations there had to be redeployed to face the Panzers advancing through Estonia; Vyborg was recaptured by the Finnish Army on 30 August 1941.

After the leeb's troops took Shlissel'burg and Tikhvin, the German government urged the Finns to take a more active part in the blockade. The government in Helsinki essentially refused. Mannerheim's biographer maintained that throughout the war, the Finnish commander-in-chief was determined not to attack Leningrad directly 'because he believed it was an action for which no government in Russia would ever forgive the Finns'.[7] In any event, December 1941 was a turning point for the Finns. The outcome of the Battle of Moscow suggested that a German overall victory was far from certain. Meanwhile, the entry into the war of the United States as an ally of the USSR suggested a profound change in the overall balance of power. The Finnish Army would not ever advance further south on the Karelian Isthmus nor beyond Lake Ladoga, south of the Svir' River.

The Red Army did not fight well in the early defence of Leningrad. The Germans were allowed to partially isolate the city and occupy a strong position around it (notably the Shlissel'burg corridor). They would not be ejected from this until the start of 1944. In some respects, however, the events of September to December 1941 can be considered a very significant Soviet victory. The Barbarossa offensive had been stopped at Leningrad, just as it would be stopped before Moscow in December. German troops had not entered the main part of Leningrad, and they would never consolidate positions further east from where they were in September (taking into account their brief occupation of Tikhvin). Hitler's forces would conduct spectacular advances in southern Russia in 1942, but in the northern and central theatres the Soviet position, while not advantageous, was now secure. It would essentially remain so until the Red Army's full-scale counteroffensive began in the summer of 1943.

10.3   Siege, Famine, Survival

The first four months of 1942 were a time of major Soviet offensive successes and – unwarranted – optimism in Moscow. There was even expectation that the war might be completed, with the defeat of Germany, in 1942. Paradoxically, it was just at this moment that the most terrible period for the population of Leningrad began.[8]

Back in the glory days of autumn 1941, Hitler and his high command had discussed what to do with the local population if the besieged city was cut off or actually fell into their hands. Hitler made his orders explicit in a directive dated 22 September 1941: 'The Führer has decided to erase the city of Petersburg from the face of the earth. I have no interest in the further existence of this large population point after the defeat of Soviet Russia.' The city would be closely blockaded and destroyed by artillery and air bombardment.[9]

The bombardment was prolonged but less effective than Hitler had expected. The Luftwaffe lacked the bomber force to cause real damage. As for the German army, the town centre of Leningrad was eighteen to twenty-two kilometres from the main artillery positions and could not be reached by their medium-range guns; in 1942 heavy artillery was committed to the siege of Sevastopol'. Some 15,800 civilians were killed by these air and artillery bombardments in the course of the whole siege.[10] This was a substantial number, but it was small compared to civilians who starved or soldiers who fell fighting on the outskirts of Leningrad.

The practical difficulties of evacuating the population had been great in the autumn of 1941, given the speed of the German advance and the exposed location of Leningrad. Nevertheless, some 490,000 people had been moved out between June and August 1941. These were workers being sent east with their factories, as part of the general evacuation of war industries that took place across western European Russia; there were also a substantial number of children. In December 1941, however, about 2,500,000 civilians remained in the city. The number is inexact because of the arrival of refugees from the west the previous summer.

In December 1941, as German troops withdrew from Tikhvin, and all along the front after the Battle of Moscow, the Soviet war leadership seemed to have assumed that the close siege of Leningrad would soon be ended. Only on 22 January 1942 did Stalin's State Defence Committee (*GKO*) issue orders to develop and prioritise the ice road across frozen Lake Ladoga (later known as the 'road of life', *doroga zhizni*) to bring in supplies and troop reinforcements and evacuate civilians. Between mid-January and mid-March 1942, another 544,000 people, the majority dependents, were evacuated over the ice. Nevertheless, February–March 1942 would be the worst period of the blockade.[11]

It would seem that there were as many as 900,000 deaths of Leningrad civilians as a result of conditions in the winter of 1941–1942. The first cases of starvation occurred in December. Most of the deaths were between then and June 1942. The register system broke down and is far from a complete source, but of 517,000 registered civilian deaths in 1942, 475,000 (92 per cent) took place in the first six months. By the summer of 1942 the civilian population of Leningrad had been reduced to 600,000, a number which could be sustained by existing food supplies. To put the course of events another way, registered civilian deaths were 107,000 in February 1942 but only 5,000 a month in the last four months of the year.[12] The worst of the siege ended in the summer of 1942. The weakest had died, but dependents could now be evacuated to the relative safety of the 'mainland' by small ships crossing Lake Ladoga. Meanwhile the garrison of Leningrad itself could be reinforced with troops ferried in from across the lake.

10.4   Unsuccessful Attempts to Break the Siege, January to December 1942

The worst months of Leningrad's 1942 humanitarian catastrophe coincided with some of the most desperate fighting on the outskirts of the city.[13] There was little that the city's garrison could do to break the siege. The essential element were now the Red Army forces that were beginning to be assembled on the Volkhov River, southeast of the blockade perimeter. The Volkhov Front was established in mid-December. At that time the Soviet high command, confident in their success after advances on Moscow, ordered the newly established army group to break the blockade. With the aid of the Leningrad garrison, its mission was 'to surround and capture [the enemy], and in the event of the enemy's refusal to surrender, to destroy him'.[14] The Volkhov Front attacked on 7 January and a week later the newly created Second Shock Army reinforced it in an operation known as the 'Liuban' offensive'. However, attacking Soviet forces were too weak to open the rail lines to Moscow, let alone destroy the forces of Army Group North. The attackers became bogged down in the woods and swamps, and in mid-March 1942 they were eventually cut off by the Germans. General A. A. Vlasov, who had been one of the heroes of the Battle of Moscow, was sent into the pocket in the following month, but he was unable to retrieve the situation. The last remnants of the Second Shock Army were destroyed in the summer (July), when Vlasov himself was captured.

By this time, early summer 1942, the overall situation on the Soviet-German front had changed again. The Soviet winter counteroffensive begun in December had petered out on all sectors on the front. The Wehrmacht had actually given up relatively little ground and the German high command was preparing a new general offensive that was more realistic than the Barbarossa campaign of 1941. For the 'second campaign', Hitler and his generals no longer expected a rapid overthrow of Soviet power in all sectors (as in Barbarossa). Instead, they planned to weaken Soviet military and economic strength in key sectors, including Leningrad, as well as to isolate the USSR from American and British supplies. As it turned out the main effort would be in the south, beginning with the May 1942 fighting around Kharkov and the Crimea, followed by an advance into the North Caucasus and towards Stalingrad. Hitler's Directive No. 41 stressed the need to concentrate for the moment on the south: 'We will refrain from the final encirclement of Leningrad and the capture of Ingermanland [the Oranienbaum bridgehead] until such time as circumstances in the enveloped areas or the availability of otherwise sufficient forces permit.'[15]

Nevertheless, on 23 July 1942 once the southern offensive seemed to be going well, Hitler issued Directive No. 45, which envisaged the capture of Leningrad by September. The operation received the codename *Nordlicht* (Northern Lights), and the new Field Marshal Erich von Manstein, who had successfully besieged Sevastopol', was put in charge of it; the forces assigned to this were a number of divisions of his Eleventh Army, along with substantial heavy artillery. Meanwhile, however, the Red Army under Generals K. A. Meretskov and L. A. Govorov had launched another major offensive in the Shlissel'burg Corridor in mid-August 1942 (the 'Siniavino Operation'). Meretskov was now commander of the Volkhov Front, and Govorov was commander of the Leningrad Front. Again, the attack did not achieve its objective of pushing the Germans back and opening the main rail lines, but it did absorb much of the Army Group North's reserves and prevent the implementation of *Nordlicht*. In any event Manstein was called away in late November 1942 to deal with the crisis at Stalingrad, marking an end to the final German attempt to take Leningrad.

10.5   The Siege Lifted, January 1943 to January 1944

The Soviet situation at Leningrad improved significantly in January 1943 (which was also in the middle of the Stalingrad battle). In Operation Spark, on 18 January, the Red Army finally recaptured the Shlissel'burg bottleneck and took control of a coastal strip on the south side of Lake Ladoga. The new corridor into Leningrad was only fifteen kilometres wide, and the emergency railway laid down in two weeks was still vulnerable to German artillery fire. This operation was carried out by the reincarnation of Second Shock Army and Eighth Army attacking from the east, outside the perimeter, and a new Sixty-Seventh Army attacking from the west, the Leningrad side. This was the first time the forces within and outside the encirclement had been coordinated to full effect, and it was also the first time the Red Army had succeeded in breaking through a heavily fortified German position. The overall coordinator was Zhukov, who had just been promoted to the rank of Marshal.

Immediately after the German surrender at Stalingrad in early February 1943, the Stavka contemplated a similar deep encirclement – this time against Army Group North. This was operation was codenamed *Polar Star*. Still under Marshal Zhukov, and involving the Leningrad, Volkhov, and Northwestern Fronts, the plan was not just to relieve Leningrad but to envelop and destroy General Küchler's Army Group North as a whole; the main force was aimed at Luga and there was a planned further advance to Narva and Pskov. The aim was to cut Küchler's main rail supply line. Had the plan succeeded, Lindemann's Eighteenth Army near Leningrad would have shared the fate of Paulus' Sixth Army at Stalingrad. However, the straightening of the southern part of Küchler's Army Group North front line (with the abandonment of the Demiansk salient) freed up enough strength to hold back the Soviets, and Zhukov could successfully argue in March for abandonment of the costly operation.

Despite this incomplete success, the balance of forces was increasingly favourable to the Red Army. The Stalingrad catastrophe and then the Battle of Kursk and the successful Soviet counteroffensive in the southern part of the front forced a continuous stripping away of troops from Field Marshal Küchler's Army Group North.[16] Meanwhile, the Russians built up their forces in the northern part of the front. As German historian Karl-Heinz Frieser put it, 'The military situation had changed into its opposite. It was no longer the besieger who threatened the besieged, but the converse.'[17] Küchler, with weak second-class divisions, few aircraft, and almost no tanks, wanted to pull back to the projected defences of the Panther line, part of Hitler's *Ostwall*, halving the length of his exposed front. But Hitler, who was supported by Lindemann, refused to withdraw.

The situation was only resolved in the new year. The 'Leningrad-Novgorod Operation' of the Second Baltic, Volkhov, and Leningrad Fronts was carried out in January and February 1944, a year after the abortive Polar Star operation. This was the first of what would be called the 'Ten Stalinist Crushing Blows'. The three earlier Russian offensives in the Leningrad region had mainly come from southwest of Leningrad, from the Volkhov River side of the Shlissel'burg corridor. The January 1944 attack was mounted by the latest version of Second Shock Army from the southwest of Leningrad, partly from the Oranienbaum bridgehead. Another attacking group came from Leningrad itself. German troops in the Shlissel'burg corridor were now hurriedly pulled out to the west. The growing partisan force played an important part in harrying the retreating enemy. The forces of the Eighteenth Army were not trapped, but much of the German siege artillery had to be abandoned. The main rail line to Moscow was opened on 26 January.

The siege of Leningrad officially ended on 27 January 1944, with major celebrations in Moscow. By the very end of January 1944 the Germans had retreated to the Luga River. The Leningrad-Novgorod Operation did not rapidly achieve all its objectives, but it did completely push the German army away from Leningrad, eventually to a new line of resistance at Narva and Lake Chud; there the Red Army would pause until the summer. Mobile operations elsewhere on the Soviet-German front in 1944 were much more successful, notably the deep offensive in Ukraine and then the destruction of Army Group Centre. The Soviet army groups there had considerably more experience of mobile warfare and much stronger armoured forces.

* * *

Leningrad was encircled for nearly three years, from September 1941 to January 1944. It was an unparalleled human tragedy. Although it is sometimes called the '900 days', the extreme period for civilian deaths was a period of three or four months in the late winter of 1941–1942. This is not an attempt to minimise the enormity of the tragedy; indeed, the number of deaths in such a short period of time makes the event even more horrifying.

To speak of a 'battle of Leningrad' is misleading; what happened was more a long series of battles or a campaign. It was not a street-by-street battle within a city, as in Stalingrad in 1942–1943, Warsaw and Budapest in 1944, or Berlin in 1945. The Germans bombarded Leningrad with artillery and aircraft, but relatively little fighting took place inside the city. This was partly because of the strength of it defences, partly because of the natural cover of the built-up area, and partly because of the unwillingness of the Germans to accept the casualties of an infantry attack. There were certainly a huge number of military losses involved in the Leningrad campaign, but for both sides these were suffered in the rugged country to the south of the city. Leningrad Front losses were 144,800 in 1941, 83,700

Figure 10.2 Soviet soldiers cheering and embracing after the siege of Leningrad was lifted, January 1944.

in 1942, and 88,700 in 1943; losses of the Volkhov Front were 298,000 from December 1941 to February 1944.[18]

Even the term 'siege' needs to be used with some care, as Leningrad was blockaded but never completely cut off from what could be called the mainland of Soviet Russia, and the supply routes there were greatly improved in January 1943. After the winter of 1941, and certainly after the autumn of 1942, there was little likelihood that the defenders would give up – or the Germans would capture the city.

The campaign was not, like the Battles of Moscow, Stalingrad, or Kursk, decisive in the conduct of the Soviet-German war. The end of the siege in January 1944 did not mark a general turning point. The question might well be asked why breaking the siege took so long. The explanation was that once the Germans had seized advanced positions (notably in the Shlissel'burg corridor) in the early, mobile phase of the war, dislodging them proved very difficult. The Soviet high command did assign very large forces to the attempts to relieve Leningrad, but it was hard to get them into place and supply them. They then had to fight their way through very difficult terrain and well-positioned enemy troops. Meanwhile, the attitude of Hitler and his High Command to the fate of Leningrad and its population in the winter of 1941–1942 was an extreme example of the racially ideological war of annihilation which they were fighting. From the Russian side, the siege of Leningrad was a remarkable feat of human endurance.

Notes

1 Strictly speaking, Ingria was the territory south of the Neva River.
2 This is the Karelian Isthmus. This name is also used for the stretch of the isthmus between Leningrad and Vyborg, which was one of the routes through which – with great difficulty – the Red Army attacked Finland in November 1939; Soviet progress was famously blocked by the 'Mannerheim Line'.
3 G. Dimitrov, *The Diary of Georgii Dimitrov* (New Haven: Yale University Press, 2003), p. 197.
4 David Glantz, *The Battle for Leningrad, 1941–1944* (Lawrence: University Press of Kansas, 2002), pp. 471–472. The fullest account of the whole military campaign, certainly from the Red Army or Russian perspective, is David Glantz's study. The opening campaign of Army Group North from the German side is detailed in the section by Ernst Klink in *Germany and the Second World War* [hereafter *GSWW*], vol. IV, *The Attack on the Soviet Union*, ed. Horst Boog, Jürgen Förster, Joachim Hoffmann, Rolf-Diter Müller, and Gerd R. Ueberschär (Oxford: Clarendon Press, 1991), pp. 631–654, 734–735. A concise Russian account is N. M. Ramanichev and B. I. Nevzorov in *Velikaia Otechestvennaia Voina 1941–1945: Voenno-istoricheskie ocherki* [hereafter *VOV/VOI*], vol. 1, ed. V. A. Zolotarev et al. (Moscow: Nauka, 1998), pp. 197–206, 235.
5 Glantz, *Battle*, pp. 462–463, 467; Richard Bidlack and Nikita Lomagin, *The Leningrad Blockade, 1941–1944: A New Documentary History from the Soviet Archives* (New Haven: Yale University Press, 2012), pp. 105–109.
6 *Velikaia Otechestvennaia: Stavka VGK. Dokumenty i materialy. 1941 god. Russkii arkhiv*, t.16 (5[1]) (Moscow: Terra, 1996), p. 259.
7 J. E. O. Screen, *Mannerheim: The Finnish Years* (London: Hurst, 2000), p. 179. On the neglected topic of Finland's role, see the articles/chapters/sections by Gerd R. Ueberschär in *GSWW*, vol. IV, *The Attack on the Soviet Union*, pp. 429–471, 941–993, along with those by Bernd Wegner in *GSWW*, vol. VI, *The Global War: Widening of the Conflict into a World War and the Shift of the Initiative 1941–1943*, ed. Horst Boog et al. (Oxford: Clarendon Press, 2001), pp. 916–923.
8 On the situation within Leningrad, especially details of the impact on the population, see Bidlack and Lomagin, *The Leningrad Blockade*; see also Glantz, *Battle*, pp. 147–148, 468.

9 Glantz, *Battle*, pp. 85–86. A 21 September Wehrmacht high command
 memorandum with a particularly cold-blooded discussion of options for
 treating the encircled population of Leningrad is printed in Glantz, *Battle*,
 pp. 481–482. See also Boog, ed., *GSWW, vol. IV*, pp. 644–646.

10 A. Z. Dzeniskevich, ed., *Leningrad v osade: Sbornik dokumentov
 o geroicheskoi oborone Leningrada v gody Velikoi Otechestvennoi voiny,
 1941–1944* (St Petersburg: Liki Rossii, 1995), p. 573.

11 For reliable estimates, see Glantz, *Battle*, pp. 147–148, and Bidlack and
 Lomagin, *The Leningrad Blockade*, pp. 270–273.

12 Dzeniskevich, *Leningrad v osade*, pp. 130, 444n39.

13 There is only a brief discussion of events in Army Group North in 1942 and
 at the start of 1943 in sections by Bernd Wegner in *GSWW, vol. VI*,
 pp. 1200–1205. For a Russian account, see Kobrin and Fesenko, *VOV/VIO*,
 vol. 2, pp. 195–212.

14 Zolotarev, *VOV/VOI, vol. 1*, p. 304.

15 Glantz, *Battle*, p. 284.

16 On the last stages of the war in the Baltic, see Karl-Heinz Frieser,
 Klaus Schmider, Klaus Schönherr, Gerhard Schreiber, Krisztián Ungáry,
 and Bernd Wegner, eds., *GSWW, vol. VIII, The Eastern Front 1943–1945:
 The War in the East and on the Neighbouring Fronts* (Oxford, Clarendon
 Press, 2017), pp. 274–292. A Russian source on this period is the chapter by
 V. O. Daines in *VOV/VIO, vol. 3*, pp. 20–32.

17 Frieser, *GSWW, vol. VIII*, p. 274.

18 G. F. Krivosheev, V. M. Andronikov, and P. D. Burikov, eds., *Rossiia i SSSR
 v voinakh XX veka: Poteri vooruzhennykh sil* (Moscow: Olma Press, 2001),
 pp. 338, 343.

11

Operation Bagration, 1944

In the aftermath of Germany's summer 1943 failure in the Battle of Kursk (Operation Zitadelle), the Soviets managed nearly a year of hard fighting to liberate Soviet territory on the southern part of the Eastern Front.[1] As part of preparing to meet the Kursk offensive, the Soviet high command had readied and subsequently unleashed paired counteroffensives to take advantage of exhausted and overstretched German forces north and south of the Kursk salient. Operation Rumiantsev (on the southern face of the salient) and Operation Kutuzov (on the northern) rolled back the Germans. Once the Soviets had momentum, the relatively flat and open terrain of southern Russia and eastern Ukraine offered few opportunities for the Germans to halt the Soviet push before the Dnepr River. Though the Wehrmacht could unleash occasional counterattacks to punish overextended Soviet forces, the Soviets advanced 500–600 kilometres from August through November 1943 along the length of the central and southern sectors of the Eastern Front. By late autumn 1943 Soviet advances had generally reached the line of the Dnepr River and managed to achieve some bridgeheads on its western bank. Their drive culminated in November with the seizure of Kiev. After a brief pause to rest and refit, the Soviet advance continued until April 1944 into and through Right-Bank (western) Ukraine, reaching the Carpathian Mountains before finally halting. As a result of the heavy fighting, both the Germans and the Soviets had concentrated much of their armour, artillery, and aviation resources in Ukraine, leaving northern sectors of the front relatively de-mechanised.[2]

This Soviet advance left a geographical anomaly. The Pripet Marshes, a morass of swamps, bogs, and forests in Belarus and northern Ukraine, split the Eastern Front into northern and southern halves.[3] South of the marshes, the Soviets had pushed forward to liberate Ukraine. The point of furthest advance in north-western Ukraine put the Soviets close to German-held Kovel', Brest, and Lublin, key points linking the northern and southern sectors of the front and blocking the path to Warsaw and then Berlin. This southern sector was quite distinct from the northern. Belarus more or less entirely remained in the hands of Germany's Army Group Centre, creating a giant salient, a 'shelf' or 'balcony' which dominated both sides' strategic considerations. While it was vulnerable to Soviet attack, it also created the potential for Germany to outflank from the north the advanced Soviet position in Ukraine.

The pause in early spring 1944 allowed both sides to consider next steps. Stalin and his generals, heartened by their nearly year-long run of successes, questioned where to focus their efforts for their next offensive. Bitter experience in the first three years of the war had taught the Soviets that offensives which were too broad and ambitious led to disaster. Even though Soviet industry was providing material resources in abundance, and Soviet commanders were increasingly capable of coordinating large-scale operations, it was still important to carefully plan for operations significant enough to contribute to victory over the Germans, but not so ambitious as to permit the Germans to carry off the spoiling counter-attacks which were their defensive specialty. While the Soviets debated the proper sector and scope for an offensive, the Germans had a more difficult problem. Anticipating correctly that a cross-channel invasion by the Western allies was coming soon, there was no possibility of accumulating resources for an offensive in the east. Instead, the issue was to how properly anticipate and prepare for a Soviet attack.

The Soviets had a series of options available to them. An attack in the north against Finland could conceivably knock that country out of the war but would not speed victory against Germany. Likewise, an offensive against Germany's Army Group North in the Baltics seemed unlikely to have great strategic significance. In the south, western Ukraine offered a potential jump-off point for offensives south-west into Romania, west into Hungary, or north-west through Brest towards Warsaw and Germany itself.

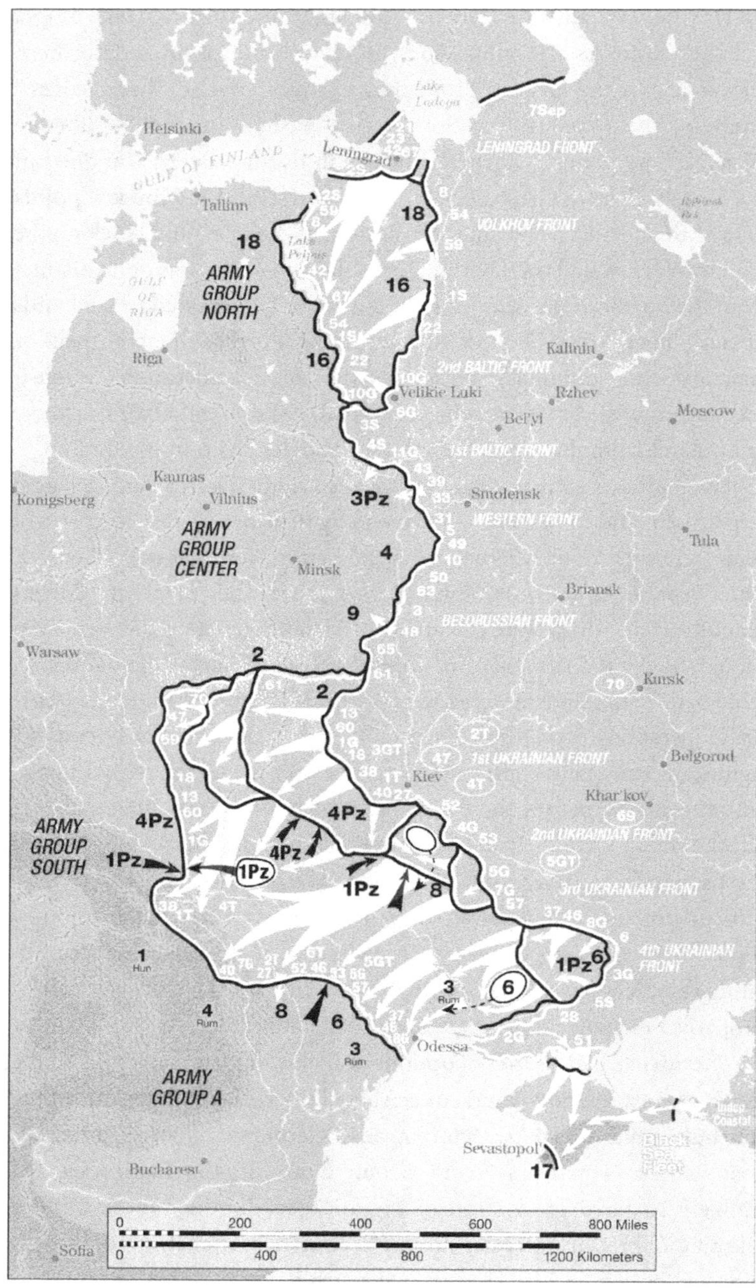

Map 10 Winter–spring campaign (December 1943–April 1944).

The Soviet high command moved instead during spring 1944 to a clear consensus on attacking Germany's Army Group Centre in Belarus. Any attack out of the Soviets' advanced position in western Ukraine, particularly moving north-west towards Warsaw or the Baltic coast, seemed too risky and subject to being cut off by a German counterstroke. By contrast, Army Group Centre seemed vulnerable to being isolated and defeated in detail. If properly executed, a Soviet offensive would not just liberate Soviet territory but potentially cut German lines of retreat, eliminating manpower wholesale from the German order of battle. In addition, it would push German airfields out of range of Moscow. Politically, an attack in Belarus offered the prospect of liberating large swathes of pre-war Soviet territory.

Tactically and operationally, the Soviet Army had grown far more proficient from its nadir in summer 1941. While its rank-and-file soldiers were not necessarily more experienced, given the high rate of casualties it had suffered, its high-ranking commanders were increasingly adept at coordinating the elements of modern warfare: using infantry, artillery, and airpower to force breaches in enemy positions, sending mechanised forces through those breaches to carry out deep penetrations, and completing victory by annihilating bypassed enemy formations and consolidating gains to be used as springboards for new advances. Perhaps most importantly, Stalin had learned over time to trust the professional expertise of his generals. While always a harsh questioner of the plans they presented him, he was willing to listen. As Stalin's reliance on the knowledge and talent of his commanders grew, Hitler moved in the opposite direction.[4]

German planning for summer 1944 fundamentally misread Soviet intentions. The problem was worst at the top, where Hitler was increasingly isolated and deluded as the fortunes of war increasingly clearly turned against Germany. His hopes turned to the development of wonder weapons and the importance of will in overcoming Germany's desperate circumstances. He thought back to Frederick the Great in the Seven Years' War, when Prussia had been saved from seemingly certain destruction by the last-minute disintegration of the anti-Prussian coalition. German generals were acutely conscious of their limited ability to carry out ambitious offensives by the spring and summer of 1944. Losses sustained at Kursk and the lengthy retreat through Ukraine, combined with the need to bolster German air defences against the Allied bombing campaign and prepare for cross-channel invasion, compelled the careful husbanding of resources. The imminent Allied invasion also drew German attention and resources west, away from the Soviets. On 3 November 1943 Führer Directive 51 decreed a fundamental reorientation of German strategy to the west to deal with an anticipated invasion by the Western Allies.[5]

When the Soviet offensive ultimately came, Hitler had fundamentally shaped German defensive doctrine in ways that proved ultimately counterproductive. In his Führer Directive 11 of 8 March 1944, he decreed a new approach of *festen Plätze* (fortified places). Key cities and towns on the Eastern Front would be fortresses, held even if threatened with or actually subject to Soviet encirclement. As such, they would be turned into breakwaters to deflect and impede Soviet advances while tying down substantial numbers of Soviet troops. While this strategy might have made sense on the southern part of the front, where relatively static German formations of infantry and artillery might hold and await relief through counterattacks by more mobile German mechanised formations, it made little sense in Belarus, where Army Group Centre had been systematically stripped of armour in order to reinforce the south. The Wehrmacht had proven highly effective in counterattacks to punish Soviet overextension. German mobile, elastic defensive tactics entailed withdrawing from danger to preserve men and equipment then counterattacking. Army Group Centre, however, lacked the forces to do that. Given its lack of motorised vehicles and reliance on horse-drawn transport, it could not even hope to withdraw faster than Soviet mechanised forces could pursue. Ironically, Hitler's directives played directly into Soviet hands. Hitler decreed that four key Belarusian towns – from north to south Vitebsk, Orsha, Mogilev, and Bobruisk – must be turned into fortresses to be held by a division or more each. The Soviets feared that German troops might escape before they could be encircled and destroyed; Hitler himself helped prevent that outcome.

Within the Eastern Front itself, the German command structure badly misread Soviet intentions. German planners focussed on the Soviet fore-post in western Ukraine, where Soviet troops stood just outside of the major communications junction at Kovel'. The

Germans agreed that the next Soviet offensive would come at Kovel'; the question was whether the Soviets would use that jumping-off point to move south-west into the Balkans, knocking German allies Hungary, Romania, and Bulgaria out of the war and cutting off Romanian oil. The Soviets could alternately opt to move north-west through Poland to cut off Army Groups North and Centre. While initial German strategy saw the Balkans as the most likely threat, emphasising Soviet empire building in a traditional Russian sphere of influence, attitudes gradually shifted over time to anticipate a Soviet attack north-west from Kovel' into Poland. Here, German strategists may have been guilty of projecting – attributing to the Soviets the desire for a single war-winning blow.[6] The Germans did not anticipate an attack on the exposed Belarusian salient. Unlike the more flat and open terrain of Ukraine that the Soviets had used for their advances in late 1943 and early 1944, Belarus's forests and swamps would ostensibly make an advance more difficult. In addition, Belarus was more distant from key German centres of gravity.

German intelligence was far better at lower levels. The three German armies in Belarus – the Third Panzer to the north-east under Georg-Hans Reinhardt, the Fourth under Gotthard Heinrici to the east, and the Ninth under Hans Jordan to the south-east – picked up on the growing Soviet forces opposite their lines and passed their concerns up the chain of command to no avail. At Army Group Centre, its commander Field Marshal Ernst Busch was in part unconvinced of the threat and in part too weak to convince Hitler of the danger. On 20 May, Hitler harangued Busch for harping on the threat to Army Group Centre and transferred almost all Busch's tanks – the LVI Panzer Corps – south to Army Group North Ukraine.[7] The three armies in Belarus were left well below nominal strength and short on heavy equipment, and Army Group Centre had almost no reserves. In sum, the Wehrmacht was almost entirely unprepared for the forthcoming Soviet offensive.

In March and April 1944 *Stavka*, the Soviet high command, began working through concepts for a spring-summer offensive and soon came to focus on Belarus. By mid-April, a rough plan was ready. After a key meeting in late May to iron out details, final directives went out on 31 May for Operation Bagration. The attack's namesake was Petr

Bagration, a Georgian prince and hero of Russia's war against Napoleon killed in the Battle of Borodino in 1812. Stalin himself a fellow Georgian suggested *Bagration* as the namesake for the offensive. The operation entailed a concentric attack by four Fronts (the Soviet equivalent of an Army Group) – clockwise from the north, the First Baltic under Ivan Bagramian, Third Belorussian under Ivan Cherniakhovskii, Second Belorussian under Georgii Zakharov, and First Belorussian under Konstantin Rokossovskii. In keeping with Soviet practice, Fronts were grouped together under the coordination of *Stavka* representatives: Aleksandr Vasilevskii for the First Baltic and Third Belorussian and Georgii Zhukov for Second and First Belorussian. First Baltic and Second Belorussian had relatively limited goals of shallow encirclements; the most important roles went to Third and First Belorussian, tasked with driving converging armoured spearheads to Minsk to cut off retreat for the entire Army Group Centre.[8]

Operation Bagration was not intended as a stand-alone operation but instead as part of a sequence of operations moving from north to south over the course of 1944. Opening with an attack on Finland, continuing with the attack on Belarus, the Soviet army would next move to an attack from north-west Ukraine into south-eastern Poland, with key roles for both the western wing of Rokossovskii's First Belorussian Front and Ivan Konev's First Ukrainian Front.

Operating under strict rules to preserve secrecy and mislead the Germans about the scale of the threat they faced, the Soviets assembled a massive and overwhelming force against Army Group Centre. For the main assault, leaving aside the portion of Rokossovskii's First Belorussian Front intended for a later attack on Kovel', the Soviets had approximately 1.2 million men, 25,000 artillery pieces, and 4,000 armoured vehicles. While the nominal strength of Germany's Army Group Centre was around 800,000, its number of actual effectives was probably closer to 500,000, with a few hundred armoured vehicles and 2,500 artillery pieces.

The cascade of Soviet summer offensives began in the far north against Finland. On 9 June 1944 two armies (the Twenty-First and Twenty-Third) of the Leningrad Front carried out massive air and artillery bombardments of Finnish defensive positions in the Karelian Isthmus, followed by ground attacks the next day. Within ten days, the

Soviets had seized Vyborg/Viipuri. Despite desperate fighting, Finnish resources were soon exhausted. Two months later, Finland asked for an armistice and formally surrendered on 19 September 1944. The Germans still did not realise the focus of the coming Soviet attack. An OKH (High Command of the Army) conference on 14 June still anticipated a major blow from the south; the Soviet attack came as a total surprise.[9]

Though much has been made of the start date of the Soviet offensive on 22 June 1944, the third anniversary of Germany's invasion of the Soviet Union in Operation Barbarossa, this was in fact only a coincidence. Soviet planning had anticipated beginning Operation Bagration at some point in the interval from 15–20 June, but logistical complications forced delay. Massive Soviet deception operations made accumulating the necessary men and equipment extremely complicated. Railroads were jammed with traffic, and equipment was moved wherever possible during the short summer nights with telltale tracks erased to hinder aerial reconnaissance.

Bagration began with massive partisan attacks against German transportation networks on the night of 19–20 June by as many as 140,000 partisans. The fundamental goal was to slow movement: to prevent German troops at the front from withdrawing out of danger and to slow the arrival of reinforcements to shore up German defences. The destruction of Army Group Centre marks the high point of Soviet partisan activity, supported by careful coordination and supply from the Soviet army. Partisans were not capable of fighting regular troops on anything close to an equal basis. They excelled instead at the destruction of infrastructure or raiding supply columns. Their personnel resources had been husbanded for just this occasion, with the Soviet central organisation for coordinating partisan activity providing huge stocks of explosives. Belarus was ideal territory for partisan operations. Unlike relatively open Ukraine, the forests and swamps of Belarus provided ample concealment. In addition, Belarusian nationalist sentiment was far less developed than in Ukraine, so there was much less competition for Soviet partisans from anti-Soviet resistance. Without an existing base of pro-Communist or pro-Russian sentiment, efforts at cultivating partisan resistance (as in the Baltic states) were hopeless. In the wake of Bagration's success, the Soviets even directed some partisans to move ahead of the advancing Soviet forces out of Soviet territory in Poland and Slovakia.[10]

When Soviet conventional forces opened their attack from 22–24 June, the assault did not hit the entire salient simultaneously but began in the north and moved clockwise around the front. The overwhelming Soviet superiority in firepower, concentrated on key points, meant that the German positional defences Hitler had insisted on were annihilated, allowing rapid Soviet armoured exploitation of the resulting gaps. In the north-east corner of the Belorussian salient, Bagramian's First Baltic Front opened the attack on 22 June northwest of Vitebsk, pushing south across the Dvina River to cut off Vitebsk from behind and prevent German withdrawal. Cherniakhovskii's Third Belorussian Front did the same in the gap between Vitebsk and Orsha, with flanking units curling out to encircle both cities. Reinhardt requested permission to withdraw his Third Panzer Army almost as soon as the attack began. Only Hitler could authorise such a step, and the Führer vacillated, first ordering that Vitebsk be held in full strength and then relenting to order only a token division to remain in the city. Efforts to break out through the rapidly closing Soviet ring from 25 to 27 June failed; 25,000 to 30,000 German troops were killed or taken prisoner. The fall of Vitebsk tore open a gap 100 kilometres wide in the German front lines. In the centre, Germany's Fourth Army held Orsha and Mogilev. While Hitler intended those as strong points around which resistance would rally, they instead were only islands in an onrushing torrent of Soviet troops, soon washed entirely away. Cherniakhovskii's Third Belorussian Front moved between Vitebsk and Orsha, Zakharov's Second Belorussian Front attacked between Orsha and Mogilev, and the right wing of Rokossovskii's First Belorussian Front operated between Mogilev and Bobruisk (though Rokossovskii was focussed on the double envelopment of Bobruisk, not on assisting the encirclement of Mogilev). For Busch's forces, remaining in place meant certain destruction; the only hope to live and fight again was for German troops, walking or in horse-drawn wagons, to retreat faster than Soviet tanks could pursue. Hopelessly isolated by the collapse of the two armies on his flanks, Kurt von Tippelskirch, temporarily in command of Fourth Army, ordered retreat on his own authority, avoiding Busch's effort to enforce Hitler's stand-and-fight directive. The last domino to fall was the Ninth Army in the south-east, centred around Bobruisk. Rokossovskii launched an

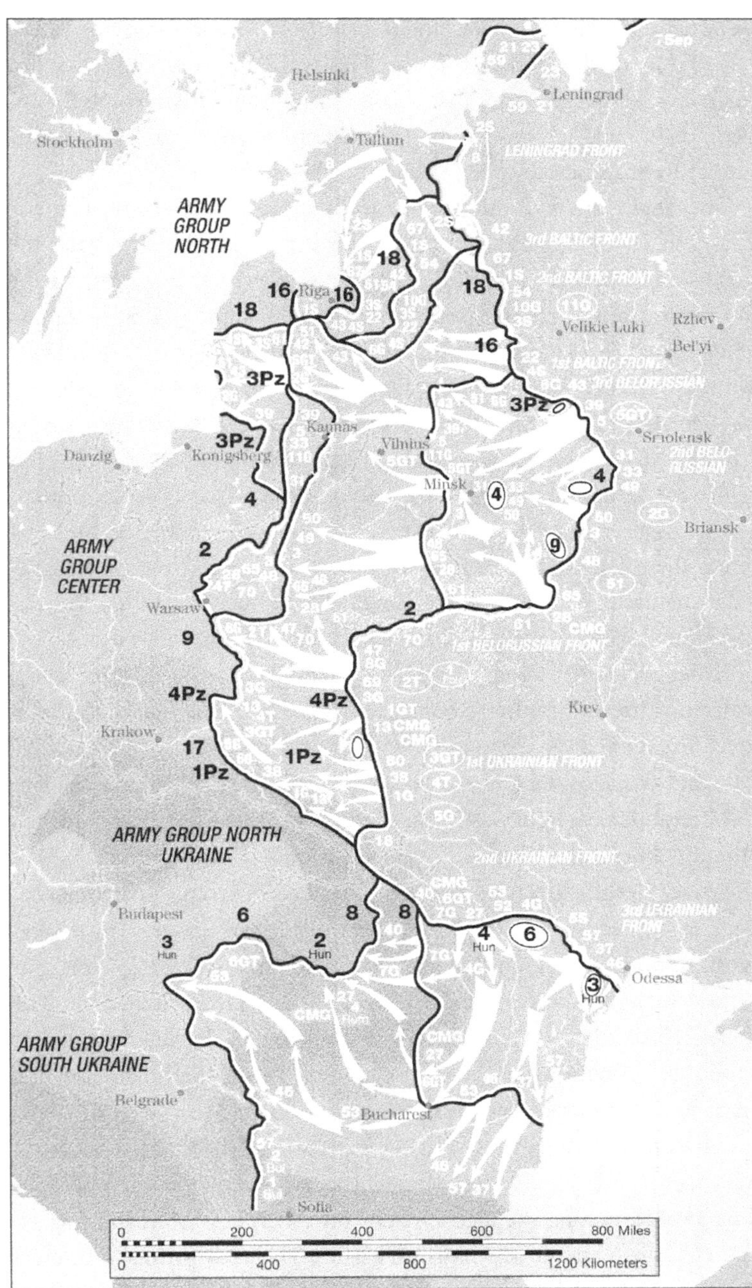

Map 11 Summer–autumn campaign (June–October 1944).

overwhelming pincer attack on Bobruisk on 24 June, moving along both banks of the Berezina River. Massive Soviet firepower assured quick breakthrough, and the Ninth Army soon disintegrated into a confused mob as conflicting orders about whether to break out or hold at Bobruisk made a bad situation even worse.[11]

The depletion of Army Group Centre prior to the Soviet attack meant that Busch had no significant reserves to plug the gaps the Soviets had opened in his line. Armour was even scarcer. Even if he had held reserves, the multiple breakthroughs made it almost impossible to halt the advance. The scale of the Soviet assault also meant that two major north-south rivers – the Dnepr to the east and its tributary the Berezina further west – were of little use: the Third Belorussian Front started its advance west of the Dnepr, and the left wing of the First Belorussian Front started west of the Berezina. Busch's lone armoured reserves consisted of the 20th Panzer Division, dispatched to him just before the offensive began. It spent a day whipsawed by contradictory orders before finally going into action around Bobruisk. With only forty operational tanks, it was too little, too late to make a difference.

Hitler sacked Busch as army group commander on 28 June 1944, replacing him with Walter Model, a master of defensive warfare, who in addition retained his command over Army Group North Ukraine. The scale and scope of the German disaster were not Busch's fault, though his obsequious deference to Hitler's senseless orders certainly made the situation worse. Model faced a clear crisis only six days into the Soviet offensive. German units at the front lines had been annihilated, encircled, or forced to retreat in varying degrees of order. The bigger question now was whether there was any hope of salvaging Minsk, or at the least avoiding another disastrous large-scale encirclement. The Soviet Third Belorussian and First Belorussian Fronts had major armoured formations converging on Minsk from the north-east and south-east, threatening not just to surround what remained of Army Group Centre but to advance further west into Poland. Hard-pressed on every front, Hitler could offer Model little in the way of reinforcements: two panzer divisions, the 12th Panzer from Army Group North, and 5th Panzer from Army Group North Ukraine. The 12th managed to meet a German column breaking out from Bobruisk, rescuing at least some German forces from encirclement. The 5th temporarily halted the

Soviets on one axis of advance but had to withdraw as the broad Soviet push threatened to leave it cut off as well. Model recognised reality and evacuated Minsk. Soviet spearheads met there on 3 July, capturing the city and trapping as many as 100,000 troops of the German Fourth Army to the east. They struggled to escape west to German lines on bad roads while constantly harassed by partisans and separated into ever smaller pockets by the Soviet advance.

By one week into the offensive, the major towns and cities anchoring the defence of Belarus had all been taken. While Model had managed to extract at least some soldiers from Belarus, there was hardly a coherent front west of Minsk. Kurt Zeiztler, head of the Army High Command, argued that Army Group North should withdraw from the Baltics to shorten the front and restore Army Group Centre. Hitler refused, and Zeiztler quit his post while suffering a nervous breakdown. The situation was truly desperate: the Third Panzer Army in northern Belarus was separated from Army Group North, Fourth Army had been annihilated, and the shattered remnants of the Ninth Army were grafted onto the Second Army facing Kovel'. Without a coherent front line, Model used judicious counterattacks to try to slow the advancing Soviets. The Soviets continued to push west past Minsk, north-west through Molodechno and south-west through Baranovichi. The Third Belorussian Front, moving north-west from Minsk, encircled Vilnius on 8 July and pushed forwards towards the Baltic shore. Hitler grudgingly granted permission for the Germans trapped at Vilnius to break out towards a relief column of the Third Panzer Army, saving a few thousand trapped soldiers.[12]

Even as one sector quieted, another exploded. By the second half of July 1944, Soviet advances in Belarus were slowing as an inevitable result of the horrific losses they had endured, as well as from shortages of fuel and ammunition. Only extreme efforts of Soviet logistics carried in Lend-Lease trucks had taken the Soviets as far as they had gone. At this point, though, the hinge of the Eastern Front around Kovel' – the sector where German intelligence had expected the main blow – finally fell victim to a Soviet offensive. On 13 July, the First Ukrainian Front under Ivan Konev moved into Galicia through Lviv and on towards Krakow. A few days later, the previously unused western wing of Rokossovskii's First Belorussian Front moved into action as well.

While part of Rokossovskii's front had encircled Bobruisk and then formed the southern pincer against Minsk, much of his army – 400,000 men – had waited until the German front was broken. They then moved into action at the south-west corner of the Pripet Marshes. Rokossovskii took only a couple of days to break German defences and advance into Poland, driving west towards Lublin. By end of July, the Soviets had reached the Vistula River and Rokossovskii turned north along its right bank, aiming for Warsaw's eastern suburbs to trap German troops east of the river. To make matters worse, to the north the Soviet First Baltic Front had broken through to reach the Baltic coast at the end of July, severing the land connection to Army Group North in the Baltics.[13]

At this point, a number of factors slowed the Soviet advance. From the Soviet point-of-view, Warsaw itself lay on the wrong (i.e., western) side of the Vistula, requiring a difficult crossing amid solidifying German resistance. In addition, more than a month of rapid advance had led the Soviet offensive to culminate (in a Clausewitzian sense of the word) as it reached the limits of human endurance and concrete supplies. Most importantly, as the Soviet Second Tank Army moved into Warsaw's eastern suburbs, it was ambushed by four panzer divisions which Model had hastily assembled to take advantage of Soviet overextension. The Soviets had to retreat in disarray to reorganise before moving on the city again.

This was the context for one of the most controversial events of the war in the East: the uprising of the Polish Home Army against German occupation. It was carefully timed to both take advantage of the Soviet approach to minimise the length of time the Polish resistance would have to fight against German regular troops and establish political legitimacy for a non-communist Poland against Soviet domination after the expulsion of the Germans. The uprising began on 1 August 1944, motivated in part by a call from Soviet radio broadcasts, but thanks to Model's defensive efforts, the Home Army's fight coincided with the Soviets being pushed back from Warsaw. Certainly the Soviets had reached the limits of their capability to advance, especially to force a crossing of the Vistula against stiffening German resistance. It is also certainly true that Stalin had no love for the Home Army and its leadership, and did not make any great effort to fight on its behalf. The Germans crushed the Polish Home Army and levelled Warsaw.[14]

Figure 11.1 Fifty-seven thousand German prisoners of war, captured during Operation Bagration, being marched through the streets of Moscow, 17 July 1944. Source: Sovfoto/Universal Images Group via Getty Images.

The destruction of Army Group Centre in Operation Bagration had a number of important results. It essentially completed the liberation of pre-1939 Soviet territory. At enormous cost, it had permanently removed a substantial number of troops from the German order of battle. Even as Germany was forced to stretch its resources across multiple fronts, the Germans counted around 300,000 men killed, missing, or captured, with an additional 100,000 wounded. As a demonstration to the world and to his own people of the scale of Soviet victory, Stalin paraded 57,000 German prisoners of war through Moscow on 17 July 1944. In order to achieve that success, however, the Soviets endured horrific losses themselves: 200,000 killed and 600,000 wounded are reasonable estimates. In combination with the Allied landings in France, Bagration helped convince the German high command, aside from Hitler and a few ideological fanatics, that the war was lost and the only hope for Germany was a negotiated settlement. Whether the Allies had any interest in a negotiated settlement is another question altogether, but this sense of the impossibility of victory and Hitler's refusal to see reason contributed greatly to a 20 July assassination attempt against him. Its failure, and Hitler's subsequent purge of any hint of disloyalty, crushed any hope of ending the war short of the complete destruction of Germany.[15]

Notes

1 There is remarkably little scholarly disagreement about the origins and conduct of Operation Bagration. Debate has revolved instead around the campaign's culmination at Warsaw and the Warsaw uprising. As a result, the operational narrative is remarkably consistent and major works present a consistent picture. Among works focussing solely on Bagration, see Gerd Niepold, *Battle for White Russia: The Destruction of Army Group Centre, June 1944* (Washington, DC: Brassey's, 1987); Steven Zaloga, *Bagration 1944: The Destruction of Army Group Centre* (London: Osprey, 1996); David M. Glantz and Harold S. Orenstein, *Belorussia 1944: The Soviet General Staff Study* (Portland, OR: Frank Cass, 2001).

Standard works on the Eastern Front with detailed coverage of Bagration include John Erickson, *The Road to Berlin: Stalin's War with Germany*, vol. 2 (London: Weidenfeld & Nicolson, 1983); David M. Glantz and Jonathan M. House, *When Titans Clashed: How the Red Army Stopped Hitler*, rev. ed. (Lawrence: University Press of Kansas, 2015); Earl F. Ziemke, *Stalingrad to Berlin: The German Defeat in the East* (Washington, DC: Office of the Chief of Military History, 1968). Erickson is particularly adept at integrating the available memoir literature; Glantz and House integrate recent archival findings from Russia.

The German official history is quite thorough and detailed. Bagration is covered in Karl-Heinz Frieser, ed., *Das Deutsche Reich und der Zweite Weltkrieg, vol. VIII: Die Ostfront 1943/44 – Der Krieg im Osten und an den Nebenfronten* (Stuttgart: Deutsche Verlags-Anstalt, 2007). It is available in English as *Germany and the Second World War, vol. VIII: The Eastern Front 1943–1944: The War in the East and on the Neighbouring Fronts* (Oxford: Clarendon, 2017).

The Soviet Union and Russian Federation have published four massive official histories of the Second World War, each to some degree a product of the political circumstances of the time. Each has merit, and the Western literature cited previously generally incorporates its major findings and interpretations. Bagration is covered in *Istoriia Velikoi Otechestvennoi voiny Sovetskogo Soiuza*, vol. 4 (Moscow: Voenizdat, 1962), 152–202; *Istoriia vtoroi mirovoi voiny, 1939–1945*, vol. 9 (Moscow: Voenizdat, 1978), pp. 40–75; *Velikaia Otechestvennaia voina, 1941–1945: Voenno-istoricheskie ocherki*, vol. 3 (Moscow: Nauka, 1999), pp. 54–80; *Velikaia Otechestvennaia voina, 1941–1945* (Moscow: Kuchkovo pole, 2012), vol. 4, pp. 345–448.

2 Erickson, *The Road to Berlin*, pp. 87–189; Glantz and House, *When Titans Clashed*, pp. 212–255. The Soviets also made failed attempts to push the Germans out of Belarus in early 1944, efforts which were largely forgotten in the Soviet Union precisely because of their lack of success: David M. Glantz with Mary Elizabeth Glantz, *Battle for Belorussia: The Red Army's Forgotten Campaign of October 1943–April 1944* (Lawrence: University Press of Kansas, 2016).

3 As is nearly always the case when researching the history of Eastern Europe, geographic names present some difficulty. Operation Bagration took place in the territory of Belarus, referred to in Russian as both *Belorussia* and the *Republic of Belarus*. Soviet military references universally used *Belorussia* for geography and unit designations. Recognizing political complications and the lack of a perfect solution, I have chosen to refer to places by their current names and military units by their historical names.

4 Seweryn Bialer, *Stalin and His Generals: Soviet Military Memoirs of World War II* (New York: Pegasus, 1969).

5 *Eastern Front 1943–1944*, pp. 489–521; Ziemke, *Stalingrad to Berlin*, pp. 313–316. For the breakdown of the Nazi system at the top, see Geoffrey P. Megargee, *Inside Hitler's High Command* (Lawrence: University Press of Kansas, 2000), pp. 192–211; Stephen G. Fritz, *The First Soldier: Hitler as Military Leader* (New Haven: Yale University Press, 2018), pp. 278–333.

6 Stephen G. Fritz, *Ostkrieg: Hitler's War of Extermination in the East* (Lexington: University Press of Kentucky, 2011), p. 406.

7 Karl-Heinz Frieser, *Eastern Front 1943–1944*, pp. 513–514; Ziemke, *Stalingrad to Berlin*, p. 314.

8 Karl-Heinz Frieser, *Eastern Front 1943–1944*, pp. 522–534; Erickson, *The Road to Berlin*, pp. 189–192, 196–215; Glantz and House, *When Titans Clashed*, pp. 256–257, 260–266; Ziemke, *Stalingrad to Berlin*, pp. 316–319.

9 Glantz and House, *When Titans Clashed*, pp. 257–259; Ziemke, *Stalingrad to Berlin*, pp. 296–303.

10 Edgar M. Howell, *The Soviet Partisan Movement, 1941–1944* (Washington, DC: Department of the Army, 1956), pp. 181–202; Leonid Grenkevich, *The Soviet Partisan Movement, 1941–1944* (London: Cass, 1999). See also Karl-Heinz Frieser, *Eastern Front 1943–1944*, pp. 534–535; Ziemke, *Stalingrad to Berlin*, pp. 303–309.

11 Karl-Heinz Frieser, *Eastern Front 1943–1944*, pp. 536–555; Erickson, *The Road to Berlin*, pp. 215–224; Glantz and House, *When Titans Clashed*, pp. 266–269; Ziemke, *Stalingrad to Berlin*, pp. 319–325.

12 Karl-Heinz Frieser, *Eastern Front 1943–1944*, pp. 555–563; Erickson, *The Road to Berlin*, pp. 224–230; Glantz and House, *When Titans Clashed*, pp. 270–272; Ziemke, *Stalingrad to Berlin*, pp. 326–329.

13 Karl-Heinz Frieser, *Eastern Front 1943–1944*, pp. 563–566; Erickson, *The Road to Berlin*, pp. 230–247; Glantz and House, *When Titans Clashed*, pp. 272–277; Ziemke, *Stalingrad to Berlin*, pp. 329–340.

14 Karl-Heinz Frieser, *Eastern Front 1943–1944*, pp. 566–584; Erickson, *The Road to Berlin*, pp. 247–290; Glantz and House, *When Titans Clashed*, pp. 276–277; Ziemke, *Stalingrad to Berlin*, pp. 340–342.

15 Karl-Heinz Frieser, *Eastern Front 1943–1944*, pp. 589–601; Glantz and House, *When Titans Clashed*, pp. 277–278.

12

The Soviet Conquest and Occupation of Germany, 1945

Operation Bagration ended with the First Belarusian Front, commanded by Marshal Konstantin Rokossovsky, capturing two bridgeheads on the western bank of the Vistula River near Warsaw in August 1944. The First Ukrainian Front, commanded by Marshal Ivan Konev, also captured a bridgehead across the Vistula further south. Both fronts then began accumulating supplies at these bridgeheads for the next deep operation that would bring them across Poland to Germany. At the time, the Red Army and the Western Allies were still 1,000 kilometres apart, with Berlin in the middle. However, Germany's strategic situation was dire. The Wehrmacht could not recover after a series of crushing defeats suffered on the Eastern Front in 1944. Army Group North was blocked deep in the Soviet rear. Army Group Centre was desperately attempting to regroup after the destruction of its main forces during Operation Bagration, and the Soviet offensive across Romania and Hungary had shattered Army Group South. All of Germany's East European allies, except Hungary, had defected: Romania, which had fielded the third-largest army of the Axis alliance in Europe, switched sides, as did Bulgaria. Two Polish armies, raised by the Soviets, were looking to liberate their country, as was a Czechoslovak corps. By 1 January 1945 the Red Army fielded 7,109,000 soldiers on the Eastern Front, to whom its East European allies added 326,525 men.[1] They were facing 2,190,000 German and Hungarian soldiers.[2]

Although Soviet generals continued to believe that the basic training of the soldier was optional because he would in any case master his trade in combat,[3] the Red Army still accumulated, during the wasteful endeavours stemming from such an attitude, a large pool of veterans with sound combat skills.[4] By contrast, the overall training of the Wehrmacht continued to be superior, but it deteriorated in parallel with the increasing casualty rate, reducing the gap in the quality of the manpower available to both the Soviets and Germans. The Soviet generals effectively learned the tricks of their profession through a long trial-and-error process and by 1944 were outperforming their German counterparts in operational art. Nor was the Soviet advantage simply on the battlefield. Soviet industry had consistently out-produced the German war economy in most major weapon categories.[5] Likewise, after the Red Army overran the Romanian Ploești region in August 1944, it deprived Germany of its main source of oil, which gravely impeded Wehrmacht logistics. In contrast, the delivery of American trucks via the Lend-Lease program boosted the mobility of the Red Army, while the supply of reliable American radios greatly improved command and control. The combination of all these factors promised an imminent end of the Third Reich.

The Germans anticipated the offensive of the Red Army in early 1945,[6] imagining it as a series of subsequent strikes, as had happened in 1944. However, in 1945 the Red Army could launch several strategic offensives simultaneously on various sections of the front. When the First Belarusian and the First Ukrainian Fronts were ready to resume their westward march, they attained an overwhelming superiority over Army Group A opposing them, surpassing it by 3.9:1 in manpower, 6.7:1 in artillery, 5.8:1 in tanks and self-propelled guns, and 7.9:1 in combat aircraft.[7] The density of Soviet artillery reached 250 guns per one kilometre of the front at the main concentrations of the offensive.[8] This was the greatest concentration of firepower the Red Army had deployed so far, and no other army obtained such artillery density during World War II.[9] As Konev recalled,

> we strove to plan our artillery attack so as to neutralize the entire tactical zone of the enemy defences … to a depth of 18–20 kilometres. By this time, we had gathered precise reconnaissance information; the enemy defences had been photographed beforehand … the enemy engineering fortifications, fire system and targets in the given sector.[10]

The First Ukrainian Front built thirty pontoon bridges over the Vistula to secure an uninterrupted flow of supplies; its engineers also built 400 dummy tanks, 500 dummy trucks, and 1,000 dummy guns for deception, placing them at the southern flank where no offensive was planned.[11]

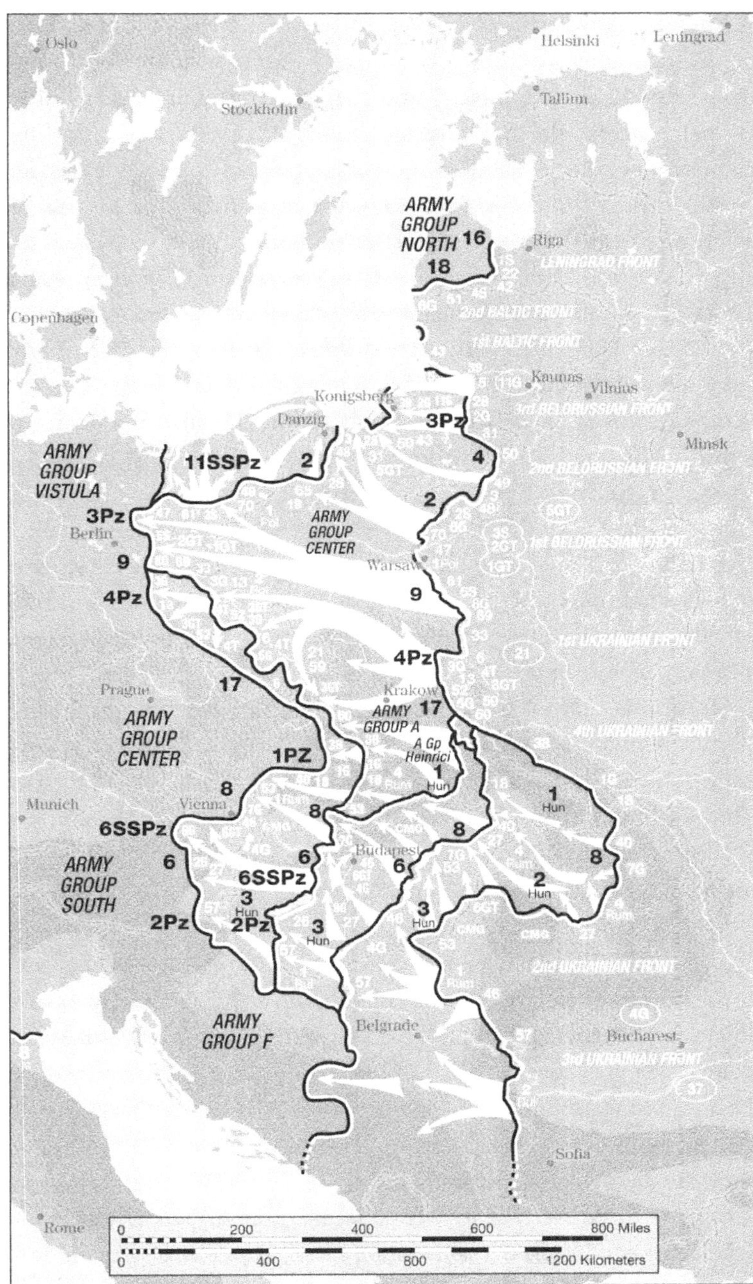

Map 12 Winter–spring campaign (December 1944–April 1945).

After a massive artillery barrage, the First Ukrainian Front and the First Belarusian Front easily broke through the German lines on 12 and 14 January 1945, respectively, and then their armour began swiftly advancing across Poland, covering at times between forty and fifty kilometres per day.[12] The Red Air Force operated almost unopposed: on 16 January, it flew 3,431 sorties in the area of the First Belarusian Front, whereas the Luftwaffe, short of both aircraft and fuel, could fly only 42 sorties.[13] The Polish Army took Warsaw on 17 January, while the Red Army entered Germany proper and on 1 February, having covered 500 kilometres within three weeks, reached the Oder River and captured important bridgeheads on its western bank. One of these, near the city of Küstrin, was only seventy kilometres away from Berlin.[14] The offensive across Poland was one of the most successful Soviet operations of World War II. This victory was attained at a relatively low cost: the Red Army's irrecoverable casualties equalled 2 per cent of the deployed manpower.[15] Yet, as Konev recalled, German soldiers 'continued to fight as before and were exceptionally staunch, sometimes to the point of fanaticism.... Nor were there as yet any signs of broken morale in the Nazi Army.'[16]

Meanwhile, the Second Belarusian Front, attacking from the Warsaw region northward, reached the Baltic Sea on 26 January, thus cutting off East Prussia from the rest of Germany. The Third Belarusian Front advanced towards Königsberg, East Prussia's capital, and by 9 February surrounded the city, along with a large adjacent area along the Baltic coast. At this point, the Red Army's stunning string of deep operations came to a halt.

As early as 1943 the Red Army General Staff learned how to coordinate the actions of aligned fronts by appointing a *Stavka* regional envoy, a high-ranking general holding broad powers. However, in 1945 Stalin spotted the opportunity to enter history as the general who finished off 'the fascist monster in its lair'[17] and began again, as he had done in 1941, intervening in operational planning. Such interventions from Moscow inevitably resulted in miscommunications, delays in the information flow, and belated reaction to events on the ground.[18] As Konev complained, 'no good came of that because, when you are given strict orders exactly when to send your tanks into the breach, they are often so out of keeping with the actual situation on the front that the rigid time-table sent down from the top just cannot be used'.[19] Stalin's interference had an even worse impact on the coordination of Red Army fronts, as secondary objectives were repeatedly prioritised at the expense of the primary ones, leading to confusion and strategic blunders.

As a case in point, the area around Königsberg was well fortified, and the Germans pinned the Soviets down at the city's outskirts for two months. Reinforced by a transfer of four armies from the Second Belarusian Front, the Third Belarusian Front assaulted the city on 6 April 1945 and took it after three days of bitter street fights. However, the Germans still resisted at the Semland peninsula around the Pillau port until 25 April. In proportionate terms, Soviet casualties during the actions in East Prussia were the heaviest of all the strategic operations initiated in 1945: the Third Belarusian Front irrevocably lost 13 per cent of its manpower, while its total casualties made up 60 per cent of the forces deployed since the start of the offensive in East Prussia.[20] Rokossovsky implied that the assault on Königsberg was unnecessary because, by that time, the German forces there retained no offensive capacity and could have been blocked until the fall of Berlin. By detaching half of the forces of the Second Belarusian Front, the *Stavka* undermined its ability to keep pace with the right flank of the First Belarusian Front which advanced directly towards Berlin.[21]

The Red Army's operational plan compiled in the last ten days of January, when it was swiftly approaching the Oder, presumed that after crossing the river, it would continue to press on towards Berlin, advancing at the maximum possible speed, leaving the Germans with no time to recover. Marshal Georgy Zhukov, who replaced Rokossovsky as the commander of the First Belarusian Front, planned to take Berlin by 16 February; Konev proposed a similar plan.[22] However, the slower advance of the debilitated Second Belarusian Front, now commanded by Rokossovsky, resulted in a 150-kilometre gap between the spearheads of the First and Second Belarusian Fronts. It was this opening that the German Army Group Vistula, deployed in Pomerania, could potentially exploit by striking at the flank of the Soviet offensive towards Berlin. Once again, the blame for this can be placed squarely at the feet of the *Stavka* and Stalin, personally.[23]

As the Red Army advanced, millions of German civilians fled westward. With East Prussia cut off from mainland Germany, the *Kriegsmarine* mobilised an enormous fleet of merchant and naval ships to evacuate East Prussian refugees and soldiers. It was the largest naval evacuation in history, one that delivered more than 1.5 million people to Germany's mainland. Yet not all of those who boarded the ships reached Germany. When the *Wilhelm Gustloff*, a flagship German cruise liner, took off from Gotenhafen in January 1945, it was overcrowded with refugees, along with German naval personnel. In total, some 10,582 people had been crammed aboard, but it was spotted by a Soviet submarine and hit with three torpedoes. The ship sank in the freezing Balic waters, taking an estimated 9,343 people down with it. It was the largest death toll in maritime history. Eleven days later, the same submarine torpedoed the liner *Steuben*, which had departed from Pillau with about 4,267 people on board, mostly wounded German soldiers and refugees; only about 300 survived.[24] Finally, on 16 April, another Soviet submarine lurking near Gotenhafen sunk the freighter *Goya*; out of the 7,000 soldiers and civilians aboard, only around 180 were rescued.[25]

By 1945 Hungary remained Germany's only ally in Europe. The Red and Romanian armies surrounded Budapest in late December 1944, trapping 79,000 Axis soldiers inside.[26] On 29 December the Red Army demanded the surrender of the Budapest garrison, but the Germans killed the Soviet truce envoy.[27] The next day, the Red Army began assaulting Budapest. It made slow and costly progress in house-to-house fighting, while German generals unsuccessfully attempted to persuade Hitler to sanction a breakout from Budapest.[28] The fascist Hungarian Arrow Cross party began hastily executing the Jewish residents of Budapest who had avoided deportation to extermination camps. They were shot on the bank of the Danube, and their bodies were thrown into the river.

The Germans undertook their two last offensives of World War II in Hungary. The first, Operation Konrad, began on 1 January 1945. The Germans attacked towards the besieged Budapest, seeking to relieve its garrison. The Red Army stopped the Germans seventeen kilometres away from the city in mid-January,[29] after which the German garrison undertook a disastrous breakout attempt on 11 February in violation of Hitler's order to hold on. As a German soldier recalled, 'like lemmings blindly driven to throw themselves into the sea, a mass of once-disciplined people, having abandoned all reason [rushed] down this road, headlong into disaster'.[30] Of 43,900 men who attempted to break out, less than 700 made it to the German lines, while half of them fell in battle and the rest were taken prisoner.[31] On 13 February the remnants of the Budapest garrison surrendered. Hungary was knocked out of the war. The Soviet offensive on Budapest that had started on 29 October 1944 was costly: the Red Army's irrecoverable casualties totalled 11 per cent of the manpower deployed at the beginning of the operation, while the total casualties constituted 44.5 per cent of the initial force.[32]

The last German offensive, codenamed *Spring Awakening*, began on 6 March 1945. Its goal was to protect an oilfield in western Hungary, the last source of oil Germany retained. Hitler argued credibly that with the loss of this area, Germany would find the 'ground cut from under our feet'.[33] After the failure of the offensive in the Ardennes, the German generals, habitually aloof from the economic side of warfare, urged Hitler to redeploy tank divisions from the Western Front to the east of Berlin against an anticipated Soviet offensive.[34] However, Hitler instead ordered their transfer to Hungary. The Soviets spotted the concentration of German tank divisions on that part of the front and correctly calculated the intended direction of the German main strike. The Germans enjoyed numerical superiority 1.5:1 in tanks and self-propelled guns, but the Soviets had more manpower and 6.5:1 superiority in artillery. They built a 30-kilometre-deep defence zone resembling the fortification belt they had built during the Battle of Kursk.[35] When the Germans struck on 6 March, during the spring thaw, they were soon bogged down in mud, Soviet fortifications, and extensive minefields. The Soviet artillery and air force then went to work grinding down the German armour. The Red Army, assisted by the Bulgarian Army, then advanced until it reached Vienna, which fell on 13 April. Hungary had suffered its second crushing defeat of the twentieth century; in World War II its army had lost between 340,000 and 360,000 soldiers dead and taken prisoner.[36]

After the disasters in Hungary, Germany was bracing for the inevitable Soviet assault on Berlin. Germany's prospects were grim. The German Ninth Army, with its 110,000 soldiers,[37] concentrated around the Küstrin bridgehead but was hopelessly outnumbered by Zhukov's First Belarusian Front, with its 908,500 Soviet soldiers and the 80,000 soldiers of the First Polish Army. Konev's First Ukrainian Front, with its

550,900 soldiers, also planned to launch an offensive on Berlin from an area well south of Küstrin.[38]

The Germans had, however, used the two-and-a-half-month respite in the Soviet drive towards Berlin to build impressive fortifications at Seelow Heights across from the Küstrin bridgehead. This was, after all, the obvious starting point of the final Soviet offensive. To impede Soviet tank actions, German engineers flooded the area before their main defensive line on the approaches to Berlin. The Soviets again reckoned on a massive artillery barrage to break through the German defences.

On 16 April 1945 both Zhukov and Konev struck, but the artillery barrage of the First Belarusian Front was ineffective because the Germans withdrew from the front trenches to the opposite slopes of the Seelow Heights. The barrage inflicted almost no causalities, and the Germans succeeded in pinning the Soviets down at the heights for three days.[39] Furious about the delay, Zhukov demanded that by 21 April his formations reach Berlin's suburbs 'at all costs ... and immediately report it to Stalin and the media'.[40] Indeed, any action prefaced by the Stalinist dictum 'at all costs' ensured that the cost was high. In contrast, the artillery barrage of the First Ukrainian Front blanketed Germans' positions across the entire depth of their defensive line, paving the way for Konev's breakthrough by the evening of the same day. After a swift advance, Konev reached Berlin's suburbs on 22 April, having covered a distance almost three times longer than that separating Zhukov from Berlin. Vasilii Chuikov, commander of the Eighth Guards Army deployed at the Küstrin bridgehead, compared the flexibility of Konev's operational method with the rigidity of Zhukov, whose actions led to 'needless losses and even failures'.[41] Nevertheless, on 24 April, Konev and Zhukov together managed to surround Berlin and demand the surrender of its garrison.[42] Having received no reply, they proceeded to launch the final assault on the capital.

In late March Goebbels recorded that 'among most sections of the German people faith in victory totally vanished. Criticism is now being directed ... at the whole conduct of the war and, unfortunately, even at the Führer personally.... Many Party members, moreover, are now beginning to waver.'[43] Goebbels speculated on the subject of organising armed resistance in the rear of the Allied armies, the so-called *Werwolf*, but his ideas as to how exactly this would work did not go beyond publishing underground newspapers and the resistance never materialised.[44] Even before the Red Army surrounded Berlin, the reserves of coal in the city were exhausted. Most of the city's buildings had no electricity, while the metro and sewerage had ceased functioning.[45] The one saving grace for the city's hard-pressed defenders was that the Red Army had paused its offensive on Berlin in February, allowing them ample time to turn Berlin into a fortress. However, according to Franz Halder, former Chief of the Army General Staff, 'no cohesive, over-all plan for the defence of Berlin was ever actually prepared. All that existed was the stubborn determination of Hitler to defend the capital of the Reich.... The city's defence was characterised only by a mass of improvisations.'[46] All the fortifications had to be constructed by hand because a lack of fuel prevented both the use of machinery and the transportation of workers to more remote sites that would have better favoured the defenders. In the end, engineering works in the 'fortress of Berlin' consisted mainly of trenches, barricades, and strongholds in the ruins of the buildings destroyed by Allied bombing.[47]

Drafting the last reserves of manpower, the Nazi Party organised the *Volkssturm* in the fall of 1944: a militia consisting of men formally unfit for active duty. A third of them were unarmed, and many of those who were received various trophy rifles, often with incompatible ammunition. They were joined by Hitler Youth, who were more motivated but untrained. In total, the Berlin garrison consisted of 60,000 regular Wehrmacht and SS soldiers supported by sixty tanks and scores of artillery batteries; the *Volkssturm* likewise numbered 60,000 men, with an unknown number of Hitler Youth militia. Against the immense Soviet superiority, such weakness was further compounded by the fact that the commander of the Berlin garrison only had authority only over the regular army but not the *Volkssturm*, SS troops, anti-aircraft batteries, or Hitler Youth.[48]

In early March 1945 Hitler and his closest entourage retreated to a bunker built in 1943 under the Reich Chancellery, eight-and-a-half metres below the surface. The bunker consisted of thirty-six small rooms; its walls were made of four-metre thick concrete.[49] By that time, Hitler was a wreck: 'hands trembling, back bent, gait shuffling, saliva dripping from the corners of his mouth, the Führer appeared much older than his 55 years';[50] 'his estimate of the means at his disposal and the fighting power of the enemy were wholly unrealistic'.[51] Proclaiming that 'the German people, if defeated, would be unworthy to survive',[52] Hitler attempted to command divisions that existed only in his imagination. He put all his hopes on the assumption that the 'perverse coalition between plutocracy and Bolshevism' could not last[53] and that a conflict among the Allies would allow Germany to snatch victory from the jaws of defeat.[54] The death of US President Franklin D. Roosevelt on 12 April was celebrated in the bunker in the firm belief that this would herald a radical change in US geopolitical strategy. This hope evaporated with the beginning of the Soviet offensive four days later.

The mood in the bunker was grim: its inhabitants, breathing air polluted with the stench of ash and decay,[55] spent their time in discussions about whether a suicide by poison or a bullet was preferable.[56] In the words of Traudl Junge, Hitler's secretary, 'An erotic fervor seemed to have taken possession of everybody. Everywhere ... I saw bodies locked in lascivious embraces. The women have discarded all their modesty and were freely exposing their private parts.'[57] To distract himself from thoughts of his looming demise, Hitler at times retreated to play with a model of Linz, designed by the architect Hermann Giesler in February 1945. He stunned the bunker inhabitants when he told them he would transform this city, one of the bleakest in Austria, into 'Europe's centre of culture' after Germany's victory.[58]

While delusion and fantasy pervaded life in the bunker, the reality above ground was that units of the First Ukrainian and First Belarusian Fronts advanced slowly to the city centre in house-to-house fighting. Stalin's overzealous effort to coordinate operations from Moscow replicated earlier strategic confusion and made the Battle of Berlin a messy affair. Competition between Konev's and Zhukov's fronts for the prestigious prize of Berlin was actively encouraged by Stalin,[59] leading to rash and costly actions. Determined to take Berlin before Konev, Zhukov sent the First Tank Army into the city without infantry support, and the tanks became an easy target for German *Panzerfausts*, handheld anti-tank weapons with an effective range of 30 to 100 metres. In fact, *Panzerfausts* destroyed up to 70 per cent of all Soviet tanks lost during the Battle of Berlin.[60]

Figure 12.1 Adolf Hitler meeting members of the Hitler Youth who were defending Berlin, 20 April 1945. Source: Popperfoto via Getty Images.

Meanwhile, the Germans observed that Soviet soldiers 'took every opportunity to infiltrate through back yards, cellar passageways, subway tunnels, and sewers. In this way many of the defence positions were stormed from behind or below'.[61] However, because the *Stavka* did not determine the operational boundaries separating Konev's and Zhukov's fronts, their formations entangled. There were numerous incidents of friendly fire when artillery belonging to one front inflicted serious casualties on formations belonging to the other front; the same was true of airstrikes by the Red Air Force. General Pavel Rybalko, one of the most competent Soviet tank commanders, demanded that the air force be withdrawn from the Battle of Berlin because its actions did more harm than good.[62] Using the confusion as a pretext, Zhukov requested that Stalin terminate Konev's advance to the city centre, thus securing the laurels of the victor for himself. Stalin eventually acquiesced, after which Konev had to restrain the deeply frustrated Rybalko from continuing with his advance.[63]

Hitler desperately ordered several relief attacks towards Berlin. Some generals, such as Walther Wenck with his Twelfth Army, did make a futile effort to comply; others, such as Theodor Busse, commander of the Ninth Army, and Gotthard Heinrici, commander of Army Group Vistula, instead marched westward to surrender their forces to the Western Allies.[64] On 25 April, Konev's soldiers met US vanguards in the city of Torgau on the Elba River; the celebration of this event by the Allies frustrated Hitler's last hope for a conflict among them.

On 29 April 1945 Hitler heard the news about the execution of Mussolini, whose corpse partisans hung upside down at Milan's square.[65] He was determined to avoid a similar plight. The next day, when the Red Army was only several blocks away, Hitler called his bunker entourage together for a brief farewell and then shot himself.[66] Before that, Hitler appointed Goebbels as Chancellor of Germany and Admiral Dönitz as President. These appointments were short-lived. On 1 May Goebbels also committed suicide, along with his wife, Magda, who had poisoned their six children.

The last-remaining German stronghold in Berlin was the governmental district, including the massive Reichstag building. On 29 April, at dawn, the Red Army vanguards crossed the Spree River over the remnants of the Moltke Bridge. The bridge was only at about 300 metres from the Reichstag, but it took the Soviets an entire day to drive the SS soldiers away from the nearby buildings before they could attack their main target. The Reichstag could have been flattened by artillery and air force, but the organisation of a massive artillery barrage required time, whereas Stalin demanded the Reichstag be taken by 1 May, the international Labour Day holiday. Pressed by Stalin, Zhukov rushed his infantry into assault at the usual 'all costs'.[67] The hoisting of a banner over the Reichstag became 'an obsession'.[68] All the units assigned to attack the Reichstag carried banners.

The first two assaults on the Reichstag at dawn and at 14:25 failed.[69] Only after the attack that started at 18:00 did the Soviets enter the building, but the Reichstag garrison continued fierce resistance.[70] A section of Soviet artillery scouts sneaked into the stairwell leading to one of the Reichstag towers, and at 22:40 they hoisted the banner over the tower while the fight in the building still continued.[71] Three hours later, an infantry section that had just arrived to the Reichstag and had not participated in the assault exploited a respite in the fight to hoist yet another banner among those flying already in and over the Reichstag. The section included two sergeants; one of them was an ethnic Russian and the other a Georgian. They were officially proclaimed the first ones to accomplish the feat of banner hoisting. Their deed was intended to symbolise the primary role of ethnic Russians in the war against

Figure 12.2 Soviet soldiers in front of the ruins of the Reichstag in Berlin, 2 May 1945. Source: Mondadori Portfolio via Getty Images.

Germany but also the contribution of Georgians to the victory; the latter was meant to please Stalin. The sergeants received 'Hero of the Soviet Union' titles, but Aleksei Berest, a Ukrainian lieutenant who led the section with the official banner, did not receive his share of glory, nor did the soldiers who had hoisted the first banner in the heat of the battle.[72] The battle in the Reichstag continued throughout the day, and only at 6:20 am on 2 May did the remnants of its garrison surrender.[73]

In the early morning of 1 May 1945 a German truce envoy, General Hans Krebs, Chief of the Army General Staff, arrived at Chuikov's headquarters and requested an armistice for negotiations, but Chuikov, under orders from Zhukov, demanded unconditional surrender. The ten-hour talks broke off with the Germans rejecting the ultimatum, but on 2 May General Weidling issued an order for capitulation.[74] However, Weidling's order did not affect the actions of German formations outside of Berlin, which attempted, sometimes successfully, to reach the territory occupied by the Western Allies. As for the top Nazi functionaries, Himmler and Göring surrendered to the Western Allies but poisoned themselves in custody before justice could be served. Martin Bormann, Chief of the Nazi Party Chancellery, was killed during an attempt to escape Berlin.[75] Heinrich Müller, Chief of the Gestapo, vanished without a trace.

In the early hours of 7 May, General Alfred Jodl signed the unconditional surrender of Germany in the French city of Reims with the termination of all hostilities by 23:01 on 8 May. This declaration prompted German forces in Prague, one of the last remaining areas under German control, to leave the city and head towards the Americans. During the night of 9 May, the Red Army made an eighty-kilometre march to Prague and entered it at dawn.[76] This was the end of World War II in Europe.

Under pressure from the Soviets, the Western Allies agreed to consider Germany's unconditional surrender issued at Reims as preliminary, with the final declaration to be signed in Berlin. The ceremony occurred in the first hour of 9 May.[77] In compliance with the provisions of the declaration, President Dwight D. Eisenhower ordered US forces to reject the surrender of the Germans and their collaborators, who attempted to flee from the Red Army to the Americans from 9 May onwards.

Despite the enormous numerical and material superiority of the Red Army over the Wehrmacht in 1945, the battles during that year were fierce. From January to April 1945, the Red Army lost a total of 800,817 men dead and missing,[78] four-and-a-half times as many as the US Army lost in Europe and the Mediterranean during the entirety of World War II.[79] The average daily casualty rate of the Red Army in 1945 was considerably higher than in 1944 and, in most categories, higher than in 1943.

Table 12.1 *Casualties of the Red Army, 1943–1945*[80]

	1943	1944	1945
Average irrecoverable daily casualties of manpower	6,335	4,833	6,208
Total average monthly casualties of manpower, 1st Ukrainian Front (percentage of the manpower engaged)	12.81	10.91	12.85
Total average monthly casualties of manpower, 1st Belarusian Front (percentage of the manpower engaged)	11.73	7,34	8.48
Average irrecoverable monthly loss of tanks and self-propelled guns	1,958	1,975	3,224
Average irrecoverable monthly loss of aircraft	1,875	2,067	2,588

12.1   The Total Cost of War on the Eastern Front

Credible German figures for casualties sustained by the Wehrmacht on the Eastern Front exist only until 1 January 1945. In this period, the number of irrecoverable casualties is recorded as 2,742,891.[81] To this number must be added two-thirds of the approximately 1,277,000 irrecoverable casualties suffered between 1 January and 30 April 1945 on all fronts.[82]

The total number of Soviet deaths accepted officially in Russia is 26.6 million.[83] This, however, is only a rough estimate based on the difference between the last pre-war census of 1939 and the first post-war census of 1959, after accounting for the assumed natural deaths and birth rates during and after the war, as well as the territorial changes that occurred in 1939–1945. The number of irrecoverable casualties of the Red Army by May 1945, including POWs, is officially stated as 11,273,026.[84] This number is, however, an inaccurate underestimation of the true total because it underrepresents (by 1.75 million) the number of POWs taken by the Germans and other Axis states.[85] Moreover, it excludes the unknown number of casualties sustained by partisans, people's militia (*opolchenie*; raised in 1941) and the NKVD (People's Commissariat for Internal Affairs) troops. It must also be recognised that some scholars have seriously questioned the methodology used by official historians in calculating the Red Army's casualties, which raise questions far beyond the obvious groups excluded from the final total.[86]

To determine the Soviet civilian irrecoverable casualties, the authors of the Russian official history simply subtracted the alleged military deaths from the total figure of population losses; this suggested the number was more than fifteen million people. They attribute this loss to either deliberate murder by the Axis or deaths from privations in the occupied regions.[87] Such an approach is misleading because this death toll includes many substantial groups who died from unrelated events or vanished – for example, the soldiers who died in the armed conflicts in 1939 and 1940, the victims of ethnic cleansing conducted by Ukrainian and Baltic nationalists, the enemy collaborators who died in battles against the Red Army and partisans, the Soviet citizens who evacuated with the Axis armies voluntarily, and the *Ostarbeiter* who refused to return to the USSR after the war. Separately, the civilian death toll attributed to the Axis occupation the victims of the Soviet regime: Germans 'repatriated' to Germany from the western borderlands in 1939–1941; the negative balance during the exchange of population with Poland and Czechoslovakia in 1944–1946; the victims of the scorched earth policy ordered by Stalin in 1941; those who died in Soviet-held territory from malnutrition, overwork, diseases, and cold; the Gulag prisoners, half of whom died in 1942–1943; the people killed by Soviet counterinsurgents in the western borderlands and in the North Caucasus in 1943–1952; those who died as a result of the Soviet deportations of 1940–1941 and 1943–1952; and victims of the famine of 1946–1947 inflicted by the Stalinist policies.

Two conclusions follow from these sets of data. First, it is clear that along with the millions of civilians killed by the Nazis, the Stalinist regime inflicted a comparable population loss on its own civilians. Second, the ratio of Soviet military deaths versus civilian losses inflicted by the Axis is far greater than the official Russian data implies. Russian official statistics deliberately misrepresent the details of the overall population loss first, to conceal the extent of Stalinist crimes, and second to obscure the ratio of the Red Army's casualties relative to the Wehrmacht's. The great disproportion of military casualties reflected the profound difference in training among German and Soviet armed forces. The Soviet Union won by its superior manpower; the more competent management of available natural resources, severely depleted by the German invasion; the more effective mobilisation of its society and economy for a total war; the better coordination of civilian and military agencies; the more rational structure of military command; and Allied Lend-Lease aid deliveries.[88] Together, these factors resulted in the superior combat capacity of the Red Army from 1943 onward, ensuring eventual victory despite the loss of many more lives in comparison to the Wehrmacht.

Notes

1 V. Zolotarev and G. Sevost'ianov, eds., *Velikaia Otechestvennaia voina, 1941–1945* (Moscow: Nauka, 1999), 3:428, p. 429.
2 Richard Overy, *Russia's War* (New York: Penguin Group, 1997), p. 257.
3 Soviet infantrymen received roughly as much entry-level training as the members of German *Volkssturm*. Alexander Statiev, *At War's Summit: The Red Army and the Struggle for the Caucasus Mountains in World War II* (Cambridge: Cambridge University Press, 2018), pp. 324–346.

4 I. Konev, *Year of Victory* (Moscow: Progress Publishers, 1969), p. 12.

5 Overy, *Russia's War*, p. 155.

6 Konev, *Year of Victory*, p. 7.

7 G. F. Krivosheev, ed., *Rossiia i SSSR v voinakh XX veka* (Moscow: Veche, 2010), p. 336.

8 Zolotarev, *Velikaia Otechestvennaia*, 3:239.

9 B. Sokolov, *Bitva za Berlin* (Moscow: Veche, 2022), p. 18.

10 Konev, *Year of Victory*, pp. 10, 11.

11 Ibid., p. 12.

12 Ibid., p. 45; Zolotarev, *Velikaia Otechestvennaia*, 3:239.

13 Zolotarev, *Velikaia Otechestvennaia*, 3:239.

14 Georgii Zhukov, *Vospominaniia i razmyshleniia* (Moscow: APN, 1969), pp. 601, 602.

15 Krivosheev, *Rossiia*, p. 337.

16 Konev, *Year of Victory*, p. 29.

17 *Pravda* (7 November 1944).

18 Zolotarev, *Velikaia Otechestvennaia*, 3:232.

19 Konev, *Year of Victory*, pp. 21, 22.

20 Krivosheev, *Rossiia*, p. 340.

21 K. Rokossovsky, *Soldatskii dolg* (Moscow: Voenizdat, 1997), pp. 384–386.

22 Zhukov, *Vospominaniia*, pp. 606, 607.

23 Zolotarev, *Velikaia Otechestvennaia*, 3:244.

24 Charles Koburger, *Steel Ships, Iron Crosses, and Refugees* (New York: Praeger, 1989), pp. 7, 105.

25 Nigel Parker, 'Forgotten Naval Disasters at Sea', www.bmmhs.org/forgotten-naval-disasters-at-sea/, accessed on 19 January 2024.

26 Karl-Heinz Frieser, ed., *Germany and the Second World War* (Oxford: Oxford University Press, 2017), p. 897.

27 Ibid., p. 901.

28 Krisztian Ungvary, *The Siege of Budapest* (New Haven: Yale University Press, 2002), p. 189.

29 Frieser, *Germany*, 8:910; Ungvary, *The Siege*, p. 195.

30 Ungvary, *The Siege*, p. 211.

31 Ibid., p. 255.

32 Krivosheev, *Rossiia*, p. 335.

33 Hugh Trevor-Roper, ed., *Final Entries 1945: The Diaries of Joseph Goebbels* (Barnsley: Pen & Sword, 2007), pp. 203, 252.

34 Frieser, *Germany*, pp. 904, 925, 956.

35 Ibid., pp. 929–931.

36 Ibid., p. 956.

37 Tony Le Tissier, *Zhukov at the Oder* (Westport: Praeger, 1996), p. 273.

38 Krivosheev, *Rossiia*, p. 347.

39 Zhukov, *Vospominaniia*, p. 643.

40 Zolotarev, *Velikaia Otechestvennaia*, 3:275.

41 Vasili Chuikov, *The Fall of Berlin* (New York: Holt, Rinehart and Winston, 1968), pp. 173, 174.

42 Zolotarev, *Velikaia Otechestvennaia*, 3:276, 282.

43 Trevor-Roper, *Final Entries*, pp. 213, 214.

44 Ibid., pp. 234, 269.

45 Zolotarev, *Velikaia Otechestvennaia*, 3:281.

46 Wilhelm Willemer, 'The German Defense', www.allworldwars.com/The-German-Defense-of-Berlin-1945-by-Wilhelm-Willemer.html, accessed on 19 January 2024.

47 Ibid.

48 Ibid.

49 Steven Lehrer, *The Reich Chancellery and Führerbunker Complex* (Jefferson: McFarland & Co., 2006), pp. 122, 123, 130.

50 Lehrer, *The Reich Chancellery*, p. 130.

51 Willemer, 'The German Defense'.

52 Ibid.

53 Frieser, *Germany*, p. 956.

54 Trevor-Roper, *Final Entries*, p. 211.

55 Lehrer, *The Reich Chancellery*, pp. 132, 136.

56 Linge, *With Hitler*, p. 193.

57 Lehrer, *The Reich Chancellery*, p. 136.

58 Frederic Spotts, *Hitler and the Power of Aesthetics* (London: Hutchinson, 2002), pp. 377, 378.

59 Zolotarev, *Velikaia Otechestvennaia*, 3:279, 284; Zhukov, *Vospominaniia*, p. 625.

60 V. Shunkov, *Oruzhie Vermakhta* (Minsk: Kharvest, 1999), pp. 138–140.

61 Willemer, 'The German Defense'.

62 Zolotarev, *Velikaia Otechestvennaia*, 3:284.

63 Ibid., 3:284, 285.

64 Willemer, 'The German Defense'.

65 Lehrer, *The Reich Chancellery*, p. 136.

66 Anton Joachimsthaler, *The Last Days of Hitler* (London: Arms and Armour, 1996), pp. 147–182.

67 Zolotarev, *Velikaia Otechestvennaia*, 3:286, 287.

68 Nikolai Iamskoi, 'Znamia No. 5', *Literaturnaia gazeta*, no. 17–18 (2001), p. 6.

69 Vladimir Piskarev, 'Kto vodruzil znamia pobedy nad reikhstagom?', *Gasyrlar avazy* 1–2 (1996), http://archive.gov.tatarstan.ru/magazine/go/anonymous/main/?path=mg:/numbers/1996_1_2/04/6/, accessed on 19 January 2024.

70 Zolotarev, *Velikaia Otechestvennaia*, 3:285.

71 Iamskoi, 'Znamia', p. 6.

72 Ibid., p. 6; Zolotarev, *Velikaia Otechestvennaia*, 3:286, 287.

73 Iamskoi, 'Znamia', p. 6.

74 Chuikov, *The Fall of Berlin*, pp. 217–244, 250–255.

75 Linge, *With Hitler*, p. 210.

76 Zolotarev, *Velikaia Otechestvennaia*, 3:293, 297.

77 Ibid., 3:298.

78 Krivosheev, *Rossiia*, p. 431.

79 The US Army suffered 176,031 combat deaths during its actions in Europe and the Mediterranean. Statistical and Accounting Branch, *Army Battle Casualties and Nonbattle Deaths in World War II* (Washington, DC: Department of the Army, 1953), p. 5.

80 Krivosheev, *Rossiia*, pp. 236, 396, 410, 518.

81 Stephen Fritz, *Ostkrieg* (Lexington: University Press of Kentucky, 2011), p. 496.

82 Krivosheev, *Rossiia*, pp. 534, 535.

83 Ibid., p. 219.

84 Ibid., p. 236.

85 V. Zemskov, 'Statisticheskii labirint', *Rossiiskaia istoriia* 3 (2011), pp. 22–32.

86 Boris Sokolov, *Rossiiskie i sovetskie voiny XX–XXI vekov* (Moscow: Novyi khronograf, 2021).

87 Krivosheev, *Rossiia*, pp. 222, 223.

88 Richard Overy, *Why the Allies Won* (London: Jonathan Cape, 1995), pp. 182–189.

Part IV

Criminality and Occupation

13

Mass Murder in the German-Occupied East, 1941–1944

The invasion of the Soviet Union – codenamed Operation Barbarossa – was the first campaign of the Second World War in which the systematic mass murder of Jews and other racial opponents was the order of the day from the very outset.[1] Since the mid-1920s, Hitler had yearned for a war against the Soviet Union and with it the destruction of Bolshevism. In his autobiographical manifesto, *Mein Kampf,* he had written, 'In Russian Bolshevism we see Jewry's attempt in the twentieth century to acquire global hegemony.' In Hitler's mind, 'Soviet Russia' was associated with the worst form of Jewish rule; it was the only country he believed to be completely controlled by Jews. The invasion of the Soviet Union in June 1941 was thus the culmination of Hitler's political and ideological programme, his defining work, the climax of his 'struggle against the Jewish Bolshevisation of the world'.[2]

Several major groups of non-combatants among the Soviet population in the territories invaded and occupied by German forces were targeted by Nazi mass-killing policies purely on the basis of their belonging to these groups (or being assigned to one or more of them by the perpetrators): Jews, psychiatric patients, Roma, urban dwellers in general (especially children, the sick, and the elderly), and captive Red Army soldiers. In fact, the range of victim groups extended even further. Inhabitants of the countryside were at serious risk of succumbing to so-called pacification operations; hundreds of thousands of residents of rural regions in Belarus, Ukraine, and Russia fell victim to German terror and reprisals carried out during the campaign waged against Soviet partisans, real and imagined. In practice, regardless of one's ethnic background, religion, physical and mental state, place of residence, or whether or not one wore a uniform, there was a very real chance of falling prey to the ubiquitous violence spread by German agencies in the occupied Soviet territories. It is perhaps hardly surprising, then, that the total number of Soviet dead in the conflict with Germany between 1941 and 1945 comes to a staggering 26.6 million people. Of these, Red Army dead account for 14.6 million, according to recent Russian figures. This leaves 12 million Soviet civilian deaths. If the 3.3 million troops who perished as POWs are deducted from the total of Red Army dead and added to the civilian toll, it becomes clear that the majority of Soviet war dead – more than 15 million people – comprised civilians and unarmed, captured soldiers.[3]

From the very first week of the German-Soviet War onwards, mass-murder operations were carried out on a gigantic scale, dwarfing all previous Nazi atrocities. Large-scale executions of Jewish men are documented for all the SS *Einsatzgruppen* – special mobile detachments of security policemen and SD (*Sicherheitsdienst*, Security Service) agents – and their respective subunits during the first weeks of the campaign.[4] During the planning phase for the German invasion of the Soviet Union, Hitler and the SS leadership could not have been certain how the Wehrmacht would react to large-scale massacres of Soviet Jews – that is, non-combatants – within its own area of operations. It is likely, therefore, that the pre-invasion orders issued in writing to the *Einsatzgruppen* were roughly compatible with the instructions issued by the Wehrmacht High Command (OKW) to the regular troops. These instructions, now known as 'the criminal orders', called for the execution of political functionaries (Red Army commissars), as well as a 'ruthless and energetic clampdown on *Bolshevik agitators, irregulars, saboteurs, Jews,* and the complete elimination of all active or passive resistance'.[5] The initial five-week period thus witnessed a dual-track approach on the part of the SS: officially, that is, according to written orders known also to the Wehrmacht, the *Einsatzgruppen* were instructed to kill leading communist functionaries (though they were not explicitly told to limit their operations to this group); unofficially, however, the *Einsatzgruppen* had evidently been supplied with additional verbal orders to include all male Jews of military-service age – or as many as possible – in the shooting operations. By the same token, the approach during the first five weeks of the campaign also demonstrates that the *Einsatzgruppen* had not received pre-invasion orders to kill *all* Soviet Jews, regardless of age or gender. Otherwise, the course of action taken by the SS commandos during these first five weeks would have amounted to insubordination.[6]

In mid-July 1941 the decision was taken to expand the scope of the killing operations to encompass the whole of Soviet Jewry, and approval was granted for the deployment of the increased manpower necessary to achieve this goal. The imminent escalation in killing could only occur after Reichsführer SS Heinrich Himmler – encouraged by the harmonious cooperation between the Wehrmacht and the SS *Einsatzgruppen* – had massively increased the number of SS troops and policemen operating behind the advancing German army. According to the original plans, the designated limit for the German military advance was a theoretical line connecting Arkhangelsk on the White Sea in the north with Astrakhan on the Caspian Sea in the south – a line some 480 kilometres east of Moscow. According to this projection, the *Einsatzgruppen*, with a mere 3,000 men, would have been expected to kill, at a minimum, all Jewish men of military-service age in an area three times the size of the territory that was actually conquered by the German army in 1941. The timetable for this mass murder was to cover twelve weeks, at which point the German planners expected the war to have been won. Due to the unforeseen military setbacks, SS troops, policemen, and regular soldiers were thus called upon from the second half of July 1941 to expand and intensify the killing in the occupied east, first and foremost in the vulnerable rear areas. Soviet Jews, as the 'pillars of the Jewish-Bolshevik system' (in the words of Eugen Müller, general for special assignment in the Army High Command (OKH)) and thus the main enemy, would be first in line in this frenzy of destruction.[7]

By the end of July 1941, at the close of this first stage of unprecedented destruction, a total of 63,000 people had been murdered by the *Einsatzgruppen* alone. More than 90 per cent of the victims of the massacres carried out by the *Einsatzgruppen* and the police regiments during these first five weeks of the campaign were Jews. In numerous instances, the murder of dozens or hundreds of Jewish men was carried out on the pretext of reprisals for one or more German soldiers having been shot from behind. Such absurd ratios were thus commonplace on the eastern front long before the Wehrmacht High Command issued its general directive of 16 September 1941, stipulating that 50 to 100 hostages be executed in retaliation for the death of every German soldier in the occupied territories.[8]

The first SS unit to make the transition to a policy of killing Jews indiscriminately, regardless of age or gender, was *Einsatzkommando 9* of *Einsatzgruppe B*. Under the command of Alfred Filbert, EK 9 arrived no later than 25 July in the Belarusian town of Vileyka, where it remained for several days. Like the other commandos of the four *Einsatzgruppen*, EK 9 had targeted primarily Jewish men of military-service age during the first five weeks of Germany's military campaign against the Soviet Union. This would change dramatically from Vileyka onwards. In two shooting operations at the end of July 1941, members of the commando shot a total of up to five hundred Jews, including women and children for the first time. The Vileyka massacres at the end of July marked the transition to genocide against Soviet Jewry. As such, EK 9 was not only the first commando within *Einsatzgruppe B* to begin systematically killing Jewish women and children, but in fact the first commando of any of the *Einsatzgruppen* to do so.[9]

By early October 1941 all the Einsatzgruppen and their respective subunits, as well as both SS brigades, had commenced killing Jews indiscriminately, regardless of age or gender.[10] Delays may have resulted from the time required for the new orders to be passed on verbally down the chain of command, from Himmler and his deputy Reinhard Heydrich, sometimes directly (as in the case of EK 9) but often via the higher SS and police leaders (HSSPF) and/or the *Einsatzgruppen* chiefs, to the individual commandos in the field. Another factor in the divergent timing of the transition to genocide was the varying zeal and interpretative will of the individual commanders. Jewish communities, furthermore, were distributed unevenly across the occupied territories; their presence and size – and, by extension, their 'accessibility' for the German killers – differed from place to place.[11]

By the end of 1941 more than 900,000 Soviet Jews had been killed by German forces. Around 460,000 of these were direct victims of the *Einsatzgruppen*. Almost as lethal as the *Einsatzgruppen* in terms of total number of Jews murdered were the twelve police battalions that made up the four police regiments. Overall, these twelve police battalions are responsible for the second largest share of murders after the

Einsatzgruppen. Then there were the SS formations active in the army group or army rear areas during 1941: the 1st SS Infantry Brigade, the 2nd SS Infantry Brigade, and the SS Cavalry Brigade. These forces killed at least 57,000 Soviet Jews in 1941. Finally, there were the Wehrmacht units deployed at the front and in the rear areas. The 707th Infantry Division alone murdered more than 10,000 Jews in Belarus in the autumn of 1941. The 707th Infantry Division may have been an extreme case among Wehrmacht formations in the occupied Soviet territories, but it was by no means exceptional. Active participation in mass shootings of Jews in the Soviet Union, either by providing shooters to the SS commandos or by carrying out killings on their own initiative, is also documented for numerous other regular German army units, including – though by no means limited to – the Signals Detachment 537 of the 286th Security Division; the 12th Company of Infantry Regiment 354 of the 286th Security Division; Infantry Regiment 691, also subordinated to the 286th Security Division; units of the 339th Infantry Division; the 62nd Infantry Division; the 454th Security Division; the 25th Infantry Division; and the 72nd Infantry Division. In many other cases, military units expressly requested the SD to shoot Jews, as did the second battalion of Infantry Regiment 350 of the 221st Security Division in mid-August 1941. On 22 September, the staff of the Seventeenth Army requested *Sonderkommando 4b* (a subunit of *Einsatzgruppe C*) to 'exterminate' all Jews in the central Ukrainian city of Kremenchug because three instances of sabotage of power lines had occurred there. As its chief of staff had made clear in an order issued on 7 September, those in command of the Seventeenth Army equated Jews with resistance and regarded 'Jews of both sexes' and 'also all ages' as fundamentally 'suspect'. In July *Sonderkommando 4a* (part of *Einsatzgruppe C*) killed 17 non-Jewish civilians, 117 'communist agents of the NKVD', and 183 'Jewish communists' in the Ukrainian town of Sokal, following a request from the Sixth Army. In other instances, the military intervened to get executions sped up, as in the case of the Eleventh Army in Simferopol later in the year.[12]

Late December 1941 marked the end of the first wave of German killing operations against the Soviet Union's Jewish population. The onset of winter weather caused the ground to freeze and made it too hard to allow for the digging of pits for the victims of the shootings. However, this proved to be only a brief respite for the Soviet Jews. The second wave of killing was launched in the early spring of 1942, on an even larger scale than the first. It lasted throughout that year, though its scale and timing varied from region to region. The context in which this second wave of shooting operations against Soviet Jews began was very different than that of the first wave the previous summer and autumn. The Wannsee Conference of 20 January 1942 had cleared the way for the mass murder of Jews in the different German-occupied territories to be placed on a centralised, pan-European footing. Technical modifications in the 'euthanasia' gas vans had opened up new possibilities for the killers, and such vans had already been deployed for murdering Jews in the occupied Soviet territories since November 1941. Meanwhile, the first death camp at Chełmno (Kulmhof) in the Wartheland had gone into operation in early December 1941, while the mass murder of the Jews of the Government General had commenced in mid-March 1942 at Bełżec extermination centre, the first to be fitted with stationary gas chambers.[13]

The dissolution of the Jewish ghettos in the occupied Soviet territories and the murder of their inhabitants continued throughout 1942. As of the end of that year, an estimated 15,000 to 16,000 'legal' Jews remained in General Commissariat Belarus in ghettos and labour camps in the region's large towns and cities. A further 6,000 to 7,000 'illegal' Jews had managed to survive by going into hiding, and some thousands escaped into the forests and joined the partisans. As of early 1943 no ghettos remained in Reich Commissariat Ukraine. Here and there, small groups of Jewish artisans were kept alive in order to serve local civilian administrations. The last of these Jews were murdered in 1943, on the eve of the German withdrawal from the region.[14] By March 1943 only 30,000 Jews were left in the whole of the Białystok District, all of them in the ghetto in the city of Białystok itself.[15] In total, around 2.6 million Jews living in the territory of the Soviet Union within the borders of 22 June 1941 were killed – that is, almost half of all Jews murdered in the Holocaust. Of these 2.6 million, all but 50,000 or so had lost their lives by the end of October 1943. At least half of all Jews killed on Soviet territory were citizens of Ukraine.[16]

Soviet Jews were the principal victims of the mass-murder campaign waged in the USSR between summer 1941 and spring 1942 by SS and

Figure 13.1 A German police officer shoots Jewish women and children from the Mizoch (Mizocz) ghetto in western Ukraine on 14 October 1942. Source: Pictures From History/Universal Images Group via Getty Images.

police forces with the active support of the Wehrmacht, but they were not the only population groups murdered there for racial-biological reasons. Soviet psychiatric patients and Roma – both regarded by the Nazis as racially inferior and thus as posing a biological threat, and both targeted in an attempt to 'purify' the newly occupied territories – were also murdered in large numbers during this period. Roma had been persecuted in the German Reich since the mid-1930s, and in some cases deported and incarcerated in concentration camps, but – much like Jews in the Reich – they had not been murdered on a mass scale. This changed during Operation Barbarossa. Given that psychiatric patients in the German Reich and the annexed Polish territories had already been killed since the second half of 1939 in the context of Nazi Germany's first mass-killing programme, the 'euthanasia' campaign, it is not surprising that patients in Soviet psychiatric clinics also fell victim to German forces from the summer of 1941.

The first mass-killing operations against Soviet psychiatric patients may have been triggered by a tour of inspection made by Reichsführer SS Heinrich Himmler. During his tour of Baranovichi, Minsk, and the surrounding area in mid-August 1941, which included the attendance of a mass shooting of Jews and alleged partisans by *Einsatzkommando 8* on the 15th, Himmler also visited the mental hospital in nearby Novinki the same day. Following the visit, Himmler – still under the immediate impression of the mass shooting that morning – requested Arthur Nebe to murder the psychiatric patients, but by other means than shooting, which was 'not the most humane way'. Instead, he instructed Nebe to experiment with new methods of killing that would be less burdensome for the perpetrators: Himmler and Heydrich feared that the mass shootings of people of all ages would have psychologically negative effects on the shooters and generate a group of brutalised men unable to reintegrate into post-war society. It was no coincidence that Himmler assigned to Nebe the task of finding an alternative to shooting: not only was he head of *Einsatzgruppe B*; as director of the Reich Criminal Police Office, he was also in charge of the Forensic Institute of the Security Police, which had played a key role in developing gassing facilities for Operation T4 in the Reich. Himmler's instructions were understood by several witnesses as a general authorisation for Nebe to kill all mentally ill people in his area of operations.[17] The tentative results of research carried out so far yield a total of at least 17,000 psychiatric patients murdered by German forces in the occupied territories of the Soviet Union.[18]

German forces marched into the Soviet Union without precise orders regarding the Roma minority but with radicalised prejudices and under the influence of experiences gathered during years of persecution. In the German Reich, Roma had already been one of the groups to fall victim to the Nazis' tendency to treat what they considered antisocial behaviour as a racial-biological threat. East of the Bug River, nomadic Roma in particular were regarded by both the Wehrmacht and police leadership as 'work-shy' and, even more ominously for the victims, as potential spies. In the climate of the siege mentality prevalent in the undermanned rear areas of the occupied Soviet territories, this translated into a blanket identification of Roma with partisans. These stereotypes prepared the ground for a murderous approach to this demographic group.[19]

A total of around 30,000 Roma were murdered in individual operations across the whole of the Soviet territories under German occupation, comprising half of those living there at the time of the invasion in June 1941. Some 6,000 Roma were killed in Belarus alone. Though the *Einsatzgruppen* did not systematically hunt down Roma in the way they did Jews, they murdered them whenever and wherever they found them. The victims were generally shot in small groups by the Security Police, though often after having been handed over by units of the Wehrmacht. It was not uncommon, furthermore, for Wehrmacht commanders to seize the initiative by expressly demanding the murder of Roma or for Wehrmacht units to conduct shooting operations themselves. After months of investigating German crimes against the Soviet Union, the latter's Extraordinary State Commission concluded that the physical annihilation of the Soviet Roma ought to be placed on a par with the murder of the Soviet Jews in terms of its totality and intentionality (though the respective dimensions are not comparable). Indeed, from spring 1942 onwards, Roma living in the rear areas of all three army groups – north, centre, and south – were treated de facto like Jews. As with the Jews, the motives for the annihilation can be found in a fatal combination of National Socialist racial ideology, which manifested itself not only in the blanket identification of Roma with partisans but also in the lack of differentiation in practice between itinerant and sedentary Roma, and a warped concept of military necessity that saw threats everywhere and envisaged the single option of further radicalisation as a response to any and all setbacks. Ultimately, Roma – like Jews and psychiatric patients – were regarded as racially inferior and as a threat to Germany's capacity to consolidate its territorial gains and eventually win a war in the east.[20]

As Germany's political and military leadership expected a swift campaign and a substantial collapse of the Soviet state, it did not anticipate having to fight a guerrilla war of any real significance. It was clear, however, that during the envisaged encirclement of entire Soviet armies, Red Army soldiers separated from their units would remain in the rear of the Wehrmacht. Additionally, the planned starvation of parts of the local population would no doubt trigger unrest. The weakness of the German security forces deployed between the main transit routes left supply lines and economic infrastructure vulnerable in the rear areas and created a power vacuum in which irregular Soviet resistance could potentially jeopardise the ultimate success of the military campaign. For these and other reasons, the Wehrmacht was not only keen to work hand in hand with the SS and police but also to react to any stirring of resistance with its own draconian measures.[21]

Even with the German military advance soon stalling, many months still passed before the first real Soviet underground groups organised themselves. Furthermore, they were often poorly equipped and insufficiently armed well into 1942 and even 1943. Until mid-1942 armed resistance frequently emanated from groups of scattered Red Army soldiers cut off from their units and acting on their own initiative. Though it would not be accurate to speak of a partisan war without partisans, the occupying forces relied from the outset on a 'preventive' approach to combating resistance, and regarded mass arrests and murder as effective instruments to this end. Already six weeks before the German invasion, on 13 May 1941, the OKW had issued a Decree on the Exercise of Martial Jurisdiction in the Area Barbarossa and on Special Measures of the Troops, which set the scene for what was to come by allowing collective reprisals against whole villages and by enabling each and every German officer to decide on matters of life and death regarding Soviet civilians without consulting superior authorities.[22]

The failure of the German offensive against Moscow and the fruits of the Soviet counteroffensive significantly improved strategic and political conditions for the Soviet partisans, which in turn led to an intensification of partisan activities. In the first months of 1942, the Germans responded to this development with a new tactic. It was devised above all by the regional military leadership in the rear area of Army Group Centre at the request of the OKH. Starting in March, the Germans organised large-scale operations – so-called *Großunternehmen* – against the partisans and their alleged accomplices. Combined forces of Wehrmacht, SS, and police encircled a given territory and then advanced inwards, gradually drawing the ring tighter and tighter, in the process confiscating cattle and foodstuffs, burning down entire villages and often massacring their inhabitants, including women and children. These operations were carried out mainly but not exclusively in Belarus and the region southwest of Moscow.[23]

Looking at the paltry weapons haul from some of these operations compared with the huge death tolls – 17 machine guns and 11 heavy weapons retrieved from at least 6,100 dead during Operation Hamburg in December 1942, 133 weapons taken from 13,000 killed during Operation Hornung in February 1943 – it is clear that the use of large-scale operations was not an effective way to fight the partisans. Describing an attack on a Soviet village in January 1943, Artur Wilke from the office of the commander of the Security Police in Minsk wrote, 'I have the inner conviction this evening that scarcely any real bandits were killed.' In fact, these operations were actually *designed* to kill Belarusian civilians rather than partisans as such. With their military fortunes in decline, the Germans resolved to wipe out those people who might conceivably provide aid to the partisan struggle behind German lines. Thus German units stuck to the roads and targeted adjacent villages (especially those bordering forested areas) during the large-scale operations, and intentionally avoided forging deeper into wooded areas where actual partisans and their bases might be encountered. As the former driver of *Einsatzkommando 8*, Georg Frentzel, later stated, 'Our objective here was to deprive the partisans in the forests of any opportunity to supply themselves with food, clothing, etc. from the villages.' The large-scale operations were a complete failure not only when it came to eliminating partisans, however, but also in their aim of cutting the partisans off from potential support networks. On the contrary, the brutality of German tactics only contributed to the growth of the partisan movement from 30,000 partisans in Belarus at the end of 1941 to 57,700 there in January 1943 and 122,600 in November 1943, which in turn led to even more desperate measures on the part of the Germans. Surprised by the number of bicycles found in partisan camps, the commander of the 1st SS Infantry Brigade, Karl von Treuenfeld, issued orders stating, 'Anyone bicycling must be shot.'[24]

The measures taken by German forces in the context of their 'pacification' campaign constituted an attack on a substantial section of the Soviet population and, simultaneously, on the national and ethnic fabric of the state. These so-called anti-partisan operations were in effect an attempt to depopulate the Soviet countryside. German forces massacred hundreds of thousands of Soviet civilians, destroying thousands of homes and, indeed, entire villages in the process – more than 600 in Belarus alone. The vast majority of the victims of these massacres had little or no connection to guerrilla resistance, and virtually all of these deaths had a racist component. This alleged anti-partisan war, waged in fact largely against Soviet peasants, cost the lives of 345,000 people in Belarus alone, its territorial focal point, of whom perhaps only 10 per cent were actually partisans. (By contrast, the Germans themselves lost 6,000 to 7,000 men in Belarus at the hands of Soviet partisans.) If we include all other Soviet territories affected – the Leningrad area, central Russia, northern Ukraine, Crimea, and parts of the northern Caucasus – the death toll as a result of German preventive terror and reprisals across the whole of the Soviet Union comes to around 640,000 people.[25]

Before the German invasion of the Soviet Union on 22 June 1941, it was clear to the Wehrmacht on exactly what scale they could expect to capture Soviet troops, and yet they neglected to make the requisite preparations for feeding and sheltering the prisoners, who were viewed by the economic planning staffs and the military leadership alike as German troops' direct competitors when it came to food. The number of extra mouths to feed was incompatible with German war aims. The obvious limitations on their freedom of movement and the relative ease with which large numbers could be segregated and their rations controlled were crucial factors in the deaths of more than three million Soviet POWs, the vast majority directly or indirectly as a result of starvation and undernourishment. In the first two months of the war, despite their severe lack of food, most Soviet prisoners still possessed a remnant of physical resilience and weather conditions were favourable. Around this time, however, the first hunger-related epidemics broke out. Already in September 1941 death rates increased considerably. In Stalag 342 (Molodechno) in Belarus, for instance, 200 prisoners a day were dying with a terrible constancy – around 6,000 per month in a single camp. From October 1941 mass mortality in all Wehrmacht camps holding Soviet POWs assumed monstrous proportions: in October, November, and December, between 300,000 and 500,000 prisoners died each month. The drastic reduction in official rations based on decisions made at the senior level to switch from a general undernourishment and neglect of the prisoners to a systematic, selective murder of most of them through starvation accelerated an intentional and sharp increase in the mortality rates in the POW camps.[26]

By the beginning of February 1942, that is, over the space of little more than seven months, two million Soviet prisoners of war had died or been murdered in German custody. This was almost 60 per cent of the 3.35 million Red Army soldiers captured during this period, most of them by the end of October 1941.[27] In Reich territory, at least 265,000 Soviet POWs died during these months; this constituted a death rate of around 53 per cent. (By contrast, death rates among Soviet and Polish *civilian* forced labourers inside Germany were well below 10 per cent.) The fact that this rate of mortality was scarcely lower than the death rate in the POW camps east of the Reich's borders sheds an unmistakeably clear light on living conditions for captive Soviet soldiers in Germany.[28] It also throws into stark relief the common fate of Soviet POWs in German captivity, regardless of their whereabouts, and refutes the claim that long transportation routes and associated supply problems were to blame for the mass mortality. Over an extended period between October 1941 and February 1942, just as many people died in a single large POW camp in the occupied Soviet territories as could be murdered during the same time by an entire *Einsatzgruppe*.[29] Indeed, as of winter 1941–1942, captured Soviet troops constituted the largest single victim group of Nazi mass-killing policies.

Alongside death by starvation – facilitated not only by deliberate under-nourishment but also by a lack of shelter and extreme exhaustion – there was a second method of annihilating Soviet POWs: mass shootings. Certain groups among the prisoners were targeted for selection and immediate execution. The so-called Commissar Order issued by the OKW on 6 June 1941 stipulated that political officers in the Red Army were to be shot on the spot, should they fall into German hands. Per this directive, as many as 10,000 Soviet political officers were murdered at the front or in the rear areas between June 1941 and May 1942. For almost all German formations that fought on the Eastern Front, there is evidence of their adherence to the Commissar Order. Reports of executions of captive Soviet political officers exist for all 13 armies, all 44 army corps, and more than 80 per cent of the almost 150 German divisions. Following the inclusion of additional cases where there are indications to this effect, the proportion at the divisional level increases to over 90 per cent of units. The Commissar Order was a blatant breach of law, for hardly any contravention of international law was more obvious than the premeditated and systematic murder of regular, uniformed prisoners of war.[30]

Despite the huge numbers involved, those Soviet prisoners of war shot by the SS, police, and Wehrmacht nonetheless comprised only a relatively small proportion of the total number of Red Army soldiers killed by their German captors. As mentioned previously, the vast majority perished directly or indirectly as a result of deliberate policies of neglect, undernourishment, and starvation while in the 'care' of the

Wehrmacht. The most reliable figures for the mortality of Soviet POWs in German captivity reveal that up to 3.3 million died from a total of just over 5.7 million captured between June 1941 and February 1945 – a proportion of almost 58 per cent.[31] Of these, at least 845,000 died in camps in the area of operations according to the Wehrmacht's own statistics, though this figure almost certainly does not include those who perished on their way to the camps, so that a total number of one million deaths in areas under military administration is more likely. Around 1.2 million prisoners died in the Reich Commissariats Ukraine and Ostland, approximately 500,000 in the Government General and up to 400,000 in the Reich.[32] To these totals must be added those prisoners who were shot immediately after being captured and, therefore, never registered as prisoners.[33] Soviet prisoners of war constituted the largest single victim group of the German war of annihilation against the Soviet Union and, after the European Jews, the largest victim group of all National Socialist annihilation policies.[34]

Around half of all Soviet civilians living under German military administration suffered from starvation, many of them on a constant basis from autumn 1941 onwards until the Wehrmacht's withdrawal from those particular territories in the autumn of 1943. These famines were at least as devastating as the more well-known famines in Nazi-occupied Europe: in Athens from the autumn of 1941 to mid-1942 (mitigated by Canadian deliveries of wheat), in the west of the Netherlands during the so-called starvation winter (*Hongerwinter*) of 1944–1945, or in the large Jewish ghettos in East-Central Europe. Furthermore, the famines in Greece and the Netherlands, unlike those in the Soviet territories, were not the result of a deliberate and premeditated German policy of starvation.[35]

No urban centre was hit worse by starvation than Leningrad, where at least one million civilians starved to death during the almost 900-day siege. After the Wehrmacht had closed the siege line around Leningrad on 8 September 1941, the only access route to the besieged city was via Lake Ladoga, Europe's largest lake. During the initial weeks of the blockade, however, the Soviet Union possessed neither sufficient transport capacity nor the necessary logistics to organise the delivery of the foodstuffs required by the inhabitants of Leningrad. Thus, from September to mid-November, only 172 tons of foodstuffs arrived in the city each day, though Leningrad's daily food demands came to 2,000 tons. During the winter, the only route into the city was across the ice that typically covered Lake Ladoga from December to April. The influx of food via this 'ice road' rescued many residents from death by starvation, but it was not enough to feed all inhabitants during the winter of 1941–1942.[36]

The winter months of 1941–1942 were in fact the bitterest of the entire blockade for the residents of Leningrad. During this period, dogs and cats largely disappeared from the city. Some residents saw no alternative but to kill and eat their beloved pets. Others did not stop at eating dead animals: in December 1941 twenty-six people were held criminally responsible for cannibalism or the sale of human flesh. In January 1942 this number increased to 366 people, and during the first half of February it rose again to 494 people. During the blockade, a total of around 1,500 people were prosecuted for this offence. The figures are nonetheless difficult to interpret, as these are only the cases that were uncovered. On the other hand, in most instances it was the corpses of persons already deceased that were processed into meat. What the figures certainly do illustrate, however, is the desperation of the people of Leningrad. The siege of Leningrad was not lifted until 27 January 1944. By that time, between 1 and 1.3 million people trapped within the siege line had starved to death.[37]

The German invasion of the Soviet Union in the summer of 1941 marked a fundamental change in both the scope and systematic nature of Nazi mass violence. Over the course of the next three years, German warfare and rule in the occupied Soviet territories were saturated in violence, causing death and suffering on an unprecedented scale. The military operations of the German-Soviet War cannot be addressed independently of mass murder in this theatre, where ten million Wehrmacht soldiers were stationed at one time or another between 1941 and 1944. The number of Wehrmacht divisions deployed on the Eastern Front in which no war crimes were committed was low, and members of the Wehrmacht may in fact have constituted the majority of those responsible for large-scale crimes carried out by the German Reich.[38]

Notes

1 For a more in-depth discussion of the following, see Alex J. Kay, *Empire of Destruction: A History of Nazi Mass Killing* (New Haven: Yale University Press, 2021), esp. chapters 3–7.

2 For the quotes, see Adolf Hitler, *Mein Kampf: Zwei Bände in einem Band* (Munich: Zentralverlag der NSDAP, 1943 [1925–1926]), pp. 751–752. On Hitler's decision to invade the Soviet Union, see Alex J. Kay, *Exploitation, Resettlement, Mass Murder: Political and Economic Planning for German Occupation Policy in the Soviet Union, 1940–1941* (New York: Berghahn Books, 2006), pp. 26–46.

3 For the figure of 26.6 million, see Mark Harrison, 'Counting the Soviet Union's War Dead: Still 26–27 Million', *Europe-Asia Studies* 71, no. 6 (2019), pp. 1036–1047. For the total figure of 14.6 million Red Army dead, see Lev Lopukhovsky and Boris Kavalerchik, *The Price of Victory: The Red Army's Casualties in the Great Patriotic War*, trans. from Russian by Harold Orenstein (Barnsley: Pen & Sword, 2017).

4 See Peter Longerich, *Der ungeschriebene Befehl: Hitler und der Weg zur 'Endlösung'* (Munich: Piper, 2001), pp. 100 and 202–204.

5 Alex J. Kay, *The Making of an SS Killer: The Life of Colonel Alfred Filbert, 1905–1990* (Cambridge: Cambridge University Press, 2016), p. 42; Alex J. Kay, 'Transition to Genocide, July 1941: Einsatzkommando 9 and the Annihilation of Soviet Jewry', *Holocaust and Genocide Studies* 27, no. 3 (2013), pp. 411–442, here pp. 413–414. Quote from 'Guidelines for the Conduct of the Troops in Russia' in Bundesarchiv-Militärarchiv, Freiburg im Breisgau (hereafter BArch-MA), RH 22/12, fols. 114–115, 'Richtlinien für das Verhalten der Truppe in Rußland', undated [19 May 1941], here fol. 114 (emphasis in the original).

6 Kay, *The Making of an SS Killer*, pp. 41–42; Kay, 'Transition to Genocide, July 1941', p. 416.

7 Kay, 'Transition to Genocide, July 1941', p. 420.

8 For the total of 63,000 killed by the end of July 1941, see Christian Gerlach, 'Die Ausweitung der deutschen Massenmorde in den besetzten sowjetischen Gebieten im Herbst 1941. Überlegungen zur Vernichtungspolitik gegen Juden und sowjetische Kriegsgefangene', in *Krieg, Ernährung, Völkermord: Deutsche Vernichtungspolitik im Zweiten Weltkrieg*, rev. ed. (Zurich: Pendo, 2001 [1998]), pp. 11–78, here pp. 54–55. On 90 per cent of the victims being Jews, see Christopher R. Browning, with contributions by Jürgen Matthäus, *The Origins of the Final Solution: The Evolution of Nazi Jewish Policy, September 1939–March 1942* (London: William Heinemann, 2004), p. 260. On reprisals as a pretext, see Dieter Pohl, 'Die Wehrmacht und der Mord an den Juden in den besetzten sowjetischen Gebieten', in *Täter im Vernichtungskrieg: Der Überfall auf die Sowjetunion und der Völkermord an den Juden*, ed. Wolf Kaiser (Berlin: Propyläen, 2002), pp. 39–53, here p. 43.

9 Kay, *The Making of an SS Killer*, pp. 57–60; Kay, 'Transition to Genocide, July 1941', pp. 412, 420–421, 424, and 427–428.

10 See Longerich, *Der ungeschriebene Befehl*, pp. 104–108.

11 Kay, 'Transition to Genocide, July 1941', pp. 425–426.

12 Ray Brandon, 'The First Wave', unpublished manuscript, 2009, pp. 1–7. On the 707th Infantry Division, see Christian Gerlach, *Kalkulierte Morde: Die deutsche Wirtschafts- und Vernichtungspolitik in Weißrußland 1941 bis 1944* (Hamburg: Hamburger Edition, 1999), pp. 617–620; Peter Lieb, 'Täter aus Überzeugung? Oberst Carl von Andrian und die Judenmorde der 707. Infanteriedivision 1941/42', *Vierteljahrshefte für Zeitgeschichte* 50, no. 4 (2002), pp. 523–557. On the active participation of other units in mass shootings, see Kay, *Empire of Destruction*, p. 72.

13 On the frozen ground, see Yitzhak Arad, *The Holocaust in the Soviet Union* (Lincoln: University of Nebraska Press, 2009), pp. 125, 157, and 251. On technical modifications in the gas vans, see Kay, *Empire of Destruction*, chapter 4. On Hitler's decision to murder all European Jews, and on Chełmno and Bełżec, see Kay, *Empire of Destruction*, chapter 8.

14 On ghetto dissolutions throughout 1942, see Longerich, *Der ungeschriebene Befehl*, p. 108. On Belarus and Ukraine, see Arad, *The Holocaust in the Soviet Union*, pp. 258 and 273.

15 Sara Bender, *The Jews of Białystok during World War II and the Holocaust*, trans. from Hebrew by Yaffa Murciano (Waltham, MA: Brandeis University Press, 2008 [1997]), p. 172.

16 Arad, *The Holocaust in the Soviet Union*, p. 525; Dieter Pohl, 'Just How Many? On the Death Toll of Jewish Victims of Nazi Crimes', in *Denial of the Denial, or The Battle of Auschwitz: The Demography and Geopolitics of the Holocaust – The View from the Twenty-First Century*, ed. Alfred Kokh and Pavel Polian (Brighton, MA: Academic Studies Press, 2012), pp. 129–148, here p. 147, n. 43.

17 Peter Longerich, *Heinrich Himmler*, trans. from German by Jeremy Noakes and Lesley Sharpe (Oxford: Oxford University Press, 2012 [2008]), pp. 533–534. For Bach-Zelewski's account of Himmler's visit, see Yad Vashem Archives, O.18/90, Statement by Erich von dem Bach-Zelewski, undated, fols. 52–55 ('humane' quote: fol. 55).

18 For the total of 17,000, see Ulrike Winkler and Gerrit Hohendorf, 'The Murder of Psychiatric Patients by the SS and the Wehrmacht in Poland and the Soviet Union, Especially in Mogilev, 1939–1945', in *Mass Violence in Nazi-Occupied Europe*, ed. Alex J. Kay and David Stahel (Bloomington: Indiana University Press, 2018), pp. 147–170, here p. 152.

19 Dieter Pohl, *Die Herrschaft der Wehrmacht: Deutsche Militärbesatzung und einheimische Bevölkerung in der Sowjetunion 1941–1944* (Munich: Oldenbourg, 2008), p. 272; Martin Holler, *Der nationalsozialistische Völkermord an den Roma in der besetzten Sowjetunion (1941–1944)* (Heidelberg: Dokumentations- und Kulturzentrum Deutscher Sinti und Roma, 2009), p. 66; Christopher R. Browning, 'The Nazi Empire', in *The Oxford Handbook of Genocide Studies*, ed. Donald Bloxham and

A. Dirk Moses (Oxford: Oxford University Press, 2010), pp. 407–425, here pp. 414–415.

20 For the total number of 30,000 and the figure of 6,000 for Belarus, see Donald Kenrick and Grattan Puxon, *Gypsies under the Swastika* (Hatfield: University of Hertfordshire Press, 2009), pp. 91 and 96. On the Extraordinary State Commission and the treatment of Roma from the spring of 1942, see Holler, *Der nationalsozialistische Völkermord an den Roma in der besetzten Sowjetunion (1941–1944)*, pp. 51, 59, and 112.

21 Dieter Pohl, *Verfolgung und Massenmord in der NS-Zeit 1933–1945*, 3rd rev. ed. (Darmstadt: Wissenschaftliche Buchgesellschaft, 2011 [2003]), pp. 124–125; Kay, 'Transition to Genocide, July 1941', pp. 418–419. On German pre-invasion expectations, see Kay, *Exploitation, Resettlement, Mass Murder*, pp. 158–163.

22 Pohl, *Verfolgung und Massenmord in der NS-Zeit 1933–1945*, p. 125. For the text of the so-called Jurisdiction Decree Barbarossa, see BArch-MA, RW 4/ v. 577, fols. 72–75, 'Erlass über die Ausübung der Kriegsgerichtsbarkeit im Gebiet "Barbarossa" und über besondere Massnahmen der Truppe', 13 May 1941, here fol. 73.

23 Gerlach, *Kalkulierte Morde*, p. 884; Pohl, *Verfolgung und Massenmord in der NS-Zeit 1933–1945*, p. 126.

24 Timm C. Richter, 'Belarusian Partisans and German Reprisals', in *Stalin and Europe: Imitation and Domination, 1928–1953*, ed. Timothy Snyder and Ray Brandon (Oxford: Oxford University Press, 2014), pp. 207–232, here p. 221 (including Treuenfeld quote); Gerlach, *Kalkulierte Morde*, pp. 907–913 (Wilke quote: p. 909; Frentzel quote: p. 911). For the weapons hauls, see Gerlach, *Kalkulierte Morde*, pp. 900–901. For the partisan figures, see Gerlach, *Kalkulierte Morde*, p. 861.

25 For 345,000 dead in Belarus, see Gerlach, *Kalkulierte Morde*, pp. 957–958; Richter, 'Belarusian Partisans and German Reprisals', p. 224. For the figure of 10 per cent and for German losses, see Gerlach, *Kalkulierte Morde*, pp. 866 and 958. For 640,000 dead across the Soviet Union, see Christian Gerlach, *The Extermination of the European Jews* (Cambridge: Cambridge University Press, 2016), p. 288, fn. 4. For a total of half-a-million dead, see Pohl, *Verfolgung und Massenmord in der NS-Zeit 1933–1945*, p. 128. On anti-partisan operations as a war against Soviet peasants, see Gerlach, *Kalkulierte Morde*, pp. 898, 907, 909, and 943; Pohl, *Verfolgung und Massenmord in der NS-Zeit 1933–1945*, p. 128.

26 See now Alex J. Kay, 'The Extermination of Red Army Soldiers in German Captivity, 1941–1945: Causes, Patterns, Dimensions', *Journal of Slavic Military Studies* 37, no. 1 (2024), pp. 80–104, here esp. pp. 83–86.

27 Christian Streit, *Keine Kameraden: Die Wehrmacht und die sowjetischen Kriegsgefangenen 1941–1945*, 4th rev. ed. (Bonn: Dietz, 1997 [1978]), pp. 128, 136, 356, n. 2, and 357, n. 5.

28 Rolf Keller, 'Arbeitseinsatz und Hungerpolitik. Sowjetische
    Kriegsgefangene im Deutschen Reich 1941/42', in *Kriegführung und Hunger
    1939–1945. Zum Verhältnis von militärischen, wirtschaftlichen und
    politischen Interessen*, ed. Christoph Dieckmann and Babette Quinkert
    (Göttingen: Wallstein, 2015), pp. 123–154, here p. 149. On civilian forced
    labourers in Germany, see Gerlach, *The Extermination of the European Jews*,
    p. 230; Pohl, *Die Herrschaft der Wehrmacht*, p. 318.

29 Gerlach, 'Die Ausweitung der deutschen Massenmorde in den besetzten
    sowjetischen Gebieten im Herbst 1941', pp. 52–53.

30 Felix Römer, 'The Wehrmacht in the War of Ideologies: The Army and
    Hitler's Criminal Orders on the Eastern Front', in *Nazi Policy on the Eastern
    Front, 1941: Total War, Genocide, and Radicalization*, ed. Alex J. Kay,
    Jeff Rutherford, and David Stahel (Rochester: University of Rochester Press,
    2012), pp. 73–100, here pp. 88 and 93.

31 Streit, *Keine Kameraden*, pp. 244–246.

32 For the regional figures, see Christoph Dieckmann, *Deutsche
    Besatzungspolitik in Litauen 1941–1944* (Göttingen: Wallstein, 2011), 2, p.
    1340. On the areas under military administration and the total of
    one million deaths there, see also Pohl, *Die Herrschaft der Wehrmacht*,
    p. 240.

33 On prisoners shot immediately after being captured, see Streit, *Keine
    Kameraden*, p. 405, n. 45. It is important to point out here that Streit's figure
    of 3.3 million dead does not include prisoners shot immediately after being
    captured; see also the discussions about 'scattered' Red Army soldiers in
    ibid., pp. 107–108, and Kay, *Empire of Destruction*, pp. 175–176.

34 In English there is still neither a single monograph nor a single collected
    volume dealing exclusively with this second-largest victim group of all
    National Socialist annihilation policies; see Gerlach, *The Extermination of
    the European Jews*, p. 5.

35 On starvation under German military administration, see Pohl, *Die
    Herrschaft der Wehrmacht*, pp. 188–194 and 198–199. On the Netherlands,
    see Ingrid de Zwarte, *The Hunger Winter: Fighting Famine in the Occupied
    Netherlands, 1944–1945* (Cambridge: Cambridge University Press, 2020).
    On Athens and Greece in general, see Violetta Hionidou, *Famine and Death
    in Occupied Greece, 1941–1944* (Cambridge: Cambridge University Press,
    2006).

36 Jörg Ganzenmüller, *Das belagerte Leningrad, 1941 bis 1944: Die Stadt in den
    Strategien von Angreifern und Verteidigern* (Paderborn: Ferdinand
    Schöningh, 2005), pp. 237–238.

37 Ibid., pp. 238–239, 241, 255, and 268–269.

38 See Alex J. Kay and David Stahel, 'Crimes of the Wehrmacht: A
    Re-evaluation', *Journal of Perpetrator Research* 3, no. 1 (2020), pp. 95–127.

14

Soviet Crimes at Times of War, 1941–1945

In 1941 the Soviet Union was ruled by a criminal regime.[1] It had come to power in a revolutionary coup in 1917, had retained power by dissolving the freely elected Constituent Assembly, and reconquered the shattered Russian Empire in a series of wars and civil wars. Fighting these wars of the Romanov succession, the Bolsheviks combined conventional warfare with terror and extrajudicial violence against perceived and actual enemies of 'the revolution'. At the end of the 1920s, the resulting new empire cemented its power through a series of onslaughts on society, often summarised by historians with terms such as 'Stalin's revolution from above', 'collectivisation', or the 'First Five-Year Plan'. They led to mass displacement, mass death, mass incarceration, and a catastrophic plummeting of living standards. In 1937–1938 the regime embarked on a second 'revolution from above' (the 'Great Terror'), which attempted to eliminate physically any remaining enemies and entrench the dictatorship in preparation for war. From 1939 onwards this reconstructed empire, which ruled through an abundance of laws but was not governed by law, expanded in an imperial outreach into eastern Europe, which was subjected to a new revolution, this time both 'from above' and 'from abroad'. The results, again, were state-sponsored mass violence, brutality, displacement, incarceration, and repression.[2]

It is hardly surprising, that such a regime, criminal in peacetime, would continue to function in extra-legal and violent ways during war. Moreover, the German war against the Soviets was not any kind of war, but a total, even totalitarian, war of extermination. Seen from the other side, it was also a war for the very survival of the Soviet regime. In such a war, all seemed fair.[3] We can distinguish several forms of Soviet criminality during its defensive war against Germany: crimes against humanity and war crimes, both perpetrated by agents of the state and often in accordance with explicitly formulated state policy; troop crimes, not guided by state policy, but often understood to be in its fulfilment by the perpetrators; and a variety of violent and criminal behaviour emanating from small group bonding, both within the military and outside of it.

14.1   Crimes against Humanity

Crimes against humanity are state crimes committed against civilians, whether or not they are citizens of the perpetrator state. They can occur during war or peace, at home or abroad. In order to qualify as crimes against humanity (rather than simple crimes perpetrated by state actors), they need to be part of a systematic attack on civilians.[4] The Soviet Union perpetrated these on a mass scale already before the Second World War – the war against the village since 1929, culminating in the man-made famine of 1932–1933; the mass deportations of 'kulaks' and diasporic nationalities; and the Great Terror of 1937–1938.[5] In the first two phases of the Second World War (the war in China from 1937 and the war in Europe from 1939), mass deportations in particular became widespread – of Koreans in 1937, of Soviet Iranians in 1938, of 'class enemies' from the annexed territories of Poland and the Baltic republics in 1940–1941. Altogether, in the period of 1937–1941, the Soviets deported some 570,000 people.[6] During the Great Terror of 1937–1938, agents of the Soviet state systematically shot some 0.7 million people and arrested 2.5 million, overwhelmingly on trumped up charges often obtained through torture. More than 160,000 died in concentration camps, not counting those who were released close to death in order to lower the mortality statistics and who died shortly after release. Overall, some 1–1.5 million Soviet citizens died between 1937 and 1938 in excess to what normally could be expected.[7]

During the 'Revolution from abroad' (1939–1941) in the newly acquired borderlands of Eastern Europe, 128,000 people were arrested, most of them sent to the labour camps of the Gulag and an unknown number shot. Nearly 22,000 Polish officers, policemen, military settlers, and other 'enemies of Soviet power' were executed in April and May 1940, a mass extermination which became famous as the 'Katyn massacre', named after one of the execution sites. The largest number of victims of the revolution from abroad, however, were neither arrested nor shot, but deported to so-called special settlements in the far reaches of the Soviet Union – some 383,000 people.[8]

Deportations differed from arrests not only in the destination of the victims – exile rather than labour camp – but also in the justification for their removal. Those arrested were accused of violating Soviet laws, often applied retrospectively to places which before their illegal annexation by the Soviets had not been subject to Soviet law at all. Deportations, on the other hand, affected people who were not accused of doing anything. They were deported because they were members of a social class or national group deemed potentially hostile to Soviet power. They were victimised not for what they (allegedly) had done, but for who they were.[9]

When the Germans attacked in the summer of 1941, many of these deportations were still under way. Sometimes echelons of cattle cars full of human cargo left their destination just before the Germans marched into a city. In a bitterly ironic twist, the victims of these crimes against humanity included a significant number of Jews, who were thus inadvertently saved by Stalin's policemen from German-perpetrated genocide.[10]

The immediate reaction of the Soviet state – and its central actor, Joseph Stalin – to German invasion was a further escalation of crimes against humanity. Stalin initiated a veritable 'great terror of 1941'. Retreating police forces emptied prisons in the western borderlands and either shot the inmates immediately or marched them away, often followed by further executions along the way. All over the Soviet Union, in its vast network of prisons and camps, people deemed potentially dangerous were shot in a pre-emptive extermination of potential trouble-makers. Behind the quickly moving frontlines, security troops executed large numbers of what they thought were 'traitors, spies, saboteurs, panic mongers, cowards and deserters'.[11]

As the immediate panic of the first half year of the war subsided and Stalin became more adept at running the war effort in coalition with his leadership team and the professionals in the army, executions became less frequent.[12] But repression continued on a high level. Between 1941 and 1945 Soviet courts and tribunals convicted in excess of sixteen million people. As one leading historian has written, 'in terms of the numbers of repressed, the wartime period has no equal in the history of the Soviet Union'.[13] Moreover, mass deportations of entire populations accused of treason and collaboration with the enemy became the order of the day: an incomplete list includes Soviet Germans in 1941–1942; Kalmyks in 1943; Chechen, Ingush, and Crimean Tatars in 1944.[14] They set the tone for a vicious counter-insurgency campaign in the western borderlands after their 'liberation', culminating in another round of deportations, albeit more selective ones again focusing on 'class enemies' rather than 'enemy nations'. An exception was the expulsion of Germans from the newly annexed Kaliningrad region as well as the greater expulsion of Germans from Eastern Europe more generally – another instance of ethnic cleansing in the wider Soviet Empire.[15]

14.2 War Crimes

The Soviet state committed not only systematic crimes against civilians clearly classifiable as crimes against humanity; agents of the Soviet state also perpetrated war crimes on a large scale. Their definition varies somewhat from crimes against humanity: war crimes break the rules of warfare and can therefore only be committed during war; they do not need to be systematic or widespread, although in the Soviet case they certainly often were; and while war crimes can be committed against civilians, they can also victimise combatants or soldiers *hors combat*.[16] The three most ubiquitous categories of Soviet war crimes during the war against Germany are executions of prisoners of war, mass looting, and mass rape.

That these occurred – and that they violated the laws of war – is not in dispute. The shooting of prisoners of war, including sometimes their mutilation either before or after the execution, is documented in a large number of sources from both sides of the front line.[17] The same is true for rape, in particular of German women at the end of the war, as well as the plunder and wanton destruction of civilian property as the Red Army advanced into Eastern and central Europe.[18] What is open to debate is the extent to which these crimes were intentional, systematic, and coordinated from above – that is, as part of a state policy (which would make those crimes against civilians into crimes against humanity).

In all three cases – prisoner executions, plunder, and rape – the situation was much less straightforward than in the case of the 'Great Terror of 1941' or the mass deportations of wartime and the immediate post-war years (if 'post-war' is the right term for what essentially was a war after the war, in many regions). In the latter, there was a clear intent from the top. There is a paper trail, with orders and the bureaucratic trappings of their implementation. These were clearly systematic, state run, intentional crimes against civilians, even if the perpetrators functioned within the confines of Soviet law.

Prisoner executions, by contrast, were more complex in their origin. They were widespread, particularly early in the war. They were exploited by German propaganda as evidence of the criminal nature of the enemy, and some German historians later followed this line of reasoning uncritically. However, there is no evidence of a systematic policy of murdering German prisoners. There is documentation of individual orders to take no captives, and there is an archival transcript of a phone conversation between Stalin and his top military leader, Georgy Zhukov, where the former suggested shooting prisoners after interrogating them under duress. Finally, there were public statements by Stalin which could, and were, read as 'signals from above' to make short work of surrendering Germans. But there is also ample evidence that many in the military leadership opposed such moves. Explicit orders to the troops survived in the archives which instruct Soviet soldiers to *stop* killing POWs.[19]

The same is true for looting. There was a state policy of looting, called 'reparations', which, however, also extended to territories which could not easily be classified as enemy territory: Manchuria or Korea are two examples. Reparations hence had strong family resemblance with organised looting, and in the Soviet requisitioning squads we can clearly see systematicity and state direction. The Soviets simply stole as much equipment as possible from regions they thought they would occupy only in the short term. Such looting only came to an end once longer-term occupation or even incorporation into the Soviet Empire became likely.[20] State policy also encouraged individual looting late in the war by creating a system where soldiers could send home, free of charge, parcels with 'gifts' they had 'acquired'. This amounted to, at least, complicity in the mass expropriation of goods from the civilian population the Red Army encountered as it marched beyond Soviet borders.[21]

But, like prisoner executions, looting was opposed by military leaders concerned with discipline, operational effectiveness, and the 'honour' and 'morality' of the Red Army. Commanders did not appreciate that their soldiers were distracted by searching for wealth rather than fighting the enemy, and they certainly did not want their trucks and tanks overloaded with civilian goods hampering effective movement. Finally, they feared that looting could negatively affect the supply of the Red Army with food, shelter, and other necessities.

Red Army soldiers not only looted in Germany; they did so elsewhere as well, including on liberated Soviet soil and when they returned to Soviet homeland during demobilisation. And they did more than that. Wherever the Red Army went, rapes followed in its wake. Red Army soldiers raped Soviet women after the liberation of villages and concentration camps where they had been held as slave labour, continuing the assaults after they returned home. They raped women in Yugoslavia and Manchuria. They even raped nurses on repatriation trains for the war disabled. These were the effects of poor control of the troops, the breakdown of command and control in the Red Army, and the proliferation of violent collectives outside state control. They were not a systematic part of war making directed or orchestrated by the state.[22]

Germany, here, was something of a special case. As the Soviet state tried to motivate an exhausted citizenry to continue fighting after years of total war and after they had liberated all Soviet territory, it unleashed a hate campaign of dramatic proportions. It fired up the soldiers with memories of what the Germans had done during the years they occupied Soviet lands. Sexual violence, sometimes implicit but often quite explicitly depicted, played a central role in this propaganda. As the Red

Army marched westward, the resulting hate unleashed itself on civilians and in particular on women. And while senior commanders often tried to stop or at least rein in these crimes, Stalin remained quiet for a prolonged period of time, offering no 'signals' that he disapproved. In fact, in a conversation with a Yugoslav communist, he uttered the oft-quoted phrase that one could surely 'understand it if a soldier who has crossed thousands of kilometres through blood and fire and death has fun with a woman or takes some trifle'.[23] It was only fairly late in the game, in April 1945, in the context of the battles for Vienna and Berlin, that Stalin explicitly reminded the Red Army that civilians were to be protected.[24]

14.3   Actors

With regards to war crimes, then, we see a contradictory and evolving role of the Soviet state and its dictatorial head, Stalin. While not ordering executions of POWs or sexual violence as normal parts of war making, the central leadership at times tolerated such behaviour and sometimes encouraged it via 'signals' disseminated by state propaganda. At the same time, and in parallel, many in the military hierarchy tried to limit the danger it posed to both the Red Army's military effectiveness and its perceived 'honour'. This contradictory and convoluted situation contrasts sharply with the crimes against humanity treated in the first section of this chapter, which were clearly ordered from above, executed within the confines of Soviet law and administrative practice, and implemented with the clear goal of reconstructing society and the ethnic and social landscape within Soviet territories.

'The state', as the organised centre of legitimate violence, was thus not the only actor driving criminal behaviour on the Soviet side of the German-Soviet War. During this war, in fact, the state's monopoly of force was severely compromised by the many men (and some women) bearing arms, uniformed or otherwise. Recent research has moved from a singular focus on the power of Soviet hate propaganda to the role of violent male bonding within small groups which often did not coincide with, but developed within, the boundaries of state-sponsored organisation.[25]

Both within the Red Army and without, small-scale violent collectives were ubiquitous during these years. Be it sub-unit bands of 'frontline brothers', be it deserters or bandits, be it improvised survival groups trying to break out of enemy encirclement, be it anti-Soviet resisters or Soviet partisans, they all shared a violent form of group formation, group reproduction, and group maintenance. Looting, rape, and wanton destruction were parts of the ways they formed and reproduced – violence against others as a form of social integration of male groups in an anarchic and brutalised environment. This is why the violence did not stop when these groups were taken back into the Soviet Union but did cease once these collectives were broken up through demobilisation, reintegration into civilian life, and police action: brutalisation was a social process more than an individual one and pacification, therefore, was necessarily a process of social deconstruction and reconstruction.[26]

Wartime violence thus eventually receded. In sharp contrast to the First World War, the war with Germany did not lead to a brutalisation of Soviet society.[27] This 'de-brutalisation' also extended to the Soviet state, which had entered the war ready to use whatever deeds necessary. While the regime remained deeply illiberal, the war led to a de-escalation of the means it used to mould the population.[28] Its policing and judicial practices became more professional, and after another round of mass deportations from the western borderlands, mass terror receded into history.[29] After Stalin's death in 1953, the Soviet Union quickly transformed from a criminal regime wielding often deadly revolutionary violence into a much more predictable dictatorship. The secret police replaced mass terror with mass surveillance and 'prophylactic' policing.[30]

14.4 Silence

Soviet crimes at times of war, then, were both widespread and complex in their origin, goals, logic, and trajectory. As I have written elsewhere, the 'Soviets deported millions of people, many of whom died; they occasionally engaged in mass shootings; and their soldiers were often undisciplined and enraged to an extent bordering on rape warfare. The Soviets were great looters, both individually and in an organized, state-run fashion'. They frequently shot prisoners of war, sometimes mutilating them in the process, as described previously, and Soviet troops 'did murder civilians during and after battle'. Nevertheless, in the context of the Second World War more broadly, there were also crimes the Soviets did not commit: there was 'no incident like the rape of Nanjing or Manila', the two iconic crimes against humanity perpetuated by Japanese forces. And while 'Stalin certainly engaged in ethnic cleansing, his regime never committed genocide', like Hitler's Germany. Moreover, 'the Soviets also very infrequently engaged in air warfare victimizing civilians' – a British and US specialty.[31]

This wider context was one reason why the criminal nature of Soviet war making has not always found its way into mainstream histories of the Soviet war. Given that their own rap sheets were far from clean after the war, the Western Allies were not keen to highlight Red Army behaviour, lest it bring their own into focus. The dominance of the more technical branches of military history in the writing of this war tended to obfuscate the criminal nature of the Red Army's behaviour, by focusing on operations, supply, and tactics. The quickly emerging Soviet myth of the Great Patriotic War, finally, whitewashed what had happened and provided a blueprint for a sanitised version of this war also for Western audiences.[32]

The simple fact that the Soviet Union won the war not against any foe but against Nazi Germany relativised its own conduct. As a historian of Eastern Europe has written, comparing anything to Nazism 'creates an illusion, making every other regime look better than it was'.[33] And in remembering this war, it was impossible to not compare the Nazis to the Stalinists. This often implicit but ever-present comparison to Germany's war made it difficult to tell the history of Soviet victory in shades of grey. As another historian has pointed out, many of those 'who were grateful to the Red Army for saving them from the effects of Fascism...did not want their liberators marked out as rapists'. The same logic applied to other crimes as the history of this war was told in stark black-and-white terms in the war's aftermath. 'There has been no neutral way to talk about the atrocities committed by the Red Army.'[34]

And while in Soviet-occupied Eastern Europe the memory of Soviet crimes was conserved only in hushed conversations in the private sphere, in pluralist societies the discourse about the just Soviet cause always competed openly with anti-Soviet counter-myths. By focusing on 'crimes against the Wehrmacht', the expulsion of Germans, prisoner executions, or the Katyn massacre, such narratives mobilised Soviet criminality to whitewash the German war of annihilation. Such apologetics focused on Soviet crimes as proof that the Germans were indeed the victims here.[35] Their existence dissuaded many historians from delving too deeply into this ethical and political morass.

It was only after the collapse of the Soviet Empire in 1989–1991 that historians could dare take a more analytical view on the many forms of criminal behaviour on the Soviet side. But such scholarly detachment is again destabilised today in the context of Vladimir Putin's dictatorship and Russia's war against Ukraine, both fuelled by a hyper-patriotic history of the Soviet war within Russia itself and triggering memories of Soviet behaviour abroad.[36] We thus again face a polarised situation where serious study of Soviet crimes at times of war falls between the front lines of accusations of Russophobia on the one hand and suggestions of apologetics for Stalinism on the other. And yet understanding the origins and logics of Soviet criminality is probably more important in this environment than ever.

Notes

1 Research and writing of this chapter has been made possible, in part, by ARC DP200101777, 'Aftermaths of War: Violence, Trauma, Displacement, 1815–1950'.

2 Jonathan Smele, *The 'Russian' Civil Wars, 1916–1926: Ten Years that Shook the World* (Oxford: Oxford University Press, 2015); Laura Engelstein, *Russia in Flames: War, Revolution, Civil War, 1914–1921* (Oxford: Oxford University Press, 2018); Joshua Sanborn, *Imperial Apocalypse: The Great War and the Destruction of the Russian Empire* (Oxford: Oxford University Press, 2014); Jörg Baberowski, *Scorched Earth: Stalin's Reign of Terror* (New Haven: Yale University Press, 2016); Jan Gross, *Revolution from Abroad: The Soviet Conquest of Poland's Western Ukraine and Western Belorussia*, expanded ed. (Princeton: Princeton University Press, 2021).

3 Mark Edele and Michael Geyer, 'States of Exception: The Soviet-German War as a System of Violence, 1939–1945', in *Beyond Totalitarianism: Stalinism and Nazism Compared*, ed. Sheila Fitzpatrick and Michael Geyer (New York: Cambridge University Press, 2009).

4 Mark Edele, 'Crimes against Humanity', in *The Routledge History of the Second World War*, ed. Paul R. Bartrop (London: Routledge, 2021), 625–638; esp. 625–626.

5 See, for example, Andrea Graziosi, *The Great Soviet Peasant War: Bolsheviks and Peasants, 1917–1933* (Cambridge, MA: Harvard University Press, 1996); Lynne Viola, ed., *The War against the Peasantry, 1927–1930: The Tragedy of the Soviet Countryside* (New Haven: Yale University Press, 2005); Anne Applebaum, *Red Famine: Stalin's War on Ukraine* (New York: Doubleday, 2017); Lynne Viola, *The Unknown Gulag: The Lost World of Stalin's Special Settlements* (Oxford: Oxford University Press, 2007); Terry Martin, 'The Origins of Soviet Ethnic Cleansing' *Journal of Modern History* 70, no. 4 (1998): 813–861; James Harris, *The Great Fear: Stalin's Terror of the 1930s* (Oxford: Oxford University Press, 2016).

6 Mark Edele, 'The Second World War as a History of Displacement: The Soviet Case' *History Australia* 12, no. 2 (2015): 17–40, esp. 26, table 2.

7 J. Arch Getty, Gabor T. Rittersporn, and V. Zemskov, 'Victims of the Soviet Penal System in the Pre-war Years: A First Approach on the Basis of Archival Evidence', *American Historical Review* 98, no. 4 (1993): 1017–1049; S. G. Wheatcroft and R. W. Davies, 'Population', in *The Economic Transformation of the Soviet Union, 1913–1945*, ed. R. W. Davies, Mark Harrison, and S. G. Wheatcroft (Cambridge: Cambridge University Press, 1994), 57–80; Mark Edele, *Stalinist Society 1928–1953* (Oxford: Oxford University Press, 2011), chapter 2; Golfo Alexopoulos, *Illness and Inhumanity in Stalin's Gulag* (New Haven: Yale University Press, 2017).

8 Mark Edele, *Stalinism at War: The Soviet Union in World War II* (London: Bloomsbury, 2021), 62–66. An important book on Katyn is Anna M. Cienciala, Natalia S. Lebedeva, and Wojciech Materski, eds., *Katyn: A Crime without Punishment* (New Haven: Yale University Press, 2007).

9 Jan T. Gross, *War through Children's Eyes: The Soviet Occupation of Poland and the Deportations, 1939–1941* (Stanford: Hoover Institution Press, 2019); Lewis Siegelbaum and Leslie Page Moch, *Broad Is My Native Land: Repertoires and Regimes of Migration in Russia's Twentieth Century* (Ithaca: Cornell University Press, 2014), chapter 7.

10 Mark Edele, Sheila Fitzpatrick, and Atina Grossmann, eds., *Shelter from the Holocaust: Rethinking Jewish Survival in the Soviet Union* (Detroit: Wayne State University Press, 2017); Eliyana Adler, *Survival on the Margins: Polish Jewish Refugees in the Wartime Soviet Union* (Cambridge, MA: Harvard University Press, 2020); Markus Nesselrodt and Katharina Friedla, eds., *Polish Jews in the Soviet Union (1939–1959): History and Memory of Deportation, Exile, and Survival* (Boston: Academic Studies Press, 2021). On the ethnic Polish majority, see Katherine R. Jolluck, *Exile and Identity: Polish Women in the Soviet Union during World War II* (Pittsburgh: University of Pittsburgh Press, 2002).

11 Edele, *Stalinism at War*, 78–80.

12 Sheila Fitzpatrick, *On Stalin's Team: The Years of Living Dangerously in Soviet Politics* (Melbourne: Melbourne University Press, 2015).

13 Oleg Budnitskii, 'The Great Terror of 1941: Toward a History of Wartime Stalinist Criminal Justice' *Kritika: Explorations in Russian and Eurasian History* 20, no. 3 (2019): 470–484, here 447–448. An earlier study is Michael Parrish, *The Lesser Terror: Soviet State Security, 1939–1953* (London: Praeger, 1996).

14 The classic study is J. Otto Pohl, *Ethnic Cleansing in the USSR, 1937–1949* (Westport: Greenwood Press, 1999).

15 Alexander Statiev, *The Soviet Counterinsurgency in the Western Borderlands* (Cambridge: Cambridge University Press, 2010); R. M. Douglas, *Orderly and Humane: The Expulsion of the Germans after the Second World War* (New Haven: Yale University Press, 2012); Nicole Eaton, *German Blood. Slavic Soil: Now Nazi Königsberg Became Soviet Kaliningrad* (Ithaca: Cornell University Press, 2023).

16 Edele, 'Crimes against Humanity', 625–626.

17 Mark Edele, 'Take (No) Prisoners! The Red Army and German POWs, 1941–1943' *Journal of Modern History* 88 (2016): 342–379.

18 Anthony Beevor, *Berlin: The Downfall, 1945* (London: Viking, 2002).

19 Edele, 'Take (No) Prisoners'. Stalin's phone conversation with Zhukov is in the Russian State Archive of Socio-Political History (RGASPI) f. 558, op. 11, d. 487, l. 73.

20 Mark Edele, 'Soviet Liberations and Occupations, 1939–1949', in *The Cambridge History of the Second World War*, ed. Richard Bosworth and Joe Maiolo (Cambridge: Cambridge University Press, 2015), esp. 497–500.

21 Mark Edele, *Soviet Veterans of the Second World War: A Popular Movement in an Authoritarian Society, 1941–1991* (Oxford: Oxford University Press, 2008), 31–21.

22 Edele, 'Soviet Liberations and Occupations', 489–494; Edele, *Stalinism at War*, 166–170. Historians have paid particular attention to rape and other troop violence of the Red Army in Germany. Classic accounts include Norman Naimark, *The Russians in Germany: A History of the Soviet Zone of Occupation* (Cambridge, MA: Harvard University Press, 1995); Atina Grossmann, *Jews, Germans, and Allies: Close Encounters in Occupied Germany* (Princeton: Princeton University Press, 2007); Oleg Budnitskii, 'The Intelligentsia Meets the Enemy: Educated Soviet Officers in Defeated Germany, 1945' *Kritika: Explorations in Russian and Eurasian History* 10, no. 3 (2009): 629–682; and Filip Slaveski, *The Soviet Occupation of Germany: Hunger, Mass Violence and the Struggle for Peace, 1945–1947* (Cambridge: Cambridge University Press, 2013). On rape in 'liberated' territories of Ukraine, Latvia, and Belarus, see Mie Nakachi, 'A Postwar Sexual Liberation? The Gendered Experience of the Soviet Union's Great Patriotic

War', *Cahiers du Monde russe* 52, no. 2–3 (2011): 423–440, here 431. On Yugoslavia, see Vojin Majstorović, 'The Red Army in Yugoslavia, 1944–1945' *Slavic Review* 75, no. 2 (2016): 396–421.

23 Milovan Djilas, *Conversations with Stalin* (New York: Harvest Books, 1962), 95.

24 Mark Edele, 'Learning from the Enemy? Entangling Histories of the German-Soviet War, 1941–1945', in *Totalitarian Dictatorship: New Histories*, ed. Daniela Baratieri, Mark Edele, and Giuseppe Finaldi (London: Routledge, 2014), esp. 200–202.

25 On propaganda, see Mark Edele, 'Paper Soldiers: The World of the Soldier Hero According to Soviet Wartime Posters' *Jahrbücher für Geschichte Osteuropas* 47, no. 1 (1999), 89–108; Lisa A. Kirschenbaum, 'Our City, Our Hearths, Our Families: Local Loyalties and Private Life in Soviet World War II Propaganda', *Slavic Review* 59, no. 4 (2000), 825–847; Karel C. Berkhoff, *Motherland in Danger: Soviet Propaganda during World War II* (Cambridge: Harvard University Press, 2012).

26 Mark Edele and Filip Slaveski, 'Violence from Below: Explaining Crimes against Civilians Across Soviet Space, 1943–1947', *Europe-Asia Studies* 68, no. 6 (2016): 1020–1035. The standard work on partisans is Kenneth Slepyan, *Stalin's Guerrillas: Soviet Partisans in World War II* (Lawrence: University Press of Kansas, 2006).

27 On World War I, see Dietrich Beyrau, 'Brutalization Revisited: The Case of Russia', *Journal of Contemporary History* 50, no. 1 (2015): 15–37.

28 On the continued illiberalism, see Franziska Exeler, *Ghosts of War: Nazi Occupation and Its Aftermath in Soviet Belarus* (Ithaca: Cornell University Press, 2022).

29 Pavel Polian, *Against Their Will: The History and Geography of Forced Migrations in the USSR* (Budapest: Central European University Press, 2022), 115–180. On professionalisation, see Peter H. Solomon, *Soviet Criminal Justice under Stalin* (Cambridge: Cambridge University Press, 1996), and David R. Shearer, *Policing Stalin's Socialism: Repression and Social Order in the Soviet Union, 1924–1953* (New Haven: Yale University Press, 2009).

30 Julie Fedor, *Russia and the Cult of State Security: The Chekist Tradition, from Lenin to Putin* (New York: Routledge, 2011), 52, 54; Mark Harrison, *One Day We Will Live without Fear: Everyday Lives under the Soviet Police State* (Stanford: Hoover Institution Press, 2016); Edward Cohn, 'Coercion, Reeducation, and the Prophylactic Chat: "Profilaktika" and the KGB's Struggle with Political Unrest in Lithuania, 1953–64', *The Russian Review* 76, no. 2 (2017).

31 Edele, 'Crimes against Humanity', 634, 628, makes the argument against genocide, based on the strict definition of the term in international law. For the counter-argument, based on a more inclusive definition, see Norman M. Naimark, *Stalin's Genocides* (Princeton: Princeton University Press, 2010).

32 The classical study is Nina Tumarkin, *The Living and The Dead: The Rise and Fall of the Cult of World War II in Russia* (New York: Basic Books, 1994). Most recently, see Jonathan Brunstedt, *The Soviet Myth of World War II: Patriotic Memory and the Russian Question in the USSR* (Cambridge: Cambridge University Press, 2021).

33 John Connelly, 'Totalitarianism: Defunct Theory, Useful Word', *Kritika: Explorations in Russian and Eurasian History* 11, no. 4 (2010): 819–835; quotation 835.

34 James Mark, 'Remembering Rape: Divided Social Memory and the Red Army in Hungary 1944–1945', *Past & Present* 188 (2005): 133–161, here 160.

35 One particular egregious example of such a history has, lamentably, been translated into English: Joachim Hoffmann, *Stalin's War of Extermination 1941–1945: Planning, Realization and Documentation* (New York: Theses and Dissertations Press, 2015).

36 See Mark Edele, *Debates on Stalinism* (Manchester: Manchester University Press, 2020), chapter 8; Mark Edele, *Russia's War against Ukraine: The Whole Story* (Melbourne: Melbourne University Press, 2023), esp. chapters 4 and 5.

Part V

Home Fronts

15

The German Home Front

When on 22 June 1941 the Wehrmacht moved into the Soviet Union, it was much more than the launch of one of the largest offensives in world history. From the Soviet perspective it was, in the words of Amir Weiner, 'the realisation of a historical nightmare, one that Soviet power expected from the moment of its inception'.[1] Germany was always considered the most likely antagonist for this nightmare, if only because the Nazi elite had implicitly and explicitly promised to invade the country from the moment the party was founded. The invasion of the Soviet Union, after all, was a vital part of Nazi Germany's long-term vision: Operation Barbarossa would not only serve to defeat and subjugate a mortal enemy; it would restore Germany's place in the world economy, open up possibilities for a new world order, and allow Nazi planners to redraw the ethnic and racial map of Eastern Europe. Following the announcement of the start of the German offensive, friends and foes alike observed surprise and nervousness among the German population but also noted that before long the mood on the home front was one of joy, pride, and confidence in victory, with Germans throughout the country placing bets on the speed with which the Red Army would be brought to its knees.[2] These optimistic sentiments were even more prevalent among soldiers, whose letters tended to express an even deeper 'understanding' of the necessity of the war with Russia.[3] To a much greater extent than scholars of Nazi Germany often realise, the attack on the Soviet Union was the regime's raison d'être – the story of the Third Reich is that of a self-professed problem-ridden European power determined to look 'East' to overcome the many challenges it faced.

Adolf Hitler never made a secret of his intentions to fight a war with the Soviet Union. He told Jacob Burkhardt, the High Commissioner of the League of Nations in the free city of Danzig, in August 1939:

> Everything I do is focused on Russia. If the West is too dumb or blind to understand this, I consider it my duty to seek rapprochement with the Russians, defeat the West, and use the amassed forces to march on the Soviet Union. I need the Ukraine, so that, unlike the last war, we won't be starved.[4]

Whether Hitler at this time truly felt that Germany was ready to launch a campaign of this magnitude remains a somewhat open question, but once the Eastern Front was opened both the troops in the field and the men and women on the German home front were expected to muster more mental, moral, and economical resources than ever before.

The six-year run-up to Hitler's 'war of world views' between 1933 and 1939 makes the German 'war effort' somewhat of a misnomer. Many of the sacrifices Germans were asked to make during wartime had already been demanded of them in the years before. As scholars like Hew Stachan have rightly stressed, the weapons German industry produced during this pre-war period would not merely be used in a swift *Blitzkrieg*; rather these measures, which touched every aspect of German society, show that the Nazi regime was gearing up for a protracted war.[5] Different Hitler Youth exercises and training courses would prepare the German youth in a not-too-subtle way for the possibility of war, ensuring that this age cohort bought into the necessity of war more wholeheartedly than their older compatriots, while at the same time readying them to colonise and subjugate Slavic lands upon German victory.[6] The Nazi economy was also steered towards a European conflict early on, and especially after the introduction of the Four Year Plan in 1936 Germans knew that they were expected to accept an economy that focused on 'cannons instead of butter'.[7] Also by that time, Germany's major industrialists had been brought into the fold, and the June 1934 'Night of the Long Knives' should at least partially be understood as Hitler's efforts to show that the socialist wing of his movement had been clipped and that private industry needed not fear its nationalisation.[8] Similar to previous

German governments, the Nazis also invested heavily in agriculture, which not only moved the country in the direction of autarky but also helped win over Germany's farmers.[9]

The German working class, meanwhile, was being prepared for the strains of a future war too. Nazi officials – along with many others – had come to understand the 'stab in the back' of the home front in 1918 as a direct result of the unwillingness to outlaw leftist organisations (such as trade unions, the German Communist Party KPD, and the Social Democratic Party SPD), following the outbreak of the First World War. It was their leadership, consisting of 'shirkers', 'cowards', and 'traitors', that kept injecting dissonant voices into the public debate throughout the conflict, which eventually proved to be Germany's undoing. In May 1933 this toxic interpretation of history was followed up by the outlawing of these parties and the forced dissolution of trade unions, but the Nazi regime also hastened to offer an alternative in the form of the German Labour Front. This organisation was tasked to align the needs of employees and employers, and even though German workers were considered to be 'malleable' enough to accept these profound changes without much push-back, the German Labour Front worked hard to secure perks for workers (improvement of the workplace, holidays, or even the promise of a car) in an effort to ensure their loyalty.[10] Looking ahead to the war itself, we see the success of these efforts. Among the ranks of the Wehrmacht, as Omer Bartov rightly emphasises, there were hundreds of thousands of former communists, socialists, and social democrats – men who in the early 1930s had formed the backbone of the opposition to Hitler's politics. On the Eastern Front these men would nevertheless go on to become prolific killers, in no way inferior to those who truly believed in the Nazi vision.[11]

The war itself opened several options for Germany. As part of the country's strategic vision, German economic planners had factored in the exploitation of the countries their Wehrmacht would conquer.[12] Each of those countries had their own job to fulfill: plants in western Europe, notably the industrial areas of Douai and Lens in Belgium, were expected to contribute to the German war economy, while German control over the Baltic Sea facilitated the shipment of iron ore from Sweden.[13] Taking central stage in Germany's exploitative agenda was the Soviet Union, which was subjected to the 'Hunger Plan'. The Hunger Plan served two intertwined purposes. First, every shipment of grain, meat, or vegetables that did not have to be sent to the troops could remain in Germany, where these goods could be distributed among the German population. Acutely remembering the unrest on the German home front caused by the Royal Navy's 'hunger blockade' during the First World War, Nazi officials were determined to keep living standards up as long as possible. Second, the systematic exploitation of the Soviet Union caused a planned famine of its population. Some twenty million Soviet citizens were expected to die as a result, as such making way for Aryan colonisation upon German victory.[14] The needs of the home front and the regime's racist vision for the Soviet Union were linked by design, presenting two sides of Nazi Germany's attempts to create a 'New Order' in Europe. It was precisely the regime's ruthless adherence to its racist principles that kept up the German standard of living for as long as it did.

The regime's efforts to alleviate the strain on the home front by racist policies certainly did not stop there. In the course of the war, millions of forced labourers from western Europe and slave labourers from eastern Europe were brought in, often by force. By late 1943 there were 7.3 million 'foreign workers' in Germany: every tenth person in the county had come from abroad. The concentration camp system played a central part in this economic 'vision' and eventually became a true pillar of the German war effort. As the war went on, SS officials were sent out to find labourers in Eastern Europe to work in concentration camps, with 'slave hunts' becoming an increasingly normal sight in countries like Belorussia and Ukraine.[15] Meanwhile, the destruction of Europe's Jews, the Holocaust, impacted the home front in two significant ways. Bringing Jews to their death required planning and resources, which meant that trains needed to transport them would not be available to carry other goods.[16] We should, however, be careful not to overestimate the extra planning that was required to achieve this: these 'special trains' could be fit into the *Reichsbahn* schedule with relative ease, if only because the speed with which their 'cargo' was brought to its destination mattered little.[17] Presenting these transports as part of the war effort, moreover, allowed those involved to play down their involvement in mass murder, with a railway worker at Auschwitz stating that 'it was my job to ensure that the wheels rolled and not to concern myself with what was transported'.[18] Germans on the home front noted the disappearance of their Jewish neighbours but also quickly came to realise that there were ample opportunities available to those prepared to look the other way. In the wake of a deportation, many a local Sunday market suddenly offered suspiciously cheap high-quality furniture or clothing. Buying these goods effectively signalled buyers' acquiescence in the regime's policies, while at the same time tying them closer to its mission and reducing the opportunity to retreat into plausible deniability.[19] The mass murder of Jews was an open secret of the German home front, and complicity and culpability were important drivers of Germany's war effort.[20]

The German home front also hardened for its own citizens. Deeply fearful of the possibly that the war could cause radical change (as had happened in Russia in 1917 – Nazi Germany's perpetual bugbear), the regime kept the home front on a tight leash.[21] Behind closed doors, Hitler vowed to brutally and instantly crush any domestic crisis and did not shun invoking the threat of imprisonment in concentration camps.[22] And even though in the course of the war the number of Gestapo officers in Germany decreased substantially – many of them were posted abroad – the threat of denunciation remained ever present.[23] It was not too surprising, then, that the longer the war lasted, the more pronounced the difference between the 'private self' and the 'public self' became. Ever more Germans decided to disappear behind the walls of their homes, feeling indifferent and resigned towards Germany's prospects. After the fall of the Third Reich, Germans readily played up these feelings, presenting them as 'proof' that they had not shared the regime's vision and a sign of inner *resistenz*.[24] Most resistance on the home front, however, remained fairly passive in nature. Listening to foreign radio programmes was as far as most Germans were willing to go, but more often Germans did not venture beyond making a symbolic gesture, such as carrying two shopping bags to avoid having to raise one's hand in the 'German greeting'.[25] Also the party badge, long worn to signify pride and belonging to the new 'People's Community', was seen less and less as the war went on.[26] None of this necessarily signalled agreement or disagreement with the way the war was going: in a self-policing state, Germans had simply learned to keep their cards much closer to their chests.

Women had to tread especially carefully. With most men drafted into the military and serving abroad, the regime was determined to ensure that women would 'uphold' German virtues on the home front.

Reports that teenage girls were prostituting themselves for scarce goods were cause for deep concern, but officials' main attention was directed at a more systemic problem. As German men were taken out of the workforce to be replaced by women or foreigners, it was not uncommon, as Jill Stephenson found, for prisoners of war and forced labourers to become 'the focus of social and sexual interest'. Working side by side with a foreign worker who could very well share your religion, age, or social background had the ability to cut right through the regime's ideas of 'racial purity', but the consequences of following up on blossoming feelings were severe. Those caught having a sexual liaison with a foreign worker faced draconian punishment: having defied the race laws – being guilty of 'polluting German blood' – would lead to years-long prison sentences, and some women were even executed for it.[27]

Two more developments came to negatively dominate life on the home front: rationing and bombing. The introduction of ration cards in August 1939 was a deeply controversial move, and witnesses remember how even Hitler himself 'flew into a rage' at the thought that its enforcement would rely on the 'policeman's truncheon and threats of imprisonment'. But as he also realised that an 'appeal to people's sense of honour' was unlikely to work in practice, the system remained in place.[28] Meat was among the first goods to be rationed, and in conjunction with the introduction of the rationing system, laws were passed to counter illicit slaughter. As with other wartime offenses, punishment was notoriously harsh, with some of those caught even receiving death sentences. But despite the outrage this caused among farmers, for whom the slaughter of an extra animal had for generations been a way to substitute their income, the regime held firm.[29] Fruit was rationed in mid-1941, vegetables in early 1942, and later that year even potatoes were subjected to rationing. Every few weeks Germans saw their rations getting smaller, and these cuts profoundly affected morale. Particularly noteworthy in that respect was that the introduction of the new rations of April 1942, which saw a decline of 200 kilocalories from the previous rations. These cuts, SD informants throughout the country noted, had a 'devastating effect' on the population. That dissatisfaction was all the greater because only a few months earlier Hermann Göring himself had vowed that as a result of the Wehrmacht's occupation of Ukraine, Germans would never again go hungry.[30] As a direct result of the rationing system a flourishing black market emerged, creating an economy that in its very nature demanded its participants put their trust in each other, rather than in the regime.[31] Rationing lay bare a number of differences that still existed in the supposedly egalitarian 'People's Community'. People in the countryside were on average still better off than their urban compatriots, while rich or well-connected people also seemingly maintained their access to goods their compatriots had not seen in years. With party officials in charge of distribution, it was moreover an open secret that these people were shamelessly enriching themselves through corruption and hoarding.[32]

Neither were the burdens of bombing equally shared. By the end of the war, close to a third of all Germans had suffered through a bombardment and half of the population had been left without water, gas, or electricity for extended periods of time.[33] Industrial areas in the west, such as the Ruhr, and urban areas, such as Hamburg and Berlin, were subject to constant large-scale air raids. Here bombing determined the pace of life and forced civilians into air raid shelters, worsening pre-existing tensions and contributing to the atomisation of society.[34] Germany's eastern provinces, on the other hand, remained out of reach for a long time, while rural areas were also mostly ignored by the bombers of the Royal Air Force (RAF) and US Army Air Forces (USAAF). Hundreds of thousands of people were evacuated there from their hometowns, and by the end of the war every fifteenth civilian had been subjected to evacuation. These evacuations were cause for considerable friction. Parents, understandably, did not want to get separated from their children, and especially those who had their doubts about the regime's ideology were hesitant to simply hand over the care of their children to Nazi officials.[35] Unused to the pace of life in the countryside, and unfamiliar with what was expected of them, young women complained about the lack of entertainment or the plain diet, while locals in turn accused them of being ungrateful and unwilling to help with chores. Having to survive in bombed-out cities, meanwhile, posed an altogether different set of problems. As Nazi officials maintained that bombardments only strengthened Germans' resolve, rather than undermined it, 'looting' in the wake of bombardments (often just scavenging for items that might have survived an attack) was not merely treated as theft but rather as a manifestation of a malicious intent to use the circumstances created by war to one's favour. With that, the accused became a *Volksschädling* ('human pest') that harmed the 'People's Community', and as such could even be sentenced to death.[36]

The Allied bombing campaign also profoundly impacted the German war effort in another way: some 900,000 soldiers manned air defences (from 1943 onwards, these 'soldiers' were mainly sixteen-year-old boys), while many more skilled workers had to remain behind to deal with bomb damage. Having to keep sixty divisions worth of troops in Germany to protect its skies – troops who, in turn, required 50 per cent of Germany's anti-tank guns (the famous 'eight-eight' guns were dual-purpose, ground-to-ground and ground-to-air) fundamentally impacted Germany's fighting strength.[37] Notwithstanding, after the war even Air Chief Marshal Arthur Harris, the commander in chief of RAF Bomber Command, had to admit that the damaging effect of the bombing campaign was 'widely overstated', even admitting that 'it was only in the last year of the war ... that our bombing really began to affect the whole German war machine'.[38]

Figure 15.1 After a raid by the US 15th Air Force, ME-109 jet fighters lay among the ruins of an aircraft factory in Obertraubling, Germany, 22 February 1944. Source: Library of Congress/Corbis/VCG via Getty Images.

After the Sixth Army's defeat at Stalingrad in early February 1943, the regime had to drop all pretence and put the entire country on a 'total war' footing. The idea of 'total war' had been introduced eight years earlier, in 1935, by General Erich von Ludendorff, one of Germany's most lauded First World War veterans. Ludendorff saw war as 'the gravest reality of a people', and although he struggled to define the exact markers of a total war, he believed that 'it can only be waged when a whole people is truly threatened in its way of life, and is determined to commit itself to it'.[39] In the run-up to the war and during its first three years, these ideas had not gained much traction among the military, both because the supposed 'stab in the back' of 1918 had made the military weary of the home front and because involving the entire population in the war effort implied that 'racially inferior' enemies could not be effortlessly defeated. Now, however, the 'total war' idea seemed to dovetail particularly well with Germany's situation. On 18 February 1943 propaganda minister Joseph Goebbels asked a packed Berlin *Sportpalast* whether his audience was ready for 'a war more total and radical than anything that we can even imagine today', receiving a resounding '*Ja!*' in reply.[40] Waging a total war, after all, had a concrete purpose, which banners hung around the *Sportpalast* conveyed: 'Total War – Shortest War'. If at this hour the German people would stand behind their military as one, it would be the surest way to end the war the quickest.

On a day-to-day basis not much changed after the proclamation of 'total war', if only because most measures that were 'introduced' were already on their way. Perhaps the most significant change was that Nazi *Gauleiter* (regional leaders) were given more powers to take direct action to streamline the war effort in their provinces. Although this did bear some fruit, it also meant that local party offices such as the *Ortsgruppe* and the *Kreisleitung* increasingly concerned themselves with military tasks, which came directly at the expense of the concerns for civilians. In practice, this meant that instead of representing a 'People's Community' based in reciprocity between the state and its citizens, they came to embody a system in which civilians 'gave' and the party 'took', without offering much in return.[41] To soften the blow, *Gauleiter* would try to alleviate the burdens of their province's civilians, which in turn immediately gave rise to accusations of '*Gebietsegoismus*', or 'regional egoism'.[42] As the war entered its final phase, grumbling became louder and resistance more open, but critically, none of that turned into mass protest, open revolt, or strikes. For better or worse, the home front remained incredibly robust, and the vast majority of Germans kept contributing to the war effort regardless of the deteriorating situation.

Heavily influenced by their propaganda, German citizens had every reason to remain optimistic until deep into the summer of 1944. Even the Allied landings in Normandy were not necessarily considered as 'the beginning of the end'. Rather, they were met with a carefully choreographed 'renewed hope' for a German victory. The thinking behind this was not that far-fetched: if the Allies could be driven back into the sea, it would take them at least two years to regroup, which would give the Wehrmacht the time to defeat the Red Army. Once that had been achieved, the Western Allies would have no choice but to sue for peace. This line of thought mirrored the hopes tied to the events of 1917, when after the signing of the Treaty of Brest-Litovsk millions of German soldiers were sent over from the Eastern to the Western Front. Even though their arrival on the Western Front eventually did not change the outcome of the conflict, it *did* show that the fortunes of war could still change at the eleventh hour.[43] As a result, as Gerhard Weinberg shows, Nazi Germany's strategy remained largely unaltered, and both Germany's late-war offensive operations (notably the Ardennes offensive) and its defensive conduct (staying put in the Kurland and East Prussia) continued to be in line with the hegemonic vision Germany had set out in 1939.[44] Germany's industrial output very much reflected these aspirations, as for both planes and tanks production numbers peaked in 1944.[45]

In the autumn of 1944, the fighting moved to German soil. Soldiers who for years had been brutalised on the Eastern Front were now ordered to defend their own territory, often conducting operations with the same disregard for their direct environment as during the fighting abroad. In the Soviet Union they had seen how their enemy used its civilians to turn the tide of war, and many German soldiers expected the same of their own population.[46] The party largely agreed with this line. In October 1944, the *Volkssturm*, the 'people's storm' militia, was established (its numbers were envisioned to reach six million), whose troops would be tasked to defend their communities. The party took the propagandist lead and oversaw recruitment, although its deployment depended on the front or the sector. In Eastern Germany many *Volkssturm* units were fully incorporated into the military command structure, while in the west they ofter operated more or less independently.[47] In some towns and cities party officials or military commanders were determined to fight to the very end; others allowed their communities to be captured after only havirg offered symbolic resistance or none at all.

Nevertheless, the final fighting was incredibly grim. More German soldiers and civilians died in the final year of the war than al previous years combined, while the bombing of their towns now reached monstrous proportions.[48] Most Germans living in the west of the country remained where they were and continued to go to their place of work. (Which other option did they have?) And it was only after the Allies had crossed the Rhine that some of them began quoting a famous passage from *Mein Kampf*: 'If a nation is led to ruin, its people not only have the right but also the duty to revolt.'[49] Few of them, however, actually turned these words into actions. Germans living in the east *did* leave their communities, but once again their behaviour was not driven by their stance towards the regime. Millions of Germans fled ahead of the Red Army, deeply fearful of the anticipated acts of hatred and revenge. Upon their arrival in the west, they were hardly received with open

Figure 15.2 Gauleiter Arthur Greise, Reichsführer-SS Heinrich Himmler, and Army Chief of Staff Heinz Guderian salute a marching Volkssturm unit, November 1944. Source: Keystone/Hulton Archive/Stringer/Getty Images.

arms, finding themselves fighting over the same limited housing as bombed-out locals, and many of them would continue to live in Nissen huts until deep into the post-war years.[50]

When Nazi Germany went to war in the autumn of 1939, it embarked on a mission its leadership had been preparing for almost two decades. Even though many Germans met the proclamation of war with feelings of alarm and dread, few of them were caught completely by surprise.[51] With the unrest on the home front during the First World War firmly in mind, the regime had used the second half of the 1930s to gradually prepare Germans for the idea of war, both in its rhetoric and in the way it structured its economy. The production of consumer goods had taken a back seat, and German factories were increasingly asked to produce military materiel. The coming of war thus did not change daily routines much, although factors such as the introduction of the rationing system and the Allied bombing campaign would soon start to grind away at home front morale. At the very least they showed that, despite the regime's best efforts, Germany's burdens were not being shared equally. The invasion of the Soviet Union – initially thought of as the decisive step in the direction of a final victory – only aggravated these feelings, as over time it demanded so many lives that many a mother or wife began doubting whether the price of war was worth the sacrifices. Graphic letters from the front, the steady arrival of foreign labourers, and the gradual disappearance of their Jewish neighbours, moreover, forced a growing number of Germans to ponder what it was they were fighting for. Few, however, allowed their minds to wander too far. Life on the home front hardened dramatically, and the only thing the regime could offer its citizens in return was their share in the spoils of war. Luxury items from France, grain from Ukraine, and goods from deported Jews all helped to buoy and pacify the home front, while at the same time tying Germans ever closer to the regime's racist mission. Nonetheless, as the war went on, more and more Germans disengaged from the 'People's Community', but despite the dissatisfaction caused by food shortages, bombing, and increased levels of suppression, Germans kept producing for the war effort. That would remain the story till the end of the war. Even in defeat the regime managed to muster hundreds of thousands of its citizens to contribute to Germany's defence, and even though many of them had by that time mentally dissociated themselves from the regime, it was only when Allied tanks rolled through their towns that they laid down their weapons or their tools.

Notes

1 Amir Weiner, *Making Sense of War: The Second World War and the Fate of the Bolshevik Revolution* (Princeton: Princeton University Press, 2002), p. 136.

2 Nicholas Stargardt, *The German War: A Nation under Arms, 1939–45* (London: Bodley Head, 2015); pp. 157–164; Heinz Boberach, ed., *Meldungen aus dem Reich: Die geheimen Lageberichte des Sicherheitsdienstes der SS 1938–1945, Band 7* (Herrsching: Pawlak Verlag, 1984), pp. 2426–2429, 2440–2441.

3 For numerous examples see Craig Luther and David Stahel, *Soldiers of Barbarossa: Combat, Genocide, and Everyday Experiences on the Eastern Front, June–December 1941* (Guilford: Stackpole Books, 2020).

4 Werner Maser, *Hitlers Mein Kampf: Geschiedenis–Fragmenten–Commentaren* (Soesterberg: Aspekt, 1998), p. 194.

5 See Hew Stachan, 'The Conduct of Total War', in *A World at Total War: Global Conflict and the Politics of Destruction, 1937–1945*, ed. Roger Chickering, Stig Förster, and Bernd Greiner (Cambridge: Cambridge University Press, 2005).

6 See Michael Buddrus, *Totale Erziehung für den totalen Krieg: Hitlerjugend und nationalsozialistische Jugendpolitik, Teil 1* (Munich: K. G. Säur, 2003).

7 See Richard Overy, *War and Economy in the Third Reich* (Oxford: Clarendon Press, 1994), and Adam Tooze, *The Wages of Destruction: The Making and Breaking of the Nazi Economy* (London: Penguin, 2007).

8 Raffael Scheck, *Germany, 1871–1945: A Concise History* (Oxford: Berg, 2008), p. 166.

9 Richard Overy, *The Penguin Historical Atlas of the Third Reich* (London: Penguin, 1996), pp. 40–41.

10 Timothy Mason, *Social Policy in the Third Reich: The Working Class and the 'National Community'* (Providence: Berg, 1993), pp. 19–40.

11 Omer Bartov, 'The Missing Years: German Workers, German Soldiers' *German History* 8, no. 1 (1990): pp. 46–65; Christopher Browning, *Ordinary Men: Reserve Police Battalion 101 and the Final Solution in Poland* (1993; repr. New York: HarperCollins, 1998).

12 Peter Fritzsche, *An Iron Wind: Europe under Hitler* (New York: Basic Books, 2016).

13 Yaron Pasher, *Holocaust versus Wehrmacht: How Hitler's 'Final Solution' Undermined the German War Effort* (Lawrence: University Press of Kansas), pp. 42–43.

14 Alex Kay, *Empire of Destruction: A History of Nazi Mass Killing* (New Haven: Yale University Press, 2021), pp. 116–145.

15 Nikolaus Wachsmann, *KL: A History of the Nazi Concentration Camps* (New York: Little, Brown, 2015), p. 417; Christian Gerlach, *The Extermination of the European Jews* (Cambridge: Cambridge University Press, 2016), p. 190.

16 See Pasher, *Holocaust versus Wehrmacht*.

17 Alfred Mierzejewski, 'A Public Enterprise in the Service of Mass Murder: The Deutsche Reichsbahn and the Holocaust', in *Holocaust: Critical Concepts in Historical Studies, Volume III: The 'Final Solution'*, ed. David Cesarani (London: Routledge, 2004), pp. 287–288.

18 Alfred Mierzejewski, 'German Railroaders and the Holocaust' *Railroad History* 186 (2002), pp. 65–67.

19 Götz Aly, *Hitlers Volksstaat: Raub, Rassenkrieg und nationaler Sozialismus* (Bonn: Bundeszentrale für politische Bildung, 2014), pp. 114–138.

20 Otto Dov Kulka and Eberhard Jäckel, eds., *Die Juden in den geheimen NS-Stimmungsberichten 1933–1945* (Düsseldorf: Droste, 2004), chapter 14, 'Das "entjudete" Dritte Reich'; David Harrisville, *The Virtuous Wehrmacht: Crafting the Myth of the German Soldier on the Eastern Front, 1941–1944* (Ithaca: Cornell University Press, 2021), chapter 2; Peter Fritzsche, *Life and Death in the Third Reich* (Cambridge, MA: Belknap Press of Harvard University Press, 2008), pp. 264–266.

21 Mason, *Social Policy in the Third Reich*, p. 21.

22 Wachsmann, *KL*, pp. 160–168, 410–425 (here 415).

23 Robert Gellately, *Backing Hitler, Consent and Coercion in Nazi Germany* (Oxford: Oxford University Press, 2001), pp. 226–229; Eric A. Johnson, *Nazi Terror: The Gestapo, Jews, and Ordinary Germans* (New York: Basic Books, 1999), pp. 310–313.

24 Mary Fulbrook, *Bystander Society: Conformity and Complicity in Nazi Germany and the Holocaust* (Oxford: Oxford University Press, 2023), chapter 10; Martin Broszat, '*Resistenz* and Resistance', in *Nazism*, ed. Neil Gregor (Oxford: Oxford University Press, 2000), pp. 241–244.

25 Jill Stephenson, *Women in Nazi Germany* (2001; repr. London: Routledge, 2013), p. 109.

26 Jeremy Noakes, ed., *Nazism 1919–1945, Volume 4: The German Home Front in World War II* (Exeter: Exeter University Press, 1998), p. 117.

27 Stephenson, *Women in Nazi Germany* (2001; repr. London: Routledge, 2013), pp. 47–48.

28 Mason, *Social Policy in the Third Reich*, p. 27.

29 Christian Tilitzki, *Alltag in Ostpreußen 1940–45: Die geheimen Lageberichte der Königsberger Justiz* (Würzburg: Flechsig, 2003), pp. 52–54.

30 Noakes, ed., *Nazism, Vol. 4*, pp. 510–519; Mason, *Social Policy in the Third Reich*, p. 27.

31 Malte Zierenberg, *Berlin's Black Market: 1939–1950* (Basingstoke: Palgrave Macmillan, 2015), pp. 47–50.

32 Lothar Gruchmann, 'Korruption im Dritten Reich: Zur "Lebensmittelversorgung" der NS-Führerschaft', *Vierteljahreshefte für Zeitgeschichte* 42, no. 4 (1994): pp. 571–593.

33 Norman Longmate, *The Bombers: The RAF Offensive against Germany 1939–1945* (London: Arrow Books, 1988), p. 359.

34 Neill Gregor, 'A *Schicksalsgemeinschaft*? Allied Bombing, Civilian Morale, and Social Dissolution in Nuremberg, 1942–1945', *Historical Journal* 43, no. 4 (2000): pp. 1051–1070.

35 Gerhard Kock, *'Der Führer sorgt für unsere Kinder . . .': Die Kinderlandverschickung im Zweiten Weltkrieg* (Munich: Schöningh, 1997), pp. 69–80.

36 Dietmar Süß, *Tod aus der Luft: Kriegsgesellschaft und Luftkrieg in Deutschland und England* (Bonn: Bundeszentrale für politische Bildung, 2011), pp. 152–168.

37 Longmate, *The Bombers*, p. 362.

38 Ibid., pp. 354, 356.

39 Erich von Ludendorff, *Der Totale Krieg* (Munich: Ludendorff Verlag, 1935), pp. 3, 6.

40 Randall Bytwerk, ed., *Landmark Speeches of National Socialism* (College Station: Texas A&M University Press, 2008), pp. 112–139.

41 Carl-Wilhelm Reibel, *Das Fundament der Diktatur: Die NSDAP-Ortsgruppen 1932–1945* (Paderborn: Ferdinand Schöningh, 2002), pp. 351–359.

42 Bastiaan Willems, *Violence in Defeat: The Wehrmacht on German Soil, 1944–1945* (Cambridge: Cambridge University Press, 2021), pp. 43–44.

43 Karl-Heinz Frieser, 'Irrtümer und Illusionen: Die Fehleinschätzungen der deutschen Führung', in *Das Deutsche Reich und der Zweiten Weltkrieg 8: Die Ostfront 1943/44: Der Krieg im Osten und an den Nebenfronten*, ed. Karl-Heinz Frieser (Munich: Deutsche Verlags-Anstalt, 2007), p. 522.

44 Gerhard Weinberg, *Germany, Hitler, and World War II* (Cambridge: Cambridge University Press, 1995), pp. 284–285.

45 Tooze, *Wages of Destruction*, pp. 627–628; Noakes, ed., *Nazism, Vol. 4*, p. 185.

46 See Willems, *Violence in Defeat*; John Zimmermann, *Pflicht zum Untergang: Die deutsche Kriegsführung im Westen des Reiches 1944/45* (Paderborn: Schöningh, 2009).

47 David Yelton, *Hitler's Volkssturm: The Nazi Militia and the Fall of Germany, 1944–1945* (Lawrence: University Press of Kansas, 2002), pp. 119–120.
48 Rüdiger Overmans, *Deutsche militärische Verluste im Zweiten Weltkrieg* (Munich: De Gruyter, 1999), pp. 238, 318; Ian Kershaw, *The End: Germany 1944–45* (London: Penguin, 2012), p. 379.
49 Longmate, *The Bombers*, p. 360.
50 Andreas Kossert, *Kalte Heimat: Die Geschichte der deutschen Vertriebenen nach 1945* (Bonn: Bundeszentrale für Politische Bildung, 2008), pp. 47–70.
51 Stargardt, *The German War*, pp. 28–34

WENDY Z. GOLDMAN

16

The Soviet War Effort

The idea of 'total war' was first broached in 1832 by Carl von Clausewitz in his history of the Napoleonic Wars and later popularised by General Erich von Ludendorff's memoir of the First World War, *Der Totale Krieg*.[1] Over time, the phrase has come to encompass many features, including mass conscription, full economic mobilisation, blurred lines between civilians and combatants, blockades, sieges, scorched earth, collective punishment of civilians, slave or unfree labour, mass murder, and totalising state control. By every one of these measures, the Soviet Union was involved in a 'total war.' After the German invasion on 22 June 1941, Leningrad was surrounded in the longest-running siege in modern history.[2] The Red Army fought along a 1,500-mile front, and in the first eighteen months, vast swathes of territory fell to the Germans and their allies. The *Einsatzgruppen* (special task forces) and the Wehrmacht visited mass destruction in the occupied areas by systematically starving the population, murdering partisans and civilians, and sending millions as slave labour to Germany. Almost one-third of the six million Jews murdered in the Holocaust were killed by the Nazis or their allies on Soviet soil. The country's losses were stunning: about twenty-six to twenty-seven million Soviet citizens died in the war, including millions of POWs who were murdered in German POW camps.[3] The heavy bombardment of Soviet cities and involvement of civilians in air defence, partisan warfare, and volunteer militias (*opolchenie*) all dissolved the line between civilian and soldier.

At the same time, the Soviet state set a qualitatively new benchmark for 'total war' in its exhaustive mobilisation of every resource, including human labour, for the war effort. In the absence of adequate food, housing, heat, and the most basic necessities of daily life, the popular slogan 'All for the Front' became a literal reality. The government, reaching the height of its power, achieved a mobilisation of resources for the front so total that the home-front population was close to collapse by the war's end.[4] In the words of one historian, 'no other population was asked to make this level of sacrifice'.[5] The nation was stretched to the breaking point. But what constitutes a 'breaking point'? What did that mean in practice?

16.1   Evacuation

In June 1941 the German *Blitzkrieg* swept over the border and quickly penetrated deep into Soviet territory. By late fall the Germans had occupied Belorussia and most of Ukraine, and were within striking distance of Moscow. Most of the country's industry, including the mines and steel plants essential to defence, and 40 per cent of its pre-war population, was located in the western territories soon to be occupied. Within two days of the invasion, the government created a new body, the Soviet for Evacuation (SE), to rescue machinery, people, grain, food, and cultural treasures under immediate threat. As the Germans advanced, the SE's mission expanded to include planned evacuations over ever-greater territory. Evacuation lasted a little over a year and occurred in two phases: the first from June to December 1941, reaching its height between July and November, and a second, smaller phase, in the summer and fall of 1942 in the south.[6] The government, establishing a policy of 'scorched earth', blew up, flooded, or blocked mines, dams, electrical stations, bridges, railroads, and industrial equipment that could not be rescued.

Throughout the summer of 1941, panic and confusion reigned in the front-line zones, and the SE faced mounting challenges, requiring mastery not only of the transfer of a single factory or locality but of an interconnected industrial base, millions of people, and even herds along a rapidly moving front. The task required close coordination among the armaments industry, railways, and larger economy. The evacuations were accomplished under severe constraints of transport and labour: the military urgently needed the rail lines and boxcars, and hundreds of thousands of workers had already left for the front. Workers were essential to the operation, often dismantling and loading the plants under heavy bombing, floods, and fires. The Communist Party, state, and economic officials understood that machines in boxcars could not produce and that evacuation would create a sharp, albeit temporary, drop in the production of desperately needed armaments. Although some evacuations were planned well in advance of occupation, others occurred at the last possible moment, placing enormous pressure on local officials. The SE was responsible for assigning the proper number of boxcars to every operation, tracking the convoys, and approving their destinations. It tracked hundreds of thousands of boxcars in various stages of loading, travel, and arrival. By mid-August 1941, less than two months after the invasion, the government reconfigured the country's Five-Year Plan to reflect the shift of industry, creating a new master plan based on the rising industrial base in the east.

Evacuation was hampered by several unalterable constraints. Foremost among these was the lack of boxcars. Even aviation and ammunition factories, which were given high priority for evacuation, showed a considerable gap between the number of boxcars they needed and the number they received. Many factories and regions received barely half the boxcars they requested. Another constraint was the amount of traffic any one rail line could bear within a given period, a number worked out mathematically by railway specialists in accordance with troop movements, food deliveries, and other essential traffic. This number, exceeded at risk of gridlock and delay, placed iron limits on loading and shipping.[7]

The journeys to the east were long and dangerous. Evacuees, provided with train tickets, were accompanied by vast streams of refugees on the roads. Massive crowds piled up at ports, river crossings, and rail junctures. Most evacuees travelled in *teplushki*, or railway cars heated by makeshift stoves but without seats, luggage racks, water, and toilets. Despite detailed health instructions, by August 1941, medical authorities were overwhelmed by the vast numbers of people in motion. Sick and healthy passengers were crammed together, and many train stations could not provide shelter, latrines, or clean drinking water. Two huge epidemics – measles and typhus –swept the evacuation routes, resulting in the death of many children and other vulnerable groups. The railway lines were bombed repeatedly and convoys were subject to painful delays and long detours. Many who were already ill or weak died in transit. Only after the massive wave of evacuees had passed were local health officials able to implement the measures needed to prevent further epidemics, including access to field latrines, boiled water, and delousing stations. Despite labour mobilisation, the return of evacuees to the liberated territories, and continuing population movements, the terrible health crisis of 1941–1942 was not repeated.[8]

By December 1941 the SE had evacuated about seventeen million people, or about 22 per cent of the population, and relocated about 37 per cent of the pre-war value of industry far to the east and south, beyond the reach of German bombers. Workers who accompanied the evacuated factories travelled for months to reach their assigned destinations. In the absence of any infrastructure, they unpacked the machines and began producing armaments under open snowy skies as the walls of the new factories rose around them.[9]

Evacuation was an audacious feat, unprecedented in the history of peace or war. Its sheer scale required great organisational coordination between the state and industry, and equally great courage and fortitude from the industrial, railway, and construction workers. Never had any state succeeded in moving and reconstructing a vast industrial base, along with millions of people, tons of grain, raw materials, food stocks, and even herds. Evacuation was made necessary by military defeat and territorial loss, but it ultimately enabled the Soviet Union to continue to produce the steel, coal, and armaments needed to win the war.

16.2   Labour Mobilisation

The evacuation of the industrial base carried huge and not-fully-anticipated consequences. In June 1941, 18 per cent of the defence industry was in the east; one year later it was 76 per cent.[10] Yet the eastern part of the country was sparsely populated. Many workers went to the front, and local residents and evacuees, were not able to fill the gap. In response, the Soviet government created a wartime labour system that was unique among the combatant nations and unprecedented in its own history. Within a week of the invasion, it established a new body – the Committee to Distribute the Labour Force, known simply as the *Komitet*. It was charged with assessing the number of available workers in every locality and mobilising them to staff industrial enterprises in need of labour. Over the course of the war, the state mobilised almost fifteen million free workers for permanent or temporary work. In addition to the *Komitet*, which mobilised about 40 per cent of all permanent workers, the Commissariat of Defence and vocational schools also mobilised draftees unfit for military service and new graduates.[11]

Initially, the government hoped to meet the labour shortage with housewives, volunteers, new vocational graduates, and workers in non-essential industries. But these sources were rapidly absorbed. In February 1942 the government passed a decree subjecting the urban, able-bodied population, including women, to labour mobilisation in their place of residence. Yet urban residents could not fill jobs in distant mines, forests, construction sites, and factories, or in the growing eastern industrial base. By summer 1942 the state began to reach beyond the urban population into the countryside to mobilise peasants. People left their homes and families and travelled hundreds, even thousands, of miles to work. Like the Red Army, the newly mobilised labour force was created from more than fifty different national and ethnic groups.

Labour mobilisation was analogous to the military draft, and failure to obey a mobilisation order was a criminal offense. According to the new wartime labour system, the industrial commissariats estimated the numbers of workers they needed for their enterprises, sending their requests to the State Committee on Defence, the highest wartime body, which then sent the requests it approved to the *Komitet* and Commissariat of Defence. These bodies, in turn, issued levy orders to provincial and republic soviets to muster the required number of people. A single levy could involve anywhere from 50 to 350,000 people, and the provinces and republics were responsible for filling numerous levies each year. The needs of the defence industry and its subsidiary branches pulled peasants off of collective farms and workers from the municipal economy, including streetcars, public baths, and local garment factories. Over time, these losses created a dearth of consumer goods and services. The government stripped and scoured every corner of the economy to provide workers and resources for defence. Women, who already held a significant percent of industrial jobs, now assumed an even greater role, as did teenagers and pensioners. Provincial and republic soviets, under intense pressure to meet the targets, often mobilised people who were too weak, ill, or disabled to cope with heavy labour. The state stripped the villages of able-bodied peasants and mobilised urban inhabitants to help with sowing and harvesting. Hundreds of thousands of teenagers, many younger than fourteen, were mobilised for vocational schools and factories far from home.[12]

Prisoners and exiles were also mobilised, although the Gulag (Main Camp Administration), like the larger economy, also suffered a shortage of able-bodied workers. Between July 1941 and September 1944, more than one million inmates were released and sent to the Red Army, leading to a 30 per cent reduction in the camp population. Many malnourished, older, or disabled prisoners were not fit for heavy labour. Those prisoners who were still fit to work made a significant contribution to heavy, unskilled jobs in construction, coal and ore mining, and timber felling. They suffered appalling death rates due to low rations and difficult working conditions. At the height of the food crisis in 1942,

Figure 16.1 A group of young women making hand grenades at a Moscow munitions plant, circa 1942. Source: Alexander Ustinov/Slava Katamidze Collection/Getty Images.

one quarter of all prisoners in the camps and colonies died. In 1944 and 1945, as the food situation in the country gradually improved, so did provisioning in the camps, and mortality dropped among both the general and the Gulag populations.[13] The state also exiled entire national groups suspected of collaboration and enrolled those fit to work into the 'Labour Army', a loose organisation under the auspices of the Commissariat of Internal Affairs (NKVD). Workers in the Labour Army were situated somewhere between free and prison labour. They were not convicted of any crime and received wages, but were confined in specially designated camps under guard. Both prisoners and workers in the Labour Army received smaller rations than free workers and suffered worse conditions.[14]

16.3 Conditions of Daily Life

Millions of people arrived in the eastern and Central Asian towns, tripling their populations almost overnight.[15] Local soviets attempted to cope with the influx of refugees, evacuees, and mobilised workers by requiring all local residents, urban and rural, to lodge newcomers and by repurposing theatres, clubs, and offices. Managers were responsible for providing housing, work clothes, clinics, bedding, canteens, daycare centres, and baths for mobilised workers, many of whom were billeted in hastily constructed barracks and earthen dugouts. People slept on three-tiered plank beds, and many accommodations lacked bedding, heat, electricity, running water, toilets, and stoves. The factories, like the barracks, were unheated, and public baths and streetcars were shut down for lack of fuel. There was no soap. Workers suffered skin infections, chemical burns, and rashes, all aggravated by the inability to bathe. Poorly clad and shod, they trudged long distances to work in snowy, freezing weather. Canteens struggled to prepare meals in the absence of sufficient food and fuel. The army requisitioned almost all horses and motor vehicles, and workers cut wood and dragged it back on sleds for the canteen kitchens.[16]

Workers, like soldiers, were bound by law to their wartime jobs. Leaving work without permission was a criminal offense. The government first established penalties in June 1940, before the invasion, for unauthorised lateness or absence. In December 1941 the penalties increased: workers in defence and defence-related industries who were absent without cause were deemed 'labour deserters' and liable to five to eight years in prison.[17] Despite these draconian penalties, many mobilised workers, facing difficult conditions, did run away. Between 1941 and 1945, no less than seven million people were convicted for absenteeism. Yet conviction meant little amid the instability and upheaval that characterised the war years. Of the seven million people convicted, one million were sentenced, and of these, only 400,000 were imprisoned. The law, ignored by workers as well as those entrusted with its enforcement, proved a poor deterrent. Managers failed to report missing workers, foremen kept spotty attendance rosters, prosecutors lacked sufficient data to charge offenders, judges hesitated to impose sentences, and collective farm managers welcomed the runaways for their much-needed labour. Although millions left their assigned jobs, the vast majority ended up contributing to the war effort in other places. In July 1945, after the war's end, everyone who was serving time for labour desertion was amnestied.[18]

In theory, the idea of assessing the number of people in every locality and assigning them to work where they were most needed seemed

Figure 16.2 Young girls assembling machine guns in a Soviet factory, 1943.
Source: Art Media/Print Collector/Getty Images.

a reasonable solution for a wartime economy under existential threat. Yet no society of such size and complexity ever managed to exercise that degree of control over labour, and certainly not when the enterprises were also forced to assume responsibility for housing, food, and clothing. By the middle of the war, numerous party officials were protesting conditions for mobilised workers, sharp conflicts over labour had developed between collective farms and industry, and provincial and republic soviets were unable to meet the levies the *Komitet* imposed. Archival records show growing lags and gaps between the numbers of people the industrial commissariats requested and the numbers the local areas were able to muster and deliver. Backlogs of unmet levies overwhelmed the new levies. Industrial managers, faced with an irremediable dearth of food, housing materials, fuel, and consumer goods, as well as intense pressure to meet their production targets, found it easier to order more workers than to improve conditions. The labour system, so critical to meeting the needs of the front, was in crisis.

16.4 Feeding the Nation

A large portion of the country's pre-war agricultural production – 38 per cent of its grain, 84 per cent of its sugar, and 38 per cent of its cattle – was located in territory occupied by the Germans. The SE began shipping grain, herds, and food processing factories out of the front-line zones immediately, but its efforts were not always successful.[19] The government, surveying its rapidly shrinking stocks, moved quickly to control the food supply. The Commissariat of Trade was repurposed to calculate available stocks and distribute them through its nationwide network of trade departments and retail stores. On 18 July 1941, less than a month after the invasion, it created a rationing system that soon encompassed all urban inhabitants and rural waged workers. Collective farmers did not receive rations on the assumption that they could provision themselves from farm produce and private plots. By late fall 1941, all ration-card holders were guaranteed at minimum bread and sugar, an entitlement which expanded to include a differentiated array of foods and consumer goods. Food was not available in stores or canteens for commercial sale; it could only be bought with a ration card. The system was built on two principles, labour contribution and vulnerability, and organised around a hierarchy of distribution that determined both the amount and type of food. The most privileged were those who expended the most calories and were most important to defence, while those in need of extra protection received supplemental foods. Soldiers received the highest rations, followed in descending order by workers, white-collar employees, adult dependents (invalids, the elderly), children, and prisoners. Bread was at the heart of the system, baked and distributed daily in relatively equal amounts to all groups. Unlike other food groups, it was not subject to substitutions. Scarcer foods groups, such as protein and fats, were provided in less-egalitarian amounts. The state also provided supplemental food through milk kitchens, extra rations and canteen meals, and refeeding programs for vulnerable groups, including children, pregnant women, nursing mothers, and workers who exceeded production norms, held hazardous or arduous jobs, or were starving or sick.[20]

Over time, the basic ration categories were repeatedly subdivided: workers in defence industries, for example, received more than other workers. Party, soviet, and economic officials were considered to be employees and, as such, received smaller rations than workers. However, they routinely allocated additional provisions for themselves in a practice called self-provisioning (*samosnabzhenie*). Drawing on stocks allocated for other groups, they established exclusive managerial canteens and requisitioned food from local farms. The practice infuriated workers and other groups, who believed that under socialism the harsh sacrifices demanded by the war should be shared equally. In 1943 the government attempted to end *samosnabzhenie* by setting firm limits on supplemental food parcels for officials, but nonetheless, the practice continued.[21]

In 1942, as the Germans conquered more territory, food stocks fell as the needs of the Red Army increased. The home front faced a food crisis. The state recognised that rations drawn from central stocks would not be sufficient to cover people's basic caloric requirements. It organised supplementary sources, including subsidiary farms, which it attached to factories and institutions, decentralised local procurement, collective and individual gardens, and collective farm markets. Of these additional sources, only collective farm markets, where peasants sold produce from their private plots, charged free market prices. Given the terrible scarcity, prices in the peasant markets were high and often out of reach for ordinary people. Throughout the war, the vast majority of calories consumed by the urban population still came from central state stocks.[22] Yet, despite the ration system and various supplementary sources, the government could not escape a painful food shortage.

As the food supply dwindled, the Commissariat of Trade was forced to cut stocks for retail stores and institutions. Local officials channelled food towards factory canteens, which became the only source of food available in many industrial towns. Canteen cooks struggled with a lack of food, fuel, and utensils. Factories began manufacturing their own spoons and pots alongside tanks and ammunition. The factory, offering food, medical care, and shelter, replaced the family as the main site of life, not only for its workers but also for their families and other urban residents. The shortages hit children especially hard. Cities reported increasing cases of acute malnutrition, many of them fatal. Officials placed numerous groups, from school children to evacuees, in factory canteens to eat at the expense of stocks allocated to workers. G. A. Liubimov, the Commissar of Trade, later attributed the survival of the country to socialised canteen dining.[23] Yet no amount of egalitarian redistribution could solve the overall lack of food. In the eastern towns, starvation-induced tuberculosis was the single leading cause of death of people of working age. The food supply reached its nadir in 1942, followed by an increase in starvation mortality in 1943 and 1944. By 1944 a huge number of workers were suffering from starvation disease (*dystrofiia*).[24] Even after the food supply improved, people continued to suffer from the toll of deprivation.

As always in times of hunger, people turned to foraging, food substitutes, and invented foods to allay hunger. The government also took the unusual step to organise scientists, nutritionists, and cooks to research food substitutes. Nutritionists invented a bitter concoction made from boiled coniferous needles containing high amounts of vitamin C to prevent scurvy. Known simply as *khvoia*, people drank glasses of the foul-tasting stuff in canteens. Unions organised workers in foraging brigades to gather edible wild greens for soups and salads, and nutritionists taught canteen cooks to make a concentration of vitamin A (carotene) from wild greens. *Uralmashzavod*, the famed tank factory in Sverdlovsk, set up a special experimental complex that produced concentrated vegetable bullion from nettles and goutweed. Canteen cooks repurposed the starchy water after boiling potatoes to create a variety of jelly-like 'desserts'. Researchers experimented with yeast as a protein substitute, and local trade departments, scientific organisations, and factories began growing and shipping tons of yeast to public canteens to add to soups. By 1945 all canteens provided a 'vitaminized course', made up of various food substitutes, to meet dietary deficiencies.[25]

16.5   Propaganda and Popular Support

Total war required painful sacrifices from the home-front population. Yet, unlike other transformative moments in history – the French revolution, the Russian revolutions of 1905 and 1917, the German and Hungarian uprisings of 1918 – when wartime discontent fuelled uprisings against the state and the system it represented, there were no mass protests on the Soviet home front. On the contrary, the degree of mass mobilisation could not have been achieved without the cooperation of ordinary people. In view of the initial military losses and the difficulty of daily life, the state's effort to rally support became critical to the war effort. People supported the war for many reasons – to repel the hated invaders, to fight against fascism, to safeguard socialism and the gains of 1917, and to protect family and country.[26] The Agitation and Propaganda Department under the Central Committee of the Communist Party was responsible for wartime propaganda. It trained and dispatched party instructors, who disseminated the speeches of party leaders, relayed news from the front, and discussed international politics, daily life, and production. At the same time, official propaganda 'from above' was accompanied by an outpouring of songs, poetry, art, and radio broadcasts 'from below' that were supported by the state. Soldiers and civilians learned K. M. Simonov's iconic poem 'Wait for Me' by heart and recited it like a prayer.[27] Young workers pioneered various shop-floor experiments to increase production. Urban residents joined voluntary militias to build barricades, defend their cities, and fight alongside the Red Army in the streets. The slogan 'A Single, Undivided Military Camp' captured the lived experience of the front and rear.

Propaganda changed in tone and message over the course of the war. After the shock of the invasion, the state struggled to explain the Red Army's failures and retreats, but over time, reporting became franker in response to people's demands for news about the front. The German failure to capture Moscow in October 1941 lifted morale, but the Red Army's subsequent advance also revealed the shocking scale of German atrocities. By 1942 the hope that German workers would rise against Hitler faded, and the state's message became overtly anti-German as evidence of the genocide of the Jews and mass murder of other civilians filtered out of the occupied territories. Journalists linked the horrors of occupation with the need for armaments in emotional articles that resonated deeply with the home front. Stalin's famous 'Not One Step Back' speech in July 1942 criticised the Red Army for retreating and promised the soldiers the weapons they needed to win. As the battle for Stalingrad began, party instructors were told, 'Don't whitewash the dangers, don't downplay the difficulties . . . . There is nowhere further for us to retreat.'[28] Workers closely followed the news from the front and organised initiatives to overfulfil output norms. By December 1942, they met Stalin's promise to the soldiers, replacing the vast stocks of equipment lost during the period of retreat.[29] After the victory at Stalingrad in February 1943, soldiers and workers were encouraged to keep personal 'accounts of revenge' to underscore the horrors and losses they experienced. One historian later noted that propagandists did not have to invent much in order to incite feelings of hatred: 'It was sufficient simply to collect and summarize the personal experience of each person.'[30] The message of the state resonated with the feelings and experiences of ordinary people to create an unusual unity of purpose.

16.6 Liberation

In the liberated territories, the Red Army discovered a wasteland strewn with rubble and corpses. The hard task of reconstruction began. The Commissariat of Trade added more than twelve million people to the ration rolls, evacuees began to return home, and the *Komitet* mobilised people for work.[31] After the liberation of Khar'kov in the summer of 1943, women canteen workers began serving more than 24,000 people who had survived occupation. In the absence of electricity, running water, fuel, horses, and motor vehicles, they hauled water from the river and cut and dragged wood from the forest on makeshift carts and sledges.[32] Their efforts were replicated in other towns. The Red Army broke the siege of Leningrad in January 1944, and evacuees began returning to restore the defence factories. In western Ukraine, Belorussia, and the Baltic states, nationalist bands that collaborated with the Germans to murder partisans, party members, Jews, and other civilians resisted the re-establishment of Soviet power. They killed those who returned to rebuild and terrorised the families of those who joined the Red Army, helped with reconstruction, or provided grain to the state. The defence factories in the east still needed workers, but the newly liberated population often resisted mobilisation for work outside their native provinces. Yet more than one million workers were mobilised in 1944 alone, some to the east, others to rebuild the newly liberated territories.[33] On 8 May 1945 the German High Command signed an act of unconditional surrender. The end to the war was announced in the Soviet Union in the early-morning hours of May 9, henceforth to be celebrated as 'Victory Day'. From one end of the country to the other, people danced in the streets and wept in each other's arms. The cost of the victory was steep, and every family had paid the price.

16.7   Conclusion

The vast majority of German divisions were concentrated in the east, and it was here that the Red Army defeated the Wehrmacht. If we think about the relationship between front and rear, one image can help us tally the cost of total war. Imagine a typical front-line soldier wearing a uniform, helmet, and boots, and carrying a gun, ammunition, a blanket, a shovel, and other standard equipment. This soldier goes into battle supported by tanks, planes, mortars, and other armaments. Now trace the supply lines back thousands of miles to the workers who manufactured the armaments and equipment, and then beyond them to those who produced the chemicals, steel, coal, and other materials that produced the armaments. Maintaining these workers, in turn, stood others, labouring in fields, forests, and peat bogs to feed, warm, and shelter them. Behind every front-line soldier stretched a vast chain of invisible labourers who 'produced' the soldier. Now imagine a transfer of resources from rear to front so complete that the labourers who produced the soldier struggled to sustain their own lives. This was total war on the home front in the Soviet Union during the Second World War.

Notes

1 See Carl von Clausewitz, Michael Howard, and Peter Paret, eds., *On War* (Princeton: Princeton University Press, 1993), and Erich Ludendorff, *Der Totale Krieg* (Munich: Ludendorffs Verlag, 1935).

2 On the siege of Leningrad, see Richard Bidlack and Nikita Lomagin, *The Leningrad Blockade, 1941–1944: A New Documentary History from the Soviet Archives* (New Haven: Yale University Press, 2007); Alexis Peri, *The War Within: Diaries from the Siege of Leningrad* (Cambridge, MA: Harvard University Press, 2017); Harrison Salisbury, *The 900 Days: The Siege of Leningrad* (Cambridge, MA: Da Capo Press, 2003).

3 On total losses, see E. M. Andreev, I. E. Darskii, and T. L. Khar'kova, 'Liudskie poteri SSSR vo vtoroi mirovoi voine: metodika otsenki i rezul'taty', pp. 36–42; on military deaths, see G. F. Krivosheev, 'Ob itogakh statisticheskikh issledovanii poter' vooruzhennykh sil SSSR v Velikoi Otechestvennoi voine', pp. 71–81; on civilian losses, see M. V. Filimoshin, 'Ob itogov ischislenniia sredi mirnogo naseleniia na okkupirovannoi territorii SSSR i RSFSR v gody Velikoi Otechestvennoi voiny', pp. 124–131, in *Liudskie poteri SSSR v period vtoroi mirovoi voiny. Sbornik statei* (St. Petersburg: Russko-Baltiiskii Informatsionnyi Tsentr' Blits, 1995). On Jewish deaths, see G. V. Kostyrchenko, ed., *Gosudarstvennyi Antisemitizm v SSSR, 1938–1953. Dokumenty* (Moscow: Mezhdunarodnyi Fond Demokratiia, Izdatel'stvo 'Materik', 2005), pp. 45–46.

4 Major works on the home front include John Barber and Mark Harrison, *The Soviet Home Front, 1941–1945: A Social and Economic History of the USSR in World War II* (London: Longman, 1991); T. M. Bulavkina and M. V. Stegantsev, eds., *Edinstvo fronta i tyla v Velikoi Otechestvennoi voine 1941–1945* (Moscow: Akademiia, 2007); Wendy Z. Goldman and Donald Filtzer, *Fortress Dark and Stern: The Soviet Home Front during World War II* (New York: Oxford University Press, 2021); A. N. Sakharov and A. S. Seniavskii, eds., *Narod i voina, 1941–1945 gg* (Moscow: Institut Rossiiskoi Istorii RAN, 2010); Robert Thurston and Bernd Bonwetsch, eds., *The People's War: Responses to World War II in the Soviet Union* (Urbana: University of Illinois Press, 2000); *Istoriia Velikoi Otechestvennoi voiny, Gosudarstvo, obshchestvo i voina, tom 10* (Moscow: Kuchkovo Pole, 2014); V. F. Zima, *Mentalitet narodov Rossii v voine 1941–1945 godov* (Moscow: Institut Rossiiskoi Istorii RAN, 2000).

5 Richard Overy, *Why the Allies Won* (New York: W.W. Norton and Co., 1995), p. 188.

6 On evacuation, see Goldman and Filtzer, *Fortress*, pp. 11–93; Rebecca Manley, *To the Tashkent Station: Evacuation and Survival in the Soviet Union at War* (Ithaca: Cornell University Press, 2009); G. A. Kumanev, 'Evakuatsiia naseleniia SSSR: dostignutie rezultaty i poteri', in *Liudskie poteri SSSR*, pp. 137–146; Iu. A. Poliakov, G. A. Kumanev, N. P. Lipatov, and A. V. Mitrofanova, eds., *Eshelony idut na vostok: Iz istorii perebazirovaniia proizvoditel'nykh sil SSSR v 1941–1942 gg. Sbornik statei i vospominanii* (Moscow: Nauka, 1966).

7 Goldman and Filtzer, *Fortress Dark and Stern*, pp. 28, 51–53.

8 Goldman and Filtzer, *Fortress Dark and Stern*, pp. 74, 263–293; Donald Filtzer, *The Hazards of Urban Life in Late Stalinist Russia: Health, Hygiene, and Living Standards* (Cambridge: Cambridge University Press, 2010).

9 I. I. Belonosov, 'Evakuatsiia naseleniia iz prifrontovoi polosy v 1941–1942', in Iu. A. Poliakov et al., *Eshelony idut na vostok*, pp. 15, 24–25.

10 V. B. Tel'pukhovskii, 'Geroizm Rabochego Klassa', in *Voina i obshchestvo, 1941–1945*, ed. G. N. Sevostianov (Moscow: Nauka, 2004), p. 9.

11 Its name was soon changed to the Committee to Enumerate and Distribute the Labour Force. Goldman and Filtzer, *Fortress Dark and Stern*, p. 385, table 5.1.

12 Goldman and Filtzer, *Fortress Dark and Stern*, pp. 164–230.

13 On the reduction of the camp population, see the report from V. G. Nasedkin, Chief of the Gulag, to L. P. Beria, 'O Rabote GULAGa za Gody Voiny (1941–1944)', in *GULAG (Glavnoe upravlenie lagerei) 1917–1960*, ed. A. I. Kokurin and N. V. Petrov (Moscow: Mezhdunarodnyi fond 'Demokratiia', Izdatel'stvo 'Materik', 2000), p. 275; on the size of the Gulag population and death rates, see Goldman and Filtzer, *Fortress Dark and Stern*, p. 386, tables 5.2 and 5.3. On prison labour, see Edwin Bacon, *The Gulag at War: Stalin's Forced Labor System in the Light of the Archives* (Basingstoke: Macmillan, 1994); Wilson T. Bell, *Stalin's Gulag at War: Forced Labour, Mass Death, and Soviet Victory in the Second World War* (Toronto: University of Toronto Press, 2019).

14 Goldman and Filtzer, *Fortress Dark and Stern*, pp. 190–194; G. A. Goncharov, '"Trudovaia Armiia" perioda Velikoi Otechestvennoi voiny: Rossiiskaia istoriografiia', in *Ekonomicheskaia istoriia: Obozrenie*, Vypusk 7, ed. L. I. Borodkin (Moscow: Borodkin, 2001), pp. 154–162.

15 Goldman and Filtzer, *Fortress Dark and Stern*, p. 381, table 2.1.

16 Goldman and Filtzer, *Fortress Dark and Stern*, pp. 176–184, 206–211, 218–219, 226–228, 244–245.

17 Martin Kragh, 'Stalinist Labour Coercion during World War II: An Economic Approach', *Europe-Asia Studies* 63, no. 7 (September 2011): pp.

1253–1273, and ' Soviet Labour Law during the Second World War', *War in History* 18, no. 4 (November 2011): 531–546.

18 Goldman and Filtzer, *Fortress Dark and Stern*, pp. 231–262, 390, table 7.2; Oleg Khlevniuk, 'Listening to the Soviet Union's "Silent Majority": The Evasion of Labor Obligations on the Home Front', *The Russian Review* 82, no. 2 (2023): pp. 1–15.

19 G. A. Kumanev, *Sovetskii tyl v pervyi period Velikoi Otechestvennoi voiny* (Moscow: Nauka, 1988), p. 311.

20 Goldman and Filtzer, *Fortress Dark and Stern*, pp. 94–127, 381–383, tables 3.1–3.4; Wendy Z. Goldman and Donald Filtzer, 'Introduction: The Politics of Food and War', and Wendy Z. Goldman, 'Not by Bread Alone: Food, Workers, and the State', in *Hunger and War: Food Provisioning in the Soviet Union during World War II*, ed. Wendy Z. Goldman and Donald Filtzer (Bloomington: Indiana University Press, 2015), pp. 1–43; William Moskoff, *The Bread of Affliction: The Food Supply in the USSR during World War II* (Cambridge: Cambridge University Press, 1990); U. G. Cherniavskii, *Voina i prodovol'stvie. Snabzhenie gorodskogo naseleniia v Velikuiu Otechestvennuiu voinu (1941–1945 gg.)* (Moscow: Nauka, 1964).

21 'Prikaz', in Rossiiskii Gosudarstvennyi Arkhiv Sotsial'noi Politicheskoi Istorii, fond 17, op. 22, d. 49, ll. 26–28; Goldman and Filtzer, *Fortress Dark and Stern*, pp. 130–139.

22 Goldman and Filtzer, *Fortress Dark and Stern*, p. 382, table 3.1.

23 Goldman and Filtzer, *Fortress Dark and Stern*, pp. 108–111, 269; G. A. Liubimov, *Torgovlia i snabzhenie v gody Velikoi Otechestvennoi voiny* (Moscow: Izdatel'stvo Ekonomika, 1968), p. 123.

24 Filtzer, 'Starvation Mortality in Soviet Home Front Industrial Regions during World War II', and Rebecca Manley, 'Nutritional Dystrophy: The Science and Semantics of Starvation in World War II', in *Hunger and War*, ed. Goldman and Filtzer, pp. 206–338. V. N. Khaustov, V. P. Naumov, and N. S. Plotnikova, eds., *Lubianka. Stalin i NKVD-NKGB-GUKR 'Smersh', 1939–Mart 1946* (Moscow: Materik, 2006), pp. 422–423.

25 Goldman and Filtzer, *Fortress Dark and Stern*, pp. 116–121.

26 On propaganda and popular moods, see Karel Berkhoff, *Motherland in Danger: Soviet Propaganda during World War II* (Cambridge, MA: Harvard University Press, 2012); Richard Bidlack, 'Propaganda and Public Opinion', in *The Soviet Union at War, 1941–1945*, ed. David R. Stone (Barnsley: Pen and Sword Books, 2010), pp. 45–68; David Brandenburger, *National Bolshevism: Stalinist Mass Culture and the Formation of Modern Russian National Identity, 1931–1956* (Cambridge, MA: Harvard University Press, 2002); A. N. Sakharov and A. S. Seniavskii, eds., *Narod i voina, 1941–1945 gg.* (Moscow: Institut Rossiiskoi Istorii RAN, 2010); Richard Stites, ed., *Culture and Entertainment in Wartime Russia* (Bloomington: Indiana University Press, 1995); Robert Thurston and Bernd Bonwetsch, eds., *The*

People's War: Responses to World War II in the Soviet Union (Urbana: University of Illinois Press, 2000).

27 K. M. Simonov, in English: https://simonov.co.uk/waitforme.
28 See www.marxists.or/russkij/stalin/t15_23.htm; RGASPI, f. 17, op. 125, d.82, ll. 19–21.
29 Evan Mawdsley, *Thunder in the East: The Nazi Soviet War, 1941–1945* (London: Bloomsbury, 2016), p. 47.
30 R. P. Sosnovskaia, *Geroicheskii trud vo imia pobedy* (Leningrad: Izdatel'stvo Leningradskogo Universiteta, 1973), p. 123; Seniavskii and Seniavskaia, 'Ideologiia voiny i psikhlogiia naroda', in *Narod i voina, 1941–1945 gg*, ed. Sakharov and Seniavskii, pp. 187–188.
31 Goldman, 'Not by Bread Alone', p. 67.
32 Gosudarstvennyi Arkhiv Rossiiskii Federatsii, f. 5452, op. 22, d. 25, ll. 9-9ob.
33 GARF, f. 9517, op. 1, d. 50, ll. 1, 8, 12, 20, 22, 24, 42, 42–43; Alexander Statiev, *The Soviet Counterinsurgency in the Western Borderlands* (New York: Cambridge University Press, 2010); Khaustov, Naumov, and Plotnikova, *Lubianka*, pp. 447, 473; Goldman and Filtzer, *Fortress*, pp. 363–364.

Part VI

Comrades in Arms

OLEG BEYDA,

GRANT T. HARWARD,

RICHARD CARRIER, AND

HENRIK MEINANDER

17

Germany and the Axis in the East

Germany can be said to have had a complex relationship with its political family of Axis countries, involving a chaotic (im)balance of elements.[1] From the very first days of Operation Barbarossa, Berlin was obliged to engage in unifying rhetoric, presenting its role within the Axis as one of *primus inter pares*. The grandiose loquacity of Dr Josef Goebbels was invoked to obscure the otherwise clear-cut desire of the Germans for sole continental domination. Necessitated by perceived cultural and racial superiority, this desire had always lain at the centre of Berlin's efforts, coexisting with a whole range of other initiatives. At the same time, Hitler's state was forced to incorporate the contradictory propaganda narrative of a unified 'European crusade against Asiatic Bolshevism'. Further complicating Germany's cross-purposed conception of alliance were competing claims, mutual animosities, and deep distrust among Hitler's would-be allies, especially in Eastern Europe.[2]

With hopes for a quick victory high until mid-December 1941, the Axis alliance seemed to be functioning smoothly despite the shortages of materiel that afflicted it. The Anti-Comintern Conference in Berlin on 25 November saw not only a formal prolongation of their larger political commitment by the participating states (Germany, Japan, Manchukuo, Hungary, and Spain) but also the induction of new members into the fold (Bulgaria, Croatia, Denmark, Finland, Romania, and Slovakia). Hitler did his best to sound upbeat, claiming the war was 'already won' and assuring his listeners that the victory would ensure 'food in great abundance and almost all the natural resources' Germany required.[3]

By the time the ink had dried on the paper in Berlin, the good news had essentially ended. Driven by domestic calculations, Bulgaria had earlier aided Hitler's efforts in Yugoslavia and Greece but abstained from a wholehearted involvement in the war against Stalin, not even severing diplomatic ties. Bulgarian King Boris III had considered opening hostilities, but by December 1941 he had dismissed the idea of sending armed troops to the East.[4] The Spanish experience confirmed Bulgarian caution. Having only arrived on the Eastern Front in October 1941, the realities of meeting better-equipped and numerically superior Siberian forces quickly dispelled the Spanish propaganda promoting a new 'imperial destiny'. In fact, the Soviet offensive in early December caused the German command to fear the whole Spanish force would be annihilated when they retreated for eleven days without orders, without their heavy equipment and without preparing minefields to slow the pursuing enemy.[5] Even in Spain's heavily controlled press, the daily reports of dead 'heroes of the Fatherland' were already passed off as the necessary price of confronting Soviet Communism.[6] Further south, Croatia's war mimicked the Spanish experience. The idealised view of an 'awakened' Croatian state 'expanding itself in the battle against barbarism from Asia' encountered a sobering reality by the end of 1941.[7] Despite being attached to a German division, the small, insufficiently trained, and poorly resourced Croatian force was always going to struggle in the high-intensity fighting, and the forced retreat from Rostov in November 1941 degraded its strength still further and led to reports of ill-discipline and a high desertion rate.[8]

Even a much larger and more sophisticated force like the Hungarian 'Carpathian Group', numbering 45,000 men and including the first-rate 'Mobile Corps' (24,000 men), which gave a good account of itself even alongside the motorised divisions of Germany's Panzer Group 1, experienced an abrupt change in attitude towards the war. As early as August 1941, the heavy casualties led to serious doubts about the future of the war as well as Hungary's commitment. The Chief of the Hungarian General Staff, Colonel-General Henrik Werth, wanted to substantially reinforce Hungary's eastern army, whereas the commander of the Carpathian Group, Lieutenant-General Ferenc Szombathelyi, argued for the withdrawal of the Mobile Corps. As Szombathelyi astutely observed, 'the war will last for a long time, we must be prepared for that and not a lightning war'.[9] The Hungarian regent, Miklós Horthy, sided with Szombathelyi and even promoted him to replace Werth. Extracting their forces, however, proved more difficult. In early September, when Horthy and Szombathelyi approached Hitler, the limited progress in the south caused Hitler to block the Hungarian withdrawal.[10]

The second half of December 1941 brought ominous complications when the European war was transformed into a global conflict. With the United States now at war with Germany and the Red Army launching a major winter offensive, the fortunes of the Axis were suddenly more imperilled than ever before.[11] It was now only a matter of time before

Figure 17.1 A Vichy French propaganda poster depicting a map of the German invasion of the Soviet Union with the slogan 'The Crusade against Bolshevism'. Source: Art Media/Print Collector/Getty Images.

the German allies would, like Hungary, start considering their options, weighing the demands of an increasingly open-ended and militarily costly commitment in the East against the dangerous political consequences of devising an exit strategy that risked 'betraying' Germany. Hitler, however, expertly exploited the mutual fears his Romanian and Hungarian allies harboured regarding their fractious border dispute to entice even larger military commitments for the Eastern Front in 1942. Not to be outdone, Mussolini promised an entire Italian army to match the Eastern Europeans.[12] Finland, on the other hand, was drawing the opposite conclusion, and in June 1942 Hitler personally paid a visit to the Finnish commander in chief General Carl Mannerheim to ensure Germany's northern flank remained actively engaged in the war.[13] That the Germans could be benevolent, cajoling, manipulating, and even menacing towards their allies was precisely the point. They were to be kept in line by both the carrot and the stick, which as one guideline from the High Command of the Wehrmacht explained in April 1942, required 'tact, political and psychological understanding, but if necessary also hardness and harsh orders appealing to their sense of honour and their national pride'.[14]

The summer of 1942 saw a major new German offensive, codenamed Operation Blue, that lead to sweeping territorial gains in southern Russia. Yet the expanding length of Germany's front required ever more troops to cover the vast distances, and while the large Axis contingents provided the solution, their imposing mass belied unresolved weaknesses in material, training, and officer quality. By November 1942 more than 300 kilometres of the Eastern Front was manned exclusively by Romanian, Italian, or Hungarian armies, presenting a tempting Soviet target as the German high command focused most of their attention on the meaningless street battles in Stalingrad. It was a predictable disaster facilitated by the hubris of the German command. The Stalingrad disaster proved the turning point for Axis involvement in the East. Even Hitler's ruthlessness towards his allies, which extended to blaming them, at least in part, for the calamity, could not reconstitute the crippling front-line losses they had sustained. Conversely, if loyalty to Hitler was based on anticipated post-war favour in a German dominated 'new order', the shifting tide meant the Axis partners had less and less to gain from remaining in Berlin's orbit.[15]

Following the destruction of the Romanian, Hungarian, and Italian contingents, it was more important than ever that Germany retain whatever foreign military aid it could, but the adverse political and military momentum was making this impossible. In the autumn of 1943 Spain felt the need to bolster its claim of neutrality, causing the Spanish dictator Francisco Franco to pull the Blue Division from the front line near Leningrad. Meanwhile, Heinrich Himmler was desperately attempting to recruit volunteers for his pan-European Waffen-SS to serve in the East. Some Wehrmacht legions, like Walloons (with 16,000 volunteers altogether), were transferred into the Waffen-SS for this purpose. Yet the relative numbers were not impressive: for example, although it is difficult to count the number of 'Germanic' volunteers precisely, the ballpark figure throughout the war was less than 50,000 (with 23,000 Dutch, 10,000 Flemish, and 6,000 Danes and Norwegians each).[16] Finally, there were the 'subhumans' from the East itself, for whom since late 1942 turncoat Soviet general Andrei Vlasov was earmarked as 'the leader.' Yet, even here, National Socialist principles overruled the military necessity, and until November 1944 Vlasov's Russian Liberation Army (ROA) remained a fictitious propaganda formation with no front-line troops (only a propaganda school in Dabendorf). What the Germans did have were dispersed 'Eastern formations', adorned in written-off German uniforms with an ROA patch on the sleeve and serving under German command. Only by November 1944 did Hitler relent, and many of these 'formations' were transferred to populate the three 'official' ROA divisions. Of the latter, only the first one was somewhat staffed, and some of its subunits saw limited action in February and then April 1945.[17]

By late 1944 the last vestiges of Germany's pan-European 'crusade' against Bolshevism were falling apart as Eastern European allies disappeared either because they changed sides or came under occupation. Finland was also under extreme pressure from the Red Army and, with no serious prospect of German retaliation, signed an armistice with the Soviet Union in September 1944. Almost immediately, the Finns turned their rifles against their former German ally in the Lapland War.

Overall, it is beyond doubt that compared with the Allies, the Axis approach to coalition warfare was poorly organised, haphazardly coordinated, and dreadfully led. Germany's relationship with its allies suffered from systematic problems, which as Richard DiNardo determined were characterised by

> language barriers, a radical difference in the degree of modernity in the level of technology and training of the Axis armies, Germany's failure to become 'the arsenal of fascism', and a lack of understanding on the part of the Axis powers, with perhaps the exception of Finland, of the relationship between national objectives, strategy and the morale of soldiers and officers alike.[18]

Yet, for all the problems, Germany's allies played an important and often underappreciated role on the Eastern Front. Already in 1941 they played major supporting roles, and the German summer offensive of 1942 simply would not have been possible without Axis contributions. Their military support behind the front was also of note, although these implicated Axis forces in their own share of war crimes. Similarly, countless Axis labourers toiled in fields, mines, and factories to support the war effort. Yet, in the final analysis, none of this mattered to a defeated and embittered Hitler, who in early January 1945 declared himself the 'victim of betrayal by our allies'.[19]

17.1   Romania's 'Holy War'

Before the Second World War, it was not obvious Romania would be Nazi Germany's most important ally against the Soviet Union.[20] Romania joined the Entente in 1916, benefited from the Paris Peace Conference in 1919, and supported the League of Nations in the 1920s. Yet, after the First World War, right-wing populism grew in Romania, in part in response to granting rights to minorities, especially Jews. In the 1930s the Legion of the Archangel Michael became one of the largest fascist movements in Europe. After 1936 Romania distanced itself from the Western Allies, adopting neutrality to draw closer to Nazi Germany.[21] In 1937 a new far-right government implemented anti-Semitic laws. In 1938 King Carol II declared a royal dictatorship, creating a fascistic one-party state. Although the king persecuted the Legionaries at home, he courted the Nazis abroad. In March 1939 Romania and Nazi Germany signed a sweeping economic agreement exchanging Romanian oil, agriculture, and timber for German arms and technicians. The next month, Great Britain and France guaranteed independence to Romania and Greece as a bluff to intimidate Nazi Germany. The Molotov-Ribbentrop pact's secret protocol assigned eastern Romania to the Soviet sphere of interest. After Nazi Germany invaded Poland in September 1939, Romania remained neutral but viewed the USSR as its greatest threat.

The shocking fall of France, followed closely by Soviet aggression, prompted Romania to embrace the Axis. The USSR demanded Romania cede (formerly Russian) Bessarabia and (formerly Austro-Hungarian) northern Bukovina or be invaded. Carol II agreed because Nazi Germany offered no support. From 28 June to 3 July 1940 the Romanian Army withdrew, resulting in armed clashes and humiliating incidents with the Red Army. Romanian soldiers accused Jews of treachery, killing hundreds while retreating. This was the de facto start of Romania's 'holy war'. The Soviet ultimatum triggered Hungarian and Bulgarian demands. Romania agreed to give southern Dobruja to Bulgaria, but it required German-Italian mediation to convince Romania to surrender northern Transylvania to Hungary. Carol II agreed, but his regime collapsed because of Legionary protests in Bucharest and Nazi skepticism in Berlin. General Ion Antonescu, who had connections with Romanian fascists and support from German representatives, forced the king to abdicate in favour of his son. The general became the *conducător* (leader) creating the National Legionary State. The Hungarian and Bulgarian occupations were less traumatic than the Soviet occupation. On 23 November 1940 Romania signed the Tripartite Pact. Nationalism, religion (Romanian Orthodox Christianity), anti-Semitism, and anticommunism pervaded society, so Romanians overwhelmingly supported allying with Nazi Germany.[22]

German planning for Operation Barbarossa assumed Romanian participation. Romania offered a forward base for attack. Wehrmacht planners were dismissive of Romanian military prowess because of valid professional reasons and spurious racist beliefs. German observers rated the officer corps as inferior, pointed to the absence of a non-commissioned officer corps, but assessed the common soldier as hardy. Consequently, German invasion plans limited Romanian involvement. The Germans kept the Romanians in the dark about the invasion. Antonescu was distracted by a political crisis. In January 1941 he used the military to suppress the Legionary Movement when it tried to seize power. In May 1941 Hitler sounded out Antonescu about Romania's stance in a future Nazi-Soviet conflict and spoke of deporting Jews beyond the Ural Mountains. On 18 June 1941 Hitler informed Antonescu of Operation Barbarossa, and Romania proceeded to mobilise two field armies, an air combat group, and a flotilla. While the Romanian General Staff drafted attack plans, it deported thousands of 'suspect' Jews to internment camps. The de jure start of Romania's holy war unleashed hell on the Red Army and Jews.

On 22 June 1941 Romanian guns joined the German barrage, targeting Soviet positions. Romania did not wait for a pretext like Finland or Hungary. Romanian Army Group Antonescu's mission was to protect the oil fields and key infrastructure from Soviet ground or air attack until the arrival of German Army Group South. In the meantime, it seized bridgeheads over the Prut River to distract the enemy and secure jumping-off points. Soviet air bombardment and Axis evacuation of some bridgeheads created an atmosphere of hysteria in cities near the front. On 29 June the Iaşi pogrom broke out after claims of 'Jewish-communist' fifth columnists, resulting in 8,000 dead. On 2 July, 326,000 Romanian and 136,000 German troops began retaking Soviet-occupied territory. Romanian gendarmes following the front received orders to 'cleanse the terrain' of Jews through mass executions and deportations. Additionally, German SS-men of *Einsatzgruppe D* arrived with instructions to annihilate communist intelligentsia behind the German Eleventh Army. Romanians expected a short war of heroic revenge. Axis forces overran northern Bukovina and northern Bessarabia as Soviet forces withdrew. The Romanian Third Army had been subordinated to the German Eleventh Army, so both crossed the Dniester River in mid-July into Ukraine. Romanian Army Group Antonescu dissolved. The Soviets fought harder for the rest of Bessarabia, but on 26 July the Romanians declared it liberated. Later, Antonescu was promoted to marshal. Romanian soldiers, gendarmes, and civilians, plus German troops and SS-men, killed 43,500 Jews in the newly liberated territory.

As Soviet resistance increased, the Germans asked the Romanians for more troops. On 10 August 1941, after crossing the Dniester, the Romanian Fourth Army attacked Odessa but failed to seize the city, becoming embroiled in trench warfare. Nonetheless, it secured the German Eleventh Army's flank. Meanwhile, Antonescu maneuvered Hitler into granting a territorial prize. On 30 August, the Tighina Agreement afforded Romania the territory between the Dniester and Bug Rivers, dubbed 'Transnistria'. The OKW (German armed forces high command) retained control of key infrastructure and local ethnic Germans. Transnistria was plundered, used for colonial projects, and deemed a dumping ground for Jews deported from Romania.[23] The Romanian Fourth Army suffered grievous losses in repeated attacks, which failed even when reinforced with a handful of German infantry and heavy artillery battalions. On 16 October, Odessa finally fell. The Stavka (Soviet high command) evacuated the city because the German Eleventh Army, supported by the Romanian Third Army, stood poised to break into Crimea. Antonescu demobilised much of his forces as Hitler promised victory. After assigning forces to support the German Eleventh Army's conquest of Crimea, the Romanian Third Army became responsible for rear area security in southern Ukraine from the Dniester to the Dnieper. The Romanians had lacked opportunities

Figure 17.2 Romanian infantry entering Odessa after the fall of the city to the Axis forces on 16 October 1941. Source: FRANCE PRESSE VOIR/AFP/Stringer via Getty Images.

to commit atrocities against Jews during the advance, particularly because the Germans diverted them away from cities, except Odessa. On 22 October, following partisan sabotage, Romanian soldiers murdered 12,000 Jews in the city and deported survivors into Transnistria's hinterland. In *Reichskommissariat* Ukraine, German commanders stressed the SS had claim over Jews, so Romanian units curbed their anti-Semitic impulses. The Romanian Army proved more competent and far more motivated than the German Army had expected.

The Soviet winter counteroffensive caused Hitler to again request help from Antonescu. The Romanians played a vital role in helping the Germans bottle up the Soviets in the Kerch bridgehead and at Sevastopol in Crimea, following Soviet amphibious landings around Christmas. Romanian troops helped retake coastal cities and took part in massacring Jews to make the peninsula *judenrein* ('free of Jews'). Meanwhile, Romanian gendarmes, Ukrainian policemen, and ethnic German SS militiamen shot tens of thousands of Jews in Transnistria. In January 1942 the OKH (German army high command) and the Romanian General Staff reassigned Romanian units from rear-area security to the collapsing front after a Soviet breakthrough at Izyum in Ukraine. At the same time, Hitler requested Antonescu remobilise the Romanian Army in the spring for a summer offensive known as Case Blue. General Iosif Iacobici, the chief of the Romanian General Staff, advocated making a minimal contribution instead. Antonescu replaced him with General Ilie Şteflea. He also made General Constantin Pantazi minister of defence (a position which the marshal had been filling himself). This triumvirate endured for two-and-a-half years. They agreed on a maximum contribution. In May Romanian forces contributed to twin German victories at Kerch and Kharkov, followed by the German assault on Sevastopol that fell two months later. Romanian manpower was vital to the German spring recovery.

Romania made the largest contribution to Case Blue of any Axis ally. After 28 June 1942, most of the divisions in Ukraine and Crimea joined in the summer offensive, as additional divisions began leaving Romania. Romanian units lacked sufficient weapons and equipment, especially anti-tank guns and heavy artillery, which made them less effective than German units.[24] The Romanian General Staff's forward headquarters in Rostov had to improvise because the OKH redirected the focus from the Caucasus to the Volga River, so most Romanian troops headed towards Stalingrad instead of the Caucasian oil fields, as planned. Most Romanians still hoped for victory, and many saw themselves as crusaders fighting for Christian civilisation against 'Judeo-Bolshevism'. Eventually Germany's Army Group B had the Romanian Third and Fourth Armies, on the German Sixth Army's flanks at Stalingrad, while Germany's Army Group A had another half-dozen Romanian divisions in the Caucasus. Romania fielded a peak of 463,000 troops east of the Dniester. On 19 November, Operation Uranus, the Soviet winter counteroffensive, smashed the Romanian armies and encircled the German Sixth Army. The Romanian Third and Fourth Armies' remnants continued to fight and were critical to German Army Group Don's attempted relief of the Stalingrad pocket before being taken off the front line. What was left of the two Romanian divisions caught with the German Sixth Army in the Stalingrad pocket fought on until 2 February 1943. The Romanians suffered 109,000 casualties and lost mountains of weapons and equipment.

Stalingrad was a catastrophe for the Romanian Army, but not until Kursk did it become clear that the tide of war had turned to most Romanians. Yet Romania maintained 110,000 soldiers on the front, mostly in the Kuban bridgehead. Many Romanian units were amalgamated into German units. On 9 October 1943, the German Seventeenth Army finished evacuating to Crimea, which Romanian troops helped hold against Soviet attacks. The Antonescu regime approached the British and Americans about an armistice but was told it would have to deal with the Soviets. The conditions and treatment of Jews in Transnistria began to improve. The Romanian General Staff tried to rebuild shattered units in Romania with limited success due to manpower and materiel shortages.

Romania again fully mobilised when the front returned to its borders. In March 1944 Soviet forces began to overrun Transnistria and northeastern Romania. The Stavka believed the first Iaşi-Chişinău offensive would force the Antonescu regime to make peace if it captured those cities. The Americans supported the Soviets. On 4 April, American bombers from Italy began hitting transportation nodes in Romania. Nonetheless, a German-Romanian line solidified along the Carpathian Mountains, Moldavian/Bessarabian hills, and

Dniester. Meanwhile, on 8 April, Soviet attacks broke through Axis defences in Crimea and overran most of the peninsula. By Sevastopol's liberation on 12 May, Romanian and German ships and aircraft evacuated most of the remaining Axis forces, but Romanian divisions suffered significant casualties and lost most of their heavy weapons and equipment. King Mihai I and a small group of conspirators finalised plans for a coup because the dictator Marshal Antonescu refused to countenance an armistice with Stalin. Trench warfare ground down German Army Group South Ukraine while air raids targeting oil refineries flattened Romanian cities. The Romanian Air Force and the German Luftflotte 4 were decimated defending Ploeşti. Meanwhile, the OKH withdrew most German panzer divisions from Romania because it needed the units in Poland. On 20 August the Stavka launched the second Iaşi-Chişinău offensive, again breaking through the Romanian Fourth and Third Armies on the reconstituted German Sixth Army's flanks. On 23 August the king arrested the marshal.

Romania turned its arms against Nazi Germany. Romanian troops defeated a German countercoup attempt against Bucharest, interned German troops across the country, and fended off German-Hungarian border attacks. On 12 September 1944 the Soviet-Romanian Armistice was signed, which required, among other conditions, Romania to provide field divisions for the Soviet Union. The Allied (Soviet) Control Commission oversaw the occupation of Romania. The Romanian Third Army was disbanded, but the Romanian Fourth and First Armies joined the Soviet Second Ukrainian Front's drive into Hungary, starting with northern Transylvania. Some Romanian troops helped push into Budapest before joining the bulk of the Romanian forces in Slovakia. The Romanian contribution rose to 248,000 troops. On 6 March 1945, under Soviet pressure, Mihai I accepted a communist-led government.[25] On 9 May Romanian forces halted short of Prague.

Romania's wartime experience was complicated. The country transitioned from neutrality to the Axis and later to the Allies. The human cost was immense. While fighting alongside the German Wehrmacht, the Romanian Army suffered 71,585 dead, 253,622 wounded/sick, and 309,533 missing (with 120,000 captured between the royal coup and the armistice). The Antonescu regime was directly responsible for the deaths of 300,000 Jews and 12,500 Gypsies (Roma) in Romania and Transnistria. In combat together with the Red Army, the Romanian Army lost 21,035 killed, 90,344 wounded/sick, and 58,433 missing. History should not be read backwards, however. Romania's nine months of coerced co-belligerency with the USSR ought not to distract from its preceding thirty-eight months of willing alliance with Nazi Germany.

17.2   Finland's 'Continuation War'

There are two overriding explanations for the Finnish participation in Operation Barbarossa: the country's exposed geographical position next to Russia and the unfinished Soviet attempt to occupy it during the short Winter War in 1939–1940.[26] Together they compelled the Finnish leadership to choose sides when it was informed of the emerging clash between the two dictatorships in autumn 1940.

Having been an integrated part of Sweden for six centuries, Finland was joined to the Russian Empire in 1809 as a Grand Duchy but was allowed to keep its Swedish laws and Lutheran faith. This gradually set in motion a national and societal yearning that during the Russian revolution in autumn 1917 resulted in a declaration of Finnish independence. Violent pro-Soviet domestic opposition followed but was crushed by a swiftly mobilised non-socialist army of civilians backed by German military intervention, which lay the groundwork for a long-lasting sense of gratitude towards Berlin among many non-socialist Finns.[27]

These Germanophile feelings would play an important role both during the 1930s and when the Finnish government, after the defeat in the Winter War in spring 1940, tried to find a solution to the growing pressure from the Soviet Union. As with many other newly born states in Eastern Europe during the inter-war period, the Finnish parliamentary democracy had been challenged by both left- and right-wing radical movements. However, neither of them would gain enough popular support to overrule the democratic constitution, which was defended by moderate non-socialist parties and the social democrats.[28]

Very few of these non-socialist political movements were outspokenly attracted by the fascist ideology. They tended to see Hitler's regime as a necessary counterweight to the Soviet Union, not least because of Germany's decisive military support to them during the revolutionary spring of 1918. In addition, the Finnish establishment was, despite Hitler's anti-democratic policy, inclined to overlook this in favour of its long-standing admiration for a perceived Germanic high culture.[29] Beyond Finland's positive bilateral relations with Germany, major Finnish political groups like the Social Democrats were increasingly anti-Soviet due initially to the conflict in 1918 but increasingly as a result of the Soviet progression into a cruel dictatorship. The view of Nazi Germany was not ignorant of Hitler's parallel behaviour but rather took account of the harsh experiences in the Winter War and the impotence of the Western powers to intercede on Finland's behalf, leaving Germany the only pragmatic choice.[30]

According to the secret protocol in the Molotov-Ribbentrop Treaty signed in August 1939, Finland was designated a Soviet sphere of interest. Thus Germany's support for Finland in the Winter War was a ruse. Due to the stubborn Finnish defence and rumours of a planned military intervention by the Western powers, Stalin decided to postpone the annexation of the country and dictated a peace treaty in March 1940 in which Finland lost one-tenth of its territory. The loss was bitter, but the Finnish army and civilian population had remained largely intact, which intensified the desire of the government to find a way of resisting future pressure from the Soviet Union.[31]

The turning point came in late July 1940 when Finnish commander in chief Gustaf Mannerheim and Finnish prime minister Risto Ryti were secretly contacted by a high-ranking SS-officer who had been sent out by Hitler to investigate how committed Finland was to defending its sovereignty if a new war would break out with the Soviet Union. The answer of the Finnish leadership was unequivocal. The country would under no circumstances surrender, which convinced Hitler that the country could be an important military ally in the planned invasion of the Soviet Union.[32]

Soon thereafter the parties reached an agreement in which Finland was secretly allowed to buy German weaponry in exchange for the transportation of Wehrmacht troops through Finnish territory up into northern Norway. Hitler's interest in Finland was also economic, and in the summer of 1940 the countries signed a wide-ranging trade agreement. German war industry needed the nickel produced at the mines in Pechenga at the Arctic Sea. In fact, when the Soviet foreign minister Molotov visited Berlin in November 1940 and required the right to conclude their own agreement concerning Finnish nickel and timber, Hitler refused to agree, arguing that Germany needed the resources for as long as the war against Great Britain continued.[33]

One month later a Finnish military emissary visited Berlin and was informed by Göring about the coming war, which had received the codename Operation Barbarossa the same day (18 December 1940). Göring invited Finland to join the war, emphasising that 'if Finland wants to exist it must advance together with Germany coherently and without hesitation'. The decision was supported by the Finnish leadership, although when the joint planning began in late January 1941 it was made clear that neither an official pact with German nor a break with the United States was possible. Hitler accepted these conditions because he was satisfied with the participation of the Finnish army, which had proven its worth in the Winter War.[34]

In December 1940 Hitler had altered his plan for the eastern crusade and decided to target Leningrad before Moscow. From this followed the agreement that the Finnish army should focus its attack towards the big lake of Onega and leave the conquest of Leningrad to the German forces. As the preparations advanced, the Finnish army was considerably strengthened by German weaponry and 1,400 Finns were recruited as volunteers into the German SS corps.[35] Unlike other German allies, and due to its strategic importance, Finland was allowed to buy German arms and other essential goods on credit. During the spring of 1941 German forces, with Finnish support, began to improve the infrastructure in the northern half of Finland for the four German divisions and one SS Brigade, which arrived in early June to conquer the Soviet harbour of Murmansk on the Arctic Sea.[36]

Simultaneously, discreet preparations for the mobilisation of sixteen Finnish divisions (470,000 soldiers) were covertly made for an offensive war that the Finnish leadership wanted to frame as an act of self-defence. This was indeed difficult to achieve, because when Operation Barbarossa began on 22 June 1941, German forces were already actively using airports and harbours in southern Finland. At first the Finnish government declared its neutrality to project its supposed impartiality; however, after intensive Soviet air attacks against Finland during the opening days of the conflict, the government could legitimately claim that the return to war was simply a result of Soviet aggression.[37]

The first ground attack from Finnish soil was launched on 29 June 1941 by the German troops in Pechenga close to the Artic Sea coast. However, the offensive towards Murmansk soon ran into problems, and in early October 1941 the German troops were ordered to establish defensive positions for winter, which had arrived earlier than usual. Further south on the German front in Finland the advance was more successful, but even here the main task to cut off the railway between Murmansk and central Russia was never achieved.[38]

On the southern half of the Finnish front the offensive was deliberately delayed. The 'brothers in arms', as the German-Finnish alliance was colloquially known, had agreed that the Finnish attack would start as soon as German forces had reached Leningrad. On 8 July the German General Staff informed the Finnish headquarters that the offensive towards the Russian metropolis would begin in two days. Accordingly, on 10 July the Finnish army hit the Soviet front with maximum force and advanced over the next five months as far east as the western shores of Lake Onega.[39]

The Red Army had to defend a huge front line from the Barents Sea in the north down to the Black Sea and was thus clearly outnumbered by the considerably enlarged Finnish army, which had been equipped with new weaponry from Germany. Finland's early military success nurtured visions of a 'Greater Finland', but gradually it became obvious that the Germans had gravely underestimated the capacity of the Soviet enemy. The newly conquered land had cost the lives of some 25,000 Finnish soldiers, and during the winter of 1941–1942, Finland was hit by a severe food shortage, which shook the fighting spirit and led many to question their belief in victory.

By early December 1941 positional warfare dominated the Finno-Soviet front and endured for the next two-and-a-half years. During that stage, the Finnish commander in chief Mannerheim declined numerous German requests to take a more active part in the siege of Leningrad. In spite of being a sworn anti-communist, Mannerheim understood that any involvement in the assault on Leningrad would so offend Soviet pride that any prospect of a future negotiated settlement would be irrevocably harmed.[40]

Figure 17.3 A Finnish machine gun crew in the forests of Karelia, spring/summer 1942. Source: Arthur Grimm/ullstein bild via Getty Images.

Compared with the German armed forces and its war industry, the Finnish army of course played only a marginal role in the huge eastward attack, which by any standard became the main front in Europe. Finnish military deaths during this war came to 70,000, which together with the losses in the Winter War rose to a total of 95,000 soldiers. In absolute numbers, these military losses were clearly less than for Hungary (300,000) or Romania (300,000), but relative to the size of the population the number of fallen Finnish soldiers (2.3 per cent) was in fact higher than the Romanian military death toll (1.6 per cent).

The Hungarians suffered by any standard the most of these three nations. More than 6 per cent (6.2 per cent) of Hungary's total population was killed during the four-year war. This comparison reveals how harshly the Hungarians were squeezed between the German and Soviet forces in the winter of 1944–1945 and how severely this hit the civilian population (264,000 deaths), of which a considerable proportion were attributable to the systematic extermination of its Jewish population. The Romanian civilian deaths (200,000) were also horrific in scale, whereas losses in Finland were only a fraction of this (2,000 civilians).[41] The reason for the astonishingly low number of Finnish civilian deaths was that the Finnish front line never collapsed and thereby the country avoided a disastrous occupation.[42]

During the large-scaled Soviet offensive on the Karelian peninsula in June 1944, which partly resulted in a chaotic retreat, the Finnish army got crucial support from the Luftwaffe and was equipped with German anti-tank weaponry. It was precisely because the Finns had proven so successful in holding their line that the Germans had been willing to deploy such valuable asserts. The Finns had held a 600-kilometre front (one-fifth of the Eastern Front) since 1941. Indeed, the German historian Bernd Wegner characterised Finland as Germany's most important military ally on the Eastern Front. Holding the northern front was strategically important, and unlike Germany's other allies in the east, Finland offered a drilled and highly motivated conscription army, which was uniquely skilled to fight in a terrain of lakes, woods, and marshes with very few roads and open fields.[43]

Even if the fighting spirit of the Finnish army was gradually diminishing and the home front suffered from food shortages during the winter of 1941–1942, the Finnish population tolerated the demands of the war and showed no sign of resistance against either its leaders or its German ally. One indication of this was that the Social Democrats remained in the government throughout the war. Another was that the communist-led resistant movement in Finland remained almost non-existent.[44]

In the German-controlled northern half of Finland the relationship between the Wehrmacht and the civilian population was remarkably harmonious. The German and Austrian soldiers there were well provisioned with food and other material resources, which in stark contrast to other German controlled areas in Eastern Europe equally benefited the civilian population. Moreover, due to the passive form of warfare in the north, the German troops and their forced labourers had the opportunity to improve the infrastructure of Lapland, which despite the destructions wrought by the retreating Wehrmacht in autumn 1944 was swiftly restored after the war. In all, it is fair to claim that Finland, for a number of reasons, suffered demonstrably less from the alliance with Germany than Hitler's other allies.[45]

Finland's involvement in this conflict – which among the population came to be known as the Continuation War – ended in September 1944 when the country withdrew from the German alliance and signed an armistice with the Soviet Union and Great Britain (the latter had declared war on Finland in December 1941). The conditions were even harsher than the treaty that ended the Winter War, resulting in not only a retreat to the borderline of 1940 but also the loss of the Pechenga land corridor in the north and a 300-million-dollar war reparation to the Soviet Union.[46] Yet, unlike other Eastern European countries, which had been occupied two or even three times during the war, Finland had once again been able to ward off the Red Army. It was thus able to restore its democratic institutions and capitalist economy with relative ease.

Indisputably, Finland was heavily dependent on German support from 1941 to 1944. Equally incontestable is the fact that the sixteen Finnish divisions that participated in the war were crucial in enabling the Germans to maintain control of the Baltic Sea and the Arctic region. This perhaps explains why Hitler showed extraordinary flexibility towards Finland, even after the Finns, as required by the armistice treaty, turned their weapons on the Wehrmacht in Lapland in September 1944. The intensive phase of the Lapland War ebbed out already by November 1944 and caused noticeably fewer military casualties (4,000 dead and wounded Finns, 3,000 Germans and Austrians) than the Wehrmacht's total losses against the Red Army by the Arctic Sea (8,300).[47]

17.3   Italy's Crusade against Bolshevism

The arrival of Italian combatants in Ukraine in August 1941 marked a watershed in Mussolini's war.[48] Until then, setbacks in North and East Africa and a disastrous campaign against Greece seriously damaged Fascist Italy's great power status. Hitler's war of annihilation against the Soviet Union was the occasion to revamp the dictator's prestige and reposition Italy's role in the war. For the Italian Royal Army (*Regio Esercito*), it was the beginning of a two-phase unplanned campaign of seventeen months, conducted in parallel with ongoing operations in Libya and occupations in France, the Balkans, and the Aegean. For the Italian people, the *campagna di Russia* took a unique place in the postwar collective memory and led to a flourishing literature as no other campaign did.[49] It also fostered myths and half-truths that are still today objects of historiographical debates.[50]

Mussolini had many justifications for joining the Nazi invasion.[51] First, he considered himself as a precursor to Hitler in the fight against bolshevism. Therefore, Hitler's attempt to destroy Stalin's communist regime left him with no other option. Second, he believed that the expected German victory would alter the balance of power in Europe in favour of Berlin and weaken Italy's place on the continent. Third, the absence of Italian troops in the East while Romania, Hungary, and Finland deployed large forces to support the Wehrmacht would damage the regime's position as the first and oldest ally of Germany. Fourth, participation would guarantee a share of the spoils but also enable Mussolini's dream of defeating Great Britain in the Mediterranean by a drive through the Middle East. Still, all these motives found their rationale in a fundamental premise: Mussolini's insatiable thirst for glory and prestige. This personality trait distorted his ability to choose caution over recklessness. Even Hitler's advice that Italy's decisive effort should be in North Africa came to no avail. Indeed, already on 30 May 1941, Mussolini ordered General Cavallero, the head of *Comando Supremo*, to prepare the deployment of an expeditionary force.[52] It would fight under German command, for better or for worse.

The *Corpo di spedizione italiano in Russia* (CSIR) was born on 9 July 1941.[53] Its order of battle totalled 62,000 men, 5,500 motor vehicles, 4,600 pack animals, 83 airplanes, 60 light tanks, and a mix of artillery, anti-tank, and anti-aircraft guns (312 pieces).[54] Most of the manpower came from two infantry divisions (*Pasubio* and *Torino*) and a *Celere* (cavalry-based) division (*Principe Amedeo d'Aosta*), with additional combat, support units, and materiel at the army corps level.[55] Despite its low level of motorisation (only one infantry division could be transported at one time), the absence of medium tanks, and the ineffectiveness of the 47/32mm gun against Soviet armour, the CSIR became an effective fighting force.[56] However, it added pressure on the meagre resources of the *Regio Esercito* and impacted negatively on the military effort in North Africa.[57]

The CSIR arrived in Romania on 5 August after a lengthy trip by train, lorry, and very long marches. Under the command of General Messe, it was initially part of the German Eleventh Army (Army Group South). The *Pasubio* clashed with Soviet troops on 11 August 1941 between the Dnestr and Bug Rivers in southern Ukraine.[58] The event set in motion a cycle that lasted until July 1942, in which the corps' units fought no less than eighteen battles, offensive and defensive, either in supportive roles for the Germans or via autonomous actions.[59] Notwithstanding the constant logistical shortcomings (of vehicles, fuel, and supplies), the rigorous Russian weather, and the inevitable wearing out of the units, the CSIR offered, within its means, a good level of fighting power – a performance often praised by German commanders.[60]

By the end of 1941, Hitler had failed to destroy the Red Army and the need for more Axis troops was unavoidable. The *Duce*'s urge to send more units finally materialised.[61] Despite a critical shortage of vehicles and weapons, and the objections of Messe, the *Armata Italiana in Russia* (ARMIR, also known as Eighth Army) came to life in May 1942 under the command of General Gariboldi. It consisted of three army corps of three divisions each (the CSIR, later renamed XXXV, the II, and the Alpine corps) and one infantry division and other units under direct command of Eighth Army, for 229,005 men.[62] The ARMIR had 16,700 motor vehicles, 25,000 pack animals, 66 aircrafts, 50 light (6 tons) tanks, and 946 guns (28 infantry, 552 artillery, 276 anti-aircraft, and 90 75mm anti-tank guns).[63] Yet the ARMIR was a large foot soldier army, as its ratio of motor vehicle to men was lower than the CSIR. Moreover, although it received some very effective and powerful guns, there were too few to increase the overall firepower that remained low. There is no doubt that a large part of this materiel could have been of better use in North Africa.[64]

The ARMIR partook in the German offensive that aimed to capture Stalingrad, and it gradually reached the Don in July and August 1942. In its first major battle (20 August–1 September), units of the XXXV and II corps repelled a Soviet attack at great cost.[65] In the following months, the ARMIR built a defensive line made up of all-around strongholds and dugouts supported by sound artillery positions. However, they were debilitated by the absence of a fortified second line and a strong mobile force capable of swift counterattack. Moreover, the launch of Operation Uranus (19 November) deprived Gariboldi of the most powerful German units that were under his command.[66] By December, flanked by the Hungarian Second Army north and the Army Detachment Hollidt south, 150,000 Italians (nine small divisions) and some German units defended a 270-kilometre front line on the Don.[67] It was operational nonsense.

The Soviet offensive (Operation Little Saturn) started with a series of minor actions before the blow of 16 December 1942 hit the II corps. Despite the stiff resistance of the Italian and German units, enemy superiority in infantry, tanks, and artillery made the difference.[68] Within days, all sectors of the II, XXXV, and XXIX (German) corps were threatened (including their lines of communication), forcing the German command to finally accept Gariboldi's request for a withdrawal that started on 19 December. Under the threat of encirclement and in terrible conditions, the remnants of the Italian divisions retreated in two separate groups (north and south) in the hope of reaching Axis lines. While numerous men died in combat and others were captured, thousands survived the ordeal. Most of the *alpini* did not have such a chance. The Soviet attack of 13 January 1943 in the Ostrogozhk-Rossosh sector targeted the Second Hungarian Army, the Alpine corps, and the German XXIV Panzer corps.[69] By 17 January, the Soviets had encircled the German corps, three alpine, and the *Vincenza* infantry divisions.[70] By the end of the month only 40 per cent (27,500) of the Italian troops made it out of the pocket.[71] On 31 January, the ARMIR left German Army Group B and ceased to be an operational force. According to the official history, between August 1942 and 20 February 1943, a total of 87,795

Figure 17.4 A column of the Italian Alpini soldiers in Russia during the retreat after their defeat on the Don, 1943. Source: Fototeca Gilardi/Fototeca Storica Nazionale/Getty Images.

men of the ARMIR were dead (or MIA) and 34,474 were injured or frostbitten.[72] The repatriation of the Eighth Army started in March, and the plan to maintain a military presence (the II corps) in the East was abandoned on 12 April.

While the CSIR fought on after the German failure before Moscow, Hitler's defeat at Stalingrad inevitably led to the destruction of the Eighth Army.[73] It is unlikely that any Italian general could have avoided the catastrophe. The return of the ARMIR's last men in May 1943 coincided with the Axis defeat in Tunisia. The *Regio Esercito* had lost its most important campaigns of the war and had no combat power left to face the imminent Allied invasion of Italy. Mussolini's war was over, and this time there was no way to turn things around as the king, influential generals, and prominent Fascists finally considered his removal from power. The quest for glory in the East proved to be his last mistake.

Notes

1 This introductory section was written by Oleg Beyda. For a general, if dated, overview of German coalition problems, see B. Mueller-Hillebrand, *Germany and Its Allies in World War II: A Record of Axis Collaboration Problems* (Frederick: University Publication of America, 1980).

2 For the country-by-country study charting non-German involvement in Operation Barbarossa, see D. Stahel, ed., *Joining Hitler's Crusade: European Nations and the Invasion of the Soviet Union, 1941* (Cambridge: Cambridge University Press, 2017).

3 V. Ullrich, *Hitler: Downfall 1939–45* (London: The Bodley Head, 2020), p. 217.

4 O. Beyda, '"Wehrmacht Eastern Tours": Bulgarian Officers on the German-Soviet Front, 1941–1942', *Journal of Slavic Military Studies* 33 (2020): 136–161; C. A. Molnar and M. Zakić, eds., *German-Balkan Entangled Histories in the Twentieth Century* (Pittsburgh: University of Pittsburgh Press, 2020).

5 X. M. Núñez Seixas, *The Spanish Blue Division on the Eastern Front, 1941–1945: War, Occupation, Memory* (Toronto: University of Toronto Press, 2022), pp. 72, 107.

6 X. Moreno Julià, *The Blue Division: Spanish Blood in Russia, 1941–1945* (Brighton: Sussex University Press, 2015), p. 225.

7 R. Yeomans, 'Croatia', in *Joining Hitler's Crusade: European Nations and the Invasion of the Soviet Union, 1941*, ed. D. Stahel (Cambridge: Cambridge University Press, 2017), p. 171.

8 A. Obhođaš and J. D. Mark, *Croatian Legion: The 369th Reinforced (Croatian) Infantry Regiment on the Eastern Front, 1941–1943* (Sydney: Leaping Horseman Books, 2010), p. 83; R.-D. Müller, *An der Seite der Wehrmacht: Hitlers ausländische Helfer beim 'Kreuzzug gegen den Bolschewismus' 1941–1945* (Berlin: Ch. Links, 2007), p. 108.

9 J. Förster, 'The Decisions of the Tripartite Pact States', in *Germany and the Second World War: Volume IV: The Attack on the Soviet Union*, ed. Militärgeschichtliches Forschungsamt (Oxford: Clarendon Press, 1998), p. 1030.

10 Förster, 'The Decisions of the Tripartite Pact States', pp. 1031–1032.

11 For succinct reading and extensive treatment, see W. Rahn, 'Japan and Germany, 1941–1943: No Common Objective, No Common Plans, No Basis of Trust' *Naval War College Review* 46 (1993): 47–68; K. H. Schmider, *Hitler's Fatal Miscalculation: Why Germany Declared War on the United States* (Cambridge: Cambridge University Press, 2021).

12 R. L. DiNardo, *Germany and the Axis Powers: From Coalition to Collapse* (Lawrence: University Press of Kansas, 2005), pp. 138–140.

13 J. Clements, *Mannerheim: President, Soldier, Spy* (London: Haus, 2009), pp. 267–268; I. Kershaw, *Hitler 1936–1945: Nemesis* (London: Penguin, 2001), pp. 524–525.

14 B. Wegner, 'The Mobilization of Germany's Allies', in *Germany and the Second World War: Volume VI: The Global War*, ed. Militärgeschichtliches Forschungsamt (Oxford: Clarendon Press, 2001), p. 906.

15 P. Gosztony, *Hitlers Fremde Heere: Das Schicksal der nichtdeutschen Armeen im Ostfeldzug* (Dusseldorf: Econ-Verlag, 1976).

16 C. B. Christensen, N. B. Poulsen, and P. S. Smith, 'Dänen in der Waffen-SS 1940–1945: Ideologie, Integration und Kriegsverbrechen im Vergleich mit anderen "germanischen" Soldaten', in *Die Waffen-SS: Neue Forschungen*, ed. J. E. Schulte, B. Wegner, and P. Lieb (Paderborn: Verlag Ferdinand Schöningh, 2014), p. 197.

17 O. Beyda and I. Petrov, *Soviet Turncoats: General Andrei Vlasov and The Russian Liberation Army, 1942–1945* (Yorkshire: Pen & Sword Books, forthcoming 2026).

18 R. DiNardo, 'The Dysfunctional Coalition: The Axis Powers and the Eastern Front in World War II', *Journal of Military History* 60 (October 1996): 713.

19 Müller, *An der Seite der Wehrmacht*, p. 21.

20 This section was written by Grant T. Harward.

21 For a reappraisal of Carlist foreign policy, see Rebecca Haynes, *Romanian Policy towards Germany, 1936–1940* (London: Macmillan, 2000).

22 For what motivated Romanian soldiers, see Grant T. Harward, *Romania's Holy War: Soldiers, Motivation, and the Holocaust* (Ithaca: Cornell University Press, 2021).

23 For more on the Romanian administration, see Vladimir Solonari, *A Satellite Empire: Romanian Rule in Southwestern Ukraine, 1941–1944* (Ithaca: Cornell University Press, 2019).

24 For operational and technical details, see Mark Axworthy, Cornel Scafes, and Christian Craciunoiu, *Third Axis, Fourth Ally: Romanian Armed Forces in the European War, 1941–1945* (St Petersburg: Hailer, 1995).

25 For details on the Soviet occupation of Romania, see Constantin Hlihor and Ioan Scurtu, *The Red Army in Romania* (Iaşi: Center for Romanian Studies, 2000).

26 This section was written by Henrik Meinander.

27 Henrik Meinander, *A History of Finland* (London: Hurst, 2020), passim.

28 Henrik Meinander, 'On the Brink or In-Between? The Conception of Europe in Finnish Identity', in *The Meaning of Europe: Variety and Contention within and among Nations*, ed. Mikael af Malmborg and Bo Stråth (Oxford: Berg, 2002), pp. 149–154.

29 Johan Östling, *Nazismens sensmoral: Svenska erfarenheter i andra världskrigets efterdyning* (Stockholm: Atlantis, 2008), pp. 13–50.

30 Timo Soikkanen, *Kansallinen eheytyminen – myyti vai todellisuus: Ulko-ja sisäpolitiikan linjat ja vuorovaikutus 1933–1939* (Turku: Turun yliopisto, 1983), passim.

31 Michael Jonas, *NS-Diplomatie und Bündnispolitik 1935–1944: Wipert von Blücher, das Dritte Reich und Finnland* (Paderborn: Schöningh, 2011), pp. 211–220.

32 Ohto Manninen, 'Ludwig Weissauer i hemliga uppdrag 1940–1943' *Historisk Tidskrift för Finland* 60, no. 3 (1975), pp. 178–181.

33 Mauno Jokipii, *Jatkosodan synty: Tutkimuksia Saksan ja Suomen sotilaallisesta yhteistyöstä 1940–1941* (Helsinki: Otava, 1988) p. 160.

34 Paavo Talvela, *Sotilaan elämä: Muistelma I* (Helsinki: Kirjayhtymä, 1976), pp. 250–267, quotation from p. 265.

35 Mauno Jokipii, *Panttipataljoona: Suomalaisen SS-pataljoonan historia* (Helsinki: W+G, 1968), passim.

36 Gerd R. Ueberschär, 'Die Einbeziehung Skandinaviens in Planung "Barbarossa"', in *Das Deutsche Reich und der Zweite Weltkrieg: Band 4* (Stuttgart: Deutsche Verlags-Anstalt, 1983), pp. 365–403.

37 Ibid., pp. 388–403.

38 Gerd R. Ueberschär, 'Kriegsführung und Politik in Nordeuropa', in *Das Deutsche Reich und der Zweite Weltkrieg: Band 4* (Stuttgart: Deutsche Verlags-Anstalt, 1983), pp. 811–825.

39 Ari Raunio, 'Jatkosota, hyökkäysvaihe', in *Sotien vuodet 1939–1945* (Pori: Satakunnan maanpuolustusyhdistys, 2009), pp. 48–63.

40 Pasi Tuunainen, 'The Finnish Army at War: Operations and Soldiers, 1939–45', in *Finland in World War II: History, Memory, Interpretations*, ed. Tiina Kinnunen and Ville Kivimäki (Leiden: Brill, 2011), pp. 153–159.

41 Boris Urlanis, *Wars and Population* (Moscow: Progress Publishers, 1971), p. 294; Támas Stark, *Hungary's Human Losses in World War II* (Uppsala: Centre for Multiethnic Research, 1995), pp. 33, 59; Mikko Uola, *Eritahtiset aseveljet: Suomi ja muut Saksan rinnalla taistelleet 1939–1944* (Jyväskylä: Docendo, 2015), pp. 160–230; 'Finnish War Victims in the Second World War: Database by National Archives of Finland', accessed 7 May 2025, www.avoindata.fi/data/en_GB/dataset/suomen-sodissa-1939-1945-menehtyneet.

42 Kari Nars, 'Suomen sodanaikainen talous ja talouspolitiikka', in *Taloudellisia selvityksiä 1966: Suomen Pankin taloustieteellisen tutkimuslaitoksen julkaisuja: Sarja A:29* (Helsinki: Bank of Finland, 1966), pp. 83–101.

43 Bernd Wegner, 'Das Kriegsende in Skandinavien', in *Das Deutsche Reich und der Zweite Weltkrieg: Band 8* (Stuttgart: Deutsche Verlags-Anstalt, 2007), pp. 963–972.

44 Meinander, *A History of Finland* (2020), pp. 9–43.

45 Ibid., pp. 255–282.

46 Ibid., pp. 275–295.

47 Ibid., p. 316; Henrik Meinander 'Страхи, надежды и спешные меры предосторожности: стратегия Финляндии в ходе войны в Заполярье, 1944–1945 гг [Fears, Hopes and Hasty Precautions: Finnish Strategies during the War in the Arctic, 1944–1945]', in *War in the Arctic: Military Operations, Everyday Life, Memory*, ed. Alexey A. Komarov (Moscow: Russian Academy of Science, 2020), pp. 47–60.

48 This section was written by Richard Carrier. In English, the essential reading is B. M. Scianna, *The Italian War on the Eastern Front, 1941–1943: Operations, Myths and Memories* (Cham, Switzerland: Palgrave Macmillan, 2019). In Italian, the best recent analysis is M. T. Giusti, *La campagna di Russia, 1941–1943* (Bologna: Il Mulino, 2016). For an incisive introduction, see G. Rochat, *Le guerre italiane 1935–1943* (Torino: Einaudi, 2008), pp. 378–399.

49 Two of the classics are M. R. Stern, *The Sergeant in the Snow* (Evanston: Marlboro Press, 1998), and N. Revelli, *Mussolini's Death March: Eyewitness Accounts of Italian Soldiers on the Eastern Front* (Lawrence: University Press of Kansas, 2013).

50 T. Schlemmer, *Invasori, non vittime. La campagna italiana di Russia, 1941–1943* (Rome: Laterza, 2019). For a global perspective, see Scianna, *The Italian War*, pp. 229–327.

51 G. Schreiber, 'La partecipazione italiana alla guerra contro l'Urss: Motivi, fatti, conseguenze', *Italia contemporanea* 191 (June 1993): 245–275; Giusti, *La campagna di Russia*, pp. 50–55; see also T. Schlemmer, 'Italy', in *Joining Hitler's Crusade: European Nations and the Invasion of the Soviet Union, 1941*, ed. D. Stahel (Cambridge: Cambridge University Press, 2018), pp. 134–139.

52 G. Bucciante, ed., *Ugo Cavallero, Diario 1940–1943* (Rome: Ciarrapico, 1984), p. 188.

53 C. De Franceschi, G. di Vecchi, and F. Mantovani, eds., *Le operazioni delle unità italiane al fronte russo, 1941–1943*, 3rd ed. (Rome: Stato Maggiore Esercito, Ufficio Storico, 2000), p. 74. See also P. P. Battistelli, *Mussolini's Army at War: Regio Esercito's Commands and Divisions* (Milan: Agrafe, 2021).

54 De Franceschi, di Vecchi, and Mantovani, eds., *Le operazioni*, pp. 537–541.

55 The extra strength came at the price of cannibalising other units in Italy. See De Franceschi, di Vecchi, and Mantovani, eds., *Le operazioni*, p. 76. For details on the units, see Scianna, *The Italian War*, pp. 87–97.

56 Yet the CSIR represented no more than 9 per cent of all non-German forces in 1941. See D. Stahel, 'Introduction', in *Joining Hitler's Crusade*, ed. Stahel, p. 12. In 1942 there were more Romanian than Italian soldiers on the front.

57 See L. Ceva, '"La campagna di Russia nel quadro strategico della guerra fascista", in Istituto Storico della Resistenza' in *Gli italiani sul fronte russo*, ed. Cuneo e provincia (Bari: De Donato, 1982), pp. 163–194.

58 Scianna, *The Italian War*, p. 102.

59 De Franceschi, di Vecchi, and Mantovani, eds., *Le operazioni*, drawing 4; see also Scianna, *The Italian War*, pp. 99–124.

60 Between 5 August 1941 and 30 July 1942, the CSIR had 1,792 dead and MIA, and 7,858 injured and frostbitten men. See De Franceschi, di Vecchi, and Mantovani eds., *Le operazioni*, p. 487.

61 Schlemmer, 'Italy', pp. 150–152.

62 De Franceschi, di Vecchi, and Mantovani, eds., *Le operazioni*, pp. 605–631. By comparison, more than half a million men fought in the campaign against Greece.

63 Ibid., pp. 192–193, 629–631. The Germans supplied 54 additional French 75mm anti-tank guns.

64 Ceva, 'La campagna di Russia', pp. 116–118; see also Rochat, *Le guerre italiane*, pp. 378–383.

65 Scianna, *The Italian War*, pp. 133–140.

66 On 17 November 1942, concerned about the defence of the mainland, both General Ambrosio, chief of the army staff, and Cavallero considered the withdrawal of one corps from Russia. See G. Bucciante, ed., *Ugo Cavallero*, p. 576.

67 Thousands of Italian soldiers were in the rear, occupied by different tasks. See Rochat, *Le guerre italiane*, p. 390.

68 Giusti, *La campagna di Russia*, pp. 243–256.

69 Scianna, *The Italian War*, pp. 179–183; see also Giusti, *La campagna di Russia*, pp. 256–263.

70 Schreiber, 'La partecipazione italiana', p. 268.

71 Ibid.

72 De Franceschi, di Vecchi, and Mantovani, eds., *Le operazioni*, p. 487; see also Giusti, *La campagna di Russia*, pp. 264–265. It was more than four times the fatalities of the longer North African campaign, and more than one-third of the military deaths between June 1940 and September 1943. Most soldiers died in captivity, and only 10,030 men returned from the Soviet camps.

73 D. M. Glantz, *From the Don to the Dnepr: Soviet Offensive Operations, December 1942–August 1943* (London: Frank Cass, 1991), p. 80.

18

The Big Three and the Eastern Front

Hitler posed a dire existential threat to Britain and the Soviet Union, and to the United States the prospect of perpetual conflict. By June 1941 Britain had been at war with Germany since September 1939, and it is not surprising the three states formed a military coalition when Hitler attacked the Soviet Union and then, in December of the same year, declared war on the United States. But the Grand Alliance that developed during the war was much more than a military coalition of convenience; it was a far-reaching political, economic, and ideological collaboration. At the heart of this collaboration were the personal roles, outlooks, and interactions of the three heads of state. Without the personal alliance of Churchill, Roosevelt, and Stalin – the Big Three, as they came to be known during the war – the Grand Alliance would have been stillborn or would have collapsed under the pressure, contradictions, and challenges of the war. It was the Big Three who ensured the survival of the Anglo-American-Soviet coalition, and no theatre was more important to this endeavour, or as difficult and divisive to navigate, than the Eastern Front.

18.1   Formation of the Grand Alliance

While the Big Three were united by a common threat prior to Hitler's invasion of the Soviet Union on 22 June 1941, it was the momentous implications of this new war in the east that united the leaders as never before and rapidly crystallised into what Churchill later called a Grand Alliance. In a radio broadcast that same day Churchill pledged unequivocal support for the USSR in the struggle against Hitler. 'The Russian danger is our danger', he told his listeners. By the end of June a British military mission had arrived in Moscow. On 8 July Churchill sent Stalin a personal message stating that Britain would give as much help to the Soviet Union as it could. This was first of a 500-message correspondence with Stalin during the war.[1] By 12 July Britain and the Soviet Union had signed an agreement on joint action in the war against Germany and promised that neither side would conduct separate negotiations with Hitler about an armistice or peace treaty.

While it was predictable that Britain would do all it could to encourage Soviet resistance to Hitler, Churchill's public enthusiasm for an alliance with Stalin was a little surprising. There was a long history of antagonism in British-Soviet relations dating back to Britain's intervention in the Russian civil war. During the 1920s Britain and the Soviet Union waged what some historians call an early cold war.[2] In the 1930s Soviet efforts to promote collective security against Nazi Germany were stymied by British appeasement of Hitler. When the 1939 Soviet triple alliance negotiations with Britain and France proved too problematic, Stalin turned to a deal with Hitler. Under the auspices of the Nazi-Soviet pact of the 1939–1941, there was extensive German-Soviet cooperation that greatly aided Hitler's war in the west.

Churchill opposed British appeasement of Hitler and welcomed Soviet occupation of Poland's eastern territories (Western Belorussia and Western Ukraine), arguing that was far better than German occupation. However, during the Soviet-Finnish war of 1939–1940, Churchill was an enthusiastic advocate of an allied expedition to aid the embattled Finns. Such an action would in all probability have led to a Soviet-Western war in Scandinavia. Fortunately, a Soviet-Finnish peace treaty was signed before the expedition could be launched. After he became Prime Minister in May 1940, Churchill tried to woo Stalin away from Hitler's embrace but to no avail. Until the peace with Germany failed, Stalin was resolved to keep his distance from Britain.[3]

Churchill was keen to encourage and support the fight against Hitler but was skeptical the Soviet Union could survive the German onslaught. Like most of his advisors, Churchill was reluctant to pour too much aid into Russia for fear that it would be wasted or captured by the Germans. But Churchill's reserve melted away in the face of staunch Soviet resistance, and he became an active proponent of allied aid to the Soviet Union.[4]

Roosevelt, too, was surrounded by advisors who thought the Germans would win in Russia in summer 1941. Nevertheless, as early as 24–25 June he announced his administration was willing to provide aid to the Soviet Union and decreed the Neutrality Act did not debar the Soviets from purchasing war materials in the United States. Crucially, at the end of July Roosevelt sent his trusted advisor Harry Hopkins to Moscow. In meetings with Stalin, Hopkins pledged American aid and asked for the Soviet Union's specific requirements. Throughout the war Roosevelt pursued a consistent policy of no-strings-attached aid to the Soviet Union. Since the Soviet Union was doing all the fighting, it deserved all the aid it could get, and Roosevelt resisted pressures to tie that aid to political or other concessions from the Soviets. In Roosevelt's view that was no way to build a relationship with Stalin or to secure a long-term Soviet-American alliance.[5]

After Hopkins' return from Russia, Churchill and Roosevelt sent Stalin a joint message proposing a conference in Moscow to discuss allied supplies to the Soviet Union.[6] This took place at the end of September, with Averell Harriman acting as Roosevelt's special envoy and Lord Beaverbrook, Minister for Aircraft Production and a strong advocate of aid to Russia, representing Churchill.

Stalin was directly and actively involved in the conference discussions, which resulted in a supplies agreement detailing the thousands of planes, tanks, and artillery pieces the British and Americans would deliver to the USSR in the coming months. The Soviets' western allies also agreed to supply thousands of tons of aluminium, nickel, and zinc, as well as an equivalent amount of steel products. This was the first of many such agreements, all of which were hailed by the Soviet press and Stalin himself. Between 1941 and 1945 the USSR's western allies supplied some 10 per cent of Soviet wartime economic needs, including hundreds of thousands of trucks, tens of thousands of jeeps, and thousands of locomotives. Allied food shipments fed a third of the Soviet population, though most such supplies were devoured by the Red Army.[7]

Figure 18.1 Female factory workers in Lincoln, UK, paint slogans and messages of support in English and Russian onto a Matilda tank in preparation for its shipment to the Soviet Union, 19 September 1941. Source: Reg Speller/ Fox Photos/Hulton Archive/Stringer/Getty Images.

At the conference with Beaverbrook and Harriman, Stalin raised the question of post-war cooperation and pursued the matter in subsequent correspondence with Churchill. Towards the end of December, Churchill's Foreign Secretary, Anthony Eden, flew to Moscow. He expected no more than an exchange of views, as well as progress on the conclusion of a wartime Anglo-Soviet treaty of alliance, but was presented with a more radical proposition. Stalin wanted two agreements with the British: a wartime agreement and an agreement on the settlement of post-war problems. To the second agreement would be appended a secret protocol on the reorganisation of European borders after the war. Stalin proposed the restoration of Europe's pre-war borders, including those the USSR had gained as a result of the Nazi-Soviet pact and a post-war military alliance in Europe to safeguard the peace, with Soviet military bases in Romania and Finland and British military bases in Western Europe. This was a rather mild spheres-of-influence agreement compared to the deals that Stalin had done or contemplated doing with Hitler, but it showed the ambition he had for the Grand Alliance even at this early stage of the war. However, Eden and especially Churchill were not prepared to enter into such negotiations.[8]

One reason for Stalin's hurry for a deal with the British was that the United States had formally entered the war following the Japanese attack at Pearl Harbor on 7 December 1941. That the United States was now fully engaged in the war was of huge, transformative importance militarily, but it also complicated political negotiations since the Americans were explicitly opposed to spheres of influence agreements and to any territorial changes in advance of a peace conference.

The US entry into the war raised the question of whether the Soviet Union would reciprocate American aid by becoming involved in the war with Japan in the Far East. Stalin was willing in principle to participate, but a Soviet war with Japan was not a practical possibility until after the Germans were defeated. Domestic political complications notwithstanding, Roosevelt accepted Stalin's decision, not least because he saw Germany as being a much greater enemy than Japan.

In addition to the question of supplies to the Soviet Union, the main issue preoccupying the Grand Alliance during this early period was the question of the Second Front. Stalin began agitating for a Second Front in northern France in his very first message to Churchill on 18 July 1941. But the British were not in a position to undertake a large-scale invasion on their own and were unwilling to risk a smaller-scale incursion to draw German troops away from the Eastern Front. When the German advance into the Soviet Union faltered in front of Moscow in late autumn 1941, Stalin interest's in a Second Front waned as the prospect loomed of a Red Army counteroffensive that would drive the Wehrmacht out of Russia. But the issue of the Second Front returned to Stalin's agenda with the failure of the Red Army's winter offensive in early 1942. In May and June 1942 Stalin sent Molotov to London and Washington to press for a firm commitment to an Anglo-American Second Front in France that year. In London Molotov was able to sign an Anglo-Soviet Treaty of Alliance, but he received only a lukewarm commitment to a Second Front from Churchill, citing concerns about the availability of sufficient resources. In Washington Molotov's arguments in favour of an immediate Second Front were given a more sympathetic reception.

The US military agreed with the Soviets that a Second Front in France was the best way to relieve the pressure on the Red Army. But at this stage of the war the British were in the driving seat of the Anglo-American alliance and would remain so until 1944 when the US supplied the preponderance of allied troops in Western Europe, as well as the bulk of the materiel. Molotov was able to secure a joint American-British-Soviet communiqué which talked about 'the urgent task of creating a Second Front in Europe in 1942', but it was clear nothing was going to happen anytime soon.

Important for the longer-term future of the Grand Alliance were Molotov's conversations with Roosevelt in Washington about post-war peace and security. Roosevelt proposed the idea of an international police force of three or four states that would maintain peace after the war. Stalin responded enthusiastically: 'Roosevelt's considerations about peace protection after the war are absolutely sound.... Roosevelt is absolutely right ... his position will be fully supported by the Soviet Government.'[9]

In summer 1942 the Germans resumed offensive action in Russia and launched a southern campaign to seize Stalingrad and the Soviet oil fields at Baku. The opening of a Second Front in the west became even more urgent. On 23 July Stalin wrote to Churchill that 'in view of the situation on the Soviet-German front, I state most emphatically that the Soviet government cannot tolerate the Second Front in Europe being postponed to 1943'.[10]

18.2   Operation Bracelet: Churchill in Moscow

As the Germans approached Stalingrad in mid-August 1942, Churchill arrived in Moscow with some bad news: there would be no Second Front in France in 1942.[11] Stalin was not pleased and accused the British and Americans of not being willing to fight and to shed the blood of their troops. Nor was Stalin mollified by the news that there would be Anglo-American landings in Northern Africa in the autumn with the aim of driving the Germans and Italians out and seizing control of the Vichy French colonies of Morocco and Algeria. Churchill justified this operation as an attack on the soft underbelly of the Axis in the Mediterranean and drew a sketch of a crocodile (the British prime minister was an amateur artist) to illustrate his point. As far as Stalin was concerned, however, the Red Army was already doing battle with the croc's hard snout. One witness to the discussion was Archibald Clark Kerr, the British ambassador to Moscow, who penned this memorable portrait of that first meeting between Stalin and Churchill:

> It was interesting to watch the impact of the two men. Clash and recoil and clash again, and then a slow but unmistakeable coming together as each got the measure of the other, and in the end, much apparent understanding and goodwill.... Now the two men know each other and each one will be able to put the right value on the messages – and they are very frequent – that pass between them.[12]

The next meeting did not go so well, and Churchill's first encounter with Stalin came close to being a complete disaster. It was saved by a long, private dinner in which the two men got to know each other personally. The conversation ranged far and wide, and the talk was helped along by a new and outstanding British interpreter, Major A. H. Birse. What they seemed to find in each other as a result of the conversation was the kindred spirit of a fellow warrior as fully engaged in the war as they were. Such intimacy and comradeship Stalin and Churchill never experienced with Roosevelt. Churchill left the meeting convinced that he had established a personal relationship with Stalin, while Molotov wrote to the Soviet ambassador to London, Ivan Maisky, that 'the negotiations with Churchill were not entirely smooth' but were 'followed by an extensive conversation in Comrade Stalin's private residence, making for a close personal rapport with the guest'.[13]

Stalin's meeting with Churchill convinced him of the importance of direct personal dealings with his British and American counterparts and made him keen to meet Roosevelt, too. But he brooded on the question of the Second Front, and as the battle for Stalingrad came to a climax, he lashed out at his western allies. On 3 October 1942 he gave a sensational statement to an American correspondent in Moscow publicly criticising Britain and United States for a lack of aid and the absence of the Second Front.

Tensions within the Grand Alliance about the Second Front coincided with an inter-allied controversy about the trial and punishment of war criminals. In October 1942 the British proposed the *post-war* punishment of war criminals. The Soviets responded by calling for war crimes trials during the war, including the prosecution of Rudolph Hess, Hitler's former deputy, imprisoned by the British since his dramatic flight to Britain in May 1941 to broker an Anglo-German peace. This was the background to an extraordinary telegram from Stalin to Maisky on 19 October 1942:

> All of us in Moscow have formed the impression that Churchill is intent on the defeat of the USSR in order to come to terms with . . . Hitler . . . at our expense. Without such a supposition it is difficult to explain Churchill's conduct on the question of the Second Front in Europe, on the question of arms supplies to the USSR . . . on the question of Hess, whom Churchill seems to be holding in reserve, on the question of the systematic bombardment of Berlin . . . which Churchill proclaimed he would do in Moscow and which he did not fulfil one iota.

Maisky tried to calm down his boss by suggesting that Churchill was seeking an 'easy war' rather than the defeat of the USSR, but Stalin was adamant that

> as a proponent of an easy war Churchill is easily influenced by those pursing the defeat of the Soviet Union, since the defeat of our country and a compromise with Germany at the expense of the Soviet Union is the easiest form of war between England and Germany . . . Churchill told us in Moscow that by spring 1943 about a million Anglo-American troops would have opened a second front in Europe. But Churchill belongs, it seems, among those leaders who easily make promises in order to forget them or break them.[14]

What is striking about this exchange between Stalin and Maisky is how personal Stalin's relationship with Churchill had become. The sense of betrayal is palpable. But Stalin's invective against Churchill was politically driven by the fear his western allies would make a separate peace with Hitler. On the western side they feared Stalin would cut his losses and end the war with Germany. Stalin calculated that a Second Front was needed to draw Britain and the United States into a bloody battle that would harden their commitment to pursue the war against Germany to the very end.

During the middle years of the Second World War there were many rumours of secret peace negotiations between Germany and one or more members of the Grand Alliance. There was no truth to these stories, but not until early 1943 did the concerns of Churchill, Roosevelt, and Stalin dissipate. There were two important turning points. First was the policy of unconditional surrender announced by Roosevelt at the Casablanca conference in January 1943. Second was the surrender a week later of the encircled German forces in Stalingrad. The Soviet victory at Stalingrad signalled that Germany was going to lose the war and that the USSR would emerge as the dominant power in continental Europe. This shifted the balance of power within the Grand Alliance. Churchill and Roosevelt were more anxious than ever to talk to Stalin about the shape of the post-war world.[15]

18.3   The Convergence Hypothesis

There is another series of reasons why Churchill and Roosevelt wanted to get closer to Stalin personally: their views of him and of the Soviet system in general had changed and become more favourable as a result of the war.

In private, Churchill and Roosevelt referred to Stalin as 'Uncle Joe'. Stalin – who had good intelligence on what was being said behind the closed doors of his western allies – would have known this long before it was revealed to him by Churchill and Roosevelt at the Tehran conference. The nickname was not patronising but a term of endearment. Churchill and Roosevelt believed that not only could you do business with Stalin; you could trust him. He was a wise and intelligent realist, and any problems in the Soviet-Western alliance were the result of the malign influence of courtiers such as Molotov – or so they believed. (In truth, Stalin was more hard line than Molotov on most issues.) Stalin was seen by Churchill and Roosevelt as a patriot rather than a communist; in other words, he was just like them. This version of the cult of Stalin's personality – which was quite widespread in western allied circles – underpinned Churchill and Roosevelt's confidence in the Grand Alliance.

Similarly, there was a perception among western leaders that the Soviet system was becoming more 'normal' during the war: state socialism was being moderated; the society was becoming more tolerant, especially of religious beliefs (important to the Christian Roosevelt and Churchill); and Russia was less revolutionary and more nationalist and hence more traditional and predictable in its state aims.

Roosevelt embraced this benign view of Russia more radically than Churchill because, unlike the British Premier, he thought past antagonisms in Soviet-Western relations were caused as much by the west as the Soviets. If the Soviet Union could be fully integrated into the community of nations, it would become a normal state and accelerate the process of its convergence with bourgeois capitalist liberal democracy. Roosevelt saw his personal relationship with Stalin as key to a strategy of integration and believed he had the guile and charm to bring him aboard the western boat.[16]

Stalin had his own (Marxist) version of the convergence thesis: during the war the advanced capitalist countries had become more state socialist, the labour movement and the left wing had strengthened, and progressive capitalist politicians favouring collaboration with the Soviet Union were now in the ascendency. Churchill and Roosevelt personified those trends, and Stalin felt he could work with them in the context of common interests, not just during the war but in peacetime, too. That did not mean Stalin had ditched his politics or his ideology. He still sought the spread of socialism and thought history was on the side of the Soviet system. But he did modify his view of how the world revolutionary process would develop. It would be more incremental and variegated and would involve a long period of peaceful coexistence between different social systems. The struggle for communism would continue, but it was not necessarily inimical to the Grand Alliance, at least in the short term. This was a point that Stalin made many times during the war, publicly and privately: the common interests and aspirations of the Grand Alliance were a fundamental not transitory phenomenon. Britain, the Soviet Union, and the United States were united in their determination to defeat and then contain Germany and Japan. The three states had a common interest in post-war peace and prosperity. The experience of the Grand Alliance had shown that it was possible for socialism and capitalism to work together for the common good.[17]

Stalin signalled his good intentions when he engineered the abolition of the Comintern in May 1943. No longer would the activities of communist parties be directed from Moscow. Henceforth, each party would find its own national path to socialism. Soviet influence would be exercised informally, especially by Stalin, who would use his influence to harmonise the communist political challenge with the post-war maintenance of the Grand Alliance. Such a strategy would not be unproblematic – the danger of a divergence of Soviet and communist goals was self-evident – but the Soviets had been handling such tensions and contradictions since the 1920s when Moscow's diplomats and Comintern officials had vied to influence Stalin and the Politburo.

18.4 Moscow and Tehran

As the Comintern was being abolished, Joseph Davies, former American ambassador to the Soviet Union, arrived in Moscow on a special mission from Roosevelt. His goal was to persuade Stalin to agree to a meet with the US president. Roosevelt was convinced that if he could meet Stalin personally, then problems within the Grand Alliance could be amicably resolved. Stalin agreed in principle to a meeting with Roosevelt but delayed committing to a date because of pressing military matters. Agreement was eventually reached that Stalin and Roosevelt would meet, together with Churchill, at a summit in Tehran.

The political path to the Tehran summit was paved by an Anglo-Soviet-American foreign ministers conference in Moscow in October 1943. The Moscow conference marked the transition of the Grand Alliance from a coalition centred on the war to one increasingly focussed on peace and the post-war world. The agreements reached at Moscow included a commitment to establish a new international security organisation to succeed the League of Nations after the war. A year later there were detailed negotiations at Dumbarton Oaks about this new organisation, which was destined to hold its founding conference in San Francisco in 1945 and call itself the United Nations.[18] Because of the detailed work done at the Moscow conference, there was no need for a fixed agenda at Tehran. Instead there was an informal, open-ended conversation in which the three leaders got to know each other and established the pattern and dynamic of their triangular relationship.

Stalin's first meeting at Tehran was with Roosevelt. They discussed a number of issues – the military situation, post-war trade, France, China – and found much common ground. The rapport between the two leaders continued in the conference plenary session, where they ganged up on Churchill and pressed the prime minister for a definite commitment and date for the invasion of France. Churchill resisted at first but later conceded that the Second Front would be opened in May 1944. In return Stalin agreed to attack Japan when Germany was defeated.

With an agreement on the Second Front in the bag, conversations between Churchill and Stalin became much friendlier. Churchill agreed with Stalin that the Soviet Union should have warm water ports and free access to the Mediterranean and the Pacific. Stalin had a highly positive conversation with Roosevelt about the president's idea for an international organisation to police the post-war world. There was consensus among all three leaders that Germany should be dismembered after the war. When the conference was over the Big Three issued a statement that they had met 'with hope and determination' and had left each other as 'friends in fact, in spirit and in purpose'.[19]

The most important decision made at Tehran concerned the date for D-Day. After the conference there was a significant increase in Soviet-Western cooperation in the military sphere. Stalin's attitude towards his western allies' contribution to the common war effort warmed considerably. In his order of the day on 1 May 1944 he noted the 'considerable contribution [of our] great allies . . . who hold the front in Italy against the Germans and divert a considerable part of German troops from us, supply us with very valuable raw materials and armaments, and subject to systematic bombardment military objectives in Germany, thus undermining the latter's military might'. When D-Day came on 6 June 1944 Stalin cabled Churchill and Roosevelt his congratulations on the Normandy landings and a few days later publicly hailed the 'brilliant success' of his western allies, stating that 'the history of warfare knows no other similar undertaking in the breadth of its conception, in its gigantic dimensions, and in the mastery of its performance'.[20]

As agreed at Tehran, the Soviets timed their summer offensive to coincide with D-Day. Operation Bagration – the campaign to liberate Belorussia – was launched on 22 June 1944. It was a stunning success, and by the end of July the Red Army had crossed into Poland and was approaching Warsaw. Anticipating that Warsaw would soon fall to the Red Army, the nationalist Polish Home Army staged an insurrection in the city. Unfortunately, the Red Army's offensive was halted by the Germans on the eastern banks of the Vistula. The insurrection continued for another two months but was brutally crushed by the Germans.

The Warsaw Uprising led to some sharp exchanges between Stalin and Churchill and Roosevelt. The two western leaders wanted to aid the uprising through airdrops. From Stalin's point of view the insurrection was a madcap adventure and the supplies would end up in German hands. He was also politically hostile to the uprising, which he saw as anti-communist as well as anti-Nazi. In the end, Stalin relented and the Soviets facilitated British and American flights to Warsaw, along with Russian supply drops to the insurgents. But it was too little too late, and Polish accusations that Stalin had deliberately halted the Red Army on the Vistula enjoyed considerable currency in the west.

The Warsaw Uprising is often seen as an important negative turning point in the history of the Grand Alliance, as the first battle of the Cold War – at stake being the post-war political future of Poland. However, at the top level of the alliance, its effects were transitory. After the uprising it was back to business among the Big Three.

In October 1944 Churchill travelled to Moscow again. This second trip is best known for the infamous Churchill-Stalin percentages agreement, which carved up Romania, Bulgaria, Hungary, Yugoslavia, and Greece into British and Soviet spheres of influence. In practice nothing happened, except that Stalin did not interfere with the British suppression of communist partisans in Greece. In any event, the main topic of discussion between Churchill and Stalin were their joint efforts to broker a deal between the Soviets and the Polish government in exile in London. Relations between Stalin and the London Poles had broken down following the Germans' 1943 Katyn discovery of the mass graves of thousands of Polish officers, executed by the NKVD in 1940. Stalin denied Soviet culpability and also insisted that Western Belorussia and Western Ukraine would remain part of the Soviet Union. In return the Poles were offered compensatory German territory in the west. Churchill supported this solution, and when he and Stalin met Mikolajczyk, the exile Polish Premier, on 13 October 1944, the two of them worked together to persuade the Pole to accept western territorial gains in exchange for losses to the USSR in the east. Mikolajczyk was willing to deal but only if he could enter reservations about the frontier question, thus leaving the matter open to renegotiation at the peace conference. Churchill tried to convince Stalin of the merits of such a deal, arguing that the Americans might take up the Poles' cause and that the continuation of the Soviet-Polish dispute would have a corrosive effect on the Grand Alliance. In the same conversation Churchill pointed out that until the Comintern had been abolished in 1943, the small countries of Europe had feared sovietisation. He himself recalled that in 1919–1920 the whole world had trembled in fear of world revolution. 'The world has nothing to fear now', replied Stalin. 'The Soviet Union does not intend to stage Bolshevik Revolutions in Europe.'[21]

18.5   Yalta

It was Roosevelt who pushed for a second summit of the Big Three. In the end its timing was determined by Roosevelt's election and inauguration as president for the fourth time in January 1945. Its venue – Yalta – was Stalin's choice. Stalin did not like flying and had not enjoyed the trip to Tehran, which was partly by plane. A meeting in the Crimea meant he could travel to the conference by train.

Like Tehran, Yalta was a very friendly gathering and the Big Three got on famously. Stalin was the dominant figure at the conference. The reasons for this were partly to do with power. Britain and the United States were invading Germany from the west, but the bulk of the fighting was still being done by the Red Army, which was approaching Berlin. By this time the Red Army had conquered or liberated most of central and eastern Europe. Stalin was not strong enough to dictate the terms of the peace, but he was well able to define and defend Soviet interests. Stalin dominated proceedings for personal reasons as well. Roosevelt was ill – he died two months later – and the junior role that Britain now played in the Grand Alliance had undermined Churchill's confidence and exuberance.

Stalin's priority at Yalta was an agreement about the future of Germany, including on reparations and dismemberment. Despite Anglo-American qualms about reparations it was agreed that the USSR would receive restitution from Germany for war damage, and a figure of $10 billion was agreed as the benchmark. In relation to dismemberment, however, Stalin left Yalta disappointed. Previous discussions with Churchill and

Roosevelt had indicated that they favoured breaking up Germany after the war. At Yalta Stalin pushed very hard for a definite commitment on dismemberment, but Churchill and Roosevelt would only agree to establish a commission to discuss the issue. From this discussion Stalin concluded that dismemberment was unlikely to materialise. After Yalta he abandoned the policy of dismemberment and became a vocal supporter of German unity.

Churchill's main concern was the resolution of the long-running dispute about the post-liberation governance of Poland. By February 1945 all of Poland was occupied by the Red Army, and just before the Yalta conference the Soviets installed a provisional government formed by the pro-communist Polish Committee of National Liberation (PCNL). At Yalta, Churchill and Roosevelt sought to persuade Stalin to establish a more representative government in Poland – one that would include pro-western politicians from the Polish government in exile in London. The compromise reached was that the PCNL government would be reorganised and broadened by 'the inclusion of democratic leaders from Poland itself and from Poles abroad'. In return for this concession the British and Americans agreed to recognise the 'Curzon Line' as the Polish-USSR border – which meant that Moscow's territorial gains under the auspices of the Nazi-Soviet pact of 1939–1941, Western Belorussia and Western Ukraine, were now formally accepted by the western powers. It was also agreed to compensate Poland for its territorial losses in the east by changing its border with Germany, although the details of the new demarcation line were left open at this stage.

Of the other decisions made at Yalta by far the most important was a confidential agreement setting out the terms for Soviet participation in the war against Japan. Stalin agreed to abrogate the 1941 Soviet-Japanese neutrality pact and to enter the Far Eastern war two or three months after the defeat of Germany. In return Churchill and Roosevelt agreed to the restoration of Russian territorial concessions in China that had been lost as a result of the 1904–1905 Russo-Japanese War.

When Roosevelt died, Stalin was very upset. As Harriman reported,

> when I entered Marshal Stalin's office I noticed that he was obviously deeply distressed at the news of the death of President Roosevelt. He greeted me in silence and stood holding my hand for about 30 seconds

before asking me to sit down.... 'President Roosevelt has died but his cause must live on' [Stalin said to Harriman]. 'We shall support President Truman with all our forces and all our will.'[22]

In response Harriman suggested that Stalin should send Molotov to the United States to meet Truman and to attend the founding conference of the United Nations – which had, of course, been Roosevelt's pet project. Stalin readily agreed, and he must have been reassured by reports from the Soviet embassy in Washington that Truman was a Rooseveltian New Dealer and a supporter of cooperation with the USSR. In Washington, Molotov had a tough talk with Truman about the Polish question, but the post-Yalta dispute about the political composition of Poland's provisional government was soon resolved by an agreement that made Mikolajczyk a deputy premier.[23]

18.6   Conclusion

The Eastern Front was the Second World War's most important battlefield. As Churchill and Roosevelt recognised at the time, it was the Soviet defeat of Nazi Germany on that front that sealed the overall allied victory. The Soviets paid a high price for their victory over Hitler, but they did not fight alone. Western allied supplies to the USSR made a vital contribution, as did American and British air, sea, and land operations against the common foe. Important, too, was the psychological boost to the Soviet war of the Grand Alliance with Britain and the United States. 'In the history of diplomacy I know of no such close alliance of three Great Powers as this', Stalin told Churchill and Roosevelt at Yalta.[24]

The experience of the Grand Alliance showed that leadership does matter and that good personal relations are essential to successful and sustained collaboration. When they allied together in 1941, Churchill, Roosevelt, and Stalin did not know how long their alliance would last or in what directions it would take them. Personal contact between the three leaders – at meetings, through correspondence, and via intermediaries – convinced them that they could work together and trust each other. At times that trust and friendship were strained but difficulties were overcome and differences resolved through compromises that respected honour and protected vital interests. The Grand Alliance, as it developed during the war, is unimaginable without the personal bond that developed between Stalin, Churchill, and Roosevelt.

Notes

1 D. Reynolds and V. Pechatnov, eds., *The Kremlin Letters: Stalin's Wartime Correspondence with Churchill and Roosevelt* (London: Yale University Press, 2018).
2 See M. J. Carley, *Silent Conflict: A Hidden History of Early Soviet-Western Relations* (Lanham, MD: Rowman and Littlefield, 2014).
3 See Dzh. Roberts, 'Cherchil' i Stain: Epizody Anglo-Sovetskikh Otnoshenii (Sentyabr' 1939–Iun' 1941 goda)', in *Voina i Politika, 1939–1941*, ed. A. O. Chubar'yan (Moscow: Nauka, 1995).
4 On Churchill's response to the German invasion of the Soviet Union, see M. H. Folly, *Churchill, Whitehall and the Soviet Union, 1940–45* (London: Macmillan, 2000), chapter 2.
5 See M. E. Glantz, *FDR and the Soviet Union: The President's Battles over Foreign Policy* (Lawrence: University Press of Kansas, 2005).
6 Ministry of Foreign Affairs of the USSR, ed., *Stalin's Correspondence with Churchill, Attlee, Roosevelt and Truman 1945–1945* (New York: E. P. Dutton, 1958), pp. 17–18.
7 On western materiel aid to the USSR during the war, see Mark Harrison's various books, starting with *Soviet Planning in Peace and War, 1938–1945* (Cambridge: Cambridge University Press, 1996). A recent Russian study is I. V. Bystrova, *Lend-Liz dlya SSSR: Ekonomika, Tekhnika, Ludi, 1941–1945* (Moscow: Kuchkovo Pole, 2019).
8 See G. Roberts, 'Ideology, Calculation, and Improvisation: Spheres of Influence and Soviet Foreign Policy, 1939–1945' *Review of International Studies* 25 (October 1999).
9 The Soviet documents on Molotov's 1942 trip to London and Washington may be found in O. A. Rzheshevsky, ed., *War and Diplomacy: The Making of the Grand Alliance* (Amsterdam: Harwood Academic, 1996).
10 Ministry of Foreign Affairs of the USSR, ed., *Stalin's Correspondence with Churchill, Attlee, Roosevelt and Truman 1945–1945*, p. 56.
11 Documentation and analysis of Churchill's trip to Moscow may be found in M. Folly, G. Roberts, and O. Rzheshevsky, *Churchill and Stalin: Comrades in Arms during the Second World War* (Yorkshire: Pen and Sword, 2019).
12 Cited by M. H. Folly, 'Seeking Comradeship in the "Ogre's Den": Winston Churchill's Quest for a Warrior Alliance and his Mission to Stalin, August 1942'. www.brunel.ac.uk/__data/assets/pdf_file/0010/185923/ET62 Folly2.pdf.

13 ' New Documents about Winston Churchill from the Russian Archives' *International Affairs* 47, no. 5 (2001): 137.

14 On the Stalin-Maisky exchange, see docs. 156–158 in O. A. Rzheshevsky, *Stalin i Cherchill'* (Moscow: Russian Academy of Sciences, 2004).

15 See W. F. Kimball, 'Stalingrad: A Chance for Choices' *Journal of Military History* 60, no. 1 (January 1996): 89–114.

16 On Churchill and Roosevelt's views on Stalin and the Soviet system, see D. Reynolds, 'Churchill, Roosevelt and the Stalin Enigma, 1941–1945', in *From World War to Cold War: Churchill, Roosevelt, and the International History of the 1940s*, ed. D. Reynolds (Oxford: Oxford University Press, 2006), and Folly, *Churchill, Whitehall and the Soviet Union*, chapter 3.

17 On Stalin's views of Churchill, Roosevelt, and the Grand Alliance, see G. Roberts, *Stalin's Wars: From World War to Cold War, 1939–1953* (New Haven: Yale University Press, 2006), chapters 6 and 8.

18 The Soviet documents on the Moscow conference are published in *Moskovskaya Konferentsiya Ministrov Inostrannykh Del* (Moscow: Politizdat, 1984). For an analysis based on western archives, see K. Sainsbury, *The Turning Point* (Oxford: Oxford University Press, 1986).

19 On Stalin's conversations with Churchill and Roosevelt at Tehran, see G. Roberts, 'Stalin at the Tehran, Yalta and Potsdam Conferences' *Journal of Cold War Studies* 9, no. 4 (Fall 2007): 6–40.

20 G. Roberts, *Stalin's Wars: From World War to Cold War, 1939–1953* (New Haven: Yale University Press, 2006), pp. 199–200.

21 The Soviet transcripts of the Churchill-Stalin talks of October 1944 may be found in Folly, Roberts, and Rzheshevsky, *Churchill and Stalin*.

22 Averell Harriman Papers, Library of Congress Manuscript Division, container 178, chronological file 10-13/4/45.

23 G. Roberts, 'Sexing Up the Cold War: New Evidence on the Molotov-Truman Talks of April 1945' *Cold War History* 4, no. 3 (April 2004): 105–125.

24 D. Reynolds, *In Command of History: Churchill Fighting and Writing the Second World War* (London: Penguin, 2005), p. 468.

Part VII

Post-war Legacies and Myth-Making

19

Germany's Selective Memory of the Eastern Front

What a contrast to the years after the First World War: whereas after 1918 the Eastern Front hardly played a role in the collective memory of the Germans, and the battlefields of Western Europe dominated the picture, after 1945 the theatre of war in Eastern and South-eastern Europe to a large extent dominated public memory – to this day. The Eastern Front stretched almost 1,600 kilometres from the Baltic to the Black Sea. Within a few months, German motorised units had advanced more than 1,200 kilometres eastwards to just short of Moscow. Millions of Red Army soldiers died or became German prisoners of war. By the end of the war, more Wehrmacht soldiers had died on the Eastern Front than in all the previous battles. It was not until 1955–1956 that thousands of men were released from Soviet captivity. In the East, at Stalingrad, the 'German catastrophe' was, in retrospect, more concentrated. But the Eastern Front was not only an area of unprecedented military violence and loss. Eastern and South-eastern Europe, occupied by the Wehrmacht, also became the scene of war crimes and crimes against humanity. The genocide of European Jews took place behind the Eastern Front. In contrast to the war on other fronts, the term 'war of extermination' should therefore be applied to the Eastern Front.

However, the collective memory of a historical event does not depend solely on its contemporary significance. Rather, it changes over time and has long since become an object of historical research itself. This applies both to the question of what exactly is worth remembering and to the meaning that is attributed to the event in retrospect. The state of knowledge and research at the time played a role, as did the social, political, and cultural context in which historical knowledge was acquired and received. Once-important events could be forgotten, while other, less central events became the focus of memory. Collective memory, public memory, is therefore inevitably selective.

This is especially true in the German case, because between 1949 and 1989–1990 we had to deal with two completely different, opposing German state and social systems: the German Democratic Republic (GDR) in the East and the Federal Republic of Germany (FRG) in the West. During the decades of the 'Cold War', the public and political visualisation of the wartime past was always dominated by the systemic conflict. Without this ideological context, the memory of the Eastern Front remains incomprehensible on both sides. The liberal-democratic Federal Republic of Germany is particularly interesting for Germany's selective remembrance of the Eastern Front of the Second World War because, within the framework of its pluralistic social order, different actors had to constantly renegotiate the collective, public memory, while in East Berlin the state party largely determined the official commemoration of the Second World War, the Eastern Front, and the role of the Red Army – all the more so because Moscow set the tone.

We will therefore approach the topic in four steps. The first is the status of the Eastern Front in West German public opinion, namely the question of the prisoners of war who remained in the Soviet Union, the 'returnees', and the veterans. The Stalingrad myth is central to this. Up until the 1970s, it shaped an image of the war (in the East) according to which the Germans saw themselves primarily as victims of this war. Second, the caesura to which the critical examination of the Second World War from the 1970s onwards led will be worked out. This debate revolved around the connection between the war and the Holocaust and the end of the 'legend of the clean Wehrmacht'. In this period the victims of Germans became the focus of remembrance. Third, a sideways glance at the GDR will illustrate the role that the war in the Soviet Union played in the socialist German state. Fourth, we will discuss how the commemoration of the Eastern Front has developed in a united Germany after the Cold War – from the early years of rap-prochement with Russia to the dramatic deterioration in German-Russian relations since the occupation of Crimea in 2014 and the attack on Ukraine in 2022.

19.1 West German Memories of the Battles 'in the East' during the Cold War

Memoirs and court testimony by German generals and officers shaped the West German historical image of the 'clean Wehrmacht' in the post-war period. German soldiers, it was said, had only done their job and, with few exceptions, had obeyed the international laws of war. Crimes were shrouded in silence, if not outright denied. In the eyes of the public, the guilty had been brought to justice at the Nuremberg trials. For the Wehrmacht, the question of guilt no longer arose; amnesty laws seemed to underscore this. The *Landser* novels of the 1950s also idealised the war experience on the Eastern Front as one of comradeship and competence. Numerous veterans' organisations cultivated this selective memory of a time in which the men endured as a long-suffering community and presented themselves as 'survivors'.[1] The ideal of the comradely German soldier was contrasted with the figure of the insidious communist partisan, as often portrayed in Nazi propaganda.

The name of one city was paradigmatic for the memory of the Eastern Front in post-war Germany: Stalingrad. Since 19 November 1942, the Red Army had trapped the Sixth Army under Field Marshal Friedrich Paulus with some 284,000 men between the Volga and the Don. The newly promoted Paulus did not shoot himself, as Hitler had suggested, but surrendered with his 91,000 soldiers. Only 6,000 would return home by 1955–1956. The sheer number of German casualties, the harshness and duration of camp life in the Gulag, and the military significance of the battle as a turning point in the war all seem to have secured Stalingrad a firm place in the 'collective memory' of the Germans. But why 'Stalingrad' and not (also) the Battle of Kursk in July 1943, which was in this period considered the largest tank battle in history? And why not the collapse of Army Group Centre in the summer of 1944, in which German casualties amounted to 350,000 men, including 158,000 prisoners of war?

The defeat at Stalingrad, according to one response, substantiated abstract interpretations that gave meaning to the war dead. The groundwork had already been laid by Nazi propaganda. The headline in the *Völkischer Beobachter* read 'The 6th Army's Battle for Stalingrad at an End / They Died So That Germany May Live'.[2] In the style of Christian redemption parables, 'Stalingrad' was ideologically elevated to the status of a sacrifice. The ambiguous concept of sacrifice in German was clearly directed at the meaningful sacrifice (*sacrificium*) that was intended, not the meaningless sacrifice (*victimus*) that was inevitably accepted. This myth of the 'heroes of Stalingrad' gave meaning to the soldiers who remained on the Eastern Front and encouraged them to fight on, so that the death of their comrades would not be in vain.

The Nazi slogans continued to have an impact beyond 1945. The Nazi master narrative of the Eastern Front *during* the war formed a starting point for public memory *after* the war. The few survivors of the Sixth Army formed associations of former 'Stalingrad fighters' in the Federal Republic of Germany and Austria in the late 1950s. They were part of a flourishing veterans' culture that was a natural part of everyday life in post-war West German society from 1950 to the 1970s. The Stalingrad Fighters, as they called themselves, had about 900 members in the 1960s (700 in Austria). They published magazines, met regularly at the national level from 1958, and gathered with relatives at memorials dedicated specifically to comrades who died in Stalingrad. In 1964 the Association of Former Stalingrad Fighters of Germany had a central memorial erected in the Hessian district town of Limburg for the soldiers who died in the battle and in captivity, yet much better known, still to this day, is the provenance and religious character of another symbolic form of remembrance. Like the memorial stone in a public space, the so-called Stalingrad Madonna in Berlin's Kaiser Wilhelm Memorial Church has been commemorating the battle since 1983.[3] The painting, created in 1942–1943, shows a seated female figure holding a child protectively under her wide coat. Reproductions can be found in many German and Austrian cities. Painted by Protestant pastor Kurt Reuben in Stalingrad as a symbol of hope for life, the painting offered a religious embellishment of the experience of death to commemorate the fallen and call for peace.

The battle was used metaphorically in different ways in the memory practices of the 'Stalingraders'. Three variants can be distinguished. First, they conflated 'Stalingrad' with a willingness for sacrifice – with no consideration for the purpose of the battle, which even in the early post-war era reflected a highly selective engagement with the realities of the war in the East. Second, in a process of meaning transfer, the

Figure 19.1 The 'Stalingrad Madonna' is an image of the Virgin Mary drawn by a German soldier, Kurt Reuber (1906–1944), in 1942 during the Battle of Stalingrad. Source: ullstein bild/ullstein bild via Getty Images.

veterans derived their special credibility as advocates for peace in Europe from the experience of suffering in the cauldron of 1942–1943. Third, the metaphor mythologised the battle not only as a turning point in the Second World War but also as a turning point in the history of the 'West', which was now threatened by Bolshevism. However, opposite interpretations were also possible: some veterans saw Stalingrad as a symbol of senseless orders and 'slavish obedience'.

It was not only the veterans who created a specific memory. The public image of the war in the East in the Federal Republic was shaped above all by popular literature with a large circulation. This is especially true of the apologetic memoirs of military leaders and the divisional histories, which since the 1950s have reinforced the distortion through the lens of the Wehrmacht. Moreover, the view 'from below', the perception of the soldiers, has been provided by published field reports since the 1950s. Supposedly authentic documents were first published in 1950 in a slim volume entitled *Last Letters from Stalingrad*, which portrayed Stalingrad as a place of horror. Beginning in the 1960s, popular historical works such as the bestseller *Operation Barbarossa*, published under the pseudonym Paul Carell by Karl Schmidt, former *SS Obersturmbannführer* and press chief to Foreign Minister Joachim von Ribbentrop, painted a picture of a rational, clean war – *with* heroism, *without* crime.[4] War criminals – according to Schmidt, it was not the German soldiers but the Soviet soldiers.

Among the traumatic experiences firmly anchored in German memory culture was a wave of spontaneous violence against the civilian population on the Eastern Front at the beginning of the Soviet winter offensive, when the Red Army entered the territory of the German Reich in late January 1945.[5] Incited by anti-German hate slogans, especially those of journalist Ilya Ehrenburg, Soviet soldiers took revenge on the German civilian population, especially as propaganda portrayed their higher standard of living compared to the USSR as a result of the raids in Eastern Europe. There was looting, pillaging, and rape. The number of indiscriminate killings of civilians, mostly by Soviet infantry, is estimated to be at least 120,000. This mass violence included the destruction of city centres and residential areas. The situation improved only in April 1945, when victory seemed certain, and the new task was to win over sections of the population to the banner of proletarian internationalism. But as late as May 1945, probably the largest mass rape in history took place in Berlin.[6] The arbitrary terror was followed by organised persecution on the orders of the command. More than a hundred thousand women were put into work battalions at the rear of the front and deported to the Soviet Union. German civilians also had to perform forced labour in the Reich. In the course of reparations, a total of 210,000 Germans, mostly young people, were deported to the USSR; one in five died in the process. The experiences of civilians in East Germany were very different from those in the West. Hatred towards the Soviets, which would have affected the civilian population, played a very different role in the ideologised German-Soviet political relationship. This ideological dimension and the experiences of (East) Germans at the end of the war contributed significantly to (West) German perceptions of the Eastern Front for decades to come.

The picture was further clouded by the demographic upheavals caused by events on the Eastern Front in the final months of the war and in the immediate post-war period. In the final phase of the war, the civilian population endured not only the harshest bombardments but also the loss of millions of homes. The advance of the Red Army unleashed a tidal wave of migration. Unlike in the West, hundreds of thousands of men and women in the East fled the fighting and prospect of Soviet occupation. The mass exodus was followed by what is known today as ethnic cleansing: the expulsion of the remaining ethnic German civilian population from the states and occupied territories of Central and Eastern Europe by order of the victorious powers. The German civilian population became the object of retaliation, geostrategic security thinking, and the goal, contrary to international law, of resolving nationality conflicts once and for all through deportation. In the final phase, the German civilian population became the victim of a process of radicalisation that did not end abruptly with surrender. Fourteen million people were forced to flee from Eastern, Central, and South-eastern Europe, and more than 600,000 lost their lives. The loss of one's homeland remained in the collective memory for a long time, even longer than the problem of being a prisoner of war, which was not solved until ten years after the end of the war with the arrival of the last 'returnees'.[7] On the other hand, the fact that flight and expulsion in the East were a consequence of their own criminal regime, which itself had pursued a ruthless policy of collective 'resettlement' and deportation since 1939, did not play a major role in German memory for decades after the war. This 'self-victimisation' also obscured the close connection between war and genocide, which was only halted by the Red Army's successful campaign. This began to change in the 1970s.

19.2 Victim Reversal: Warfare and the Holocaust

Until well into the 1960s and even into the 1970s, the memory of the Eastern Front fit into the context of a victim narrative of the Second World War and National Socialism, in which the Germans presented themselves primarily as victims: as victims of Nazi terror, Anglo-American bombing, and excessive violence on the part of the 'Russians'. The stories of Soviet terror, mass rape, flight, and expulsion also fit politically into the period of confrontation between the West and the 'Eastern Bloc'. Last but not least, this self-victimisation had a clear exculpatory function. It distracted people from their own role in establishing a dictatorship with genocidal aims.

Since the 1970s the history of remembrance of the Second World War has changed, with serious consequences for the meaning attributed to the Eastern Front. Several actors can be distinguished. First, the (academic and non-academic) reappraisal of the Nazi era and war crimes led to a different view of the Eastern theatre of war, especially the role of the Germans. After the Jews, Soviet prisoners of war were the largest group of victims of Nazi policies. Of the more than 5.6 million Soviet soldiers captured, some 3 million died in the custody of the Wehrmacht. Until the 1970s it was taboo to research the fate of Soviet prisoners of war. The communist soldiers were 'no comrades', according to the title of a standard work published in 1978.[8] Research conducted by the Military History Research Office (MGFA) in Freiburg im Breisgau initially met with little public response. On the other hand, the four-part television series *Holocaust – The Story of the Weiss Family*, which was broadcast in Germany and Austria in 1979, had an enormous impact on the West German population. The US miniseries, which dramatised the genocide through the fate of fictitious Berlin Jews, greatly popularised knowledge of the murder of European Jews, the concentration camps, and the gas chambers – despite criticism that it trivialised and commercialised the subject – and introduced the term 'Holocaust' into public discourse. And it cast a dark light on the Eastern Front, which was suddenly portrayed as the scene of mass murder perpetrated by Germans. In public memory the perpetrators were primarily the approximately 3,000 members of the *SS Einsatzgruppen*, a small group of ideologically trained special units under *Reichsführer SS* Heinrich Himmler. The mass of German soldiers, on the other hand, were said to have had nothing to do with these crimes.[9] They were the troops of the ideological war, not the Wehrmacht. After all, more than seventeen million soldiers were involved. There was hardly a German family that did not have a relative who had served in the Wehrmacht.

This 'legend of the clean Wehrmacht' was first publicly challenged by a travelling exhibition organised by the Hamburg Institute for Social Research between 1995 and 2004. The programme was titled 'Crimes of the Wehrmacht: Dimensions of the War of Extermination, 1941–1944'.

The exhibition and its revised versions from 1995–1999 and 2001–2004 focused on the Wehrmacht's involvement in the extermination of European Jews, the plundering of occupied territories, and the mass murder of civilians and Soviet prisoners of war.[10] It became clear that the Wehrmacht leadership had issued criminal orders that violated the Geneva Conventions, the Hague Land Warfare Convention, and the customs of war. In the aftermath, a younger generation of historians confronted the German public with the gruesome facets of the 'war of extermination' that had raged primarily in the Eastern theatre. New sources such as trial documents, Wehrmacht files, and letters from the front disproved the myth of the apolitical, abused soldier. Institutionalised historiography also responded to the public debate, which was by no means limited to historians. The MGFA continued its series *Germany and the Second World War* and organised an international conference on the subject in 1999.[11] The Institute of Contemporary History launched the project 'The Wehrmacht in the National Socialist Dictatorship', which led to numerous individual studies, such as a study of five divisions in the Soviet Union and a highly publicised summary entitled 'Crimes of the Wehrmacht'.[12] In addition to new depictions of the battle of Stalingrad, which included the Soviet side, the siege of Leningrad by the Eighteenth Army in the fall and winter of 1941–1942 also aroused interest.[13] A documentary was broadcast simultaneously on German and Soviet/Russian television in the early 1990s.[14] At the memorial service for the victims of Nazism on 27 January 2014, ninety-five-year-old Russian writer Daniil Granin spoke about the Leningrad blockade. The Eastern Front had mutated into an arena where the criminal warfare of the German military and its many connections with the Nazi regime became abundantly clear to a wider audience. Remembrance was one thing; compensation was another. When compensation for former forced labourers was discussed in Germany around 2000, Soviet prisoners of war were initially ignored. It was not until 2015 that the Bundestag decided to pay a symbolic 2,500 euros to each of the nearly two thousand survivors.

It was no longer about casting Germans as victims but about recognising the victims of Germans. The identification of the politicised post-war academic generation(s) with these 'actual' victims formed the basis for a committed confrontation with the past and a distancing from the previous generation. Giving the victims a voice was the (historical-didactic and museological) credo. Of course, the emotional identification with the victims had a downside: it largely ignored the perpetrators.[15] This focus on the victims of the Eastern Front fundamentally differentiated the collective memory in the Federal Republic from that in the GDR.

19.3 A Sideways Glance at Memory in East Germany

In the Soviet occupation zone and in the GDR, which was founded in 1949, the public image of the Eastern Front during the Second World War was shaped by two factors: the dependence on Soviet power and the ideological framework of interpretation it provided. The victory over the Wehrmacht in the 'Great Patriotic War' was a victory over fascism, which was intended to significantly underpin the rule of the Communist Party of the Soviet Union, which legitimated itself not least through its anti-fascism. The fact that German anti-fascists had defeated Hitler's dictator-ship alongside the Soviet Union was part of the founding myth of the GDR. In view of the political and military balance of power and the significance of the victory, the trivialisation or idealisation of the German military campaign was out of the question, as was criticism of the Soviet military. The excess violence committed by the Red Army in 1945 were just as taboo as the fate of German prisoners of war in the Soviet Union's prison camp system until 1955. While the memory of the Eastern Front in the Federal Republic was marked by anti-communism, in the GDR the Marxist-Leninist view of history and the premise of class struggle deter-mined the interpretation. Accordingly, the Wehrmacht was seen as an instrument of power of the German monopoly bourgeoisie.

On the other hand, it was clear from the beginning that the campaigns of the Wehrmacht, especially in Eastern Europe, had criminal features and that Hitler's soldiers were waging a war of extermination. The link between the military and politics was undeniable. Significantly, propa-ganda always referred to the Wehrmacht as the 'fascist Wehrmacht'. While generals and admirals in the Federal Republic remained silent about the crimes, the criminal war and the influence of the fascist regime were among the central themes of the memoirs of former Wehrmacht officers published in the GDR.[16] The GDR presented itself as an anti-fascist response to the experience of war and dictatorship, while externalising any historical responsibility to the 'fascist' Federal Republic. It was therefore only logical that 8 May 1945 was officially celebrated as the 'Day of Liberation' (by the Red Army). In the Federal Republic, this formula only became widely accepted at the end of the 1980s, after President Richard von Weizsäcker's speech in the German Bundestag on the fortieth anniversary of the liberation of Berlin. In retrospect, Weizsäcker had spoken of a 'liberation' from National Socialism that demonstrated the success of the second German democracy. Until then, the end of the war and the capitulation had been equated with a 'defeat' that gave no cause for celebration.

The fact that this selective, pro-Soviet memory of the war in the East contradicted the personal memories of some of those affected was another matter. Which citizen of the GDR had fought in the 'anti-fascist' resistance? In the Federal Republic, different social groups – veterans, refugees and expellees, political parties – had to agree time and again on how the West German memory of the war in Eastern Europe should be shaped. The East German government, on the other hand, had to use all historical and political means at its disposal to anchor the pro-Soviet orientation in the collective memory of East German citizens. Monuments to the Red Army and the 'Victims of Fascism', Soviet military cemeteries, and military parades were as much a part of this as education in schools and memorial sites such as the former Buchenwald concentration camp. The camp was turned into a place of communist resistance, supporting the Red Army in its fight against Hitler. There was no place in this selective memory for the Holocaust. The genocide of the Jews did not fit into the Marxist-Leninist worldview. The universalising talk of 'fascism' also consistently ignored the specificity of German fascism, namely anti-Semitism.

19.4   The Eastern Front: From a United Europe to the War against Ukraine

The 1990s and 2000s saw a shift in public memory of the Second World War in general and the war on the Eastern Front in particular. The end of the Cold War, the unification of the two German states in 1990, the collapse of the Soviet Union in 1991, and a generational change transformed the basic conditions of the German (and European) culture of remembrance. The Nazi war and genocide remained (and remain) its negative fixed point. The universalisation of 'Auschwitz' was, of course, linked to the human rights legitimisation of military interventions, initially in the Yugoslav wars of the 1990s. One striking event signalled the change in Germany. For the first time, a German chancellor – Gerhard Schröder – attended the Victory Day parade in Moscow in 2005 after being invited to the sixtieth D-Day anniversary celebrations in France in 2004. On 9 May 2010, Angela Merkel watched the parade of Russian, French, Polish, British, and American soldiers alongside Putin. The 'Joint Commission for the Study of the Recent History of German-Russian Relations' was founded in 1997 with the aim of promoting academic research into German-Russian history in the twentieth century and helping to strengthen mutual trust between Russia and Germany.[17]

The German-Russian Museum was established in 1991 in Berlin-Karlshorst, via a joint initiative of the German and Russian governments, as a place of common remembrance of the Second World War. Since 1967 the 'Museum of the Unconditional Surrender of Fascist Germany in the Great Patriotic War 1941–1945' has been located on the site where the supreme commanders of the Wehrmacht signed an unconditional surrender in the presence of representatives of the Soviet Union, the United States, Great Britain, and France on the night of 8–9 May 1945. In 1995, the first permanent exhibition after the redesign dealt with the 'Memory of a War'. The current permanent exhibition 'Germany and the Soviet Union in the Second World War' was opened in 2013. The museum is the only one in Germany with a permanent exhibition commemorating the war of annihilation against the Soviet Union.

In (German) research today, the war in the East is discussed not least in terms of its significance for the end of the war and the Nazi regime. The large-scale commemorations of the anniversary of D-Day on 6 June 1944 in Normandy suggest that the landing of the Western Allies ushered in the final phase of the war and thus the end of Nazi rule in Europe. Contrary to this Western narrative, it was not only Soviet and post-Soviet historiography that emphasised the decisive role of the Red Army; their great offensive, which began in the summer of 1944 and reached the pre-war borders of the German Reich in January 1945, contributed significantly to the collapse of National Socialism.

German-Russian relations deteriorated drastically with the annexation of the Ukrainian peninsula of Crimea in violation of international law in the spring of 2014. This has not been without consequences for the official commemoration of the Red Army and its contribution to the defeat of Nazism on the Eastern Front. This was already evident during the celebrations of the seventieth anniversary of the end of the war in 2015. The crisis has charged the symbolic act of remembrance with current political significance, thus linking the representation of the past with the interpretation of the present. The Russian side, for its part, used the 9 May military parade on Red Square to stage military power.[18] This created a dilemma for German politics: on one hand, politicians across the political spectrum continued to see themselves as having a historical responsibility to remember the role of the Red Army in 1945 or, more broadly, the significance of the USSR/Russia in the Second World War. On the other hand, no one wanted the commemoration to be exploited for Russian interests. Participation in the ceremony in Moscow on 9 May 2015 was ruled out, as was any official participation in the counter-commemoration in Gdansk, which was attended primarily by Eastern and South-eastern European states and hosted by Polish president Bronislaw Komorowski – an event at which Ukrainian president Petro Poroshenko also appeared. On 10 May 2015 German Chancellor Angela Merkel and Vladimir Putin laid wreaths at the Tomb of the Unknown Soldier in the Alexander Garden near the Kremlin. The common denominator was, on the one hand, mourning for the crimes committed by the Germans *during* the war and, on the other hand, appreciation for the reconciliation between the two peoples *after* the war. Merkel recalled the starving inhabitants of besieged Leningrad, the abused and murdered Soviet civilians, concentration camp inmates and prisoners of war, and a scorched-earth war in which the Wehrmacht and SS literally wiped out countless villages and towns. Foreign Minister Frank Steinmeier and his Soviet counterpart Sergei Lavrov laid wreaths at Volgograd; at the Russian military cemetery in Rossoshka, not far from Volgograd; and at the Central Memorial of the Russian Federation in memory of the Battle of Stalingrad – as a sign of shared responsibility for peace in Europe.

The war against Ukraine has made a joint German-Russian commemoration of the Second World War and the victims of the Eastern Front impossible. Military aggression and increasingly autocratic rule on the Russian side have been accompanied by the radicalised politics of history. Putin instrumentalised the past for a post-Soviet state patriotism designed to legitimise his rule, unite society with pride for the 'glorious' struggle, and strengthen belief in Russia's destiny as a great power under a strong leader. The Soviet Union's victory over Germany became a founding myth of contemporary Russia, which no longer allowed dissent. The revival of old enemy images, the rehabilitation of Stalin, and imperial ambitions ensure a divided memory and a common reappraisal of the war on the Eastern Front are a distant prospect. The German-Russian Historical Commission has suspended its work.[19] The former German-Russian Museum was renamed 'Museum Karlshorst' in protest on 24 February 2022; the Ukrainian flag flies in front of the building. It remains to be seen to what extent the war will change the memory of the Eastern Front once again. It is quite possible that the war against Ukraine will bring the country even more into focus as the site of a criminal war whose victims post-Soviet Russia claims as its own.

Notes

1 For further reading, see Jörg Echternkamp, *Postwar Soldiers: Historical Controversies and West-German Democratization, 1945–1955* (New York: Berghahn Books, 2020).

2 *Völkischer Beobachter*, 4 February 1943. See also Christina Morina, *Legacies of Stalingrad: Remembering the Eastern Front in Germany since 1945* (Cambridge: Cambridge University Press, 2011).

3 See Joseph B. Perry, 'The Madonna of Stalingrad: Mastering the (Christmas) Past and West German National Identity after World War II' *Radical History Review* 83 (2002): 7–27.

4 Paul Carell, *Unternehmen Barbarossa: Der Marsch nach Rußland* (Frankfurt am Main: Ullstein, 1963).

5 Norman Naimark, *The Russians in Germany: The History of the Soviet Zone of Occupation, 1945–1949* (Cambridge, MA: Harvard University Press, 1995).

6 Antony Beevor, *The Fall of Berlin 1945* (London: Penguin Books, 2020), p. 410.

7 Ike Scherstjanoi, ed., *Russlandheimkehrer: Die sowjetische Kriegsgefangenschaft im Gedächtnis der Deutschen* (Munich: Oldenbourg, 2012).

8 Christian Streit, *Keine Kameraden: Die Wehrmacht und die sowjetischen Kriegsgefangenen 1941–1945* (Bonn: J. H. W. Dietz, 1978). This work has had numerous new editions, most recently in 1997.

9 H. Krausnick and H.-W. Wilhelm, *Die Truppe des Weltanschauungskrieges: Die Einsatzgruppen der Sicherheitspolizei und des SD 1938–1942* (Stuttgart: DVA, 1981).

10 Hamburger Institut für Sozialforschung, ed., *Verbrechen der Wehrmacht: Dimensionen des Vernichtungskrieges 1941–1944 – Ausstellungskatalog* (Hamburg: Hamburger Edition, 2002).

11 H. Boog, Jurgen Forster, Joachim Hoffman, Ernst Klink, and Rolf-Dieter Muller, *Germany and the Second World War, Vol. 4: The Attack on the Soviet Union* (Oxford: Oxford University Press, 1998), first published in German 1983; K.-H. Frieser, ed., *Germany and the Second World War, Vol. 8: The Eastern Front 1943–1944 – The War in the East and on the Neighbouring Fronts* (Oxford: Oxford University Press, 2017), first published in German in 2007; J. Förster, 'Wehrmacht, Krieg und Holocaust', in *Die Wehrmacht: Mythos und Realität*, ed. R. D. Müller and H. E. Volkmann (Munich: Oldenbourg, 1999), pp. 948–964.

12 Johannes Hürter, 'The Wehrmacht during the Nazi Dictatorship', Leibniz Institute for Contemporary History, Institüt fur Zeitgeschichte, München-Berlin, www.ifz-muenchen.de/en/research/ea/research/the-wehrmacht-during-the-nazi-dictatorship; Christian Hartmann, *Wehrmacht im Ostkrieg: Front und militärisches Hinterland 1941/42* (Munich: Oldenbourg, 2009); Christian Hartmann, Johannes Hürter, and Ulrike Jureit, eds., *Verbrechen der Wehrmacht: Bilanz einer Debatte* (Munich: C. H. Beck, 2005).

13 Jörg Ganzenmüller, *Das belagerte Leningrad 1941 bis 1944: Die Stadt in den Strategien von Angreifern und Verteidigern* (Paderborn: Schöningh, 2007).

14 Guido Knopp, Valerij Korsin, Anatolij Nikiforow, and Harald Schott (directors), *Der verdammte Krieg – Das Unternehmen Barbarossa – IV. Der Kampf um Leningrad*, D-ZDF/SOW-TV, 1991.

15 Ulrike Jureit and Christian Schneider, *Gefühlte Opfer: Illusionen der Vergangenheitsbewältigung* (Stuttgart: Klett-Cotta, 2010).

16 Dorothee Wierling, 'The War in Postwar Society: The Role of the Second World War in Public and Private Spheres in the Soviet Occupation Zone and Early GDR', in *Experience and Memory: The Second World War in Europe*, ed. Jörg Echternkamp and Stefan Martens (New York: Berghahn Books, 2013), pp. 214–228.

17 Horst Möller and Aleksandr O. Cubar'jan, 'Mitteilungen der Gemeinsamen
    Kommission für die Erforschung der jüngeren Geschichte der deutsch-
    russischen Beziehungen', www.degruyter.com/serial/mkeg-b/html?
    lang=de.
18 Cf. Jan C. Behrends, 'Russlands geschichtspolitischer Sonderweg. Der
    "Große Vaterländische Krieg" und die Feiern am 9. Mai 2015',
    Zeitgeschichte-Online, May 2015, www.zeitgeschichte-online.de/kommen
    tar/russlands-geschichtspolitischer-sonderweg.
19 Cf. 'Gemeinsame Kommission für die Erforschung der jüngeren Geschichte
    der deutsch-russischen Beziehungen', www.deutsch-russische-geschichts
    kommission.de.

20

The Politics of War Memory in the USSR and Post-Soviet Russia

> The Soviet Union could not recognize the First World War since the Bolsheviks had opposed it; thus the Second World War took its place.
>
> George Mosse, *Fallen Soldiers*

Shortly after Vladimir Putin concluded his second term as president of the Russian Federation, Evgenii Briun, the country's leading specialist in the study of drug and alcohol abuse, made an extraordinary claim. Briun, who headed the Moscow Scientific and Practical Center of Narcology, sought to debunk a widespread stereotype which held that Russians were uniquely prone to alcohol abuse. To this, Briun countered that Russians 'drink no more and no less' than peoples of other countries. The difference, reported Briun, and the reason for the misconception, was simply that Russians have been celebrating victory in the Second World War much longer than other nations. In Briun's analysis, 'soldiers, having grown accustomed to drinking at the front, celebrated victory, and this celebration has lasted a very long time'.[1]

Briun's proclamation, implausible though it may be, underscores an essential feature of contemporary Russian political culture: the deeply entrenched memory of the 'Great Patriotic War', which has become a cornerstone of post-Soviet national identity. In no other country is the war victory observed with such a mix of official pomp and genuine popular reverence. Each year on May 9 – Victory Day – hundreds of thousands of Russians of all ages, clad in victory-themed regalia and brandishing placards of relatives who fought in the war, take part in what has become the country's most important public celebration. From the nationally televised festivities in Moscow to the more intimate commemorative gatherings in small towns and rural localities, the collective remembrance of victory unites the country like no other event.

This chapter situates contemporary Russian war memory in its twentieth-century historical context, exploring how and why the war victory gained such prominence, and drawing out certain continuities and discontinuities across the Soviet/post-Soviet divide. Given the immense scale of Soviet wartime losses – some 27 million dead and the destruction of roughly 70 thousand villages and 1,700 larger towns and cities – and the unusually heavy-handed instrumentalisation of history under Putin, the Second World War was bound to play a prominent role in Russian memory culture. Yet, as this chapter will show, the precise character of Russian war memory and its utility for the Kremlin as means to legitimate political authority, foster national unity, and frame geopolitics derive overwhelmingly from decades of Soviet-era commemorative practices.

The objective here is not to rectify distortions of historical truth but rather to elucidate the mechanisms by which states repurpose the past in the service of the present. Such a focus on 'official' memory can shed light on not only how historical narratives are created and disseminated but also dynamic processes of adaptation in response to shifting political landscapes, social pressures, and international contexts. Soviet war memory, as elsewhere, was the product of internal debate and deliberation as the leadership wrestled with what were often pan-European issues of representation. This chapter thus approaches the myth and memory of the Great Patriotic War as a particular manifestation of a universal impulse to 'make sense' of war in the modern world.[2]

20.1   Setting the Stage: Stalinist War Memory

News of Germany's capitulation reached Moscow in the early hours of 9 May 1945. As in other European cities, spontaneous celebrations erupted, with Soviet citizens flooding streets and public squares, singing, dancing, laughing, and crying. The following month, a grand parade was held in Red Square. The June procession included iconic scenes, later immortalised in a series of paintings and photographs. Among these was the memorable entrance of Marshal Georgii Zhukov into the square on the back of a famed grey-white horse named Idol and Soviet soldiers' dramatic casting down of Nazi standards at the base of Lenin's Mausoleum. The euphoria of victory remained palpable. As a soldier who participated in the parade recalled, 'almost everyone cried. Women. Children. Even the assembled ranks of the victorious heroes! They wept from the most acute excitement, from delight, from joy!'[3]

By the end of 1947, however, the tone of Victory Day celebrations had shifted decisively. In December the Presidium of the Supreme Soviet re-designated 9 May so that it became a 'working' rather than 'non-working' holiday. This was indicative of a more general late-Stalinist approach to war memory that was at once 'amnesiac' and 'war-obsessed'.[4] The period from 1945 until Stalin's death in 1953 witnessed near-constant deliberations over plans for major war memorials in Moscow and the USSR's 'hero-cities', only for most of the projects never to see the light of day. The Communist Party authorised the release of significant literary and cinematic works centred on the war, such as Aleksandr Fadeev's novel *The*

Figure 20.1 Red Army soldiers dumping Nazi banners at the foot of Lenin's Tomb during the Victory Day parade celebrations in Moscow, June 1945. Source: Sovfoto/Universal Images Group via Getty Images.

Young Guard (1946) and films like *The Third Blow* (1948), *The Battle of Stalingrad* (1949), and *The Fall of Berlin* (1949). And yet it also precipitated the war theme's decline in popular culture. Filmmakers, for instance, produced nine war films in 1946, but that number had dwindled to zero by 1951. The celebratory rhetoric surrounding Victory Day remained, even as the leadership downgraded it to a 'working holiday'.

Stalinist war memory was therefore paradoxical, by turns exalting and diminishing the war's place in Soviet public culture. In part, this was a by-product of the post-war myth-making taking place among all former belligerents. As in Western Europe and the United States, Soviet political leaders and mass media combed the wartime experience for 'usable' elements, repurposing these in a way that presented an overwhelmingly positive image of the country at war. While features of the resulting Soviet war myth fluctuated over time – for example, Stalin's military leadership and the role of the Western allies – many of the essential ingredients to victory established at this time remained constant into the late 1980s. These included the overall guidance of the Communist Party, the Soviet economic and political system, cooperation among Soviet nations, the inspiring role of Marxist-Leninist ideology, and the unity and steadfast patriotism of the Soviet people.

Like the war myths that were appearing throughout Europe and North America by 1948, the Soviet myth of victory served to contain potentially disruptive memories that could threaten social stability and undermine political legitimacy. Stalinist authorities discouraged the writing of war memoirs and remained wary of recollections that might draw attention to the brutal methods and terrible human toll required to achieve victory. Consequently, there were concerted efforts to mask over the traumatic legacies of the war in both official and popular culture, while the visible wounds of war, exemplified by the many war invalids reduced to begging, were systematically cleared from public view.[5]

Similarly, the Party worked to suppress memories recalling errors in leadership, instances of collaboration and defeatism, and localist framings of the war effort – that is, the elevation of local authority and experiences at the expense of the Kremlin's leadership and its overarching narrative of all-Soviet heroism. This centralising impulse reconfigured commemorations in major Russian urban centres like Leningrad, a city that had suffered under a 900-day siege during the war and where early celebrations had stressed the war's local dimensions. By 1949 authorities had dismantled several locally conceived war monuments, shuttered the Museum of the Defence of Leningrad, scrapped plans for a major war memorial, and circumscribed public discussion and publications tied to the city's wartime experience.

In non-Russian Union republics, a process of homogenisation also unfolded. Republic-level authorities and intellectuals were granted leeway to mediate the central war myth in a way that exalted the 'titular' Soviet nation (Ukrainians in the Ukrainian SSR, Kazakhs in the Kazakh SSR, and so on), while simultaneously diminishing the participation of others. This pattern of ethnic minority exclusion implicitly contrasted the heroism of titular peoples with groups suspected of disloyalty. State narratives minimised or consigned to oblivion the wartime contributions of the hundreds of thousands of Crimean Tatars, Chechens, Kalmyks, Volga Germans, and others who faced mass deportation during the war due to Kremlin suspicions over their collective potential for collaboration. Acceptable modes of ethnic heroism therefore came to centre on 'Russian', titular 'non-Russian', and overarching 'Soviet' modes.

Although scholars have long contended that Soviet war memory deliberately subordinated the wartime role of the titular nations to overall ethnic Russian leadership, the actual dynamics were more complex and ambiguous. Provided that republican cultural producers did not present the wartime valour of titular peoples as *surpassing* that of the Russian people, representations could broadly suggest parity with the Russian nation, thereby fostering an image of a laterally (rather than hierarchically) arrayed 'Soviet people'. However, any narrative or commemoration linking the heroism of titular nations during the war to unique ethnonational histories or legacies of the pre-Soviet past faced strict censure. Such digressions into the pre-revolutionary era had to conform to a broader historical framework that privileged ethnic Russian guidance and pre-eminence in the realms of culture, science, and military achievement before 1917.

The Soviet victory narrative similarly absorbed the unique contributions and sufferings of Soviet Jews. This tendency had analogues across formerly occupied Europe, where the post-war years saw the distinctiveness of the Jewish experience subsumed to narratives stressing national victimhood and resistance. For its part, Soviet media recognised Jewish contributions until very late in the war and offered Soviet readers glimpses into the horrors of the German extermination program, at times inciting calls for the establishment of Jewish military formations within the Red Army. 'I am convinced', wrote one Soviet soldier, 'that the Jews will fight the Fascists with a hatred ten times greater, both as patriots of the motherland and as the avengers of the blood of their brothers, sisters, fathers, and mothers, wives and children'.[6]

The ensuing marginalisation of the Jewish wartime experience, which accompanied the notorious anti-Semitic campaigns of the late-Stalin era, stemmed from multiple factors, including widespread anti-Semitism among party rank and file. The creation of the state of Israel in 1948 raised Stalin's suspicions over the supposed divided loyalties of Soviet Jews, while anxieties within the leadership over prior Nazi characterisations of the USSR as the hub of 'Judeo-Bolshevism' did little to counteract the erasure of specifically Jewish heroic narratives. By 1948–1949, with few exceptions, official accounts were universalising Jewish wartime suffering as an expression of the more general ordeal endured by all 'citizens of USSR'.[7]

But the production of Stalinist war memory involved much more than erasure and silencing; nor was its function solely about producing a sense of the past in which Soviet citizens could rejoice. The Stalinist leadership sought not to suppress the war's remembrance but rather to channel its expression into the pressing tasks of restoring political legitimacy and ideological conformity, mobilising economic recovery, and waging the Cold War. Moreover, post-war ideologists and propagandists utilised the war's memory in a way that legitimated not only the Bolshevik Revolution but also the upheavals of the 1930s – the collectivisation of agriculture, Stalin's breakneck industrialisation program, and mass political repression. From the vantage point of 1945, collectivisation, five-year-plan industrialisation, show trials, purges, and the Gulag were validated as necessary preconditions for the apocalyptic clash of 1941–1945.

Arguably the most important factor shaping post-war commemorations was the fledgling Cold War. Early Soviet war memory developed in reaction to the war narratives then emerging in the United States, Britain, and France, where Soviet wartime successes were often attributed to the miscalculations of Hitler, Russian climactic conditions, and Soviet soldiers' fear of their own government. This view of the Eastern Front emanated from within the US Army Historical Division and its 'Halder Group', the latter named for Franz Halder, the former head of the German Army General Staff, whose reflections became a key source in the development of official US war memory. Already in the months after May 1945, the propaganda department and Soviet Lecture Bureau were instructing their members that the main struggle emerging between the USSR and its former allies was 'over the interpretation of victory, over which countries participated in the war and to what extent'. The overriding objective of propagandists and public lecturers was therefore to 'demonstrate the role of the Red Army, the role of our Soviet Union ... [as] the decisive factor in achieving this victory'.[8]

It was in this context that Soviet historians, ideologists, and propagandists crafted a myth of victory that was a mirror image of Western depictions. Rather than the formidable Russian winter, the use of Soviet troops as cannon fodder, or a reliance on traditional Russian nationalism – all factors central to Western accounts – Soviet myth-makers asserted the primacy of the leadership of the Communist Party and Stalin, the Soviet political and socioeconomic system, supranational unity, and the ideological bedrock of Marxism-Leninism. In a far cry from his midnight victory toast of 24 May 1945, in which the Soviet leader credited the Russian people with victory, Stalin's 'summation' speech of February 1946 affirmed the paramount role of the Soviet system, the Red Army, and 'the single collective body' of Soviet people.[9] The Cold War context also explains why many of the first significant Soviet war memorials appeared not in the USSR but in Central and Eastern Europe, where the Soviet victory myth held an overwhelmingly geopolitical significance.

During the final years of his life, Stalin's personal role in leading the war effort took on grandiose proportions as his personality cult came to fuse with, if not entirely subsume, the war narrative. Public representations increasingly depicted the leader, glimmering in the white military tunic of his late-cultic persona, as not simply the architect of victory but as its embodiment. This process is well attested by Yerevan's Victory Monument (1950), one of the last significant war memorials of the Stalin era. The memorial itself consisted of a granite pedestal adorned with artistic embellishments. However, the memorial served as a mere foundation for what was the largest Stalin monument in the USSR.

The impact of the Stalin cult's absorption of the victory myth was twofold. On the one hand, it simplified Soviet war memory and masked over many of the ideological tensions that were developing within it. The cult of Generalissimo Stalin superseded contestations between the centre and periphery, 'Russian' and 'non-Russian', front-line solider and partisan, veteran and non-combatant, stabilising Soviet war memory in the process. In the longer term, however, the close association of the war victory with the personality cult meant that any future attempt to augment the victory myth and its public commemorative edifice had to first grapple with the Stalin question. This challenge would preoccupy Stalin's successors as they attempted to refashion the war's memory for a new, post-Stalin era.

20.2   Filling the Void: Origins and Development of the Victory Cult

The nature and prominence of the war's commemoration in the first post-Stalin decade is the subject of some debate among scholars. Many highlight an air of hesitation and uncertainty in the war's official representation, evidenced by Victory Day's continued 'working' status, the relatively sparse state of monuments, and the 'Thaw' era's nuanced artistic depictions of the war, which gave Soviet readers and filmgoers unprecedented scenes of front line confusion, defeatism, and officer incompetence, complicating efforts to promote an unambiguously heroic war myth. Conversely, some scholars suggest a more linear trajectory, arguing that the war's prominence 'seemed only to intensify as the Soviet Union moved away from both the October Revolution and the war itself'.[10] More recent scholarship, examining regional and societal variation, suggests that the intensity of the war's commemoration during the 1950s and early 1960s varied by community and geography. Within the military, the Komsomol, among veterans, and in certain localities, a rich commemorative discourse emerged that predated the more centralised and grandiose 'war cult' of the Brezhnev years (1964–1982).

Archival evidence supports the view of an uneven pattern of war veneration during these years, with a high degree of variability across the USSR; however, it also confirms an overwhelming commitment on the part of the leadership towards leveraging the war's memory as a post-Stalinist source of political legitimacy and patriotic loyalty. Already in June 1955, Georgii Zhukov, newly appointed as Defence Minister, sent a memorandum and draft resolution to the Central Committee (CC) proposing the development of large-scale war monuments and memorial complexes throughout the country – a project the Ministry of Culture promptly endorsed. By the time Nikita Khrushchev launched his assault on key aspects of Stalin's legacy during his 'Secret Speech' in early 1956, the CC was overseeing plans for a national victory memorial in Moscow and formulating a special commission to explore the larger question of the war's 'immortalisation' across the USSR.

However, the decoupling of Stalin from the victory narrative proved a significant obstacle to these objectives. The Secret Speech detailed Stalin's wartime 'mistakes', including the deportations of ethnic minorities and strategic blunders, while underscoring the collective role of the Party and Soviet people in winning the war. Not coincidentally, popular responses to the speech tended to home in on the revelations about Stalin's war leadership. Reports on the public mood indicate that although some were horrified by Stalin's actions, many others viewed his wartime role as an unassailable, even redemptive, aspect of his rule. Such divisive reactions to the Secret Speech, and the mass protests it inspired within the Communist bloc, prompted the leadership to pursue a more nuanced portrayal of Stalin, particularly his role in wartime. Already in June 1956, for example, a CC resolution called for a 'balanced' understanding of Stalin, downplaying his ability to affect the course of the war and stressing the role of a 'Leninist core of leaders' who operated as a check on Stalin's wartime foibles. For the next several years, a series of commissions on war histories, monuments, and patriotic education struggled with the ambiguous line on Stalin, slowing the development of the war's large-scale veneration before 1961, when Khrushchev intensified his campaign against the personality cult.

The Twenty-Second Party Congress that year ended the official ambiguity over Stalin's war record, clearing the way for a complete overhaul of the war's public commemoration. This began with the removal of Stalin's body from Lenin's Mausoleum amid congressional proceedings and the subsequent targeting of key remaining emblems of the personality cult. Most conspicuously, in November, the Supreme Soviet decreed the renaming of the city of Stalingrad to Volgograd. Such moves to further extricate Stalin from the victory myth had been quietly in preparation in the lead up to the congress. In March 1960, at the urging of Khrushchev and his ideological chief Mikhail Suslov, the CC formulated a special commission, headed by Leonid Brezhnev, to evaluate the state of the country's war graves and monuments. In July Brezhnev's commission submitted its report 'On the Immortalisation of the World-Historic Victory of the Soviet People in the Great Patriotic War 1941–1945', proposing the radical expansion of the war's remembrance across the USSR. Among other things, this included establishing myriad new war memorials, commemorative rituals, and the reconstitution of 9 May as 'a ubiquitous, nationwide' and 'non-working' holiday. These initiatives were to be implemented in time for the twentieth anniversary of victory in 1965. Unfortunately for Khrushchev, who was ousted from power in October 1964, the expansive system of commemoration his leadership envisioned would come to fruition only under his successor, Brezhnev.

Historians typically regard the twentieth anniversary of Victory Day in 1965 as initiating the commemorative cult of the war. It certainly reassured the leadership of the war's utility as a source of patriotism and political legitimacy. KGB surveillance of the event captured a sense of overwhelming gratitude towards the Party, the state, and Brezhnev personally for reinvigorating the war's national prominence. Some respondents urged the Party to take the war's public veneration further, noting how this would 'raise the authority of our Party and government'. Such early, positive indicators drove the expansion of the war's commemoration into the 'full-blown' cult of the late 1960s to early 1980s, during which the war victory increasingly overshadowed the Bolshevik Revolution as the central defining event of the Soviet project.

The late-socialist war cult was therefore less a break with the memory politics of the Khrushchev years than their realisation, albeit reconfigured in a way that could co-opt the support of ultra-conservative 'neo-Stalinists', whom Brezhnev's commitment to 'stability' in the ranks had allowed back into the fold. In his anniversary report, Brezhnev mentioned Stalin only in passing, as a concession to this hard-line faction. But the main ingredients for victory remained Party leadership, the Soviet system, and the multinational unity of the Soviet people. The Brezhnev leadership likewise rebuffed attempts to revive the cult of Generalissimo Stalin or to incorporate elements of Russian nationalism into the war's memory, as some ultra-conservatives desired. In the name of balance and stability, however, Brezhnev permitted neo-Stalinists within CC structures, like the notorious Sergei Trapeznikov, to suppress overt critiques of Stalin's war leadership and roll back the Thaw-era trend of critical or morally ambiguous portrayals of life in wartime. After 1965 even academic histories of the war that delved too deeply into Stalin's failures came under fire. One of the better-known examples was historian A. M. Nekrich, whose 1965 monograph *June 22, 1941* highlighted Stalin's responsibility for the country's unpreparedness at the time of the German invasion. Despite its stress on party leadership and the heroism of the Soviet people, the book's negative assessment of Stalin led to Nekrich's expulsion from the Party in 1967 and subsequent emigration to the United States.

The war cult thus embodied a 'patriotic compromise' between rival ideological factions. It resisted the hyper-conservatism of neo-Stalinists and Russian nationalists while nevertheless advancing core conservative priorities – Soviet patriotism, love for the motherland, anti-Westernism, and most importantly youth indoctrination. The promotion of these ideals aimed to counter not only the disruption wrought by de-Stalinisation but also, it should be noted, the global tectonic shifts of the 1960s, such as intergenerational conflict and the development of transnational Jewish memory following the Auschwitz and Eichmann trials earlier in the decade. The war's memory also served to deaden the inevitable Western influence brought on by détente. In one sense, then, the war cult served as a counter-measure to the global trends of cultural liberalisation, political dissent, and emerging collective memory of the Holocaust, positioning the Soviet victory myth as a distinct and ideologically cohesive alternative.

In the two decades that followed the landmark 1965 jubilee, the war's veneration became a ubiquitous feature of Soviet life. The war cult instituted an array of commemorative rituals and sparked a proliferation of museums, monuments, histories, films, novels, memoirs, and television series, all reinforcing the myth of the Great Patriotic War. While rooted in the commemorative policies of the Khrushchev years, the late-socialist war cult diverged in key respects from the preceding era. Its prioritisation of blandly patriotic productions contrasted sharply with the human-centred dramas that emerged during the Thaw, although notable exceptions abounded, such as Elem Klimov's starkly realist *Come and See* (1985), produced during the tail end of the cult and based on an earlier memoir collection. By the 1970s the war cult was also centring the aging Soviet leadership, particularly Brezhnev, whose minor wartime role as a political officer was transformed into a major heroic feat. Official portraits adorned the Soviet leader with an ostentatious array of medals and decorations while the city of Novorossiysk, the site of Brezhnev's purported heroic action, was granted 'hero-city' status in 1973. But the war cult's most

Figure 20.2 *The Motherland Calls* is a neoclassicist and socialist realist war memorial sculpture on Mamayev Kurgan in Volgograd, Russia. Completed in 1967, it was designed primarily by sculptor Yevgeny Vuchetich and stands eighty-five metres high. Source: Archive Holdings Inc.

indelible features were the roughly 100,000 (according to official figures) monuments and sprawling memorial complexes that dotted the country, such as the Stalingrad battle memorial, with its colossal sword-wielding centrepiece *Motherland Calls*. Although the late-socialist boom in war monuments is often regarded as a defining feature of the long Brezhnev years, many of the most significant projects had been under development since the late 1950s.

By the time Mikhail Gorbachev ascended the post of general secretary in 1985, the war cult's repetitive patriotic messaging and omnipresence had paradoxically become a hindrance to its ability to inspire and mobilise Soviet society in an ideologically cohesive manner. This does not indicate the popular rejection of the war myth, however. As anthropologist Alexei Yurchak has demonstrated, Soviet citizens, particularly the youth, derived a variety of meanings from state commemorative practices, many if not most of which were harmonious with the official narrative.[11] Likewise, historian Catherine Merridale, through oral history work conducted more than a decade after the collapse of the USSR, has noted the effectiveness of the war cult as a propaganda campaign. The veterans Merridale interviewed tended to repeat the cult's phraseology rather than assert long-suppressed memories at odds with the official line.[12] All this suggests that despite the war cult's heavy-handedness, Soviet citizens actively engaged with and internalised significant elements of the victory myth during late socialism.

20.3 Decline and Reinvention: The End of the USSR and Beyond

Gorbachev's efforts to reform the Soviet system jolted the politics of memory. His policy of openness, which encouraged a more candid exploration into past silences and distortions, aimed to foster a more honest and dynamic political culture. This objective inadvertently undermined the victory myth. While Gorbachev appears to have genuinely believed in the fundamental elements of the myth, as well as its social and political utility, his *glasnost* policy enabled journalists and historians to push the boundaries of their mandate to investigate the 'blank spots' of Soviet history, which subjected the war narrative to unprecedented scrutiny. By 1990 open criticism of the Soviet war effort encompassed the disastrous early defeats of 1941, Soviet authorities' callous disregard for soldier and civilian casualties, and Soviet culpability for various war-related atrocities, including the 1940 massacre of Polish prisoners of war at Katyn. Such revelations, coinciding with the end of the Cold War, fed a growing anti-communist sentiment in the country, which held that Nazism and Soviet socialism shared many core characteristics, an idea reaffirmed in Vasily Grossman's long-suppressed war novel *Life and Fate*, finally published in the Soviet Union in 1988. Consequently, the war myth became a key site of contestation between the Soviet state and many of its constituent republics, contributing to growing fissures within the Union. Despite these complications and the Soviet collapse in 1991, the war narrative retained significant resonance, particularly among older Russian-speaking populations, for whom the war victory remained the regime's signal achievement.

Unlike Gorbachev, the first president of the Russian Federation, Boris Yeltsin, had few qualms about demolishing foundational communist-era myths. However, Yeltsin understood the victory myth's enduring importance among nationalists, a resurgent neo-communist opposition, and broad swaths of ordinary Russians. Thus, rather than embrace the liberal, anti-communist narrative, Yeltsin pursued a 'middle ground'.[13] His administration attended to the war's tragic elements – notably acknowledging the Holocaust as a uniquely horrific event – and criticised the Soviet state's mismanagement of the war effort, while simultaneously celebrating the mass heroism of the Soviet people. In commemoration of the fiftieth anniversary of victory in 1995, the Yeltsin leadership oversaw the completion of Moscow's Victory Memorial on Poklonnaya Hill, stripped of its communist iconography and incorporating a Russian Orthodox church, a mosque, and eventually a synagogue. This inclusivity reflected the multi-confessional, civic orientation of post-Soviet Russian nationhood as Yeltsin's government envisioned it.

And yet the war's memory was never a central focus of Yeltsin's presidency, preoccupied as it was with dismantling the broader Soviet legacy and navigating the political and economic turbulence of the post-Soviet transition. The continual, critical re-evaluation of the Soviet war myth also contributed to a growing sense of disillusionment and pessimism, exacerbated by Russia's first war in breakaway Chechnya. Yeltsin's approach thus proved ill-suited to fostering a robust and patriotic sense of Russian national identity. Among nationalists and other conservative circles, such ambivalence fed an emerging counter-narrative of the war, which parroted Soviet patriotic rhetoric and imagery while replacing the Soviet myth's ideological scaffolding with a Russian national gloss. Some variants of the counter-narrative even restored Stalin's place as the architect of victory, only this time not as the ethnic Georgian communist leader of the multinational USSR but as a defender of the Russian imperial heritage. Although a marginal tendency during the 1990s, this counter-narrative set the stage for the dramatic reinvention of the war myth under Vladimir Putin.

Putin's restoration and recasting of the war myth in a Russian national guise thus developed in reaction to the more critical posture of the late 1980s and 1990s.[14] The Putin leadership did not simply reverse the prior era's public criticism of the victory myth; it established the war's memory as the linchpin of Russian historical memory and national identity. By foregrounding the 1945 victory, Russian state memory culture shifted attention away from the more complicated and problematic aspects of the communist past. In effect, by reducing the legacy of the Soviet period to victory in the war, political and cultural elites sought to smooth over the revolutionary ruptures and traumatic upheavals that punctuated Russian history in general and the communist era in particular. In place of a historical narrative defined by social, political, and ideological division, the government fashioned an overarching national story of war, which positions the Great Patriotic War as the culmination of a thousand-year string of Russian military triumphs. Domestically, this official project has co-opted a very real popular yearning to honour the wartime generation and its achievements, subsuming grassroots commemorations to a dominant myth of state designed to legitimate political authority and foster a patriotic sense of what it means to be Russian.

Like its Soviet-era predecessor, Russia's reimagined war myth has geopolitical dimensions as well, which became increasingly acute in the wake of Russia's 2014 annexation of Crimea. The war's mythology has become fundamental to Russia's global self-image as an ideological and military bulwark against new forms of fascism and militarism. According to this logic, where Russia and the Russian people are the natural heirs to the Soviet legacy of the victory over fascism, those whom the Russian government perceives to be enemies are cast as latter-day embodiments of the fascist menace. In the twenty-first century, such historical parallelism has underpinned Russian foreign policy maneuvers and the various wars of Soviet succession, none more so than the Russian-Ukrainian War, the bloodiest European conflict in decades, waged by Russia under the pretext of 'de-Nazification'. Under Putin's stewardship, therefore, the recalibrated war myth served not only as a pillar of Russian national identity but also as a tool of foreign policy, invoking the Soviet legacy of victory over fascism to justify and frame Russia's actions at home and abroad.

Whatever the Putin leadership's role in fostering a dominant myth of state around the Soviet victory in the Second World War, Russia's politics of war memory cannot be understood in isolation from the intensive, Soviet-era cultivation of victory culture that preceded it. The Kremlin's frequent recourse to the war theme as a source of political legitimacy, mass patriotism, and framing mechanism in geopolitics and military interventions stems directly from the entrenchment of the war's memory amid decades of Soviet myth-making.

But while it is tempting to draw a straight line from the Soviet commemorative cult to the instrumentalisation of war memory in Russia's conflict with Ukraine, the discontinuities are paramount. Among numerous other things, the Russian national-imperial rebranding of the war myth – along with the associated implication that the millions of Ukrainians who fought alongside other Soviet peoples in the Great Patriotic War were in fact 'Russians' – represents a significant departure. Contrary to the Russian state war narrative and its implicit and explicit justifications for war against other former Soviet peoples, the Soviet myth of victory – albeit within limits – celebrated diversity.

Notes

1 'Glavnyi narkolog Moskvy: rossiiskoe p'ianstvo – mif, v strane prosto dolgo otmechali pobedu v voine', *NEWSru*, 30 December 2008, www.newsru.com/arch/russia/30dec2008/mif.html.
2 Due to space constraints, citations will be kept to a minimum. Key works on Soviet and post-Soviet war memory include J. Brunstedt, *The Soviet Myth of World War II: Patriotic Memory and the Russian Question in the USSR* (Cambridge: Cambridge University Press, 2021); V. Davis, *Myth Making in the Soviet Union and Modern Russia: Remembering World War II in*

Brezhnev's Hero City (New York: I. B. Tauris, 2018); M. Edele, *Soviet Veterans of the Second World War: A Popular Movement in an Authoritarian Society 1941–1991* (Oxford: Oxford University Press, 2008); L. A. Kirschenbaum, *The Legacy of the Siege of Leningrad, 1941–1995: Myth, Memories, and Monuments* (Cambridge: Cambridge University Press, 2006); I. Mijnssen, *Russia's Hero Cities: From Postwar Ruins to the Soviet Heroarchy* (Bloomington: Indiana University Press, 2021); N. Tumarkin, *The Living and the Dead: The Rise and Fall of the Cult of World War II In Russia* (New York: Basic Books, 1995); A. Weiner, *Making Sense of War: The Second World War and the Fate of the Bolshevik Revolution* (Princeton: Princeton University Press, 2002); D. J. Youngblood, *Russian War Films: On the Cinema Front, 1914–2005* (Lawrence: University Press of Kansas, 2006); and the individual contributions in D. L. Hoffmann, ed., *The Memory of the Second World War in Soviet and Post-Soviet Russia* (New York: Routledge, 2022).

3 Brunstedt, *The Soviet Myth*, p. 73.

4 Ibid., pp. 73–74; Kirschenbaum, *Legacy*, p. 117.

5 Edele, *Soviet Veterans*, pp. 93–94.

6 Y. Arad, *In the Shadow of the Red Banner: Soviet Jews in the War against Nazi Germany* (Jerusalem: Gefen Books, 2010), p. 9.

7 Weiner, *Making Sense of War*, pp. 209–216.

8 GARF (State Archive of the Russian Federation) R-9548/1/12/39, 50–51.

9 Brunstedt, *The Soviet Myth*, p. 93.

10 Weiner, *Making Sense of War*, p. 380.

11 A. Yurchak, *Everything Was Forever, Until It Was No More: The Last Soviet Generation* (Princeton: Princeton University Press, 2013), passim.

12 C. Merridale, *Ivan's War: Life and Death in the Red Army, 1939–45* (New York: Metropolitan Books, 2006), pp. 321–335.

13 N. Koposov, *Memory Laws, Memory Wars: The Politics of the Past in Europe and Russia* (Cambridge: Cambridge University Press, 2017), pp. 207–237.

14 Koposov, *Memory Laws*, pp. 238–99; J. McGlynn, *Memory Makers: The Politics of the Past in Putin's Russia* (London: Bloomsbury, 2023).

A Guide to Further Reading

Part I Conceptions of War

Corum, James S., *The Roots of Blitzkrieg: Hans von Seecht and German Military Reform* (Lawrence: University Press of Kansas, 1992).

Dyakov, Yuri and Tatyana Bushuyeva (eds.), *The Red Army and the Wehrmacht: How the Soviets Militarized Germany and Paved the Way for Fascism, from the Secret Archives of the Former Soviet Union* (Amherst, NY: Prometheus Books, 1995).

Ericson, Edward E., III, *Feeding the German Eagle: Soviet Economic Aid to Nazi Germany, 1933–1941* (Westport, CT: Praeger, 1999).

Habeck, Mary, *Storm of Steel: The Development of Armor Doctrine in Germany and the Soviet Union, 1919–1939* (London: Cornell University Press, 2003).

Haslam, Jonathan, *The Soviet Union and the Struggle for Collective Security in Europe, 1933–1939* (New York: St. Martin's Press, 1984).

Haslam, Jonathan, *The Spectre of War: International Communism and the Origins of World War II* (Princeton, NJ: Princeton University Press, 2021).

Johnson, Ian O., *Faustian Bargain: The Soviet-German Partnership and the Origins of the Second World War* (New York: Oxford University Press, 2021).

Kershaw, Ian, *Hitler 1936–1945: Nemesis* (London, Penguin, 2000).

Kotkin, Stephen, *Stalin, Volume II: Waiting for Hitler, 1929–1941* (New York: Penguin Press, 2017).

Kuromiya, Hiroaki, *Stalin, Japan, and the Struggle for Supremacy over China, 1894–1945* (London: Routledge, 2023).

Leach, Barry, *German Strategy against Russia 1939–1941* (Oxford: Oxford University Press, 1973).

Müller, Rolf-Dieter, *Enemy in the East: Hitler's Secret Plans to Invade the Soviet Union* (New York, 2015).

Reese, Roger R., *Stalin's Reluctant Soldiers: A Social History of the Red Army, 1925–1941* (Lawrence: University Press of Kansas, 1996).

Roberts, Geoffrey, *The Soviet Union and the Origins of the Second World War: Russo-German Relations and the Road to War, 1933–1941* (London: Macmillan Press, 1995).

Stone, David R., *Hammer and Rifle: The Militarization of the Soviet Union, 1926–1933* (Lawrence: University Press of Kansas, 2000).

Strohn, Matthias, *The German Army and the Defence of the Reich: Military Doctrine and the Conduct of the Defensive Battle 1918–1939* (Cambridge: Cambridge University Press, 2010).

Part II Opposing Forces

Dunn, Walter S., Jr., *Hitler's Nemesis: The Red Army, 1930–45* (Mechanicsburg: Stackpole Books, 2009).

Dunn, Walter S., Jr., *Stalin's Keys to Victory: The Rebirth of the Red Army in WWII* (Mechanicsburg: Stackpole Books, 2006).

Edele, Mark, *Stalin's Defectors: How Red Army Soldiers Become Hitler's Collaborators, 1941–1945* (Oxford: Oxford University Press, 2019).

Glantz, David M., *Colossus Reborn: The Red Army at War, 1941–1943* (Lawrence: University Press of Kansas, 2005).

Glantz, David M., *Stumbling Colossus: The Red Army on the Eve of World War* (Lawrence: University Press of Kansas, 1998).

Harrisville, David, *The Virtuous Wehrmacht: Crafting the Myth of the German Soldier on the Eastern Front, 1941–1944* (Ithaca and London: Cornell University Press, 2021).

Hill, Alexander, *The Red Army and the Second World War* (Cambridge: Cambridge University Press, 2017).

Kühne, Thomas, *The Rise and Fall of Comradeship: Hitler's Soldiers, Male Bonding and Mass Violence in the Twentieth Century* (Cambridge: Cambridge University Press, 2017).

Megargee, Geoffrey P., *Inside Hitler's High Command* (Lawrence: University Press of Kansas).

Merridale, Catherine, *Ivan's War: Life and Death in the Red Army, 1939–1945* (New York: Metropolitan Books, 2006).

Reese, Roger, *Why Stalin's Soldiers Fought* (Lawrence: University Press of Kansas, 2011).

Römer, Felix, *Comrades: The Wehrmacht from Within* (Oxford: Oxford University Press, 2019).

Rutherford, Jeff and Adrian Wettstein, *The German Army on the Eastern Front: An Inner View of the Ostheer's Experiences of War* (Barnsley: Pen and Sword, 2018).

Shepherd, Ben H., *Hitler's Soldiers: The German Army in the Third Reich* (London: Yale University Press, 2016).

Wette, Wolfram, *The Wehrmacht: History, Myth, Reality* (Cambridge, MA: Harvard University Press, 2006).

Part III Campaigns

Beevor, Antony, *Berlin: The Downfall 1945* (London: Viking, 2002).

Boog, Horst (ed.), *Germany and the Second World War, Volume IV: The Attack on the Soviet Union* (Oxford: Clarendon Press, 1998).

Dick, C. J., *From Defeat to Victory: The Eastern Front 1944* (Lawrence: University Press of Kansas, 2016).

Duffy, Christopher, *Red Storm on the Reich: The Soviet March on Germany, 1945* (New York: Atheneum, 1991).

Dunn, Walter S., Jr., *Soviet Blitzkrieg: The Battle for White Russia, 1944* (Mechanicsburg: Stackpole Books, 2008).

Frieser, Karl-Heinz (ed.), *Germany and the Second World War, Volume VIII: The Eastern Front 1943–1944 – The War in the East and on the Neighbouring Fronts* (Oxford: Clarendon Press, 2017).

Fritz, Stephen G., *Ostkrieg: Hitler's War of Extermination in the East* (Lexington: University Press of Kentucky, 2011).

Gerasimova, Svetlana, *The Rzhev Slaughterhouse: The Red Army's Forgotten 15 Month Campaign against Army Group Centre, 1942–1943* (Solihull: Helion, 2013).

Glantz, David M., *The Battle for Leningrad 1941–1944* (Lawrence: University Press of Kansas, 2002).

Glantz, David M. and Jonathan M. House, *Stalingrad* (Lawrence: University Press of Kansas, 2017).

Glantz, David M. and Jonathan M. House, *When Titans Clashed: How the Red Army Stopped Hitler* (Lawrence: University Press of Kansas, 2015).

Mawdsley, Evan, *Thunder in the East: The Nazi-Soviet War 1941–1945* (London: Bloomsbury, 2016).

Megargee, Geoffrey, *War of Annihilation: Combat and Genocide on the Eastern Front, 1941* (Oxford: Rowman & Littlefield, 2006).

Noble, Alastair, *Nazi Rule and the Soviet Offensive in Eastern Germany, 1944–1945: The Darkest Hour* (Eastbourne: Sussex Academic Press, 2010).

Reid, Anna, *Leningrad: The Epic Siege of World War II, 1941–1944* (New York: Walker & Company, 2011).

Roberts, Geoffrey, *Stalin's General: The Life of Georgy Zhukov* (New York: Random House, 2012).

Rutherford, Jeff, *Combat and Genocide on the Eastern Front: The German Infantry's War, 1941–1944* (Cambridge: Cambridge University Press, 2014).

Stahel, David, *Operation Barbarossa and Germany's Defeat in the East* (Cambridge: Cambridge University Press, 2009).

Stahel, David, *Retreat from Moscow: A New History of Germany's Winter Campaign, 1941–1942* (New York: Farrar, Straus and Giroux, 2019).

Statiev, Alexander, *At War's Summit: The Red Army and the Struggle for the Caucasus Mountains in World War II* (Cambridge: Cambridge University Press, 2018).

Töppel, Roman, *Kursk 1943: The Greatest Battle of the Second World War* (Helion: Warwick, 2018).

Ziemke, Earl F., *Stalingrad to Berlin: The German Defeat in the East* (New York: Barnes & Noble, 1968).

Ziemke, Earl F. and Magna E. Bauer, *Moscow to Stalingrad: Decision in the East* (New York: Military Heritage Press, 1988).

Part IV Criminality and Occupation

Baberowski, Jörg, *Scorched Earth: Stalin's Reign of Terror* (New Haven: Yale University Press, 2016).

Beorn, Waitman Wade, *Marching into Darkness: The Wehrmacht and the Holocaust in Belarus* (Cambridge, MA: Harvard University Press, 2014).

Berkhoff, Karel, *Harvest of Despair: Life and Death in Ukraine Under Nazi Rule* (Cambridge, MA: Harvard University Press, 2004).

Browning, Christopher R. and Jürgen Matthäus, *The Origins of the Final Solution: The Evolution of Nazi Jewish Policy 1939–1942* (London: Arrow Books, 2004).

Edele, Mark, 'Soviet Liberations and Occupations, 1939–1949', in *The Cambridge History of the Second World War*, ed. Richard Bosworth and Joe Maiolo (Cambridge: Cambridge University Press, 2015), esp. 497–500.

Edele, Mark, 'Take (No) Prisoners! The Red Army and German POWs, 1941–1943' *The Journal of Modern History* 88 (2016): 342–379.

Edele, Mark and Michael Geyer, 'States of Exception: The Soviet-German War as a System of Violence, 1939–1945', in *Beyond Totalitarianism: Stalinism and Nazism Compared*, ed. Sheila Fitzpatrick and Michael Geyer (Cambridge: Cambridge University Press, 2009).

Enstad, Johannes Due, *Soviet Russia under Nazi Occupation: Fragile Loyalties in World War II* (Cambridge: Cambridge University Press, 2019).

Kay, Alex J., *Empire of Destruction: A History of Nazi Mass Killing* (New Haven: Yale University Press, 2021).

Kay, Alex J., *Exploitation, Resettlement, Mass Murder: Political and Economic Planning for German Occupation Policy in the Soviet Union, 1940–1941* (Oxford: Berghahn Books, 2006).

Kay, Alex J., Jeff Rutherford and David Stahel (eds.), *Nazi Policy on the Eastern Front, 1941: Total War, Genocide and Radicalization* (Rochester: Rochester University Press, 2012).

Longerich, Peter, *The Unwritten Order: Hitler's Role in the Final Solution* (Stroud: Tempus, 2005).

Polian, Pavel, *Against Their Will: The History and Geography of Forced Migrations in the USSR* (Budapest: Central European University Press, 2022).

Rhodes, Richard, *Masters of Death: The SS Einsatzgruppen and the Invention of the Holocaust* (New York: Vintage Books, 2003).

Schulte, Theo, *The German Army and Nazi Policies in Occupied Russia* (Oxford: Berg, 1989).

Snyder, Timothy, *Bloodlands: Europe between Hitler and Stalin* (New York: Basic Books, 2010).

Statiev, Alexander, *The Soviet Counterinsurgency in the Western Borderlands* (Cambridge: Cambridge University Press, 2010).

Willems, Bastiaan, *Violence in Defeat: The Wehrmacht on German Soil, 1944–1945* (Cambridge: Cambridge University Press, 2021).

Part V Home Fronts

Barber, John and Mark Harrison, *The Soviet Home Front 1941–1945: A Social and Economic History of the USSR in World War II* (London: Longman, 1991).

Berkhoff, Karel C., *Motherland in Danger: Soviet Propaganda during World War II* (Cambridge, MA: Harvard University Press, 2012).

Braithwaite, Rodric, *Moscow 1941: A City and Its People at War* (New York: Alfred A. Knopf, 2006).

Edele, Mark, *Stalinism at War: The Soviet Union in World War II* (London: Bloomsbury, 2021).

Goldman, Wendy Z. and Donald Filtzer, *Fortress Dark and Stern: The Soviet Home Front during World War II* (Oxford: Oxford University Press, 2021).

Harrison, Mark, *Soviet Planning in Peace and War 1938–1945* (Cambridge: Cambridge University Press, 2002).

Hartmann, Christian, *Operation Barbarossa: Nazi Germany's War in the East 1941–1945* (Oxford: Oxford University Press, 2013).

Moorhouse, Roger, *Berlin at War: Life and Death in Hitler's Capital, 1939–45* (London: Bodley Head, 2010).

Overy, Richard, *War and Economy in the Third Reich* (Oxford: Oxford University Press, 2002).

Stargardt, Nicholas, *The German War: A Nation under Arms* (New York: Basic Books, 2015).

Steinert, Marlis, *Hitler's War and the Germans: Public Mood and Attitude during the Second World War* (Athens: Ohio University Press, 1977).

Stites, Richard (ed.), *Culture and Entertainment in Wartime Russia* (Bloomington: Indiana University Press, 1995).

Stone, David R. (ed.), *The Soviet Union at War 1941–1945* (Barnsley: Pen and Sword, 2010).

Tooze, Adam, *The Wages of Destruction: The Making and Breaking of the Nazi Economy* (London: Viking, 2006).

Vaizey, Hester, *Surviving Hitler's War: Family Life in Germany, 1939–48* (New York: Palgrave Macmillan, 2010).

Part VI Comrades in Arms

Axworthy, Mark, *Third Axis Fourth Ally: Romanian Armed Forces in the European War, 1941–1945* (London: Arms and Armour, 1995).

Beyda, Oleg, *For Russia with Hitler: White Russian Émigrés and the German-Soviet War* (Toronto: University of Toronto Press, 2024).

Carley, Michael J., *Silent Conflict: A Hidden History of Early Soviet-Western Relations* (Lanham, MD: Rowman and Littlefield, 2014).

Folly, Martin, Geoffrey Roberts, and Oleg Rzheshevsky, *Churchill and Stalin: Comrades in Arms during the Second World War* (Yorkshire: Pen and Sword, 2019).

Folly, Martin H., *Churchill, Whitehall and the Soviet Union, 1940–45* (London: Macmillan, 2000).

Glantz, Mary E., *FDR and the Soviet Union: The President's Battles over Foreign Policy* (Lawrence: Cornell University Press, 2005).

Gooch, John, *Mussolini War: Fascist Italy from Triumph to Collapse 1935–1943* (Dublin: Penguin, 2020).

Harward, Grant T., *Romania's Holy War: Soldiers, Motivation, and the Holocaust* (Ithaca: Cornell University Press, 2021).

Kinnunen, Tiina and Ville Kivimäki (eds.), *Finland in World War II: History, Memory, Interpretations* (Boston: Brill, 2012).

Lunde, Henrik O., *Finland's War of Choice: The Troubled German-Finish Coalition in World War II* (Havertown, PA: Casemate, 2011).

Meinander, Henrik, *Mannerheim, Marshal of Finland: A Life in Geopolitics* (London: Hurst & Company, 2023).

Müller, Rolf-Dieter, *The Unknown Eastern Front: The Wehrmacht and Hitler's Foreign Soldiers* (London: I. B. Tauris, 2007).

Reynolds, David, 'Churchill, Roosevelt and the Stalin Enigma, 1941–1945', in *From World War to Cold War: Churchill, Roosevelt, and the International History of the 1940s*, ed. David Reynolds (Oxford: Oxford University Press, 2006).

Reynolds, David and Vladimir Pechatnov (eds.), *The Kremlin Letters: Stalin's Wartime Correspondence with Churchill and Roosevelt* (London: Yale University Press, 2018).

Roberts, Geoffrey, 'Stalin at the Tehran, Yalta and Potsdam Conferences' *Journal of Cold War Studies* 9, no. 4 (Fall 2007): 6–40.

Roberts, Geoffrey, *Stalin's Wars: From World War to Cold, 1939–1953* (New Haven: Yale University Press, 2006).

Rzheshevsky, Oleg (ed.), *War and Diplomacy: The Making of the Grand Alliance* (Amsterdam: Harwood Academic, 1996).

Scianna, Bastian Matteo, *The Italian War on the Eastern, 1941–1943: Operations, Myths and Memories* (Cham: Palgrave, 2019).

Stahel, David, *Joining Hitler's Crusade: European Nations and the Invasion of the Soviet Union, 1941* (Cambridge: Cambridge University Press, 2016).

Vehvilainen, Olli, *Finland in the Second World War: Between Germany and Russia* (London: Palgrave Macmillan, 2002).

Part VII Post-war Legacies and Myth-Making

Brunstedt, Jonathan, *The Soviet Myth of World War II: Patriotic Memory and the Russian Question in the USSR* (Cambridge: Cambridge University Press, 2021).

Echternkamp, Jörg, *Postwar Soldiers: Historical Controversies and West-German Democratization, 1945–1955* (New York: Berghahn Books, 2020).

Edele, Mark, *Soviet Veterans of the Second World War: A Popular Movement in an Authoritarian Society 1941–1991* (Oxford: Oxford University Press, 2008).

Fedor, Julie, Markku Kangaspuro, Jussi Lassila, and Tatiana Zhurzhenko (ed.), *War and Memory in Russia, Ukraine and Belarus* (Cham: Palgrave, 2017).

Goltermann, Svenja, *The War in Their Minds: German Soldiers and Their Violent Pasts in West Germany* (Ann Arbor: University of Michigan Press, 2020).

Hoffmann, David L. (ed.), *The Memory of the Second World War in Soviet and Post-Soviet Russia* (New York: Routledge, 2022).

Morina, Christina, *Legacies of Stalingrad: Remembering the Eastern Front in Germany since 1945* (Cambridge: Cambridge University Press, 2011).

Müller, Rolf-Dieter and Gerd R. Ueberschär, *Hitler's War in the East 1941–1945: A Critical Assessment* (Oxford: Berghahn Books, 2009).

Prince, Michael K., *War and German Memory: Excavating the Significance of the Second World War in German Cultural Consciousness* (Plymouth: Lexington Books, 2009).

For EU product safety concerns, contact us at Calle de José Abascal, 56–1°,
28003 Madrid, Spain or eugpsr@cambridge.org.